D0804452

SEINFELD

Master of Its Domain

SEINFELD

Master of Its Domain

Revisiting Television's Greatest Sitcom

Edited by

DAVID LAVERY

with Sara Lewis Dunne

continuum

NEW YORK • LONDON

2006

The Continuum International Publishing Group Inc
80 Maiden Lane, New York, NY 10038

The Continuum International Publishing Group Ltd
The Tower Building, 11 York Road, London SE1 7NX

www.continuumbooks.com

Copyright © 2006 by David Lavery

All rights reserved. No part of this book may be reproduced, stored in a retrieval system, or transmitted, in any form or by any means, electronic, mechanical, photocopying, recording, or otherwise, without the written permission of the publishers.

Printed in the United States of America

Library of Congress Cataloging-in-Publication Data

Seinfeld, master of its domain : revisiting television's greatest sitcom / edited by
David Lavery with Sara Lewis Dunne.
    p. cm.
Includes bibliographical references and index.
ISBN-13: 978-0-8264-1802-9 (hardcover : alk. paper)
ISBN-10: 0-8264-1802-3 (hardcover : alk. paper)
    1. Seinfeld (Television program)   I. Lavery, David, 1949–   II. Dunne, Sara Lewis.
PN1992.77.S4285S43   2003
791.45'72—dc22   2005030744

Contents

IV. "It is so sad. All your knowledge of high culture comes from Bugs Bunny cartoons": Cultural, Pop Cultural, and Media Matters

V. Afterword

VI. "Get out!": Back Pages

Preface

"Part of Popular Culture"
The Legacy of *Seinfeld*

David Lavery and Sara Lewis Dunne

> The idea that you have two guys who have never written a show, being run by a network executive that had never had a show, leading to a show that has a unique and unusual feel—this is a model that all the networks subsequently ignored and never did again—except for HBO. I think HBO—I don't know if they really knew that that's how our show evolved, but that's a network that hires people that they like and says that's the end of their job. We like you; do what you think you should do, and it leads to much more distinctive programming.
>
> —Jerry Seinfeld, "How It Began"

I

In "The Van Buren Boys" (8014), a Season Eight episode of *Seinfeld*, J. Peterman assigns Elaine the task of writing his autobiography. When it becomes apparent while sitting in his prosaic apartment, watching the world-famous globe-trotter watch television and search for a coupon for plant food, that his real life is actually very boring, she tells him a Kramer story about his escape from an unlikely gang, street toughs devoted to the eighth president of the United States. Peterman suggests they buy Kramer's stories and use them in *his* life writing. Although they eventually give Kramer his stories back—he quickly discovers that he can't really be Kramer without them—in "The Muffin Tops" (8021) Peterman's book *is* published, and Elaine has a confession to make to Kramer:

> Elaine: Kramer, ahem, remember that whole deal with you selling Peterman your stories for his book and then he gave them back to you?

Kramer: Vaguely.

Elaine: Well, I was kind of, he he he, short on material and I, um, I put them in the book anyway.

Kramer: You put my life's stories in his autobiography?

Elaine: Kramer, listen, it is such a stupid book. It doesn't matter.

Kramer: Oh no. Sure. It matters. Wow. I've broken through, huh. *I'm part of popular culture now.* Listen, I've got to thank Mr. Peterman. [my italics]

Inspired, Kramer starts showing up at Peterman's book signings and launches yet another scheme: Peterman reality tours, with Cosmo himself as tour guide.

After a slow beginning, *Seinfeld* broke through, too, developing into master of its domain, one of the most commercially successful sitcoms in the history of television,[1] being named by *TV Guide* as "The Greatest Show of All Time," and becoming itself "part of popular culture," its language, jokes, characters, situations now part of the water cooler vocabulary of two, even three, generations. With *Seinfeld* likely to run in syndication for several more decades, it may well remain common currency for a half century.

II

Seinfeld was, however, not without its detractors. Much talked about in the popular press during its original run (1989–1998), especially in the run-up to its final episode,[2] it was frequently both blamed and praised.[3]

Blame. Writing in the decidedly-left periodical *The Progressive*, Elayne Rapping examines *Seinfeld* and co-conspirators like *Friends* (1994–2004) and *Mad About You* (1992–1999) and finds them all to be alarming signs of the times in the dawning Information Age: "Call me a hopeless Puritan," Rapping writes, "[b]ut I see, in this airwave invasion of sitcoms about young Manhattanites with no real family or work responsibilities and nothing to do but hang out and talk about it, an insidious message about the future of Western civilization" (37). Ron Rosenbaum, writing in *Harper's Bazaar*, laments the "*Seinfeld* mania . . . that has swept through the media like a warm and fuzzy hurricane." In *Glued to the Set: The 60 Television Shows and Events That Made Us What We Are Today*, Steven D. Stark compared *Seinfeld* to *Home Improvement* (1991–1999) and found it wanting, the television equivalent of "sophomoric talk radio" (285). Roseanne Arnold (Roseanne Barr), whose series *Roseanne* (1988–1997) ran contemporaneously with *Seinfeld* on ABC, found her rival pretentious: "They think they're doing Samuel Beckett instead of a sitcom" (quoted in Wild 1).

Praise. Novelist Jay McInerney (in *TV Guide*) answers his own titular question "Is *Seinfeld* the Best Comedy Ever?" with a definite yes. Salon.com's Joyce Millman, while admitting an early distaste for the show, describes it as "Faster, smarter, darker and more unpredictable than any other network sitcom around, . . . a gasp-for-breath funny portrayal of bad behavior." Even some conservatives loved it: Rob Long, offering his tribute in the right-wing organ *National Review,* found *Seinfeld,* a series that inspired laughs at the expense of the handicapped, the homeless, the elderly, the retarded, suicides, abortion, and a variety of minorities, the near-perfect culture wars antidote to obsessive PCness. And Bill Wyman, also writing in Salon,[4] dismisses the carpers' complaints as a complete misunderstanding of *Seinfeld*'s intent and profound significance:

> *Seinfeld* was not really about how evil humanity is, though it's about that to some extent. The show is really about the joy of charting, in exquisite, unrelenting, almost celebratory detail, the infinitely variegated human interactions that, closely watched, will ultimately tell the story of the disintegration of our species.

III

Despite all the critical give and take, surprisingly, *Seinfeld* has to date inspired only one book-length study, *Seinfeld and Philosophy: A Book About Everything and Nothing.*[5] In David Wild's *Seinfeld: The Totally Unauthorized Tribute,* we do read, however, of several other volumes in the works:

Seinfeld *Friendship: Bond or Bondage*
Soup Nazis, Big Salads, and Other Food Issues: Seinfeld's *Hearty Appetitive for Disaster*
Jerry: Stand-Up Guy or Peter Pan with a Punch Line?
The Cosmetology of Kramer: Men Are from Mars, Cosmo Is from . . . ?
Elaine Benes: Tomboy or Time Bomb Waiting to Go Off?
George Costanza: Angst in His Sweatpants
Wash & Weary: The Dirty, Messy Truth about Jerry's Cleanliness
Newman's Own: Big Man, Bigger Problems
Crazy Joe Davola and the Insanity Defense
The Seinfelds and the Costanzas: Two Approaches to Parenthood from Potty Training On
"The Panties Your Mother Laid Out for You": Sexual Perversities in Manhattan
Seinfeld *of Dreams*
Elaine's Dancing: Movement or Madness?
Zen and the Art of Seinfeld

Elaine's "Get Out" Gesture as a Reflection of Postfeminist Rage
Frank and Estelle Costanza: Can This Marriage Be Saved?
Homoeroticism on the West Side: Jerry and George—A Love Story for Our Times?

To the best of our knowledge, none of these tomes has seen print, and since the series was to have been a project of Pendant Publishing (the New York house, former employer of Elaine Benes and George Costanza, publisher of Cosmo Kramer's coffee-table book on coffee tables, which went out of business when Mr. Lippman forgot his handkerchief and, his hand covered with snot, was unable to shake hands and seal the deal for the Matsushimi takeover ["The Opposite," 5022]), most likely they never will.

Though these must-read-TV books will now never appear in our universe, as fans of imaginary books of television criticism,[6] we like to think they do occupy a shelf in some library (zealously guarded by Mr. Bookman) or in a Brentano's (where Uncle Leo might shoplift them or George might make them forever-flagged bathroom reading material), not in our reality, of course, but in *Seinfeld*'s "sitcosmos" (the term is David Marc's, from *Comic Visions*). After all, the Sein-verse has its own alternate reality movies, such flicks as *Prognosis Negative* ("The Dog," 3004), *Checkmate* ("The Movie," 4013), *Rochelle, Rochelle: The Movie* ("The Smelly Car," 4020), *Death Blow, Cry, Cry Again* ("The Little Kicks," 8004), *The Other Side of Darkness, The Pain and the Yearning* ("The Comeback," 8013), and *Sack Lunch*[7] ("The English Patient," 8017). Why not books as well?

IV

As this, hopefully real, book was in its final stages of development, the long-awaited *Seinfeld* DVDs came out. To date, rich-in-extras boxed sets of Seasons One through Four have been issued. Film scholar Thomas Doherty was thinking of movie DVDs when he wrote of how the "tantalizing wraparound extras— outtakes, 'making of' docu-shills, theatrical trailers, concealed 'Easter-egg' trea-sures, rock videos, and other tasty ancillary material" possible on DVDs have completely changed "the relation of the motion-picture spectator to the object of attraction." Thanks to the DVD, Doherty observes, a new relationship with the medium, "both homespun and starstruck," becomes possible: "you and the auteur, shoulder to shoulder, planted on your living-room couch, munching pop-corn and hoisting a brewski, sharing a private tutorial in film studies laced with E! Entertainment gossip" (178). Television DVDs, multiplying by the day, including collections of some of the medium's worst shows, offer similar pleasures, even if the small screen is supposed to be auteurless.

Neither the authors or editors of this volume have begun to assimilate the *Seinfeld*iana to be found on the series DVDs. The insights come in various forms: "Yada, Yada, Yada" (episode commentaries by the cast, Larry David, and writers like Larry Charles and Peter Mehlman); "Inside Looks" (interviews with actors, writers, directors, and studio execs concerning selected episodes); "Notes About Nothing" (MTV "Pop-up Video"–influenced on-screen background information on each episode); "Not That There's Anything Wrong with That" (outtakes and bloopers); "In the Vault" (deleted scenes); and "How It Began" (an hour-long documentary on the making of *Seinfeld*).

Allow us, however, to at least offer our own notes on what is to be gleaned from a quick tour of the DVDs, remembering, of course, that the oral history of the series offered there is not necessarily an objective record and hardly the last word to be said about *Seinfeld*'s creation and development.

The original plan was for a special—ninety minutes about a standup comic. That it evolved into "ninety hours" still astounds Seinfeld ("How It Began").

Seinfeld declares the "gaps in society where there were no rules" to be the series' specialty ("Inside Look" for "The Seinfeld Chronicles," 1001).

In real life, it was actually Jerry who was relying on David to be the writer—the opposite of the situation on the show, where George, the David-inspired character, doesn't have a clue how to write for TV ("How It Began"). (In real life, David had written for *Fridays* and *Saturday Night Live*.)

David comments several times on how individual episodes—"The Contest" (4010), for example—came out of his notebook ("Inside Look" for the episode). Others comment on David's notebook as well. (On David's HBO series *Curb Your Enthusiasm*, the notebook makes several appearances.)

That *Seinfeld* was filmed on the same stage as *The Dick Van Dyke Show* (1961–1966) gave both Seinfeld and David a sense of their own show's place in TV history ("Inside Look" for "The Seinfeld Chronicles," 1001).

Julia-Louis Dreyfus has never seen the *Seinfeld* pilot, in which she did not appear ("Inside Look" for "The Seinfeld Chronicles," 1001).

David still hates the pilot because of network interference in its creation ("How It Began").

Richards admits not knowing how to play Kramer at first and being envious of the comfort Alexander and Seinfeld felt in their characters ("Inside Look" for "The Seinfeld Chronicles," 1001).

Jerry initially thought the wacky neighbor was a cliché ("How It Began").

The form of episode titles ("The Chinese Restaurant," 2011, "The Little Kicks," 8004) was the result of Seinfeld not wanting writers spending time and creative energy on them ("Inside Look" for "Male Unbonding," 1004). Only "Male Unbonding" lacks a "the."

David was quite aware of the untypical-for-television continuity *Seinfeld* was developing but saw no "downside" in it ("Inside Look" for "The Stakeout," 1002).

NBC was extremely unhappy with the eventless "The Chinese Restaurant" and held it back until late in the season, but Alexander and others felt that it was the first episode that truly defined the show ("Inside Look" for the episode).

Richards was hurt by being left out of "The Chinese Restaurant"; later, Alexander would be similarly upset about not appearing in "The Pen" (3003) ("Inside Look" for both episodes).

Richards observes that Kramer first became Kramer in "The Statue" (2006)—in the scene in which he pretends to be a detective ("Inside Look" for the episode).

Beginning with "The Busboy" (2012), Seinfeld began to selflessly write himself out of episodes and give the big laughs and scenes to the supporting cast ("Inside Look" for the episode).

David recalls his terror at the television reality of having to turn out first thirteen (Season Two) and then twenty-two (Season Three) episodes ("How It Began").

Larry Charles recalls that writers thrived on the challenge of weaving together different story ideas that were brought to the writers' table into single episodes ("Inside Look" for "The Baby Shower," 2010).

Elaine's father ("The Jacket," 2003) was based on David's real-life encounter with the intimidating writer Richard Yates, author of *Revolutionary Road* ("Inside Look" for the episode).

With "The Revenge" (2007), Richards began to realize his hope "to *do* funny, not just talk funny" ("Inside Look" for the episode).

NBC executive Warren Littlefield pushed getting Elaine and Jerry back together, and the "this, that" arrangement of "The Deal" (2009) was the result. When Jerry went on tour immediately after the season, he received resounding "No's!" to his question to audiences about whether they should continue to be lovers, and by Season Three they were again "just friends" ("Inside Look" for the episode).

David claims that they worked the censors the way a coach manipulates a referee, complaining about small, insignificant "calls" so that they could get away with more important envelope-pushing matters—like the use of "it" to refer to the penis ("It moved") in "The Note" (3001) ("Inside Look" for the episode).

The ending of "The Parking Garage" (3006), in which Kramer's long-misplaced car fails to start, was a nonscripted perfect moment ("Inside Look" for the episode).

Again and again we learn that the events of episodes like "The Pen" (3003) or "The Café" (3007) had their origins in the actual experiences of the writers ("Inside Look" for those episodes).

Jerry explains that by Season Three the governing principle of the series on a daily basis had become "Let's not do anything you might do on another show" ("Inside Look" for "The Café," 3007).

The famous line uttered in "The Boyfriend" (3017) by Jerry over a prostrate, de-pantsed George—"And you want to be my latex salesman"—was improvised ("Inside Look" for the episode).

When David and Seinfeld visited the set of *Murphy Brown* (1988–1998) so Kramer could make a cameo appearance ("The Keys," 3022), they were both struck that it seemed like a real sitcom, while they always thought of their own show as "an amateurish version of a real sitcom" ("Inside Look" for the episode).

Writer Peter Mehlman cites his brother's observation that it was not the show's edgy material that distinguished it but that it did it "in mixed company" ("Inside Look" for "The Contest," 4010).

The addition of the oft-repeated, now famous "not that there's anything wrong with that" in "The Outing" (4016)—Larry Charles came up with the line—saved an episode they considered abandoning by transforming its possibly offensive tone into satire ("Inside Look" for the episode).

The "rhymes with a female body part" name "Delores" was actually contributed by an audience member ("How It Began").

"We'll go watch them slice this fat bastard up": this line from "The Junior Mint" (4019), a violation of every network rule about likability and identifiability, was, according to Seinfeld, a watershed for the series: "We were really out of the barn and running wild" ("Inside Look" for the episode).

If future *Seinfeld* DVDs are comparable to those so far released, by the time all are available—all nine seasons, all 180 episodes—we should have at our disposable a superb resource for examining not only the much neglected sitcom genre but television creativity itself.

V

The present volume about the Seinfeldian universe cannot hope to map that sit-cosmos as fully as the several thousand imaginary pages of *Seinfeld* criticism David Wild envisioned, but it does explore some of the same territory. Jerry, George, Elaine, and Kramer are all examined at length, friendship is considered,

Jerry and George's masculinity is called into question, taboo and awkward subjects are brought into the open, food is simmered, parents are discussed. These and more subjects—*Seinfeld* in syndication, intertextuality, nothingness, Jane Austen, ethnicity, J. Peterman, *Seinfeld* in the Netherlands—are all given their due in a book intended to be not only an intellectual exploration of all things *Seinfeld* but a guide to the *Seinfeld* sitcosmos as well. Its editors hope that both "scholar-fans" and "fan-scholars" (to borrow Matt Hills's important distinction in *Fan Cultures*) will find it both illuminating and useful.

The book's first part, "'Giddy-up!': Introductions," provides three essay overviews of the series, by Albert Auster, noted television scholar David Marc, and Bill Wyman, as well as a miscellany of "Reflections on *Seinfeld*" by a variety of critics.

In Part II, "'Maybe the dingoes ate your baby': Genre, Humor, Intertextuality," Michael Dunne on *Seinfeld*'s intertextuality, Barbara Ching on the existential dimensions of the sitcom, Dennis Hall on the contemporaneous cultural phenomena of Jane Austen and *Seinfeld,* and Amy McWilliams on the series' revisioning of expected genre formulae all look at *Seinfeld* as a text among texts.

"'If I like their race, how can that be racist?': Gender, Generations, and Ethnicity," Part III, offers Joanna L. Di Mattia on the show's "homosociality," Matthew Bond on "Parents and Children on *Seinfeld*," and Jon Stratton on *Seinfeld*'s Jewishness.

Part IV, "'It is so sad, all your knowledge of high culture comes from Bugs Bunny cartoons': Cultural, Pop Cultural Matters, and Media Matters," endeavors to situate the *Seinfeld* sitcosmos in a variety of contexts. Geoffrey O'Brien considers it as a 1990s phenomenon; Sara Lewis Dunne cracks its food codes; Eleanor Hersey offers a cultural studies critique of the character of J. Peterman on the show; Elke van Cassel analyzes why *Seinfeld* never quite made it in the Netherlands; and Michael M. Epstein, Mark C. Rogers, and Jimmie L. Reeves scrutinize *Seinfeld* as a highly successful syndicated program.

In an afterword, David Lavery and Marc Leverette reflect upon the nature of rereading *Seinfeld* as a syndicated text and in light of Larry David's *Curb Your Enthusiasm.*

"'Get out!'," *Master of Its Domain*'s back pages, offers several appendixes, including Betty Lee's systematic "*Seinfeld* Glossary," a comprehensive episode and situation guide that identifies directors and writers and catalogs each main character's situation in each show, and a brief log of intertexts and allusions in *Seinfeld.* A composite bibliography and an index complete the volume.

Notes

1. First season episodes of *Seinfeld* drew audiences in the 15 million range. By Season Seven, the typical audience for the series had increased to over 30 million per episode. See the essay by Epstein, Rogers, and Reeves in this volume for more on *Seinfeld* economics.

2. For an excellent discussion of *Seinfeld*'s finale, see Joanne Morreale's "Sitcoms Say Goodbye: The Cultural Spectacle of *Seinfeld*'s Last Episode."

3. "Reflections on *Seinfeld*," included in Part One below, collects a variety of observations from a variety of sources on *Seinfeld*.

4. Wyman's essay is included in this volume.

5. Edited by William Irwin, *Seinfeld and Philosophy* was the founding volume in a hugely successful Open Court Press series in which academic philosophers cogitate on popular culture. *Seinfeld,* we should note, did motivate several other fannish books: Fretts's *The Entertainment Weekly* Seinfeld *Companion* (1993), Golub's *The Seinfeld Aptitude Test* (1994), Gattuso's *The Seinfeld Universe: An Unauthorized Fan's Eye View of the Entire Domain* (1996), Wild's *Seinfeld: The Totally Unauthorized Tribute* (1998), in addition to comprehensive special-issue episode guides from both *TV Guide* and *Entertainment Weekly.*

6. See Angela Hague and David Lavery, eds., *Teleparody: Predicting/Preventing the TV Discourse of Tomorrow.*

7. Thanks to the following exchange between Elaine and her current boyfriend, Blaine, we do learn a bit about this particular imaginary film:

> Elaine: Oh, c'mon, Blaine. I mean, look at the poster for *Sack Lunch.*
> Blaine: It's a family in a brown paper bag.
> Elaine: *(laughing)* Don't you wanna know how they got in there?
> Blaine: No.

Acknowledgments

This book's gestation was almost a decade, and, needless to say, it is a delight to finally see it in print.

My thanks to Sara Dunne for all her help along the way and for her fine essay.

My gratitude to Jon Stratton and to the Curtin University of Technology for making it possible to reprint Jon's excellent essay.

My thanks to all the book's other authors—Michael Dunne, Albert Auster, Bill Wyman, David Marc, Dennis Hall, Amy McWilliams, Joanna Di Mattia, Barbara Ching, Geoffrey O'Brien, Matthew Bond, Eleanor Hersey, Michael Epstein, Jimmie Reeves, Mark Rogers, Marc Leverette, and Betty Lee—for their contributions and especially for their patience.

I especially want to thank David Barker at Continuum for being receptive to our proposal and making it possible for the book to find a home. Thanks, too, for Gabriella Page-Fort for her hard work on the manuscript.

My family, all *Seinfeld* fans, have been, as usual, more supportive than I deserve. Thank you Joyce and Rachel.

Most of all, I want to acknowledge my daughter Sarah Caitlin Lavery. Only a little older than *Seinfeld*, she knows the series as well as I do and, an aspiring writer herself, toyed with writing an essay for the book to be called "Growing Up *Seinfeld*." This book is dedicated to her. (I hope, one day, she writes that essay.)

—David Lavery

I want to thank David Lavery, a gentleman, a scholar, and a helluva fellow, for inviting me to be part of this project. I also want to acknowledge the encouragement and support of my husband, Michael Dunne, and my friend, Dennis Hall, who first urged me to publish the original version of my essay about the food in *Seinfeld*.

—Sara Lewis Dunne

I

"Giddy-up!"
Introductions

ALBERT AUSTER (Fordham University)

Much Ado About Nothing

Some Final Thoughts on *Seinfeld*

This essay originally appeared in *Television Quarterly*, no. 29 (1998): 24–33.

Back when *The Mary Tyler Moore Show* went off the air in 1977 there were quite a few voices raised in protest and even more in sorrow. Feminists, especially, were practically grief-stricken. As one woman wrote years later, "Mary Richards made it OK—OK to be a single woman. OK to be over 30, OK to be independent. She made it acceptable to stay home alone and watch her if you had a mind to."

Only a few years later the end of a series became a national event. When *M*A*S*H* aired its final episode, "Goodbye, Farewell and Amen," in 1983, it was not only cause for despair, it was also the basis for the largest audiences ever gathered to watch a single television episode. Ten years later, *Cheers'* demise aroused similar feelings and a large audience, but not as large as the one for *M*A*S*H*'s finale. Although failing to eclipse *M*A*S*H*'s final episode's rating. *Cheers* fans certainly matched it in the hyperbole with which they lamented its departure. For example, novelist Kurt Vonnegut said that, "I would say that television has produced one comic masterpiece, which is *Cheers*. I wish I'd written that instead of everything I had written."

Barely five years later, we had the finale of another highly rated, critically acclaimed series, *Seinfeld*. This time, when the announcement was made of the series ending, it caused not only sorrow in some quarters but consternation: a sense that a national calamity was upon us. Indeed, *People* magazine headlined the news with the words "A Stunned Nation Prepares for Life Without *Seinfeld*."

Behind all this hype, however, one sensed a note of hysteria, especially from the TV networks. Ever since the late '80s the networks have anxiously watched their audiences decline. In 1998 that hysteria took on megabuck dimensions when NBC, faced by the loss of *Seinfeld* and with no immediate successor in sight, agreed to pay $13 million per episode for its hit doctor series *ER*.

Similarly, faced by the possible loss of its perennial and only certain top ten prime-time hit, *Monday Night Football*, ABC agreed to pay practically double what it had previously paid for the rights to broadcast the games. These events, coupled with the end of *Seinfeld*, lead one to believe that behind some of the hoopla surrounding the end was increasing the need to deliver large audiences and thus convince advertisers of the continued relevance of the networks.

Another dimension that seemed to be overlooked in the "Festivus" of grief (to those uninitiated into the *Seinfeld*ian universe this was the yuletide holiday created by George Costanza's father) surrounding *Seinfeld*'s demise was the fact that despite its huge audiences many people just didn't get it.

For example, a literate and sophisticated couple (she is a published poet with a Ph.D. in English and has written a book on Faulkner, and he is a retired successful businessman), friends of my wife and me, would often ask us (knowing we both taught media studies and I was a TV critic) what was good on television. And we would inevitably reply: *Seinfeld*.

Invariably, they would dutifully go and watch the series and then, when we met again, would ask us what we saw in it. This happened a number of times with other highly intelligent people of our acquaintance, with generally the same results. When questioned a bit further as to why they disliked the series, the consensus was that they couldn't see spending time with such unlikable people.

Nor were our friends alone. Maureen Dowd in her Op-Ed page column in *The New York Times* once denounced the show for being the last vestige of '80s Yuppie self-indulgence. And *New York Magazine* television critic John Leonard in his brief epitaph on the series demise hardly bothered to hide his disdain. He commented, "The passing of *Seinfeld*, that Cheez Doodle of urban fecklessness into cryogenic syndication, inspires no tear in this cave. Jerry, George, Kramer and Elaine never spoke for my New York. . . . in *Seinfeld* I always miss the snarl and the edge, not to mention real politics and real work . . . I know we're all so postmodern hip that we can be ironic about our own nostalgia—but nostalgic about our own irony?" Of course, Leonard and Dowd might certainly be accused of just a bit of over-the-top peevishness in their reactions to the sitcom which in other places had been referred to as "the defining sitcom of our age."

On the surface, it certainly doesn't seem to reflect well on our culture and society that its so-called defining contemporary comedy was one that dealt in such excruciating minutiae as getting a table in a Chinese restaurant, finding a parking space, or locating the perfect piece of fruit. As a matter of fact, if your heart was set on watching a show that really dealt with life's quotidian, then arguably there's no better place to start than reruns of *Ozzie and Harriet*. However, it was *Seinfeld*'s special genius to reveal the fact that God (or more precisely in *Seinfeld*'s case, the Devil) really did reside in the details.

This is especially true in times such as these when, whether or not Saddam really permits U.N. arms inspectors to get inside his palaces, and sex and subpoenas are topic number one on the Washington, D.C., agenda. They also seem beyond the power of the average citizen to exert much influence over. As a result, daily experience looms larger and larger in our minds because it is something over which we do presumably have at least some semblance of control. In addition, it is undoubtedly in small letter rather than capital letter experiences that we often gain some of life's more piquant pleasures as well as its equally bittersweet frustrations and disappointments.

Indeed, nothing can cast a pall over a day faster than finding out the milk you counted on for your morning coffee has turned sour overnight; or brighten it more quickly than discovering that the check you've been expecting came in the mail. As a result, when Jerry Seinfeld and his co-producer Larry David proposed their show about nothing to NBC executives back in 1989, little did they know that they had latched onto the veritable cultural tiger's tail.

Beside seizing on its little portion of a cultural phenomenon, the success of the show was also in no small measure due to its writing and its actors. The writing of each episode was compared by one critic to "the twisted strands of DNA." Thus, one of the particular hallmarks of *Seinfeld* was to make four often disparate story lines, each seemingly headed off toward its own individual left field, end in one place without violating *Seinfeld*'s cardinal rule of "no hugging, no learning."

For example, the *Seinfeld* episode titled "The Boyfriend" (3017), ranked fourth in *TV Guide*'s list of all-time best series episodes, in which both Elaine and Jerry vie for the attentions of former New York Mets baseball star Keith Hernandez, and George tries to get his unemployment benefits extended by fabricating a bogus job, ends in a scene where Kramer and the recently seen-for-the-first-time Newman (did we ever really learn his first name?) do a takeoff on the Kennedy assassination's Zapruder film.

Certainly other sitcoms have used the backstory–front story approach to great advantage, perhaps none better than *Seinfeld*'s predecessor in NBC's crown jewel Thursday night 9:00 p.m. time slot, *Cheers*. However, what set *Seinfeld* apart from these other series was its ability to have the final scene turn into a socko punch line ending that summed up the previous action and left you scratching your head in wonder at the brilliance of the program's inventiveness.

For that matter, not very many sitcoms equaled *Seinfeld* for the consistency and quality of its surreal situations. Sitcoms would have to go a long way to best Kramer and George's father's invention of the male bra (or, as Kramer called it, "the bro" ["The Doorman," 6016]); the churlish bubble boy who asks Susan to take off her top ("The Bubble Boy," 4006); and perhaps most over-the-top of all, the death of George's fiancée from licking toxic glue on the cheap wedding invitation envelopes he forced her to buy ("The Invitations," 7022). This episode has been the most frequently criticized of all *Seinfeld* shows for going a bit too far.

None of those story lines and fantastic moments would have meant anything without the gifted ensemble that emerged over the years to play them. Lost now in all the hosannas over the passing of the program was the fact that when it debuted back in July of 1989 as *The Seinfeld Chronicles*, it was a show without Elaine (Julia Louis-Dreyfus), and Kramer (Michael Richards), rather than being the mooch and the constant intruder into Jerry's apartment that he would later become, was a recluse who hadn't been out of his apartment for ten years. Also forgotten in all the *post hoc* praise was the fact that the show, which one early critic termed "mildly amusing," was clobbered when it was opposite *Home Improvement*.

Clearly, in its first years, and not until after it was salvaged by placing it in the surefire time slot after *Cheers,* the program was a cult favorite and an acquired taste. Much of that early popularity was in no small part due to such things as the misadventures of George Costanza (Jason Alexander), whose whining and self-destructiveness would made Dostoyevsky's underground man seem like the paragon of narcissism.

George's style included such kamikaze antics as getting fired from one job because he had sex with the cleaning lady ("The Red Dot," 3012); and trying to get a date with actress Marissa Tomei practically moments after the death of Susan. Indeed, by comparison no one but a lord of losers like George could make you believe that his boss at the New York Yankees, the famously autocratic George Steinbrenner, was a cuddly version of Mr. Magoo.

Equaling George's outrageous behavior, and undoubtedly surpassing him as the source of the show's original claim on the public's affections, was the hyperkinetic Kramer. Nothing, except perhaps Ed Norton's (Art Carney) balletic arrivals at Ralph and Alice Kramden's apartment in *The Honeymooners,* compared to the whirling dervish entrances of Kramer into Jerry's apartment to serve himself a bowl of cereal, or inform Jerry of his latest scheme for rickshaws to be pulled by the homeless ("The Bookstore," 9017).

Perhaps most unforgettable of all were Kramer's brief but always doomed attempts at normalcy. For example, in the unjustly overlooked story line in the much praised episode "Bizarro Jerry" (8003), Kramer starts working at the firm of Brandt-Leland (despite not being hired and not getting paid), which starts his and Jerry's relationship deteriorating into a parody of the classic pattern of the nagging housewife and the workaholic husband. Ultimately, it was Kramer's aptitude for physical comedy (joyfully reminiscent of such silent clowns as Keaton and Chaplin), coupled with his zany schemes and eccentric friends, that provided each episode with its unique bit of Dadaist counterpoint.

In the very same "Bizarro Jerry" episode in which Kramer starts his job, Elaine discovers a group of friends who are the mirror opposites of Jerry and his friends, and despite the show's no hugging, no learning *obiter dicta*, we do gain just a bit of insight into the real Elaine. Originally added to the cast to provide the show with a bit of "estrogen," and given a history as Jerry's ex-girlfriend, the smart, diminutive, feisty Elaine has more than her fair share of zany adventures and weird jobs. Indeed she is the "best man" at a lesbian wedding ("The Subway," 3013), finds her nipple exposed in the picture she includes in her personal Christmas card ("The Pick," 4012), and works as the personal assistant to the eccentric millionaire Mr. Pitt, who is so aristocratic he eats his Snickers bars with a knife and fork ("The Pledge Drive," 6003).

Nonetheless, despite these comic misadventures, Elaine is the only character on the show who seems to know or care that there is a world beyond the hermetically sealed universe of Monk's coffee shop and Jerry's apartment, so beloved of Jerry, George, and Kramer. However, despite yearning for the "Bizarro Jerry" world of her friend Kevin and his pals Gene and Feldman, where in contrast to Jerry's world everyone is nice to one another, goes to the ballet, and reads books together, she's been so shaped and tainted by her association with Jerry, George, and Kramer, she's become a total misfit in polite society.

It's this struggle with conventional society that was also the hallmark of Jerry Seinfeld's character on *Seinfeld*. In interview after interview, Jerry cited the movie *Lenny* (1971) as one of his major comic inspirations. Now, nothing could be more different than the blessed life of this child of middle-class Long Island parents, who graduated from Queens College and practiced and polished his stand-up routines in Yuppie comedy clubs, and the tortured existence of the so-called "sick" comic who grew up and learned his craft in a world of strippers and burlesque comics, and whose brief but legendary career ended in the drugged-out vortex of criminal prosecutions and paranoia.

It was the now legendary NBC programming chief Brandon Tartikoff who originally dismissed the *Seinfeld* show's chances of success with the comment that it was too Jewish and too New York. Nevertheless, besides their both being young, Jewish, and urban, Bruce and Jerry also shared, in varying degrees, a kind of alienation from the middle-class world. It is the virtual condition of every comedian's life that he works while most of the rest of the world sleeps and that the seeds of his/her art are bred in a kind of ironic detachment from everyday life. Therefore, in a term borrowed from the gay ("not that there's anything wrong with that") world, the comedian is continually at odds with straight society.

The fictional Jerry's long string of dates and relationships that never seem to work out, his moderate success as a stand-up comic, his generally good "buffer zone" relationship with his parents in Florida, and his spotlessly neat and clean Upper West Side bachelor pad testify to both his middle-class background and his aspirations. But the fictional Jerry's conventional tendencies are constantly at war with, and undermined by, his ultra-fastidiousness (Jerry breaks up with women for such petty reasons as eating peas one at a time ["The Engagement," 7001], liking Dockers pants commercials ["The Phone Message," 2004], and using a toothbrush that accidentally fell into the toilet bowl ["The Pothole," 8016]), fear of commitment, and self-absorption.

These latter traits reached epic proportions in the very same episode in which George's fiancée dies. Jerry, facing a life alone with Kramer, thinks he's in love with Jeannie Steinman (Janeane Garofalo), who has his initials, loves cereal, and riffs on brunches and shirt collars just like him ("The Invitations," 7022). In a rare moment of self-awarness, he concludes that "Now I know what I've been waiting for all these years—myself," only to break up with her when he also realizes that he hates himself.

Added to this was Jerry's often reluctant, petty outlaw behavior. Jerry thinks nothing of mugging an old lady for a marble rye bread ("The Rye," 7011); he makes out with a date during a screening of *Schindler's List* ("The Raincoats," 5019); he's hunted by the public library for a twenty-year overdue copy of *Tropic of Cancer* ("The Library," 3005); and when advising someone about breaking up a relationship, he suggests the brutal approach of doing it like removing a Band-Aid, "one motion, right off" ("The Ex-Girlfriend," 2001). As a result, despite Jerry's best efforts, he seems to be in a kind of perpetual unconscious guerrilla struggle with respectability.

This latter battle was one of the guilty pleasures of *Seinfeld*. In recent years, television drama and comedy emphasized either the dastardly conduct of the rich, such as in *Dallas* and *Dynasty*, or the dysfunctional behavior of the working class found in *Roseanne* and *Married . . . with Children*. *Seinfeld* was unique in that it examined the not-so-discreet churlish charm of the bourgeoisie. In contrast to the generations of family- and friends-style sitcoms, whose characters, despite frequent misunderstandings, were ultimately generous and mutually supportive of one another, Jerry, George, Kramer, and Elaine never missed an opportunity to compete with, lie to, and backstab one another.

Not only did the fearsome foursome wreak havoc on each other, it usually extended to anyone in their wake. Heading the long list of *Seinfeld's* victims—which included the likes of Jerry's friend Babu, who was deported back to Pakistan because Jerry forgot to file his visa application ("The Visa," 4014)—was George's Job-like fiancée, Susan Ross (Heidi Swedeborg). Even before their fatal engagement, she had to endure Kramer's misplaced Cuban cigar burning down her parents' cabin ("The Bubble Boy," 4006), as well as the later embarrassment of the discovery of love letters from novelist John Cheever to her father found in the cabin's ashes ("The Cheever Letters," 4007); losing her job at NBC; and the breakup of a lesbian relationship—all because of George.

This cycle of devastation even extended to their own families. For example, when Jerry's parents heard that the dreaded Costanzas are about to move to their condominium in Florida, they move in with Jerry, thus putting an end to his precious "buffer zone" ("The Showerhead," 7015). Similarly, when Jerry buys his father a new Cadillac, it results in the condo's board, of which he is president, voting to impeach him à la Watergate—they think he must be embezzling funds, because they don't believe a mere comedian could afford to buy his father such an expensive car ("The Cadillac," 7014). Indeed, though Jerry Seinfeld himself claimed *Abbott and Costello* as another of his comic muses (and the series' use of dialogue and language confirms this), the main characters'-stick-in-the-eye approach to one another, and everyone else, seemed more akin to the *Three Stooges*.

Nothing, however, rivaled *Seinfeld* for its version of postmodern etiquette. There was, for instance, the *Seinfeld* guide to dating that includes how many dates you have to have before it is still proper to break up a relationship over the phone rather than in person (only two); how long after sleeping with a woman you have to keep dating her (three weeks); and for those needing guidance on the subject, the information that the longer you know someone, the shorter you have to wait for them in the street; that you only have to keep a thank-you card for two days (unless you have a mantle); and you should never "degift" (take back something you give) or "regift" (give away something you receive).

Less frequently acknowledged, but nonetheless an essential ingredient of quite a few *Seinfeld* episodes, were mild satiric jabs at political correctness (especially ironic in a show supposedly about nothing). For example, Kramer is beaten up at an AIDS walkathon for refusing to wear a red ribbon ("The Sponge," 7009); George's father's car is vandalized when George parks in a disabled parking spot ("The Parking Space," 3021); and in an episode that prompted a network apology,

Kramer is attacked when he stomps on a burning Puerto Rican flag during the Puerto Rican Day Parade ("The Puerto Rican Day," 9020). The inspiration for these incidents is neither conservative nor liberal politically; instead, they seemed inspired by the series' radical individualism, or, put in a showbiz idiom, "Screw 'em, if they can't take a joke!"

Unfortunately, this indifference to politics and society did have its downside. For example, black characters in their infrequent appearances on the series rarely rose above the level of caricature. Thus, lawyer Jackie Chiles, the series' parody of Johnnie Cochran, seems an *Amos 'n Andy* lineal descendant of George "Kingfish" Stevens and Algonquin J. Calhoun.

If the series did have one strong point in its dealings with race, it was with the embarrassment and uneasiness that middle-class whites often feel about the issue. As a result, in one episode Elaine, because she's afraid of being considered a bigot, goes through all sorts of contortions in order to discover the race of the somewhat-swarthy man she's been dating (Jerry thinks he's black ["The Wizard," 9015].

Of course, Elaine's racial guessing game is mild in comparison to the larger question that often plagued the series—the extent to which the series went to hide not only its cultural Jewishness but any sort of religiosity. Though the series, apropos of Tartikoff's caveat, is replete with Jewish body language and syntax (George's head slappings and comments like "Again with the keys"); references (Bar Mitzvahs, the Holocaust, Florida condos, and Elaine being referred to as having *shiksappeal*), nevertheless, *Seinfeld* was always the artful dodger in explicitly acknowledging its Judaism. As a result, we have a funeral of a relative from Krakow without a yarmulke in sight ("The Pony Remark," 2002). When George wants to convert to "Latvian Orthodox" in order to impress a woman ("The Conversion," 5011), it's never really made clear what religion he wants to convert from.

All of these elements, both positive and negative, came together in the series' intellectually consistent, but generally less than hilarious, final episode. It was a conclusion that some finale mavens rated as inferior to *Mary Tyler Moore*'s sign-off, but better than *M*A*S*H*'s, and undoubtedly the equal of *Cheers*' curtain call. Nevertheless, the hoopla that surrounded the show paid off in Superbowl-type ratings that almost equaled *Cheers*' final episode (which, to be fair, is quite good, given the fact that the champion *M*A*S*H*'s and *The Fugitive*'s finales never had to contend with the inroads of cable).

There was, in addition, one other record set by the passing of *Seinfeld*. Some sort of Guinness mark must have been achieved for shortest post-TV-finale attention span by the modern media hype machine. In less time than it took to say "get out," that colossus had made a 180-degree turn, and was in overdrive about another story—the death of Frank Sinatra on May 14, 1998. In the heat of the coverage of the death of the man whose voice had become the soundtrack for millions of lives worldwide, the ballyhoo over *Seinfeld* faded like a snowstorm in July.

As a matter of fact, in what seemed like less than a nanosecond, the Upper West Side had been exorcised by images of Hoboken on the television landscape—memories of the antics of Jerry, George, Kramer, and Elaine were replaced by nostalgia about the hijinks of Rat Packers Frank, Dino, Sammy, Peter, Joey, and Shirley, and "ring-a-ding-ding" substituted for "yada, yada, yada."

The hype meltdown aside, *Seinfeld*'s finale's most solid achievement was to manage to conclude without violating the consistency of the series' major characters or its major themes. This was perhaps a bit more difficult for *Seinfeld* than either for *M*A*S*H, Mary Tyler Moore,* or *Cheers.* In those earlier finales, there was the end of the Korean War, the purchase of the TV station by a media conglomerate, and the closing of the bar to serve as justifications for these programs' bittersweet conclusions. For *Seinfeld*, there was no such easy rationale.

Also in comparison to *MTM, M*A*S*H,* and *Cheers,* where fans and critics cited certain episodes such as "Chuckles the Clown Bites the Dust," "Abbyssinia, Henry," etc., as highlights of the series, but left it for later generations to decide which of them were "classics"—*Seinfeld*'s fans, along with a number of entertainment periodicals and critics, had already constructed an elaborate pantheon of the series' most inspired episodes and anointed them as the *Seinfeld* canon. As a result, there was hardly any room for additions, which made the task of any final episode much more difficult.

The final episode, however, if not fall-on-the-floor funny, was still amusing and, in this most self-referential of all series, must have set a record for self-references. Concocted under a cloak of secrecy that the media claimed rivaled the Manhattan Project, former co-executive producer and head writer Larry David created a virtual concordance of some of the series' major moments, characters, and themes. Receiving curtain calls were story lines such as *The Jerry Show*, George and Jerry's self-reflexive show about nothing, which they had tried unsuccessfully to peddle to the network in the series' fourth season. Characters included lawyer Jackie Chiles, the Bubble Boy, Susan Ross's parents, and others, all of whose appearances, as character witnesses, were occasioned by the trial of the foursome for violating the Latham, Massachusetts, "Good Samaritan" Law

In addition, David, in a bow to the show's most ardent fans, even included moments that alluded to their dreams of how the series should end. Thus, to those who believed that the show's rightful consummation should have been Jerry and Elaine's wedding, there was a moment when the corporate jet on which they are flying seemed to crash and Elaine appeared about to confess her abiding love for Jerry, only to squelch it moments later when they were saved.

Finally, in an homage to the only love affair the show really ever had—its passion for symmetry—the finale's concluding moments made a bow to the series' origins with Jerry in a jailhouse jumpsuit (George and Kramer in attendance, but Elaine nowhere in sight) doing his stand-up routine for the cons, spouting trademark insouciant lines such as "So, what's the deal about the 'yard'?"

This final allusion to the fictional and the real Jerry's beginnings in stand-up may be to some extent a suggestion about his immediate future. However, one might not go wrong in predicting another sitcom in the not-too-distant *Seinfeld* future. As a matter of fact, after the show's finale a very sober, almost solemn Jerry (in contrast to the *Cheers* cast, which was boisterously and blissfully drunk in its curtain call on the *Tonight Show* after its finale) appeared with Jay Leno to talk about his future. Upon his entrance, the studio audience's standing ovation was so intense and so prolonged that it prompted him to wave and seem to head offstage teasingly shouting, "OK, come on, let's do another season."

Whether Jerry Seinfeld can resist the future siren call of the sitcom better than the likes of equally talented stand-ups who starred in hit sitcoms (Bill Cosby, Bob Newhart) remains to be seen. What is not moot is that in a sitcom world where there is so much unrelieved similarity, *Seinfeld* stood out because of its originality and steadfast insistence on being true to itself. This makes it especially noteworthy in a medium where we've become so inured to the sameness of sitcoms that some teenagers can even shout story lines back to the screen à la *The Rocky Horror Picture Show.*

Seinfeld was also special because it continued and kept alive a tradition inherent in *The Mary Tyler Moore Show, M*A*S*H,* and *Cheers:* that at its very best the sitcom has the potential to become an authentic American comedy of manners. In this, *Seinfeld* succeeded by becoming the television comedy that pointed out the imprecision of our contemporary relationships and gave a name to the sources of our modem urban anxiety.

As a result of these efforts, *Seinfeld* achieved something that not even *Mary Tyler Moore, M*A*S*H,* and *Cheers* ever accomplished, which was to create adjectives akin to the literary-inspired Dickensian and Kafkaesque. Hereafter, something is *Seinfeld*ian—or in its more common usage, an event or character is "just like a *Seinfeld* episode"—when it breaks the fourth wall of conventional expectations to reveal the potential of the everyday as a source of both art and philosophy. So, despite its best efforts at adhering (even on to the very last) to its rule of "no hugging, no learning," *Seinfeld* left us with a very rich legacy after all.

DAVID MARC (Syracuse University)

ʃeinfeld

A Show (Almost) About Nothing

This essay appeared in somewhat different form in *Comic Visions: Television Comedy and American Culture.* Second edition. Malden, Massachusetts: Blackwell, 1999: 199–203.

Back in the early days of TV, when intellectuals were still making believe that the home screen wasn't the center of American culture, "nothing" was a very popular topic among high-culture writers. There was Jean-Paul Sartre's *Being and Nothingness,* a topic that took the French philosophe well over six hundred pages to explain. Samuel Beckett was writing plays such as *Waiting for Godot* and *Endgame,* which held literally hundreds of theatergoers glued to their seats for hours as they searched for significance in apparently meaningless conversations. If movies were your thing, you could stare at a Stan Brakhage film, such as the *Weir Falcon Saga,* for up to six hours at a time and not even hear a sound of any kind, much less some pithy dialogue. TV meanwhile, with its endless stream of heavily plotted soap operas, cop shows, and sitcoms, was establishing a reputation for itself as Idiot's Delight Number One.

Perhaps it's a case of trickle-down culture, but barely a half century later, the biggest hit on TV turned out to be a sitcom that described itself as a "a show about nothing." Has Jerry Seinfeld succeeded in bringing situation comedy to the existential abyss so coveted by post–World War II intellectuals? I don't think so. After watching a couple of hundred episodes I've come to the conclusion that *Seinfeld* handles a number of topics beyond being and nothingness. These include: being Jewish in America, being a straight white single guy with middle-class values living in the inner city, being more successful than your friends, and being full of wisecracks utterly bereft of political or social idealism.

Like Jack Benny, George Burns, and Roseanne before him, Jerry Seinfeld is a Jewish stand-up comedian starring in a sitcom about the life of a stand-up comedian who happens to have the same name in so-called real life. Like his predecessors, Seinfeld likes to shuffle back and forth across a metaphoric proscenium, speaking sometimes directly to the audience as a stand-up comic and at other times indirectly as a dramatic character living a fictional life. Of these four Jewish comedians, Jerry is the only one whose sitcom identity is established as Jewish. This is ironic, because Seinfeld is perhaps the least Jewish of them. He is at first glance Jerry the American, one of TV's "us," a televisually acceptable, collegiately dressed SWM. But he has also identified himself as one of mytho-America's "them," a New York Jew, a sarcastic, wisecracking cynic with an overbite, living on the margin of the middle state. While he's better looking than Alfred Kazin, he does live in the same neighborhood.

In its semidetached Jewishness, *Seinfeld* shares more with the early fiction of Phillip Roth (especially *Goodbye, Columbus* and *Portnoy's Complaint*) than with the openly Jewish American sitcom characters that could be found in shows such as *The Goldbergs, Rhoda,* or *Bridget Loves Bernie.* Like Alexander Portnoy, Jerry lives out a dilemma that is simultaneously his deepest source of anxiety and his richest resource of strength. He can do more than pass for a successful American; he *is* a successful American, militantly bourgeois in attitude and bank account, apparently freed of the burdens of millennial suffering, and ready and willing to take on the high-end problems of sexual gratification, unchecked consumerism, and dinner at good restaurants in the post-Auschwitz universe. Yet somehow, like the early Roth characters, Jerry cannot help but be heir to the legacy of the Diaspora. His sense of humor, the very asset that has allowed him entrée to an advantaged hedonistic secular life among the *goyim,* remains rooted in a marginal point of view that grows out of exclusion. Jerry needs exclusion and, without his Jewishness, he is unexcludable.

The Jazz Singer is perhaps the most seminal of all Jewish American texts, and its themes pervade *Seinfeld.* In the 1927 film, Al Jolson is split between two identities: He is born Jakie Rabinowitz, scion of a cantorial dynasty whose wanderings have recently landed the tribal gene pool on the Lower East Side of early-twentieth-century Manhattan, U.S.A. He attempts, however, to remake himself into the all-American Jack Robin, an entertainer who has forsaken the ghetto shul for the bright lights of American show business. Jack gets his big break to star on Broadway. But just when he thinks he has fully transcended the entire chosen people/"*oy-how-vee-suffad*" thing, his heritage harkens him back and he cannot resist.

His father, whom he has not seen in twenty years, is sick. There is no one to sing the service on Yom Kippur. Against all American reason, Jolson dons his prayer shawl and does the family business, missing opening night on Broadway, choosing to sing "Kol Nidre" rather than "Toot, Toot, Tootsie, Good-bye." The remarkable and bizarre ending of *The Jazz Singer* finds Jakie/Jack wearing black-face, singing mammy songs to a sold-out Broadway theater, despite his having committed the greatest of all show business sins: the show did not go on. Does he marry his gentile girlfriend and spawn children who will not have the Right of Return? We do not know. This is perhaps the only musical ever made in Hollywood that simply drops the love-interest story in the middle of the movie without ever resolving it. It was just too hot to handle. Jerry, like Jakie, goes out with shiksas, but thus far hasn't married one either.

Seventy years later and several miles uptown, Jerry is no Yeshiva boy, but he is also under no illusions about transcending his Jewishness. He has learned the lesson of *The Jazz Singer* well. Like Jolson, he enjoys the money and the small-nosed glamour girls. But no matter how American his show business success makes him, he takes it for granted that he will always carry a second psychological passport. He is neither embarrassed by his Jewishness (à la Walter Lippman) nor enamored of it (à la Norman Podhoretz). He accepts the cards that were dealt him and makes the most of his hand, moving seamlessly between two spheres of consciousness with as much grace and refinement as he can muster. He would never do something so stupid as to agree to a New York opening on Yom Kippur. He'd fire his agent before making a boneheaded blunder like that.

His best friend, George (Jason Alexander), would like to enjoy the American garden of gentile delights the way Jerry does, but he cannot. He remains a prisoner of the Bronx. Round, balding, and bespectacled, he is not only physically removed from goyish ideals of televisual masculinity, but psychologically mired in a tangle of neuroses that he has inherited wholesale from his father (Jerry Stiller). "Next to George," Joshua Ozersky wrote in a recent doctoral dissertation, "Jerry seems like Lee Marvin." And this is exactly what Jerry wants. The flexible Jerry is more successful than George at the two most important pursuits in single-American culture: making money and getting laid.

George is a sitcomic flourish at the fiction of Isaac Bashevis Singer. There is George the *schlemiel*: he meets an attractive woman on the subway and goes with her to a hotel room, only to find himself handcuffed to the bed without his clothes. There is George the *schlmazel*: when he is accused of racism for telling an African-American coworker that he resembles Sugar Ray Leonard, he finds himself compelled to stop black people on the street to try to befriend them ("The Diplomat Club," 6020). But above all, there is George the *nebbish*: we learn in one typical episode that all the principal characters masturbate frequently ("The Contest," 4010). But only George gets caught by his mother (Estelle Harris) while doing it.

What does a man seeing successful figures at both the bank and the mirror see in a friendship with such a broadly defined American failure? Jerry the American needs George around to remind him of his Jewishness, which, despite any difficulties it might present, is after all the secret engine of his professional success—the source of his humor. Though George has no experience as a writer, Jerry takes him as his collaborator in creating a new television sitcom ("The Pitch," 4003).

If George speaks to Jerry's Jewishness, Elaine (Julia Louis-Dreyfus) speaks to Jerry's peculiar position as a straight white man living the cosmopolitan life. An outwardly graceful but internally haggard New Yorker, Elaine enhances the suggestion of Jerry as the enlightened postfeminist American guy. A former lover, she is now one of his best friends—and as such offers proof of just how erect his consciousness is.

Elaine's chief identity is that of Single American Working Woman. Like her sitcom sisters Mary Richards and Murphy Brown, she has yet to find a man worth slowing down for. Unlike them, however, Elaine lacks a position in the lucrative television industry. Murphy and Mary both work in TV; when we meet Elaine, she is working in publishing. Enough said. Ultimately, she must work at a succession of jobs for neurotic and borderline psychotic men who derive much of their pleasure in life from being her boss. Elaine lacks a traditional ethnic identity, but instead is principally hyphenated as a single-American. This stands in contrast to George's ethnic hyperbole, leaving Jerry just where he likes to be: in perfect balance at the American middle. He has girls, money, and power enough to play philosopher-king among the working stiffs (be they characters in the cast or the audience).

Jerry's perfect balance in the order of things is emphasized yet again by his physical positioning between tall, ectomorphic, manic Kramer (Michael Richards) and short, endomorphic, monopolar George. Kramer functions in the sitcom as a kind of postmodern Ed Norton, entering and leaving Jerry's unlocked apartment at will. (The unlocked door of the inner-city apartment has somehow endured from *The Honeymooners* to *Seinfeld* as a theatrical convention that defies all rationalizations of verisimilitude.)

Kramer's susceptibility to every identity that passes him by—entrepreneur, gambler, chef, playboy, hot tub owner—puts him in a state of constant self-image chaos in sharp contrast to Jerry's elegantly constructed self. Remarkably, Jerry, the least marginal of the four characters, is the only one who is specifically and repeatedly identified as a Jew.

Jerry defies both of the popular stereotypes about Jews: he is neither a left-leaning do-gooder nor a tough-minded businessman. He is a man committed to only one thing: detachment. He makes fun of Elaine when she stops going out with an attractive man who is an opponent of abortion rights ("The Couch," 6005). He makes fun of Marxists when Elaine starts dating one ("The Race," 6010). He makes fun of fascists when George is mistaken for a neo-Nazi leader ("The Limo," 3018). But positing no political beliefs of his own, and glad to take potshots at anyone who does, he leaves the viewer with the impression that anyone stupid enough to be committed to believe in anything, as opposed to nothing, deserves ridicule.

Seinfeld then is not so much a show about nothing as a show that advocates nothing. As such it may be remembered as the perfect period piece of the American 1990s. How will the 1990s be remembered in the twenty-first century? Only the syndication numbers will tell.

BILL WYMAN

Seinfeld

A version of this essay originally appeared on Salon.com on January 7, 2002.

The very idea of art has been so discombobulated by popular culture over the past five decades that notions of technical mastery, of dizzying scrupulousness and hallucinogenic detail, have lost a lot of force. Degrees of precision in classical sculpture and painting—the breathtaking emotions and the dizzying details—seem to have no counterpart in the present age. You don't have to be a cultural nostalgist to concede that, if nothing else, the artists of the past seemed technical masters of their media in a way that almost nothing today approaches.

In the mechanical or structural sense, the modern era has its areas of artistic precision. But these are most often hidden behind a patina of sparseness or repetition, as in our great skyscrapers. There are technicians, sometimes acclaimed, at work in film (Steven Spielberg, Ridley Scott), but they are emotionally crude, low on subtext, and too often manipulative. Technical mastery in pop music seems less important than ever, from a metal god shredding his electric guitar on stage to Elton John elbowing out the masters of Broadway for the latest hit musical. Even the innovators in futuristic pop—the turntablists and collagist producers—adhere to the treasured rock 'n' roll verities of down-and-dirty productions. Indeed, the modern age has come to make us view technical brilliance in the arts a bit suspiciously. Why? Are our artists today just not detail-minded? Do they lack the patience, the imagination, to work on such a precise level? Is detail on that level just not part of contemporary culture?

On the other hand, it's possible that the people in previous eras looked at Michelangelo's frescoes in the Sistine Chapel, gazed at a Bernini statue or a Van Dyck portrait, and took it for granted. These works were part of the tapestry of the age, and after the novelty wears off, the art—and this was often public art—faded into the background.

Perhaps today we take things for granted as well. What if the true cultural brilliance of our time existed right under our noses? It might be something that was well liked and even respected, but might not be recognized for its mastery. It might be something that we'd not even suspect of such artistry, precision, and meticulous attention to detail. It might be a TV show. It might even be a sitcom. It might be . . . *Seinfeld.*

I didn't watch *Seinfeld* for most of its run. I sneered at broadcast television. Friends met every Thursday to hoot over it, but I never deigned to join them. It wasn't until its last year on the air, sometime in 1999, that I happened to catch a scene—a rerun, as it turned out—that brought me up short.

George Costanza, Jerry Seinfeld's friend, is sitting in a car with a woman outside her apartment, late at night. The dynamic was appreciable in an instant: a tubby bald guy with a nice looking woman, the date winding down.

You could see the emotional accounting of the moment trip through the woman's mind: *He's a schlub, but he's obviously willing to please; I don't have to get up that early in the a.m.; it's been months since I've been laid; I don't have to go out with him again; my friend downstairs is out of town, so there's no chance of her busting me with him; it may be just that I had two glasses of wine but he's not that bad looking*

And you could see her all-but-perceptibly shrug when, in the end, the bottom line appeared, and it favored the schlub.

Sitting next to her was George, enduring the calculations; he was at an age, 30-ish, by which such moments were familiar. He waited patiently. Then came the shrug. The woman turned to him. "Would you like to come up for a cup of coffee?" she asked.

This seconds-long moment was already an exquisitely brutal and compressed masterpiece of conception and acting. And at this point, with the tension exquisitely tight, we, the viewers, were sighing with nervous relief for the schlub—this is how guys like George get lucky, after all; it's not pretty, but it works for them—when George broke into our reverie.

"Coffee?" he scowled. "No! It keeps me up all night!"

The woman looked at him with a burst of disbelief, and then her face flickered with the quick realization that she'd lucked out—been given an inadvertent reprieve by someone who was a bigger loser than she'd appreciated. "OK," she said, and got out of the car.

George remained in his seat, stunned at what he'd just said and marveling savagely at the urges that moved him.

That scene was my introduction to the show, and I quickly saw how a significant part of it was created along those lines: tableaux of human fecklessness imagined and wrought and presented with an adamantine clarity no less intoxicating than the smooth stone of "Apollo and Daphne" or the riotous imagery on the dominant wall of the Sistine Chapel.

There are great movies released every year, great rock albums, great TV shows. *The Simpsons* is as dense as—even denser than—*Seinfeld,* but its deliberate cartooniness and shotgun approach to humor, however devilish, limit its timelessness. *Will & Grace* and *Frasier* are both scintillatingly written and mischievously themed, but both have a too-small worldview. On cable, sitcom-style series like *The Larry Sanders Show* or *Absolutely Fabulous* were conceived and written by creators with malevolent worldviews and a fine ear for human foibles. Yet even against them the mordant eye and literary deviltry of *Seinfeld* holds its own, and it did it, swimming upstream, so to speak, in a much more mainstream medium.

It's not just that, put simply, *Seinfeld* is about how evil humanity is, though the show certainly makes that point. I think its message is a slightly more elevated one. From the direction to the acting and the writing, the show is all about the joy of charting, in exquisite, unrelenting, almost celebratory detail, the infinitely variegated human interactions that, closely watched, will ultimately tell the story of the disintegration of our species.

The show, for those who are unfamiliar with it, features a guy named Jerry who makes a decent living as a stand-up comic. (The star is stand-up comedian Jerry Seinfeld; I'm using the present tense because it's still viewable on a daily basis in many markets.) We never see him practice, and his interest in his work seems deliberately casual. He has some unspoken code of his art—he looks down at certain other comedians—but he's not too edgy himself.

He doesn't run with a fast showbiz crowd; rather, the great part of his existence is spent in the company of a loser friend of his from high school, an ex-girlfriend, and an unconventional mooch across the hall.

The friend, George Costanza, is played by Jason Alexander. He can't keep a job and is devoid of talents or ambition in an almost systematic way—which is to say, he determinedly devotes more time and effort to *avoiding* work than he does actually working. He is so amoral as to sometimes seem almost a monster, ready to lie, cheat, or steal to give himself a slight edge up in a world he firmly believes dealt him the worst of hands.

The ex is Elaine Benes (Julia Louis-Dreyfus), a not-unattractive woman whose laudable penchant for confrontation is taken to almost sociopathic levels and who in this way functions as the closest thing the show has to a traditional male figure.

And the mooch is Kramer (Michael Richards), a gangling elf across the way who doesn't work but seems blessed with a cosmic guardian angel, though he, like the others, is more often taunted by fate than rewarded by it. (And in the *Seinfeld* worldview, fate is nothing more than the world the characters make for themselves.)

Show lore has it that Seinfeld and a stand-up pal, Larry David, were considering a sitcom offer from NBC when David came up with an idea about a sitcom "about nothing." This idea is at once contemptuous and arrogant in the extreme; in an odd way, the pair thought themselves so superior to the medium that they could do a show about *nothing* and it would still be better than the dreck that was on TV. NBC took the bait.

Another widely accepted bit of *Seinfeld*iana is that Costanza is a stand-in for David, who quickly became the show's executive producer. (David left before the last season but came back to write the final episode.) George may be the show's most precise realization—born a white male in the most fabulously wealthy country in the history of the world, George uses nothing of what nature gave him in a resentful, infantilizing war against reality. To him, life is a very long line to get some necessity, and he views virtually everyone around him with the suspicion and hostility of a Soviet housewife waiting all day for a loaf of bread.

George is capable of eating an éclair he finds in a garbage can; pushing children and the elderly out of the way if he thinks he's in danger; smiling when he learns his dreaded fiancée has died; taking advantage of—even physically combating—the infirm or physically handicapped; and lying and then sticking to the lie even though everyone in his immediate vicinity knows he's not telling the truth. He's selfish and self-pitying, cheap and reflexively untruthful, and lives in a world of such flattened ambition that even his fantasies are pathetic. "I always wanted," he says elegantly in "The Marine Biologist" (5014), "to pretend that I was an architect."

Seinfeld watches the four cast members go about their lives, debating the tiniest of life's details. The first lines between Jerry and George in the show's very first episode are a fabulously reductionist sample of Jerry's stand-up humor, as he takes aim at a new dress shirt George is wearing: "To me, that button is in the worst possible spot. The second button literally makes or breaks the shirt. Look at it: it's too high, it's in no-man's-land. You look like you live with your mother."

What followed was eight and a half seasons of this stuff. Jerry tries to find out why his date didn't eat her pie at dinner ("The Pie," 5015). George schemes to find a way to sleep without detection at work ("The Nap," 8018). Elaine plots to rid herself of her reputation as the office skank ("The Bookstore," 9017). Jerry and George devise a means of allowing Jerry to break up with a girlfriend and date her roommate ("The Switch," 6011). Kramer take up golf and hires himself a caddy ("The Caddy," 7012)—or forms a company and hires himself an intern

("The Voice," 9002). Some episodes are now legendary for the existential punch—the four spend an entire episode waiting for a table at a Chinese restaurant ("The Chinese Restaurant," 2011), or looking for a car in a parking garage ("The Parking Garage," 3006), or trying to get to a dinner party ("The Dinner Party," 5013). In perhaps the slyest of these, George tells the merciless parents of his late fiancée that he has a house in the Hamptons and then finds himself driving the implacable pair out there to see it, even though both he and they know it doesn't exist ("The Wizard," 9015).

As in the set piece with George and his date, over and over again we see modern-man agonists, swept up by banal urges about the most minor of comforts as they solidly trump once-stronger and more atavistic ones. Jerry, relentlessly chary of germs, tosses clothing items that touch bathroom fixtures and could never again kiss a woman whose toothbrush he saw fall into the toilet.

Nothing was too small-minded for Seinfeld and David to tackle, from discussions of the most minute of human behaviors to . . . well, to other minute behaviors: constipation and masturbation, evasion and prevarication, the pettiest envies and the most banal euphemisms. George tries to give Elaine a sweater he got cheap because it had a spot on it ("The Red Dot," 3012), then plots to fail an eye test so he can get books on tape ("The Fatigues," 8006). Elaine ponders her bragging rights when she dates a guy who's gone to medical school but hasn't yet technically gotten his doctor's license ("The Abstinence," 8009). Jerry forgets the name of the woman he's dating ("The Junior Mint," 4019); another he drugs, not to rape her but to play with her toys—her *real* toys, not metaphorical ones ("The Merv Griffin Show," 9006).

The emotional relations between friends and lovers become a bottomless abyss of ontological inquiry. What defines a male friend (going to the airport? helping you move? being a "come with" guy who goes with you to the laundromat?) and what doesn't (calling him to say thank-you for hockey tickets and washing your underwear together, among other things).

In a remarkable scene early on, Jerry and Elaine, determined to sleep together again, rationalize it in a hysterical discussion about "this" (i.e., their friendship) and "that" (i.e., sex) ("The Deal," 2009). Foreplay is reduced to a ballet of sophistry.

In the late-twentieth century, Seinfeld and David argue, man is unmanned and woman unwomanned by these new urges. In their place is a moral code that much of the time emanates exclusively from a concern with the utterly trivial. Jerry obsesses about a woman with a Chinese name who isn't Chinese ("The Chinese Woman," 6004) and another who is "too good" ("The Sponge," 7009). Forced to choose between a woman and making a funny voice—a voice found amusing only intermittently by his friends—he chooses . . . the voice ("The Voice," 9002). The message is clear: once rampant and fecund, bound in exploration and battle, we are now epicene and unwanted, not increasingly genetically forced into solitariness but in fact quite content with remaining solitary.

We don't make war, we shove for position; we don't mate, we bump around in the dark. And in place of the big pictures and magnificent vistas seen by those who built our society, we are obsessed with the small and the trivial, even the microscopic. We are at once appalled by procreation and strangely drawn to the act that produces it.

You don't have to agree or disagree with this thesis to enjoy the show, but you must marvel at the Herculean ingenuity that created the set pieces that follow the characters' moral prestidigitation.

After a while it's hard not to see virtually everything the show did leveraged against this worldview: the characters seem to operate almost as characters in a hellish, upside-down version of a miracle play, the saints replaced by sinners, their deeds endlessly examined.

We see them making every effort to do *anything* but break out of their characters. Most fulfillingly, in *Seinfeld* we knew that the group never would succeed. For one, it was obvious that the sensibilities behind the show were much too rigorous to allow any *Friends*-like shenanigans. Elaine would not get back together with Jerry; instead, her sexual adventures will keep her the slightly awe-inspiring alpha male of the group. George would never marry, for so many reasons. (When his doomed fiancée rebukes him for his odd obsession with toilets, he marvels that he ever considered marrying her: "We don't even share the same interests" ["The Postponement," 7002].) Kramer would never see a brilliant idea come to fruition; and Jerry, well, Jerry would continue to hang out with his friends, eat cereal, and identify an infinite number of character flaws that would rule out one vivacious, shapely, attractive woman after another.

And time and time again, their own behavior came back to bite them on the ass. In perhaps the show's most slicing scene, Seinfeld meets the perfect mate—Janeane Garofalo, the perfect girl, who's *exactly like him*—only to discover how quickly observational humor wears thin ("The Invitations," 7022). A woman, breaking up with George, says, "It's not you, it's me" ("The Lip Reader," 5006). This is a line George has heard before, coming out of his own mouth. He bursts into a rage—an unattractive rage, not a mock sitcom rage—and tells her: "That's *my* line. Don't tell me it's not me; it *is* me. It's *me!*" She concedes the point; it's another small Pyrrhic victory for Costanza, in a life full of them.

You can look at *Seinfeld,* of course, as the Ur-sitcom—a bunch of people sitting around doing nothing, as David and Seinfeld intended. In the fourth season, this creation tale was laid out in a season-long arc that saw them pitching just such a sitcom on NBC. And the idea of "nothing" would be a sly recurring motif as the show went on.

"Nothing" is a nice way of describing star Seinfeld's innocuous brand of comedy as well. This, too, became a running joke, as Jerry's brand of observational humor came under withering fire from his friends; from lesser comics like the parasitical Kenny Bania; and even from his dates. (One woman breaks up with Jerry because she didn't find his act funny ["The Ex-Girlfriend," 2001]. "I can't be with someone if I don't respect what they do," she drawls. "But you're a cashier," he responds.) And "nothing," too, is that vast wasteland of most broadcast TV, which was assertively supposed to be about something but most often amounted to nothing.

But even joking about how *Seinfeld* is about nothing, few critics actually spent time examining what the show was really about. What that something was was obvious but nonetheless disturbing. Could the show have been made—could two writers in actual life have gotten away with designing a new show—about what *Seinfeld* is really about? Something that bleak, that uncompromising? And, once proposed, could its creators have been allowed to drive home that thesis with the densest underpinning in the history of the medium, something almost playlike in its attention to details, thematic denseness, and near poetic devotion to the theme?

Could they have said, that is, We'd like to do a *situation comedy* about man's inhumanity to man? The petty desires, the arrant cruelties? The lack of perspective, the meaningless hostility? The lack of commitment, of sympathy; the confusion, the hostility, the isolation; the impossibility of love; the futility of even attempting to break out of the molds we've stuffed ourselves into?

The creators quit at the top of their game and departed with one of the most widely misunderstood works of art of our time, the final episode of *Seinfeld.* In that now infamous episode, you will remember, the group scores a free trip to Paris on an NBC jet. A bumbling Kramer nearly causes a plane crash—a nice feint at those rumors that the show would kill off the characters. The foursome is forced down at a New England town (the cradle of spiritual individualism), where they watch amusedly, as they would in New York, as a fat guy is robbed.

But they're caught in a local Good Samaritan Law and put on trial, at which local prosecutors call in a good chunk of the show's supporting players to act as character assassins; Teri Hatcher testifies that Seinfeld just wanted to know whether her breasts were real; a virgin testifies about the group's masturbation contest; a woman in a wheelchair tells how George gave her a cut-rate wheel-chair; an elderly woman relates how Seinfeld stole the loaf of bread out of her hand; a Pakistani immigrant tells how he was deported after Jerry carelessly didn't give him his mail with his immigration papers in it.

And on and on. The four are convicted with dispatch and sent off to a cell together.

Jerry looks at George: "That button, it's in the worse possible spot . . ."

The group had come full circle, adding a new level of existential desperation to their predicament. They'd been in the same vicious circle already but didn't recognize it; in an insular, uncaring world, they'd acted alone, as if they didn't need or want to relate to others, and then in the end found themselves in a spot where they got their wish—and then continued on as if nothing had happened.

A downer! cried the critics. Well, duh. Scriptwriter David's semiotic coup in this episode was to try, in a last parting burst, to get the audience to consider the implications of a show about nothing that dominated the most powerful medium of its time. Finally, almost in desperation, he criminalized the act. Sometimes, he was insisting, nothing is something.

Reflections on Seinfeld

Frank McConnell. "How *Seinfeld* Was Born." *Commonweal*, issue 9, February 1996: 19.

C. G. Jung famously described the unified self as a quartet, or quaternity, of mutually tensioned personalities: the Animus, the striving, male part; the Anima, the nurturing, female part; the Syzygy, the "ego," organizing impulse; and the Shadow, the dark, feared, often-denied other inside all our dreams. Elaine, who constantly screws up finding the right guy; George, who constantly screws up finding any woman; Jerry, ironic and detached, who tries mainly to keep his balance; and Kramer, anarchic and maladroit (what the hell does he do for a living?), who nevertheless gets, as if by magic, all the girls and money and success everybody else wants—mainly by not even trying.

Jung would have loved this show. The four main characters are so perfectly a single, self-conscious self, so perfectly a comic projection of our own daily negotiations with the world, that it's difficult to believe the writers didn't, sometime, flip through a copy of *Psyche and Symbol*.

Well, actually, not so difficult. Comedy has its own wisdom, older and wiser—and more fully human—than psychology. *Seinfeld* just built, like all art worth the name, on an established tradition and came up with something new and fine.

Ron Rosenbaum. "Nothing Personal: Deprogramming the Cult of *Seinfeld*." *Esquire*, issue 8, August 1993.

St. Martin's Press recently announced plans to publish something called *The I Hate Madonna Handbook* (by Ilene Rosenzweig). Now I myself don't hate Madonna, but I still love the idea: a kind of revenge of the fan on the cult of celebrity, perhaps even presaging a long-overdue popular revolt against the tyranny of the stars over our imagination.

In any case, this set me to thinking about what I'd entitle my contribution to the rebellion. I didn't have to think long; the title suggested itself instantly: *The Horror of Seinfeld.*

Is *horror* too strong a word for what is, after all, only a depressingly insipid stand-up comic and his painfully tame sitcom? I don't know. There was a memorable bit on one of the classic *SCTV* shows of the mid-'80s in which Count Floyd, the inept and transperantly insincere kiddie-horror-show host, learns that his station has supplied the wrong film for his show: Instead of the usual cheapo monster movie, he's sending out Bergman's *Persona* to the kids.

"Aaahoooooh!" Count Floyd howls gamely after the first reel. "Pretty scary, huh, kids? These people are *very* depressed. Let me tell you, kids, being that depressed can be *really scary.*

Thus the horror of *Seinfeld.* It leaves me that depressed. Not only depressed but lonely; it suddenly seems the entire nation has succumbed to the *Seinfeld* mania that has swept through the media like a warm and fuzzy hurricane.

Elayne Rapping. "The *Seinfeld* Syndrome." *The Progressive*, September 1995: 37–38.

Call me a hopeless Puritan. But I see, in this airwave invasion of sitcoms about young Manhattanites with no real family or work responsibilities and nothing to do but hang out and talk about it, an insidious message about the future of Western civilization. It's not that I'm such a big fan of the way industrialism has structured our work and family lives. But these new sitcoms—which seem to be functioning as cheering squads for the end of work and family life as we, and the media heretofore, have known it—don't offer much in the way of replacement. In fact, what I see as I watch them is a scary commercial message on behalf of the new economic system, in which most of us will have little if any paid (never mind *meaningful*) work to do, and the family ties (remember that old show?) that used to bind us, at least as economically dependent on the wage of a breadwinner (remember that old term?), have become untenable.

"What, me worry?" ask these clever series, as mantras to get us through our pointless postindustrial days. To which I answer, under my breath, "But I do. I do."

Jay McInerney. "Is *Seinfeld* the Greatest Sitcom Ever?" *TV Guide*, June 1–7, 1996: 14–18.

It's easy to forget after seven seasons just how strange *Seinfeld* seemed at first. Remember the show in which Jerry and George are trying to come up with an idea for a TV show to pitch to NBC? . . . Kramer . . . proposes a show in which Jerry plays a circus manager. The characters will be circus freaks. "People love to watch freaks," says Kramer. Like the candy mint that is also a breath mint, *Seinfeld* is both of these things. It's a show about nothing in particular, which is to say, everyday life as we know it. And Jerry is the bemused ringmaster of a genuine freak show.

"We are all queer fish," F. Scott Fitzgerald once said. The revelation of *Seinfeld*, as distinct from most sitcoms, is that normal life is actually quite peculiar. Kramer, lurching around Jerry's apartment like a cross behind Baby Huey and Frankenstein's monster, isn't the only freak; Newman, the Pillsbury Sourdough-boy, certainly qualifies. And George is neurotic enough to make Woody Allen seem positively serene and Waspy. I know people like this, but before *Seinfeld*, I don't recall seeing anyone like George or Elaine or even Jerry on TV.

Steven D. Stark. "A Tale of Two Sitcoms." *Glued to the Set: The 60 Television Shows and Events That Made Us Who We Are Today.* **New York: Free Press, 1997: 282–87.**

The *Seinfeld* evocation of early male adolescence did reflect deeper cultural strains. This country has always venerated "bad boys," from Huck Finn to Holden Caulfield. Moreover, many psychologists consider that preteen stage of life, when one is acutely aware of being powerless, as the time when individuals are most subversive of the society at large. That sentiment fit a nineties cultural mood, as America became full of the defiant, oppositional anger that often characterizes the early adolescent—witness the tearing down of public figures with the ready help of the tabloid press, and the flocking to antiestablishment talk radio, whereon the humor grew more derisive by the day. In a similar vein, one could imagine the whole *Seinfeld* cast of perpetual adolescents on the Clinton White House staff workng with George Stephanopolous or Craig Livingstone. Yet boys will be boys: Maybe that's why much of the country viewed the Clinton administration's missteps as benignly as they viewed George Costanza's.

Because this country has always had tendencies that remind observers of a 14-year-old boy, no one would blame *Seinfeld* alone for society's failure to grow up and take care of its real children, its current ambivalence about paternal authority, or its vulgarity and exhibitionist inclinations. Yet the show definitely played a role, along with its cultural cousin. In much the same way that *Roseanne* had domesticated tabloid television for the masses, *Seinfeld* did the same for sophomoric talk radio, as embodied by fellow Manhattanites Stern and Imus.

Rob Long. "Jerry Built: The Success of *Seinfeld* Was an Implicit Rebuke to PC Pieties—and a Confirmation of America's Unpredictable Spirit." *National Review*, issue 9, February 1998: 32–33.

[*Seinfeld*] is also a pretty smutty little half-hour, which is one of the reasons conservatives are uneasy about it. Conservatives have a hard time with smut, sadly. They associate it with the excesses of the 1960s and 1970s—young people grooving on sex and drugs and tinny music, bad haircuts, that sort of thing. But the true legacy of those years wasn't music or intoxicants; it was piety. Insufferable, caring, toasty-warm piety. The adjective "nurturing" to describe a relationship between adults; the phrase "handicapped"; the smoothing out of all the rough edges of life—"challenged" for slow, "homeless" for alcoholic, "white wine" for bourbon-rocks, and "life partner" for . . . well, you know.

Seinfeld is gleefully free of cant. There are no messages, positive or otherwise, delivered in an episode except the only one that matters: Laugh. Enjoy. And tune in next week. We are the kings; they are the clowns. Implicit in the series is the understanding that our moral and spiritual life is our own affair. Jerry and friends are strictly for laughs. . . .

WHY, then, does it work? Why is Jerry Seinfeld, comedian, richer than Jack Welch, corporate titan? Perhaps because there is something in the American spirit that loves a misfit. Perhaps because *Seinfeld* once produced an episode in which the central characters disrupted the life of a handicapped—and insufferable—boy. Perhaps because after years of pious liberal nonsense, the American viewing public relished the naughty pleasure of apolitical laughter. *Seinfeld* isn't a show about nothing; it's a show about nothing pompous.

Joyce Millman. "600,000 an Episode, and Worth Every Penny." *Salon*, issue 16, May 1997.

Maureen Dowd's attack on *Seinfeld* in Wednesday's *New York Times* was almost as surreal as an episode of the show itself.

Writes Dowd: "A friend of mine rants, 'Why don't the characters just move to penthouses on Fifth Avenue? How can they be playing smart Jewish people hanging out in a diner eating all the eggs they want for $3.99 when they are the most highly paid TV actors of the late 20th century? Why don't they just tie Jerry Seinfeld's compensation to how the Knicks do next year?'" Apparently Dowd's "friend" has never heard the term "suspension of disbelief." I wonder if her friend also has trouble watching the cast of *ER* perform surgery, knowing full well that not one of those people ever graduated from medical school.

Dowd has some sort of thesis about *Seinfeld* being the last bastion of evil yup-piedom, as proven by greedy Jason Alexander, Julia Louis-Dreyfus, and Michael Richards, and their "breathtaking $600,000-a-week salaries" (actually, that's $600,000 an episode), and she drags in special guest stars to prop up her argument.

She quotes *New Republic* literary editor Leon Wieseltier: "*Seinfeld* is the worst, last gasp of Reaganite, grasping, materialistic, narcissistic, banal self-absorption." (And all along, you thought it was just a really funny show.) . . .

Waiter, reality check! *Seinfeld* is no defense or glorification or symbol of Yup-pie values. It's a satire, a farce, a comedy about people who have *no* values. Jerry, Elaine, George, and Kramer are self-obsessed, oral-fixated, envious, untruthful, mean—they're not Yuppies, they're babies! They grope around the grand playpen of childish behavior that is New York City, getting into one *Alice in Wonderland*–meets–the Marx Brothers situation after another. *Seinfeld* is as much a "reflection of the what's-in-it-for-me times" as *Rugrats.* Actually, *Rugrats* might be more politically aware.

Lewis Grossberger. "A World in Peril." *Mediaweek,* January 12, 1998: 30.

The end is nigh and this time the media person means it. The portents are not just portending; they're screaming at us and waving their arms wildly. Millions of innocent chickens mercilessly whacked in Hong Kong, killer trees stalking America's mediocre politicians, the specter of the tragic *Titanic* once again grip-ping a nation's imagination, Oprah Winfrey getting sued for libel by a ham-burger, David Brinkley selling out. These omens—horrific though they may be—are nothing compared with The Death of *Seinfeld,* which now threatens to plunge the globe into a shattering depression in every sense the word can muster.

Consider the economics. *Seinfeld* is the most profitable program on NBC, if not the planet, earning $200 million a season—40 percent of the network's profits—and the linchpin of its crucial Thursday-night prime-time schedule. Without *Seinfeld,* Thursday could collapse. If Thursday goes, Friday could follow, then Saturday and before long the entire week would be decimated, setting in motion a terrifying domino effect that would wipe out the entire calendar. A world without calendars would make global warming and the year 2000 computer crisis look trivial. No one would know what date to write on their checks. People would say, "Thank God it's Friday," and it would only be Wednesday. *Monday Night Football* could crash into *Saturday Night Live.*

Elizabeth Lesly, with Ronald Grover and I. Jeanne Dugan. "*Seinfeld:* The Economics of a TV Supershow and What It Means for NBC and the Industry." *Business Week,* issue 2, June 1997: 116–22.

It is the first TV series to command more than $1 million a minute for advertising—a mark previously attained only by the Super Bowl. Its growing strength has helped a smart network dominate prime time—and news, mornings, and late nights, too. It has shattered the ceiling of what a network will pay to keep a show and even its supporting actors. It effortlessly creates cultural artifacts and major tourist attractions out of the quotidian things of its characters. It has so permeated popular consciousness that the august *New York Times* op-ed page warned recently that the show was contributing to the coarsening of American life. It will cost NBC about $120 million to bring it back for its ninth season. That's more than 10 percent of NBC's entire prime-time budget for 26 shows. But it probably is worth every penny, even before you start counting the $180 million or so the network will get from advertising alone.

Seinfeld is the rarest commodity in the entertainment business—a sure thing. The show's strategic importance to NBC reaches far beyond just the network's profit on the show. NBC has leveraged *Seinfeld* and its prime-time strength in such a way as to put considerable distance between it and other broadcast and cable networks. Indeed, by delivering the key demographics advertisers seek, NBC last year was nearly seven times as profitable as ABC, the only other network to make money in 1996. . . .

All the while, NBC has been busily using *Seinfeld*-generated lucre to diversify into cable networks and international markets and to snare the long-term rights to hugely expensive future events such as the Olympic Games. "It almost defies logic what the value of that program is" to NBC, says top media buyer Betsy Frank of Zenith Media Services, who buys ad time for such clients as General Motors and Toyota's Lexus. "*Seinfeld* is one of the most important shows in history."

Liza Schwarzbaum. "Much Ado About Nothing." *Entertainment Weekly,* issue 9, April 1993.

The philosophy of *Seinfeld,* as articulated by its star and its anhedonic executive producer and cocreator, Larry David, is, "No hugging. No learning." Which means Seinfeld and his TV pals are not about to learn or teach any important life lessons, and there will not be any Very Special Episodes. After 68 installments, neither Jerry, George, Elaine, nor Kramer has yet figured out how to sustain a successful romantic relationship . . . George still can't hold down a job . . . Kramer still hasn't got the hang of taming his hair . . . and Elaine (the only one with a 9-to-5 job; she works as a reader in a publishing company) is still hanging out with these losers. "My advice to her," says Louis-Dreyfus, "is this: Get away from these guys as quickly as you can!"

Anyhow, hugging has never been a *Seinfeld* thing because, face it, Jerry is not what you'd call a hugger. "There are many things I'm embarrassed to do [on the show], usually something with a woman," he says. Like, kiss her? "Yeah, I'm still having a little trouble with that. I go to great lengths to keep myself from feeling at all awkward—because I hate it. Comedians are generally very self-conscious people. There is nothing like having your own show; I can't recommend it more highly to you. To be able to go, Nahhhh, I don't think I want to do that."

Ken Tucker. *"Seinfeld." Entertainment Weekly*, issue 10, January 1992: 58–60.

Surrounded by these edgy characters, Jerry is free to stand around with a blank, raised-eyebrow stare—he's Jack Benny in Nikes. (As hysterical as the show is, it doesn't do much good to quote jokes from *Seinfeld*—so much of it has to do with the actors' expressions and reactions.) As a stand-up comedian, Seinfeld has always presented himself as a low-key, pleasant young man, the undisputed leader of the didja-ever-notice school of comedy. Laid-back mildness is essential to Seinfeld's nightclub appeal, and you can experience it every week in the brief stand-up bits that frame each episode of *Seinfeld*.

On his own, Seinfeld can be a tad too whimsical, and I think we have to assume that a lot of the shrewd sharpness that has done so much to enliven *Seinfeld* this season is due to cocreator and writer Larry David. Like Michael Richards, David was once a performer and writer on ABC's *Saturday Night Live* rip-off, *Fridays* (1980–82). On *Fridays*, David was little more than a glowering nerd—Woody Allen trying to be Travis Bickle; as the id behind *Seinfeld*, though, David has channeled his style, which is one of comic frustration, into these genial but driven characters, giving the show an urgency it wouldn't otherwise have.

John Docker. *"Seinfeld." Museum of Broadcast Communications. Encyclopedia of Television*, second edition. Edited by Horace Newcomb. New York: Fitzroy Dearborn, 2004.

Seinfeld also recalls a long comic tradition of farce that descends from Elizabethan drama. In the plays and the jigs following, the audience was presented with a contestation of ideals and perspectives. Whatever moral order is realized in the play is placed in tension with its parody in the closing jig. There the clown dominated as festive Lord of Misrule, creating, for audiences to ponder, not a definite conclusion but an anarchy of values, a play of play and counterplay. Similarly, *Seinfeld* continuously presents an absurd mirror image of other television programs that, like Shakespeare's romances, hold out hope for relationships despite every obstacle that tries to rend lovers, friends, kin, neighbours apart, obstacles that create amidst the comedy sadness, pathos, and intensity.

The possible disadvantage of a genre like absurdist farce is repetition and sameness, comic action turning into ritualised motion. Seinfeld himself comments that in *Seinfeld,* "You can't change the basic situation or the basic characters." Nevertheless, he rejected the suggestion that even the show's devotees think the characters are becoming increasingly obnoxious and the jokes forced (*TV Week,* March 4, 1995). While some contemporary satirical comedy such as *Married . . . with Children* may have fatally succumbed to this danger, *Seinfeld* remains one of the most innovative and inventive comedies in the history of American television.

Carla Johnson. "Lost in New York: The Schlemiel and the Schlimazel in Seinfeld." *Journal of Popular Film and Television* **22.3 (1994): 116–124.**

In *SeinLanguage,* Seinfeld writes:

> Like it or not, things represent us. Most of the time, people's things even look like them. . . . [E]verything you have is really a layer of clothing. Your body is your innermost and truest outfit. Your house is another layer of wardrobe. Then your neighborhood, your city, your state. It's all one giant outfit. We're wearing everything. That's why in certain towns, no matter what you've got on, you're a bad dresser. Just for being there. Some places you're better off just moving instead of changing. (103)

In Seinfeld's world, there is really nowhere to go. He writes, "I love to travel. Much more than I've ever enjoyed getting anywhere. Arrival is overrated" (67). The show features establishing shots of the familiar Seinfeld haunts: Jerry's apartment and Monk's. Interior shots show the small rooms in which the sidekicks congregate—Jerry's efficiency apartment with the kitchen and living room blended into one; the crowded restaurant with the familiar booth just big enough for the four pals, who are eternally subjected to eavesdropping by those in breath-close, neighboring booths. A recurring claustrophobic image is created by tight shots of any number of the group pressed together in a car. Even scenes located at Elaine's health club reveal a space no larger than the misnomered "Fitness center." Leslie Fiedler, writing in *Saul Bellow and His Critics*, describes the "gradual breaking up of the Anglo-Saxon domination of our imaginations; the relentless urbanization which makes rural myths and images no longer central to our experience" (Wisse 78). The *Seinfeld* camera rarely travels outside the confines of rooms, multilevel buildings, and compact cars.

Joanne Morreale. "Sitcoms Say Goodbye: The Cultural Spectacle of *Seinfeld*'s Last Episode." *Journal of Popular Film and Television*, fall 2000, v28 i3: 108.

Sitcoms are all about relationships. In *Seinfeld*, the most important relationship was between discourse and viewer. In a show about characters who were shallow, self-centered, and neurotic, who were afraid of intimacy, the text's discourse created a pseudo-intimacy with the viewer, one that ultimately formed the basis for social relationships. The closing episode became a cultural marker, a basis for "real" discussions with friends and colleagues. Ultimately, it suggested that mediated relationships have become the ground for actual ones, that virtual participation in a media event has become the basis for community, that television viewers are all, like the characters on *Seinfeld*, guilty as charged. *Seinfeld*'s final episode parodied the superficiality and self-absorption of its audience. At the same time, the cultural spectacle surrounding *Seinfeld*'s departure created a deep sense of nostalgia. Viewers mourned the loss of *Seinfeld* even before the last episode aired. They felt nostalgia for *Seinfeld* because, like all commodities, it reminded them of a past moment when they "imagined possession would bring happiness but which, now that it has arrived, is experienced only as the ache of unfulfilled expectations" (Herron 2). The disconcerting closing episode made apparent that there would be no future, no fulfillment, and no redemption for the *Seinfeld* Four, nor for the viewers who watched the show. The characters showed no remorse, and the final shot depicted Jerry, clad in an orange uniform, conducting his opening monologue from within a prison of his own making. According to Jerry Seinfeld, "The stage experience is very pure. It's very empirical. An authentic moment in your life" (Collins 4). Thus *Seinfeld* ended the way it began, with a stand-up comedian performing his act, stripped of all of the artifice of the sitcom form.

Katherine Gantz. "Not That There's Anything Wrong with That: Reading the Queer in *Seinfeld*." Originally published in *Straight with a Twist: Queer Theory and the Subject of Heterosexuality*. Calvin Thomas, ed. Urbana, Illinois: University of Illinois Press, 2000: 165–90.

Seinfeld's narrative design would, at first glance, seem to lack the depth necessary in character and plot to facilitate a discussion of the complexities of homoerotic male relationships. The sort of nonspecific, scattered quality of the *Seinfeld* text, however, makes it well suited to the fluid nature of a queer reading, whose project is more concerned with context than fixity, more with potential than evidence. Nonetheless, *Seinfeld* is full of both context and evidence that lead the text's critics toward a well-developed queer reading. *Seinfeld* enjoys a kind of subculture defined by a discursive code that unites its members in a common lexicon of meaning. The narrative restricts its focus to the foursome, containing and maintaining the intimate bonds between the show's three men and its one woman (the latter being clearly positioned as sexually incompatible and socially separate from the others). Directly related to this intense interconnection, the foursome often causes each member's inability to foster outside heterosexual romantic interests. . . .

All of these relationships are in motion amid a steady stream of other discursive and iconic gay referents. Their visibility admits the "knowing" viewer into a queerly constructed *Seinfeld* universe while never being so explicit as to cause the "unknowing" viewer to suspect the outwardly "normal" appearance of the show. Reading the queer in *Seinfeld* sheds a revealing light on the show's "not that there's anything wrong with that" approach to representations of male homoeroticism. While sustaining a steadfast denial of its gay undercurrents, the text playfully takes advantage of provocative semiotic juxtapositions that not only allow but also encourage the "knowing" spectator to ignore the show's heterosexual exterior and instead to explore the queerness of *Seinfeld.*

Irwin and Cara Hirsch. "*Seinfeld*'s Humor Noir: A Look at Our Dark Side." *Journal of Popular Film and Television* 28.3, fall 2000.

The absence of redeeming, positive, humanistic values of the characters on *Seinfeld* sets them apart from other sitcom series. The genius in the writing is the creators' awareness that viewers identify with the immaturity, narcissism, and venality of *Seinfeld.* The primary characters reflect the worst civilized (nonviolent) qualities that exist within most people, and these are flaunted with cynical humor. The message given by the creators is that this represents an exaggeration of what most middle-class, educated, and apparently evolved people are like. They seem to have succeeded in getting audiences to acknowledge their similarity with these characters, to resonate with and to accept some universally shared inhumane qualities, and to develop a sense of humor and acceptance about this darkness. *Seinfeld* is most decidedly not a show about "nothing"; it is a show dedicated to the exposure of some of the worst and most hidden aspects of the neat, well-manicured majority.

David Zurawik. "A 'Too-Jewish/Not Jewish-Enough Jew for the '90s—
Seinfeld." The Jews of Prime Time. **Hanover, New Hampshire: Brandeis University Press/University Press of New England, 2003: 202.**

Seinfeld was the first series in the history of the medium with a clearly identified leading Jewish character to become number one in the Nielsen ratings, making it the most popular series on all of television. . . .

Seinfeld found the largest audience of any network series during the entire decade and made Thursday nights on NBC the most profitable evening in the history of network television at the peak of the show's popularity. And, in terms of sociology, what about the profound relationship that many of the viewers in the twenty million or so households that tuned in to *Seinfeld* every week formed with this TV Jew and his New York friends?

It did not happen very often, but at its best moments, *Seinfeld* offered as informed an exploration of Jewish identity as any sitcom except *Brooklyn Bridge.* And, unlike *Brooklyn Bridge,* which in dealing with nostalgia and the fondly remembered past had less sociological relevance and potential impact, *Seinfeld* was offering its mass audience a look at a significant part of baby-boomer Jewish life as it was lived in 1990s America.

James Wolcott. "Blows and Kisses." *The New Yorker,* **issue 15, November 1993: 107–109.**

The critic Leslie Fiedler once wrote that among Jews words have "the impact of actions, not merely overheard but *felt,* like kisses or blows."

The loudest squeals come from Jason Alexander's George, who mostly beats up on himself. Short, stocky, losing his hair, he can't sit without giving the impression of being stewed in a pot. Paranoid, hypochondriacal, sexually insecure, he traces his low self-esteem to his parents, a screeching pair of psychological castrators straight out of the family-dinner flashback in *Annie Hall.* His squawks of annoyance and anxiety, his declarative hand chops are familiar gestures from the Woody Allen playbook. But where Woody is usually monopolizing the debate, working solo no matter who is sharing the screen, George and Jerry are equal partners when it comes to figuring out women. They compare notes, commiserate, come up dry. "They're working on a whole other level from us," Jerry says.

II

"Maybe the dingoes ate your baby": Genre, Humor, Intertextuality

MICHAEL DUNNE (Middle Tennessee State University)

Seinfeld *as Intertextual Comedy*

This essay originally appeared in somewhat different form in *Intertextual Encounters in American Fiction, Film, and Popular Culture*. Bowling Green, Ohio: Popular Culture Press, 2001: 159–68.

I n the discursive field surrounding the concept of postmodernism, debate has raged about many issues, including whether there even *is* such a phenomenon. It seems to me, however, that a recurrent element of arguments on all sides of these issues is an assumption that allusion, quotation, referencing, or what I have been calling "intertextual encounters" abound in the texts of various kinds on which some might be willing to bestow the title *postmodern* or that others might deny that classification to. Thus, Robert Morris asks in *Critical Inquiry* (1988): "To what other text can one assign that iconophilia, . . . that lust for the represented, and that appetite for the quotation than to the text of poststructuralism?" (346). The answer *no other sort of text* is clearly implied in Umberto Eco's "Innovation and Repetition: Modern and Post Modern Aesthetics" (1985) when he writes, "It is typical of what is called postmodern literature and art . . . to quote by using (sometimes under various stylistic disguises) *quotation marks* so that the reader pays no attention to the content of the citation but instead to the way in which the excerpt from a first text is introduced into the fabric of a second one" (176). In this respect, if in no others, Eco is joined by Fredric Jameson, who notes, in *Postmodernism, or, The Cultural Logic of Late Capitalism* (1991), "the emergence of new kinds of texts infused with the forms, categories, and contents of that very culture industry so passionately denounced by all the ideologues of the modern, from Leavis and the American New Criticism all the way to Adorno and the Frankfurt School." And Jameson goes on to explain that "The postmodernisms have, in fact, been fascinated precisely by this whole 'degraded' landscape of schlock, kitsch, of TV series and *Reader's Digest* culture, of advertising and motels, of the late show and the grade-B Hollywood film, of so-called paraliterature, with its airport paperback categories of the gothic and the romance, the popular biography, the murder mystery, and the science fiction or fantasy novel; materials they no longer simply 'quote,' as a Joyce or a Mahler might have done, but incorporate into their very substance" (2–3). In other words, all these critics— and numerous others—see evidence of a postmodern sensibility at work when they recognize the presence of frequent and perhaps ironic intertextual encounters. Nowhere is this assumption more valid than in the more sophisticated comedy available on American television in the 1990s.

In a rerun of *The Simpsons*, broadcast just before the close of the last millennium (December 19, 1999), for example, Homer and Marge sit at a piano during the show's opening and closing sequences singing "Those Were the Days," like Archie and Edith Bunker on *All in the Family*. Homer even holds a cigar in his hand, as Archie always did. Significantly, the song's lyrics have been updated for this new setting. Gone are Herbert Hoover and the old LaSalle that functioned as symbols of the good old days from Archie's perspective in the 1970s. In their place are Fleetwood Mac and 8-track tapes, symbols of the 1970s that seem— despite the presence of the gender ambiguities and welfare state politics that troubled Archie back then—like the good old days to Homer in the 1990s. Surely there is a thematic lesson about historical relativism implicit in the way these lyrics are used in *The Simpsons*. But there is an even more striking intertextual lesson. Without some knowledge of 8-track tapes and Fleetwood Mac, the lyrics are senseless, as the entire sequence is without equal knowledge of *All in the Family*. This deliberate evocation of television knowledge is apparent, too, when the episode moves beyond the parodic introductory sequence into the diegetic narrative about how Lisa got her first saxophone. This story is generated when Bart accidentally tosses Lisa's instrument out the window and it is run over by two huge semis. Once the saxophone is squashed enough for narrative purposes, a kid wearing a rain slicker rides up on a tricycle, squashes the sax some more, and then falls over sideways. The appropriate music from *Laugh-In* plays on the sound track, and audience members with sufficient intertextual memory of Arte Johnson doing the same thing on *Laugh-In* get the joke created by writers who obviously remember Rowan and Martin's show. We should observe further that the potential appreciative audience for these jokes is huge, since the original viewers of *Laugh-In* have been substantially augmented by thousands of young people who have seen the show only in cable reruns. Thus a quintessential postmodern intertextual TV encounter takes place on an episode of *The Simpsons*.

While it would probably be productive to track the many intertextual encounters of this sort sprinkled throughout *The Simpsons*, it seems to me even more productive to devote this attention to the successful television program organized around comedian Jerry Seinfeld. While *The Simpsons'* candidacy for such scrutiny seems apparent, *Seinfeld's* inclusion may seem less plausible. After all, *Seinfeld* (1989–1998) was ostentatiously billed as "the show about nothing." Even so—or, perhaps, therefore—*Seinfeld* can easily be seen to share the "iconophilia," the "appetite for the quotation," the ironic use of "quotation marks," the creation of "texts infused with the forms, categories, and contents of [the popular] culture industry" that characterize the field of postmodern TV comedy more generally. Furthermore, we can see in the show the fondness for allusion and reference and the overt and covert textual self-consciousness that mark the classic popular songs and animation discussed elsewhere.

Seinfeld is filled with all sorts of references and allusions to high and popular art, history, politics, and consumer culture. In the episode entitled "The Jacket" (2003), for example, George can't get the song "Master of the House," from *Les Miserables*, out of his head, to the annoyance of Elaine Benes's very scary father. From a simple narrative perspective, any song would probably fill the bill as an irritant here, but the bright catchiness of this particular tune contrasts effectively with Lawrence Tierney's intimidating performance as Mr. Benes, and the timeliness of the allusion to a current Broadway hit show contextualizes the joke in the discourse of contemporary New York popular culture. Timeliness is also a key factor in the episode called "The Checks" (8007), when Elaine hooks up with Bret, a potential new boyfriend who thinks of the Eagles' hit "Desperado" as "his" song. Because this song dates back to the mid-seventies, this precise allusion effectively situates Bret as a classic-rock-listening Yuppie. When Elaine proposes another Eagles song, "Witchy Woman," as a candidate for "their" song, historical resonance continues to be a crucial component of the communication between *Seinfeld*'s writers (Steve O'Donnell, Tom Gammill, and Max Pross) and their audience. The same may be said for the theme song from the comic television show *The Greatest American Hero* (1981–1983), the theme from which George uses for his answering machine message in "The Susie" (8015). The original show, starring William Katt, never offered much in the way of plot, character, or even laughs, but David Mandel, author of "The Susie," must have watched the show nevertheless and had the theme song stuck in the back of his mind all those years, like "Master of the House." Clearly, Mandel assumed that many *Seinfeld* viewers would remember this airy pop tune also.

A more contemporary connection is established through another TV show, *Melrose Place*, in "The Beard" (6014). Not only is *Melrose Place* (1992–1999) closer in time to *Seinfeld* historically, it is also more significantly involved in the plot. In "The Beard" Jerry is interested in dating Sergeant Channing, a female police officer who is a fan of *Melrose Place*. Sergeant Channing's fondness for this show makes perfect sense in 1995, since *Melrose Place* consistently scored among the top ten TV ratings favorites at the time. When Jerry claims that he has never watched *Melrose Place*, the cop challenges him to take a lie detector test. Jerry successfully lies that he knows nothing about *Melrose Place* characters Sidney, Michael, Jane, Billy, Jake, and Allison, but he eventually breaks down under questioning, crying out, "Did Jane sleep with Michael again?" It turns out that Jerry has been secretly watching *Melrose Place* all along, a fact that destroys his chances with Sergeant Channing and annoys Elaine because it has deprived her of the chance to discuss with Jerry a show to which she is as devoted as Channing—and Jerry. The episode ends with Jerry, Elaine, George, and Kramer sitting on Jerry's couch in front of the TV as the theme from *Melrose Place* plays, a scene that the episode's writer, Carol Leifer, clearly must have assumed to be familiar in the same living rooms where people gathered to watch *Seinfeld.*

Popular films supply other easily accessible intertexts for *Seinfeld* episodes. Elaine blows her chance to get soup from the Soup Nazi in the episode of that title when she does an impression of Al Pacino in *Scent of a Woman* (1992). Jerry and Elaine blow their chances to become godparents in "The Bris" (5005) through their bad impressions of Marion Brando in *The Godfather* (1972). When George sees his father without a shirt on in "The Doorman" (6016), he is offended at the sight of Frank's developing breasts. George tells Jerry that the experience was his "own personal *Crying Game*" (1992). At the grave of George's fiancée, Susan, Jerry offers a moving speech to her parents. Later Jerry admits to George that the words he spoke actually came from *Star Trek II: The Wrath of Khan* (1982) and that they actually applied to Mr. Spock's death, not to Susan's. In all of these cases, writers and readers alike are assumed to have seen—or at least heard about—the same popular films, and so these films can serve effectively as intertexts for a wide variety of comic plots. Perhaps the high point in this sort of cinematic referencing occurs in "The Raincoats" (5019), when Jerry and his girlfriend Rachel are detected "making out" at *Schindler's List* (1993). The comic plot requires that Jerry and Rachel become sexually frustrated because Jerry's parents are staying in his apartment and because Rachel lives with her conservative rabbi father. In one sense, any movie house could provide the fictional couple an opportunity for sexual privacy, but a crowded theater showing the Academy Award–winning film about the Holocaust is the ideal choice diegetically because of Jerry and Rachel's Jewish backgrounds, and intertextually because of the near worshipful adulation with which *Schindler's List* was publicly viewed at the time of this episode's original broadcast (1994).

Most fans of *Seinfeld* would anticipate, however, that the show's most comprehensive intertextual encounters involve Superman. As Mary Kaye Schilling and Mike Flaherty point out in *Entertainment Weekly*'s special-edition glossary for *Seinfeld*, "Though [Jerry] frequently references other superheroes, the Man of Steel is his undisputed fave and chief source of pop-cultural metaphors" (23).

Thus, in "The Caddy" (7012) Jerry explains that Elaine's old high school nemesis, Sue Ellen Mischke, is her Lex Luthor, Superman's arch rival. In "The Secret Code" (7007), we learn that Jerry's ATM password is Jor-El, the name of Superman's father. In "The Face Painter" (6021), George describes his complicated emotional encounter with Siena, who just may be deaf in one ear, by saying that "It's like when Superman reversed the rotation of the earth to save Lois's life." Lois Lane also figures in "The Race" (6010), an episode with a particularly rich Superman intertext. Lois's name gets invoked in the script simply so that Jerry can say to his girlfriend of the week that he runs "faster than a speeding bullet, Lois." As the title of the episode implies, the plot involves a foot race between Jerry and an old high school acquaintance, Duncan. The climax occurs as Jerry outraces Duncan in the slow motion popular in *Superman* films while the sound track plays the familiar *Superman* theme.

As Umberto Eco's discussion of postmodernism leads us to expect, references and allusions in *Seinfeld* are drawn indiscriminately from all aspects of culture. Eco notes that "the media are relying on—and presupposing—the possession of pieces of information already conveyed by other media" (172), and *Seinfeld* responds by having Elaine characterize herself in "The Bookstore" (9017) as being like Tina Turner in her relations with Zach, a coworker and unsatisfactory boyfriend. Elaine doesn't sing or dance well in high-heeled shoes, and so she is unlike Tina Turner in the most obvious ways, but Elaine is hoping that she can get other people in her office to view her as an emotionally abused woman, and so she may seem to resemble the Tina Turner familiar to viewers of 1998 TV talk shows. Similarly, when Kramer accidentally gets vanity license plates that spell "ASSMAN" in "The Fusilli Jerry" (6019), the characters speculate about whom the plates could actually be intended for. When George suggests Wilt Chamberlain, the reference has nothing to do with professional basketball but with *A View from Above*, the 1991 autobiography in which Chamberlain claimed to have had sex with 20,000 women. Higher up the cultural ladder, we learn in "The Scofflaw" (6013) that a traffic cop wearing an eye patch sees the multiticketed Newman as his Moby-Dick and in "The Secret Code" (7007) that Maya Angelou volunteers at a charity soup kitchen. Although these references mostly involve simple name recognition, the intertextual encounters are at least partly literary. The same may be said of the intertextual encounter in which the old love letters saved from the wreckage of the Ross vacation cabin turn out to be letters from John Cheever to Susan's father ("The Cheever Letters," 4007). While John Cheever was assuredly a widely recognized fiction writer, his appearance as a reference here is clearly attributable to the publication of *The Journals of John Cheever*

(1991), in which the famous author wrote about his alcoholism and homosexual love affairs.

A similar referential mixture—this time, of celebrity with politics—is at work when Estelle Costanza compares her brassiere-clad husband to J. Edgar Hoover in "The Doorman" (6016) and when George describes an embarrassing encounter with a girl by telling Jerry in "The Phone Message" (2004), "So I just stand there like . . . remember how Quayle looked when Bentsen gave him that Kennedy line? That's what I looked like." Some political knowledge may be relevant in both cases, but an ear for the news of the day is probably all that is really required to participate in this rhetorical community. The same may be said when Elaine's boss, Mr. Pitt, ends the episode called "The Gymnast" (6006) looking like Adolph Hitler addressing a Nazi rally. Pitt is admittedly wearing Austrian-looking riding clothes (because he had earlier hoped to go horseback riding in the park), and he has a thick black mustache on his upper lip (because he accidentally touched himself with ink-stained fingers), but Mr. Pitt is nothing like Hitler in any significant way. The intertextual joke is purely visual, and it requires little knowledge of history or politics. In fact, the less one knows about the Second World War, the funnier the joke is. Funny or not, however, it is apparent that the writers, Alec Berg and Jeff Schaffer, intended to communicate with their audience intertextually through this image.

Other allusions and references are more diegetically functional. In "The English Patient" (8017) Elaine is one of the few Americans who will admit in 1997 that she finds the 1996 Academy Award smash *The English Patient* boring. In this respect *The English Patient* serves as *Schindler's List* does in "The Raincoats" (5019), as the movie that everyone is supposed to admire. "The English Patient" surpasses "The Raincoats" in terms of intertextual organicism, however, since the comic plot of the former also requires a character named Neil to be so badly burned by a crepe that his gorgeous girlfriend will take him to England for burn treatment. All parallels to the plot of *The English Patient* are surely deliberate. In "The Boyfriend" (3017) Kramer and Newman act as conspiracy nuts caught up in a bizarre tale about how baseball star Keith Hernandez spat on them following a 1987 Mets game at Shea Stadium. Using a golf club as a pointer, Jerry enacts the role of a Zapruder film analyst to demonstrate that Hernandez could not have been solely responsible and that there must have been a "second spitter" on the grassy knoll outside the stadium. As it turns out, there was a "second spitter"—Roger McDowell, whom Newman had taunted throughout the game. Many assassination buffs would love to have such a clear answer to all their questions about what actually happened when John Kennedy was killed in Dallas. Since—like Larry David and Larry Levin—we have all heard these questions asked and probably seen the Zapruder film analyzed, our shared intertextual encyclopedia permits the writers to make a new joke out of old material.

Another tragedy—the 1994 O. J. Simpson murder case—provides the intertext for several episodes of *Seinfeld*. In "The Big Salad" (6002) Kramer fears that he has inadvertently incited former baseball player Steve Genderson to murder. In a direct parallel to the O. J. case, Kramer and Genderson are seen on television fleeing from the police in a white Bronco just as Al Cowlings and O. J. did. In "The Maestro" (7003) Jackie Chiles, a recurring character based on O. J.'s flamboyant attorney, Johnnie Cochran, represents Kramer in a lawsuit based on Kramer's having been burned by a cup of too-hot caffe latte sold to him by Java World. In addition to the Cochran parallels, this episode alludes to the controversial 1994 lawsuit in which Stella Liebeck was awarded $2.9 million in compensation for the too-hot cup of McDonald's coffee that spilled in her lap. Jackie Chiles/Johnnie Cochran also appears in "The Caddy" (7012) in a case based on Sue Ellen Mischke's having caused a traffic accident by wearing a brassiere on the outside of her sweater. In an obvious reference to the gloves that didn't quite fit O. J. Simpson in his trial, Jackie asks Sue Ellen to try on a bra in court. As in the O. J. case, the garment does not fit, and so the defendant wins the case.

Other sustained references include the film *Midnight Cowboy* (1969) in "The Mom and Pop Store" (6008) and *The Merv Griffin Show* (1962–1986) on the episode of the same name. However, the point should be clear without further discussion that *Seinfeld* often engaged in both localized and extended cultural references of the sort popular in Warner Brothers' cartoons. "The Merv Griffin Show" (9006) episode points to still another way in which *Seinfeld* resembles those cartoons and other forms of self-conscious intertextual encounters. In this episode Kramer transforms his apartment into the set of *The Merv Griffin Show* and interacts with his friends as if he were a talk-show host and they were his guests. The writer of this episode, Bruce Eric Kaplan, even works Jim Fowler of *Wild Kingdom* into the script because Fowler is such a regular guest on actual shows of this kind that his presence establishes an especially convincing intertext. In this way Kaplan reminds viewers that *Seinfeld* is also a TV show, a part of what Mimi White calls the "all-encompassing present text" of television. Kramer helps writers give similar reminders in several episodes. In "The Keys" (3022) Kramer moves to California and gets a small part on *Murphy Brown* (1988–1998). In "The Opposite" (5022) Kramer appears on *Live with Regis and Kathy Lee* (1989–2000) to promote his new coffee-table book. In both episodes stars easily recognizable from their own hit television shows help to remind viewers that *Seinfeld* is also a television show. Although less obviously identified with television, Kramer's possible appearance in a Woody Allen film in "The Alternate

Side" (3011) and his accidental Tony Award in "The Summer of George" (8022) signal "show business" even so, and thus indicate textual self-consciousness rather than referential opacity. As Eco claims, when a spectator is "aware of the quotation, the spectator is brought to elaborate ironically on the nature of such a device and to acknowledge the fact that he has been invited to play upon his encyclopedic competence" (171).

Other intertextual invitations of this sort are issued when episodes refer to the diegetic Jerry's career as a comedian. This happens when Jerry appears on *The Tonight Show* in "The Trip, Part I" (4001), along with George Wendt and Corbin Bernsen, who play themselves. When Jerry appears on *Tonight* again in "The Showerhead" (7015), host Jay Leno also appears in a cameo role. In a variation on this theme, Bryant Gumbel interviews Jerry on the *Today* show in "The Puffy Shirt" (5002). When Jerry is booked to appear on Charles Grodin's talk show in "The Doll" (7016), he hopes to get comic mileage out of a barbecue sauce bottle that looks like Grodin. Beyond television appearances, Jerry claims to be substituting for Carrot Top at Bally's in Atlantic City in "The Money" (8012), an episode in which his parents reiterate their advice that he give up comedy and enter the management training program at Bloomingdale's. In "The Little Jerry" (8011), the previous but related episode, Jerry's parents encourage him to get out of comedy and into advertising. The cumulative effect of these incidents is to remind viewers that a comedian named Jerry Seinfeld is playing a character named Jerry Seinfeld on a television show of that name. In intertextual terms, this self-consciousness is acute.

Seinfeld also signals its nature as a TV sitcom in various covert ways. "The Bizarro Jerry" (8003) episode creates a competing group of three male friends for Elaine, each more decent and normal than Jerry, George, or Kramer. On the allusive level, some viewers are probably reminded of Superman's bizarro opposite. On the level of comic plot, viewers are entertained to see Elaine struggling to choose between the two trios of totally opposite friends. But the most compelling effect of the episode is to remind viewers of what Jerry, George, and Kramer are really like week after week and thus to remind viewers of why we are attracted to this particular sitcom rather than to its dozens of competitors. When Elaine and George temporarily switch personalities in "The Abstinence" (8009), there is considerable comic delight in seeing George as bright and efficient, but this delight results primarily from knowing how ineptly he usually acts, from comparing the usual and the unusual intertextually. Through a similar switch in the previous episode, "The Chicken Roaster" (8008), sleep deprivation and switched apartments turn Jerry temporarily into Kramer. It is surely fun to watch a manic

Jerry and a composed Kramer, but it is fun mostly for those who are used to the opposite, status quo.

The most overtly self-conscious episodes of *Seinfeld* are those focused on George and Jerry's efforts to develop their own sitcom, just as the most overtly self-conscious song lyrics are the ones about writing songs. In "The Pitch" (4003) Jerry and George try to interest NBC network executives in putting on a TV show "about nothing." The difficulties that Jerry and George encounter in this episode seem comic rather than tragic or dramatic because viewers know that the two friends—or their real-life counterparts, Jerry Seinfeld and Larry David—will triumph in the end. Otherwise, we would not be watching all of this action on *Seinfeld* right now. This recognition intertextually points the audience toward comedy in "The Checks" (8007) also, even though Jerry and George seem to have tremendous difficulties trying to interest Japanese TV executives in their unproduced show. The apex of overt textual self-consciousness, however, must be "The Pilot" (4022). In this episode the network has finally given Jerry and George a chance to make an episode of their sitcom. As actors read for the parts of George, Elaine, and Kramer, viewers are reminded of these diegetic characters' distinguishing, humorous qualities. At the same time, the episode suggests that Jason Alexander, Julia Louis-Dreyfus, and Michael Richards must also have read for their parts once upon a time. That Jerry will play Jerry on the pilot episode just as Jerry Seinfeld plays Jerry on *Seinfeld* merely confirms this conjunction between the highly successful "show about nothing" and its intertextual matrix, especially the "all-encompassing present text" of television.

In her essay "Crossing Wavelengths: The Diegetic and Referential Imaginary of American Commercial Television," from which this phrase is derived, Mimi White conjectures that "[r]egular television viewers are the 'best' viewers, capable of deriving the greatest potential satisfaction from any single show because they are in the advantageous position of understanding the rules of the game" (61). These are the viewers best equipped to connect "The Pilot" intertextually to the ongoing *Seinfeld* series; to appreciate it when Jerry gets a shot on *The Tonight Show*, complete with a guest appearance by Jay Leno; and to learn that Jerry watches *Melrose Place* just as they do. These are also the viewers ideally situated to appreciate highly self-conscious TV comedy shows like *The Simpsons* (1989) and *The Larry Sanders Show* (1992–1998), starring Garry Shandling.

BARBARA CHING (University of Memphis)

They Laughed Unhappily Ever After

Seinfeld and the Sitcom Encounter with Nothingness

I. Seinfeld and Sartre

George: The show is about nothing.
Jerry: Well, it's not about nothing.
George: No, it's about nothing.
Jerry: Well, maybe in philosophy. But even nothing is something.

("The Pitch," 4003)

W hen George and Jerry have this argument, they are proposing a sit-com to NBC executives at the network headquarters. While George righteously insists, Jerry rightfully senses that the philosophy of nothingness won't amuse these decision makers. He already suspects that they will prefer "something" more conventional, and within the events of the actual sitcom, the network never approves a show about nothing. But what makes *Seinfeld* so compelling is its charting of the space between the two abstractions of nothing and something. Indeed, outside of philosophy-averse network headquarters, Seinfeld's sitcom makes an appeal to philosophy almost inevitable. In particular, philosophers and critics have begun to explore the relationship between Sartre, the philosopher of nothingness, and Seinfeld, the comedian of nothingness. Jennifer McMahon, for example, analyzes the parallel between Sartre's theory of subjectivity and *Seinfeld*'s portrayal of human relationships. While she argues that the sitcom better portrays the value of friendship than the philosopher does (91), Theodore Schick notes that the final episode, which locks the four main characters in a shared jail cell, shows "a curious similarity to *No Exit*. Is Hell other people, as Sartre's play suggests?" (184).[1] Television critics, too, publicized the parallel: in her review of the finale for *Bad Subjects*, Annalee Newitz compared the episode to "a pop version of Jean-Paul Sartre's ultra-dark existentialist play," echoing Caryn James in *The New York Times*, who called it a "road company version of *No Exit*," and Frank McConnell in *Commonweal*, whose review of the finale was entitled "No Way to Exit?: *Seinfeld* as Sartre." Certainly, as the series closed, Jerry and his friends behaved as if they would live unhappily ever after. At the same time, in Sartre's philosophy, their very function as comic actors is to keep the audience from experiencing such existential malaise.

While philosophers regularly note the connection between laughter and "nothingness,"[2] Sartre's approach connects jokes to narrative structure. Comedians, according to Sartre, mute our despair by provoking laughter at the people and situations that threaten our hopes for dignity and meaning. This pleasure, he argues, allows us to avoid questioning the very existence of meaning in favor of focusing on limited situations in which meaning fails. The hope for a happy ending—comedy writ large—can thus survive. Because both jokes and more structured comedy provoke laughter, Sartre makes no theoretical distinction between a stand-up comic's unconnected stream of gags and the ageless comic plot in which guys get girls and live happily ever after. Laughter quarantines disappointment from despair, and comedy, as a literary genre, structures the blinking instinct of laughter (825).[3] To Sartre, both comedy and laughter are inextricable and fundamentally conservative; their endlessly repeatable and ever pacifying pleasures keep us from imagining radical changes in the status quo. Had he seen them, Sartre surely would have found the conservative dynamic at work in archetypal American sitcoms: after a contrived volley of one-liners and zany situations, television families, in their cozy houses or familial offices and bars, live happily ever after over and over. Moreover, sitcom stardom reinforces Sartre's claim that famous comedians inextricably enmesh themselves in the conservative structure of comedy. Specifically, Sartre argues that comedians cannot be separated from the roles they create (827). If he had only known about syndication! Sitcom stars, he might then argue, reinforce the constricting happiness of this vision by dint of repetition. Jerry Seinfeld brings this role-playing to its logical conclusion by inserting his comic persona, a comedian playing a comedian, into the long-running narrative of a sitcom.

Sartre outlined this theory of comedy and comedians in *L'Idiot de la famille (The Family Idiot)*, his massive biography of the nineteenth-century novelist Gustave Flaubert. Flaubert's comedy, Sartre asserts, exposes the confinement of a conventional happy ending. The novelist attempted to write about nothing as an escape from the hollowness of the bourgeois world he knew. At this point, it need hardly be mentioned that *Seinfeld,* too, proclaimed itself a show about nothing.[4] In *Seinfeld,* the jokes and plots never take the tidy shape of the comedic ending; in fact, several episodes vent hostility toward the happy home. Treasured family cabins get burned to the ground ("The Bubble Boy," 4006), and lighting out for new territory offers little satisfaction: the sunny vistas and sitcom studios of L.A. make the golden West intolerable ("The Trip," 4001). Elaine cannot even abide optimism. She rejects one boyfriend because he likes "Desperado," the Eagles' country-rock warning against nihilism ("The Checks," 8007). In the final season, when she discovers that her beau David Puddy listens to Christian rock, she admits that she prefers lovers who have no beliefs ("The Burning," 9016). Although Sartre argues that Flaubert cracked this foundation, *Seinfeld* shows that there is no exit from the edifice that houses middle-class dreams. In other words, *Seinfeld* owes its existence to the familiar (and familial) triumph of hope and despair that is the *something* of comedy. As Northrop Frye noted in his description of comedic form, "dramatic comedy, from which fictional comedy is mainly descended, has been remarkably tenacious of its structural principles and character types" (163).[5] Sartre, too, with his focus on Flaubert, implicitly recognizes that literature and its history reveal the philosophy of comedy. In this essay, then, I will juxtapose *Seinfeld*'s continued jokes about creating a "show about nothing" to the narrative formed by nine-years' worth of episodes to demonstrate that the show inevitably participates in the formal structure of comedy even as it jokes against it.[6]

II. Arrested Development

The rest of the story need not be shewn in action, and indeed, would hardly need telling if our imaginations were not so enfeebled by their lazy dependence on the ready-mades and reach-me-downs of the ragshop in which Romance keeps its stock of "happy endings" to misfit all stories.

—George Bernard Shaw, "Epilogue to *Pygmalion*"

Seinfeld's last episode clearly entwined Jerry's conflicted desire to put a show about nothing on NBC with NBC's desire to normalize Jerry Seinfeld. Although this episode placed the four main characters on an aborted private flight to Paris, I am not arguing that Jerry Seinfeld and Larry David designed the show as an engagement with Sartrean comic theory but rather that Sartre's theory of comedy, because of its emphasis on nothingness, serves particularly well to highlight the paradoxes posed by a comedy about nothing. After all, Seinfeld and cowriter Larry David deliberately set out to break the sitcom mold, and in this quest they struggled with an even more powerful comic power than the bourgeoisie Flaubert longed to shock. As David Marc notes, television is fundamentally a comic medium not only in its reliance on the ancient dramatic structure that leads to a happy ending in the foundation and social reinforcement of the family but also in its quintessentially American optimism (xv, 13, 15). Economic pressures further reinforce the normative structure: while American television comedy expresses a pragmatic and domestic faith in "working things out," the commercials that surround and support it loudly insist that life gets better every day, thanks to the things you can buy and take back to your happy home. In fact, Geoffrey O'Brien, in *The New York Review of Books,* argued that *Seinfeld* was the definitive sitcom of the '90s precisely because of the huge sums it could command from advertisers (13). Given this reality, the comedian may declare that his comedy is about nothing, but Seinfeld's jokes and his show would be judged by the social, artistic, and economic norms that comedy, perhaps especially situation comedy, constantly conveys. By the final episode, Jerry wants to be on television so badly that he would consent to the National Broadcasting Corporation's preference for comedy in the most traditional sense of the word.

In retrospect, we know that *Seinfeld's* success, like Flaubert's novels, did not unleash a transformative encounter with nothingness. Nevertheless, a backward glance reminds us just how radically ungeneric *Seinfeld* appeared at its July 1989 premiere. In 1988, *Harper's Magazine* commissioned five hot young television writers to imagine the sitcom that would define the '90s. Although *Entertainment Weekly* and other writers would later christen *Seinfeld* with that title (16), it is remarkable just how far from *Seinfeld* the team from *Harper's* wandered and how close to the classic sitcom form they remained. What they envisioned, *Gas, Food, Lodging,* did hit the road. It was a program about laid-off ex-Yuppies forced to sell the McMansion; they replace it with a trailer and set off to experience America. These writers wanted to get the sitcom out of "some damn living room" and made a point of excluding children (50), but they don't imagine forgoing the heterosexual consumerist couple in a domestic environment. They just put it on wheels. *Harper's* also hired Judy Hart Angelo and Gary Portnoy, theme song writers for *Cheers* and other sitcoms, to write lyrics for a *Gas, Food, Lodging* theme. The melody would be "upbeat," they noted, and the words stress the bright future to come: "The future may not always be / Right there where the eye can see / But if you search you just might find / Forgotten roads of a different kind." In this show, all roads lead to a happy home; in contrast, *Seinfeld* repeat-edly and ultimately imprisoned its characters. Likewise, *Seinfeld*'s "theme song," such as it was, made no promises for bright tomorrows. It simply and wordlessly riffed as it underscored the stasis of its characters' lives.

In the early years of *Seinfeld*, the show seemed determined to demonstrate that stand-up (and situation) comedy, just as Sartre would have it, flows from the same trivially unhappy source: the quixotic struggles of a comedian in conflict with the entrenched banality of the status quo. In the first seven seasons, the weekly installments opened and closed with Jerry's stand-up routine. The "story" that unfolded between the routines demonstrated that Jerry drew his inspiration from the failures he and his friends experienced. They are a group of New Yorkers ostensibly looking for love and normality even as their inflated sense of singularity requires them to reject the responsibilities and compromises entailed in living happily ever after. Rather than gathering around the family dinner table, they eat the unremarkable, perhaps even monastic fare sold by Monk's diner.[7] Boys meet girls and lose them—even poison them—with such regularity that no viewer could rationally expect a happy family to form. Of course, irrational hope is another matter. The ultimate irony of the show demonstrated the futility of refusing the dogged belief in comedy's coupling. "Even nothing is something," Jerry had pronounced out of desperation; he learned in the final episode (9022) that even "nothing" must hold out the promise of romance. When the NBC executives suddenly call him to revisit his pitch, he hears that NBC's new presi-dent insists that *something* should happen between the characters of Elaine and Jerry. George tries to reject this primrose path but Jerry readily agrees. (Even though he and George failed to include Elaine in the pilot they planned because they could not imagine what a woman character would say or do.)[8] In fact, the actual pilot ("The Seinfeld Chronicles," 1001) revolved around Jerry, George, Kramer, and a quickly fizzling romance for Jerry. In the second episode, the series introduced a hypothetical romantic tension between Jerry and Elaine. Neverthe-less, Jerry adamantly insists to his parents that he and Elaine are only friends and he actively but ineptly pursues another woman. In "The Deal" (2009), Jerry and Elaine attempt to resume a sexual relationship without romance, bragging that they have found a formula for combining lust and friendship, but they quickly, and without explanation, give up on the idea. In any case, it doesn't need to make sense outside of the long-standing cultural logic that NBC insists on: Elaine's role in the show adds the necessary "something" even as her relationship with Jerry continually amounts to nothing.

Romance, in every sense of the word, maybe especially the sense that leads to marriage with children, inspires faith in the future. At the most exalted level, romantic quests express the hopes of an entire culture. *Seinfeld*, in contrast, obsessed only on unholy grails. None of the four main characters progresses or changes; they learn nothing and acquire nothing of particular value or glamour. While Jerry covets a girlfriend's toy collection ("The Merv Griffin Show," 9006) and J. Peterman (one of Elaine's bosses) haunts Sotheby's for Kennedy (or is it Camelot?) relics ("The Bottle Deposit," 7020), *Seinfeld*'s plots thwart and ridicule these desires. Even as Jerry and friends seek true love, they reveal their incapacity for it. In one of the show's most hilarious incidents, Elaine confesses to her rabbi neighbor how intensely she envies George's engagement; he then broadcasts her dismay on *his* television show ("The Postponement," 7002). Once George becomes engaged, Jerry convinces himself he wants to marry his female double, Jeannie Steinman, only to discover how much he dislikes his mirror image ("The Invitations," 7022). Nevertheless, he continues to search for the ideal mate. As Thomas Hibbs has observed, rather than replacing the sentimental, happily-every-after family-oriented structure of traditional American sitcom, *Seinfeld* places its characters in a hovering state of "perpetual adolescence" (151).[9] No wonder, Hibbs claims, that masturbation plays such an "essential" role on the show (169); to him, it exemplifies arrested development. And although Hibbs does not cite Sartre, Sartre claims that we have license to laugh at comedians precisely because they exemplify arrested development. Adults, by definition, are taken seriously. Sartre names his massive tome on Flaubert *The Family Idiot* after the domestic immaturity of comedians. When Salon.com television critic Joyce Millman argued that *Seinfeld* was "the greatest sitcom of all time," she cited the fact that "Jerry, George, Elaine and Kramer . . . behaved like eternal teenagers" as support for her praise. George calls himself King of the Idiots, and Jerry calls him Biff, after the eternally adolescent older son in Arthur Miller's *Death of a Salesman*. "We're like children. We're not men," Jerry whines as he and George share yet another lunch at the diner ("The Engagement," 7001). This exchange inspires George to get engaged, and it also opens the clip show that builds up to the finale. The emphasis on arrested development serves to explain every laughable memory that follows and both opens and culminates the *Seinfeld* narrative. While they languish in jail, a literally arrested development, "the New York Four" repeat their offenses as reruns even as the time limit on their sentences creates hope for their reformation. The last conversation we hear reiterates the opening exchange in the first episode (the *true* pilot). Jerry begins to criticize the placement of the second button on George's shirt. "Look at it—it's too high, it's in no-man's-land." "Haven't we had this conversation before?" George responds. No doubt, this theme, if not this very conversation, repeats itself as long as they consider themselves arrested adolescents instead of men.

III. Laughing Stocks and Bondage

For not getting out of it, I have chosen it.

—Jean-Paul Sartre

The New York Four stay out of it for a good run. "Get out!" is one of Elaine's favorite exclamations, and from the first line of the first show, Jerry uses the circular flight from domesticity as a punch line and a philosophy. He's supposedly doing stand-up, but he could just as well be posing questions to a school of peripatetic philosophers: "Do you know what this is all about? Do you know why we're here? To be out. . . . People . . . you know how many people come home at night . . . We should go out . . . This is what they're talking about. This whole thing . . . we're all out. No one is home." However, built into the plot of this series is a thoroughly bourgeois audience who cannot bear this encounter with undomesticated comedy: the NBC executives and spectators of the pilot aren't "out"; they watch from their snug and smug homes ("The Pilot," 4022). The exceptions, NBC president Russell Dalrymple and executive Susan Ross, suffer for their attraction to the *Seinfeld* foursome. Dalrymple gets lost at sea when he joins Greenpeace to impress Elaine ("The Pilot"). Susan becomes engaged to George only to die from the sealing compound on the cheap wedding invitations he insisted she choose ("The Invitations," 7022). When they finally agree to sponsor the series, the new NBC team resists contamination by requiring that Jerry and Elaine eventually go home together and stay there happily ever after. Jerry envisioned as much at the end of his first monologue, at the end of the first episode: "Once you're out, you wanna get back." Indeed, "The Outing" (4016), the show in which a newspaper reporter takes Jerry and George for a gay couple, reveals a hysterical commitment to the heterosexual model. George capitalizes on the misunderstanding to break up with yet another girlfriend—"I'm out, baby! I'm out!" But when this gambit fails, he quickly resorts to another extreme: the fantasy of possessing a repellent excess of male sexuality. He makes the impossible claim to be a porn star named Buck Naked.[10]

But no matter how tenuously or strenuously the Seinfeld foursome clings to heterosexual coupledom, they seem incapable of making the sort of commitment that could lead to the happily-ever-after lives of Shakespearean or suburban comedy. Even in the final episode, when they think their private plane is about to crash, they cannot confess to love, although we are teased with the possibility. Instead, George admits that he cheated in the infamous "contest" to see who could abstain the longest from masturbation, and Elaine stammers "Jerry, I've always . . . I . . ." The declarations are all aimed at Jerry, but they lead nowhere, as if he is the empty space in this circle. In fact, Jerry's very manhood is questioned by the Romanian gymnast with whom he has a brief sexual fling ("The

Gymnast," 6006). Expecting especially exciting maneuvers from this exotic contortionist, he is disappointed by the banality of their encounter. Although he intends to break off their relationship, she beats him to the punch line. She invokes what she calls the Romanian ideal of the comedian, a man so virile that no other can compare. "You may make people laugh, Jerry Seinfeld," she says, "but you are no comedian." The comedian, in other words, embodies a procreative life force that Jerry negates. The laughter he provokes leads to nothing but a one-night stand. In theory, he is incapable of forming a series; in practice, of course, we watched it. Nevertheless, episode after episode contrasts *Seinfeld*ian recreation with procreation or even destruction.

The characters occasionally announce their plans to change; no new life ever forms. Instead, dead-end relationships occur throughout the series. The "Soul Mate" (8002)/"Bizarro Jerry" (8003) episodes highlight Jerry's emptiness and thus the hollowness of the foursome he centers. During a sidewalk rant against her circle of women friends, contented mothers who are urging her to reproduce, Elaine meets Kevin, an attractive potential partner who professes to share her aversion to procreation. He undergoes a vasectomy in hopes of pleasing her; when he tells her this news, she realizes that perhaps her resolve is not so firm after all. Shortly thereafter, she decides that she and Kevin should just be "friends" (even though he reverses the vasectomy). He readily agrees to a platonic relationship and begins to incorporate her into his circle of male friends, George and Kramer look-alikes. Morally, however, the resemblance founders. These men are altruistic and intellectual, lovers of books and the arts, while Jerry and friends consume entertainment: television shows, movies, and sports events. Elaine quickly begins to prefer the interests of Kevin's friends to the inane obsessions of Jerry's crowd. But her fear of convention overcomes her when the three men gather in a clinch around a familial bag of groceries. Elaine then gets out, rejoining the dinner table at Monk's and the emotionally barren social arrangements of Jerry's quartet. Likewise, when they learn that Susan has died, Jerry, Elaine, Kramer, and George can think of nothing better to do or say than suggesting that they eat yet another meal out. When Jerry briefly dates a dermatologist, he feels insecure in the face of her calling, particularly since his parents have questioned his ability to make a living as a comedian. Jerry soothes his ego by calling the doctor a "pimple popper" until he learns that she preserves life by curing fatal skin cancer ("The Slicer," 9007). At this point, he can no longer suppress his fear that his comedy serves no purpose; nevertheless, he copes by construing his ability to enrage the doctor as confirmation of his comedic talent. Metaphorically, his parents and the Romanian gymnast were right all along: his comedy is no way to make a life.

If anything motivates Jerry's friends, it is a Flaubertian disdain for embour-geoisement; in their minds, chasing the sitcomic American dream would render them indistinct from the common herd. This is Elaine's objection to mother-hood: childbirth, she complains, has "been done to death" ("The Soul Mate," 8002). A similar desire for distinction inspires George to suggest creating a sit-com about nothing as he and Jerry brainstorm for an idea to present to NBC executives. "Everybody's doing something; we'll do nothing," he argues. While Jerry showed no interest in George's earlier suggestions—that Jerry play a gym-nastics coach whose son disappoints him by showing no interest in the sport, or an antique dealer who involves himself in the lives of his customers—the invidi-ous comparison seduces him. He even takes George along to his first meeting at NBC. When the executives express skepticism, George again insists upon the concept's singularity: "If you want to keep on doing the same old thing, then maybe this idea is not for you. I, for one, will not compromise my artistic integ-rity" ("The Pitch," 4003). As George storms out, Jerry, desperate to retain NBC's interest, latches on to an idea of Kramer's that he had previously rejected: "How about this: I manage a circus." "People want to watch freaks," Kramer had prom-ised, even though he claims to be afraid of clowns ("The Opera," 4008). Still, "freakdom" reveals the hard core of the singularity that seduces Jerry.

These notions come back to haunt Jerry when the gymnast insults his man-hood as they are leaving a circus performance. As if to undermine even Jerry's demotion to clown, Kramer simultaneously passes a kidney stone and stuns the crowd with his cries of agony. We're probably still laughing, but the narrative trajectory that joins "The Pitch" (4003) to "The Gymnast" (6006) says that peo-ple only want to watch freaks frolic; freaks in pain make a circus that Jerry can't manage. Without laughter, as Sartre notes, despair overtakes hope, and without hope, no one will watch a show about nothing. Indeed, this romantic failure fore-shadows the comedic failure of the finale. Jerry needs a laughing audience, but each time he chooses to get out, he loses some.

IV. The Art of Delay

If I had known, going into college, that I was going to become a comedian, I would have studied philosophy, English, and history.

—Jerry Seinfeld (*Jerry Seinfeld on Comedy*)

In his analysis of the comic plot, Northrop Frye notes how often these stories test social principals by pitting "the rhetoric of comedy" against "the rhetoric of jurisprudence." In traditional comedy, young love replaces repressive and anti-quated authority. Frye thus describes the ritual wedding that brings comedy to its end as a judgment about "what should be." Such judgment naturally also entails a statement about what shouldn't be, and Frye duly notes that darker comedies often expel the "blocking" characters who can't be assimilated into the society symbolized by a newly wed family. What Frye didn't see, but that Sartre clearly states, is that the comic persona itself is the one found guilty, even scapegoated. In Sartre's words,

> whether it consist of pure and simple elimination or banishment (expulsion, quar-antine, incarceration) the measures taken have three inseparable characteristics: the community, whatever it had been before, groups together; it unifies itself with an action for which each individual assumes complete responsibility, it purifies its intersubjectivity through the suppression of the disturbing element and for a certain time, it achieves a high degree of integration. (812, my translation)

How better to describe the spectators and jury in the final episode's trial? A dispa-rate group of individuals who had been deceived, dumped, or annoyed by Jerry and friends unites to condemn the self-centered behavior of the New York Four. Ostensibly the friends are on trial for watching a carjacking without coming to the aid of the victim. As in the sitcom Jerry and George proposed, the characters did nothing but joke about the situation.[11] They are charged with violating the "Good Samaritan" (3019) Law, so, as the prosecutor says, the trial will be about character (although *Seinfeld*'s arrested plot development also comes in for some criticism). In a show so obsessed with semantics, it can be no accident that Art Vandalay, the name George assumes to substantiate many of his desperate lies and impersonations, turns up as the judge who arrests the development of this sitcom. He jails the foursome for their antisocial behavior and, perhaps, their artistic vandalism. As the final episode closes, we see Jerry forced to further delay his sitcom plans. Instead, he reverts to stand-up comedy, now performing before an impassive crowd of prisoners. People aren't laughing anymore.

Until this point, though, our own laughter abets the crime of doing nothing, but it also expresses our hope for "something," and finally, so does the show about nothing. In the initial meeting with NBC executives, George's claim to artistic integrity sounds like his usual self-serving bluster; after all, he is afraid of these married men with jobs, "wearing suits and ties." By the time the final episode aired, it could be argued that if "even nothing is something," that "nothing" began as the art of delay. By practicing this art rather than rushing into "some-thing" (such as his ever-postponed marriage to Susan), George did in fact main-tain a perverse sort of artistic integrity. He introduced this so-called integrity in the second episode ("The Stakeout," 1002), when he went with Jerry to the office of a woman with whom Jerry hoped to begin a romance. While they enjoy good fortune in meeting the woman, George quickly reverses it when he awkwardly explains that they are there to meet with an acquaintance in the import/export business: "Art Vandalay," a refinement of his first impulse, "Art Core." He is enacting comedy's necessary obstacle to romance, and he evidently prefers to avoid the objectionable extremes of the hard core by stereotypically muddling in the midst of things. But if the art of delay arrests development, it may not dither indefinitely. Even the man named for delay, Judge Art Vandalay, determines that laughter had better be about something. He hopes that the New York Four will repent and reform while they are locked away. Comedy, this punishment implies, must eventually arrive at the heart of the matter. Or, as Shaw, Sartre, and other skeptics might put it, it must finally bend its shape to the cultural demands of romance.

Shaw called his *Pygmalion* a romance, but only to tweak his audience's desire to see his flower girl and Henry Higgins form a family. But from the play's London premiere to *My Fair Lady* (which Shaw did not live to see), the audience had its way. Had Jerry Seinfeld in fact had the prescience to study "philosophy, English, and history," he would have encountered many variations on that dictate. On the other hand, scriptwriter Larry David already articulated a commercial logic behind this ending: "I asked myself, 'Where could I send them for a year or two with the possibility of them coming back?' The first thought was a biosphere. But that struck me as a little too crazy. Then I said, 'Hey, what about prison?' They could be in jail for a year, then get out and everything would be the same" (*Seinfeld, Seinoff* 103). He never promises that they will live happily ever after, but sitcoms don't end in jail cells. They have reunion shows. Going out and getting out still remain possibilities for the New York Four, but the judge and NBC have made their wishes clear. That was seven years ago; and in spite of Larry David's plan, it appears that the comedy of Art Vandalay still prevails. In the shadows of domestic bliss, we've seen the promise of something many times over, but we ain't seen nothing yet.

In fact, we do not know whether the structure of comedy can be radically altered, and we don't know why no comedian, whether standing up in front of an audience, sitting down in front of a blank page, or mugging for the sitcom camera, has permanently done so. Frye imagines that comedy's stable form reflects a long-standing human desire for communal integration and an orderly, gradual transmission of power through the formation of new families. Shaw claims that comedy has simply corrupted our imaginations to make us want what comedy traditionally provides (even though life itself seldom conforms). Sartre darkens the claim by arguing that since comedy reinforces power, power reinforces comedy. Seinfeld, too, made his jokes with this philosophy, and tried to make nothing from it, but ended with "something" still firmly entrenched. As both Sartre and *Seinfeld* show us, we are either laughing at the prisoners of comedy or we are in the judge's chambers condemning them. In the meantime, the comedian does time.

Notes

1. Vincent Brook convincingly points out a "'no exit' motif" running throughout the series (56).

2. For example, Kant asserts that "laughter is an affection arising from a strained expectation being suddenly reduced to nothing."

3. See Peter Caws for further discussion of Sartre's theory of comedy.

4. See also Eric Gans, who makes the link to Flaubert: "Whether or not Seinfeld and David were aware, in creating their 'series about nothing,' of Flaubert's expressed desire to write 'a novel about nothing,' in their success they have become Flaubert's true successors."

5. Well before *Seinfeld*, Grote argued that American sitcoms marked the "End of Comedy" in their fundamental commitment to situations, rather than plot progressions, and in their aimless extension over as many seasons as they could acquire an audience: "The ending of the traditional comedy is the promise of a new life, a celebration, a wedding, a possible baby, a new and better world. The only ending that the sitcom allows is death. Because the series format is designed to last forever without significant change, obviously no ending is planned. But the series still must end sometime, and they end in most odd manners. When they go off the air, they just do not come on one day. Those series that do choose to make an ending always do so by making a change that destroys the situation" (103).

6. Morreale, too, notes that the highly self-referential finale shaped the sitcom "by destroying its central premise that it was a show about nothing. Instead, it became about something—about the nature of the sitcom and sitcom characters, articulated in a manner that afforded the audience . . . none of the pleasure of a happy ending" (112).

7. Gantz argues that this coffee shop is an example of a "queerly coded" space, "a name that conjures up images of an exclusively male religious society" (170).

8. Gantz also discusses this scene (171).

9. See also Rapping.

10. See Gantz for a thorough discussion of homosexual themes in the show.

11. Noted by Morreale (111).

DENNIS HALL (University of Louisville)

Jane Austen, Meet Jerry Seinfeld

> "I made up my mind on the subject. I planned the match from that hour; and when such success has blessed me in this instance, dear papa, you cannot think that I shall leave off match-making."
>
> —Emma Woodhouse (10)

> The worst dates are often the result of a fix-up. Why do we fix people up? Because *you* think they'll have a good time? Who the hell are you? It's a little power trip isn't it? You're playing God.
>
> —Jerry Seinfeld (13)

The divine Emma, literature's matchmaker par excellence, and the mortal Jerry, amourial maladroit, were among the most popular characters to engage the enthusiasm of American audiences in the 1990s. The characters in Austen's novels and in Seinfeld's television show tapped a deep vein of interest in a realistic comedy of manners and humors that endures particularly within the middle classes, despite, indeed, because of the assaults of the culture of postmodernism. While the Jane Austen revival proved an impressive hit, Jerry Seinfeld—author, comedian, player, character, and television show—was, of course, the biggest and most influential comedic phenomenon of the 1990s. Jane Austen, I want to argue, manifests what may be called the "Enlightenment project" (Harvey 14), while Jerry Seinfeld exhibits the postmodern project. To see how these two cultural enterprises meet and diverge allows one better to appreciate both the reappearance of Austen and the endurance of Seinfeld.

At the height of Seinfeld's popularity, American popular culture simultaneously indulged an enthusiasm for entertainments based upon what were once thought classic works, a wider phenomenon of which the Jane Austen survival is a significant part (Hall). Despite its profusion, ephemerality, and seemingly infinite variety, postmodern popular culture exhibits a distinct taste for looting and refashioning—"re-presenting" I believe we are now obliged to say—the artifacts of the past. The more orthodox the work, apparently, the greater the delectation. The practice, of course, has been going on for years. Thomas Hine, who has compiled a CD-ROM collection of nonverbal quotations for a new edition of Bartlett's, observes that "Clearly, 'high' Western culture is not dead. Quite the contrary. We're swimming in it. We live our lives in a great sea of communication and manipulation, where fragments of high culture are constantly being repeated, combined, repackaged, and adapted" (37). Few days elapse without our confronting, in one form or another, evocations of *The Thinker, The Scream, The Ninth Symphony, The Ride of the Valkyries, The Parthenon,* or *The Governor's Palace at Williamsburg.* Fragments of these and the like are, of course, the building blocks of postmodern pastiche.

The mid-'90s, however, revealed a marked increase in the exploitation of whole works, of classic literary narratives that are engaging the attention, perhaps even the *jouissance,* of mass audiences. Consider: Almost the entire Merchant-Ivory canon. A stunning Art Deco film version of *Richard III* (Richard Loncraine, 1995), followed by an *Othello* (Oliver Parker, 1995) blurbed as "one of the great erotic thrillers of our time," and Kenneth Branagh's rollicking *Much Ado About Nothing* (1993), a movie made possible by the earlier popular success of his *Henry V* (1989). A grunge *Romeo and Juliet* (Bazz Luhrmann, 1996) to which teens actually flocked. A brave, even relentless series of film versions of the work of Henry James. A realistic rendering of *The Last of the Mohicans* (Michael Mann, 1992) led the way to Demi Moore's conversion of *The Scarlet Letter* (Roland Jaffé, 1995) into a sexual fantasy à la Russ Meyer's *Vixens* and to Ted Danson's transformation for television of *Gulliver's Travels* (Charles Sturridge, 1996) into a sentimental domestic tragedy worthy of *The Donna Reed Show.* And only fair to mention, I suppose, *Muppet Treasure Island* (Brian Henson, 1996),whose anachronistic gags are apparently as uproarious to those under 8 as they are tedious to those able to recall the feeling of adventure in reading Stevenson's tale.

In addition to basing productions on specific literary works, film and television in the '90s were much given to period pieces that invoke the texture or, if you will, the feeling of authenticity associated with literary works, indeed often leaving viewers wondering in vain what famous eighteenth- or nineteenth-century work they are based upon; we might call this the John Jakes syndrome, after the success of his Civil War epics marinated in the aura of *Gone with the Wind.* A movie called *Restoration* (Michael Hoffman, 1995), about a man who marries a mistress of Charles II, vied with *Braveheart* (Mel Gibson, 1995) for audiences, as did an action epic called *Cutthroat Island* (Renny Harlin, 1995), in which Geena Davis unbuckles her swash for the PG-13 crowd. And a good many are watching *The Madness of King George* (Nicholas Hytner, 1995) and *Jefferson in Paris* (James Ivory, 1995) on video, and some re-rent *Dangerous Liaisons* (Stephen Frears, 1988) and *Amadeus* (Milos Forman, 1984) more often than they are willing to admit.

Patrick O'Brian's novels of late-eighteenth-century seafaring sustain a large following (recently brought to the screen in *Master and Commander: The Far Side of the World* (Peter Weir, 2003), and historical romances continue to outsell by a wide margin anything pretending to be "serious fiction," whatever that oxymoron may mean. Both of these lists, of course, could be much longer, but the trend is clear, and it continues into the new millennium.

In this context film versions of *Pride and Prejudice* (Simon Langton, 1995), *Sense and Sensibility* (Ang Lee, 1995), *Persuasion* (Roger Michell, 1995), and *Emma* (Douglas McGrath, 1996) drew critical acclaim, and much more significantly, these films captured very large theatre, television, and video rental audiences. The plot of *Clueless* (Amy Heckerling, 1995), a delightful tale of Beverly Hills High School airheads, closely follows that of Austen's *Emma*. Moreover, sales of Austen's books are on the rise; indeed, the Folio Society began seducing membership with a seven-volume boxed set of "The Complete Novels of Jane Austen, Worth \$199, Yours for \$9.95" (5).

A host of explanations for this prodigy compete for our assent. Most of them in some sense work, and in their accumulation they do go a long way, I must admit, in accounting for the very big business a movie like *Emma* has done and in suggesting something of its cultural meaning. It *is* a woman's film, although no *Thelma and Louise* and also popular with men, notwithstanding the arguments about who now determines which movie tickets are bought. It *is* a form of acedia, for it is often easier and cheaper for producers to use traditional narratives firmly planted in the public domain, if not in the popular consciousness. In a culture that consumes narratives at the rate we do, some recycling is inevitable; as Hine notes, "What familiarity breeds isn't contempt. It's reuse" (37). It *is* a coffee-table movie: long running time, lots of costumes, beautiful interiors, gorgeous natural scenes, lots of dialogue, and no violence—well no physical violence, no bashing and blood. It *is* a movie that exhibits wit for audiences dulled by the ubiquity of the vacuous and the vulgar. It *is* a movie that portrays social difference through syntax and gesture rather than volume and riot. It *is* a movie that represents genuine sexual tension, but "the sexuality," as one critic of the novel points out, is "in the minds and speech and emotional intensity of the characters, in the mental urgency of every encounter" (Brown 51). Sex is not signed in skin; it is a movie to which one can take one's middle and high school children without squirming at the site of every unoccupied sofa or cleared dining room table. And it *is* a movie about manners. Now, I have heard it seriously argued that the Austen movies are popular because they reflect good manners in an age of ubiquitous boorishness. While readers of Judith Martin's Miss Manners column may be pleased, these are, I think, comedies of manners in the more traditional sense. *Emma* and the other Austen narratives have far more to do with the testing of conventions that bind and loose individuals and social groups rather than simply with etiquette, the forms of civil speech and behavior.

One NPR commentator, however, provides a more fruitful approach in his suggestion that there is a fundamental similarity between the Jane Austen movies and the *Seinfeld* television series. While one might not wish to characterize *Seinfeld* as a "women's" show, it is not a "men's" show, for the scripts and dialogue carefully avoid most of the pitfalls of sexism in its exploration of relationships between men and women. Elaine is as strong a character as any on the show, and Jerry's monologues about dating as often as not apply to women as well as men. While clearly not the coffee table TV of *Masterpiece Theatre*, *Seinfeld* is free of violence and very much given to delivering its social commentary via gesture and especially through careful manipulations of language. While sometimes vulgar, it is full of wit and is never vacuous. Sexuality is a major concern of *Seinfeld*, yet it plays out this concern in the speech, emotional intensity, and mental urgency of the ensemble cast of characters; indeed, the show's treatment of sexual themes is downright decorous compared to much of what passed for situation comedy in the 1990s.

Finally and more to the point, *Seinfeld*, like *Emma* and most of the Austen canon, is comedy of humours and manners, in many respects after the precedents of Ben Jonson, Oliver Goldsmith, and Richard Brinsley Sheridan (Harmon & Holman 107–108, 429). This is not to suggest that the antics of Jerry and Elaine, George and Kramer are analogs of the interactions of Emma and Mr. Knightly, Harriet Smith and Robert Martin, Frank Churchill and Jane Fairfax, as is the case in the direct borrowing in *Clueless*. Rather, both are testing conventions, finding out what brings people together and drives them apart. The audiences for both are fascinated by, perhaps even share, the narcissism of a small group of young adults who are groping to find, or to forge for themselves, their identities and their relationships within a social milieu. The environment is relatively stable in the Austen narratives, where the trick is to discover how the system works, while the environment in the *Seinfeld* series is relentlessly mutable, where the effort is to discover if there is a system that works at all. Still, *Seinfeld* portrays the same struggle between sense and sensibility—and for essentially the same stakes—inscribed in the idiom of the mid-1990s.

An interest in communication, particularly the efficacy of language, perhaps most clearly links both of these cultural enterprises and their audiences. I think it significant that Deborah Tannen's *You Just Don't Understand. Women and Men in Conversation* (1990) and *Talking from 9 to 5: Women and Men in the Workplace: Language, Sex, and Power* (1994), John Gray's *Men Are from Mars, Women Are from Venus* (1992), and Jerry Seinfeld's *SeinLanguage* (1993) are among the decade's bestsellers; they are a few of the many indices of the growing and almost technical interest in a crisis in communication that defines the market for both Austen's and Seinfeld's material. Their divergence on this point of common interest, however, points to other significant differences between *Seinfeld* and works like *Emma* and their uses and gratifications for audiences. Consumers of Austen experience, if you will, enjoy the reactionary pleasures of texts in which language in the final analysis works. For the narrative's author and for her characters, the ironies are fixed in that they finally deliver clear meaning. Consumers of *Seinfeld*, on the other hand, explore the pleasures of texts that finally demonstrate the many ways language does not work.

Most notably, an Austen narrative is governed by a strong sense of an ending, while the *Seinfeld* TV series perforce remains open-ended. The characters in both are fundamentally decent people; neither traffics in serious ridicule or anything close to genuine evil. Yet the readers and viewers of an Austen narrative know that the characters will survive, whatever befalls them, reasonably intact. And viewers of *Seinfeld* are equally certain that the characters will continue to endure their angst. Resolution in the achievement of identity and the accommodation of social convention drives Austen's novel and readers from the outset, while demonstration of the protean self and the mutability of human relationships propels *Seinfeld*, from Jerry's opening monologues through the brief urban dramas that sustain the attention of his viewers. Horace Walpole observed that "this world is a comedy to those that think, a tragedy to those that feel" (quoted in McMaster 38), and such typical *Seinfeld* episodes as "The Junior Mint" (4019), "The Bubble Boy" (4006), "The Wallet" (4004), "The Bris" (5005), "The Contest" (4010), and "The Yada Yada" (8019) play close to the threshold between thought and feeling; they could easily be tearjerkers, and would be if extended into another episode or if sensibility were given freer rein. Comedic thought prevails in *Seinfeld* by insulating the viewers from feeling through not only the episodic structure of the whole enterprise, but also through the fragmentation within episodes (commonly three or four story lines), the extravagant dialogue, and frequent sight gags.

Comedic thought is sustained in Austen by engaging feeling, by, if you will, taming it. In Austen's narratives both sense and sensibility are exhaustively played out, and while sense triumphs, it comes to recognize the power and even the value of sensibility. Personal satisfaction and social order are represented as finally harmonized, and both are achieved through exercises of reason and sentiment, will and language—human capacities available to individuals through which they can and do construct their identities and a sufficiently satisfying social order. In *Seinfeld*, sense and sensibility remain scarcely distinguishable in the antics of an ensemble dedicated to a kind of existential irrationality and whose members perpetually endure personal frustration sustained as much by their own indecision and linguistic confusion as by the intrusions of a chaotic society.

In sum, Austen manifests the Enlightenment project, while Seinfeld exhibits the postmodern. The Enlightenment project, whatever else may be said of it, is dedicated to a purposeful and instrumental rationality (Harvey 15); it recognizes human creativity and "the pursuit of individual excellence in the name of human progress" (Harvey 13). One's identity and lot in life, however narrow their scope, are seen in large measure as dependent upon the individual as well as the community. The postmodern project, whatever else may be said of it, seeks to shatter such optimism, recognizing the inevitable "revolt of human nature against the oppressive power of purely instrumental reason over culture and personality" (Harvey 13). At "the core of postmodernist philosophical thought" is the insistence "that we should, in the name of human emancipation, abandon the Enlightenment project entirely" (Harvey 14).

As David Harvey and others have noted, a renewal of the Enlightenment project—considerably modified to be sure—is underway (359), and I think the popularity of the Jane Austen movies is a piece of that cultural action. The enjoyment of movies like *Emma* is part of a widening expression of discontent with the indeterminacy, ephemerality, fragmentation, and the rest of the confusion characteristic of the condition of postmodernity—the condition that *Seinfeld* so efficiently exhibits.

Postcapitalism is erasing concrete differences in the ways people can actually live their lives by flooding its markets with the ephemeral differences of commodified signs, produced and consumed not so much for their utility as for their power to signify. Having lost so much control over self and environment to the culture of postcapitalism, the appeal of the Enlightenment paradigms of rationality and self-determination is increasingly powerful. Significantly, this turn to the Enlightenment tradition has recourse to whole narratives rather than isolated quotations, articulated models rather than a profusion of fragments. The Enlightenment project seeks more to know *how* than to know *what*.

Moreover, the enthusiasm for Enlightenment narratives responds to the communications crisis spawned by the postmodern traffic in commodified signs, which is reflected in an insatiable appetite for irony, a taste for self-reflexivity, a penchant for jargon, an addiction to textual looting, and an indulgence of incoherence. In this regard all of Austen's work stands in stark contrast to *Seinfeld*. *Emma*, for example, presents itself and is commonly taken as a text in which meaning, however narrow its scope, is inherent, reliable, and authentic. It is taken as an unabashed exercise of intentionality on the part of its author and as a demonstration of how plain sense can function to promote human happiness—a remarkable vision of human power in the face of the palpable failures of written spoken language to communicate in the 1990s.

David Harvey suggests that a renewal of interest in the Enlightenment project may provide a platform for a useful cultural critique of postmodernism: "On that critical basis it becomes possible to launch a counter-attack of narrative against image, of ethics against aesthetics, of a project of Becoming rather than Being, and to search for unity within difference" (359). If a taste for Jane Austen, as a representative of the Enlightenment project, has become a practical part of that critique, as I think it has, then a cultivated interest in Jerry Seinfeld, as a representative of the postmodern project, will complete the critical dialogue, as I think it must.

AMY McWILLIAMS (Texas A&M University)

Genre Expectation and Narrative Innovation in Seinfeld

I n the fall of 1997, *Seinfeld* aired "The Betrayal" (9008). The episode was advertised as "backward," and the scenes ran from conclusion to opening, with each segment making clear what had happened in the previous one. This particular episode draws attention to the expectation for and disruption of linear narrative in an obvious way, but plot structure has always been a playground for *Seinfeld*'s creators. The show was, infamously, about nothing. Tracking the everyday escapades of its four lead characters, it taught no moral lessons and held no opinions on major world issues. Rather, it reveled in both the ridiculous and the ordinary (as well as the ridiculous in the ordinary), creating a world where simple objects such as raincoats, Pez dispensers, and toilet paper wreaked havoc and accepting the gift of a pen was tantamount to declaring World War III.

The world of *Seinfeld* was not without predecessors; its characters and events grounded the show firmly in the tradition of situation comedies. The writers presented these familiar elements, however, in a narrative structure that both depended on and refuted viewer expectations—and that was where the true innovation of *Seinfeld* lay. While not every episode drew as much attention to plotting as "The Betrayal," the plots of *Seinfeld* always made us very aware that they are plots. In other words, the writers of *Seinfeld* create plots that draw attention to themselves all the time; they took the typical story line for a thirty-minute show and tweaked it in a number of ways. This attention to plotting allowed *Seinfeld* to avoid other generic expectations as well, for the show did not have to come to a moral, a main theme, or even a conclusion at the end of each episode. *Seinfeld* was not, in the end, a show about nothing; it was a show about shows—a parody of the sitcom genre.

From the beginning, *Seinfeld* depended on its comic predecessors, drawing on familiar elements of the sitcom to create and populate its world. Parody has been defined as "[R]epetition with critical distance that allows ironic signaling of difference at the very heart of similarity" (Hutcheon 26). This was precisely what *Seinfeld* presented: a repetition of familiar patterns and formulations that achieved, in its deviations from the norm, a critique of the very genre in which it participates. As with all parodies, the series grounded its criticism in familiarity. The characters are variations on those we've seen before: Jerry, the "straight man" for much of the quartet's comic banter; George, the neurotic best friend; Elaine, the token female character; and Kramer, the wacky neighbor. Jerry stands at the center of the group, providing an almost normal but still neurotic axis for the action, much as Bob Newhart's characters on *Newhart* (1972–78) and *The Bob Newhart Show* (1982–90) or Alex Rieger (Judd Hirsch) on *Taxi* (1978–83). George serves as the prerequisite sidekick for Jerry. Watch almost any sit-com in history and you'll find such a character, from Ethel (Vivien Vance) on *I Love Lucy* (1951–57) to Ralph (Don Most) and Potsie (Anson Williams) on *Happy Days* (1974–84) and Al Borlen (Richard Karlan) on *Home Improvement* (1991–99). Elaine is the only woman who returns every week; other than the mothers, she's the only female that sticks around at all. Surrounded by men, she is the ex-girlfriend, the resident expert on the female gender, and the sometime sexual object of all three of her comrades. (In "The Tape" (3008), for example, an erotic message she leaves in jest on Jerry's tape recorder causes all three men to see her in a new light.) Her peers include Mary Richards (Mary Tyler Moore) from *The Mary Tyler Moore Show* (1970–77), Margaret Houlihan (Loretta Swit) from *M*A*S*H* (1972–83), and Sally Solomon (Kristen Johnston) from *3rd Rock from the Sun* (1996–2001). And, finally, there is Kramer, who may well be the long-lost brother of Christopher Lloyd's Jim Ignatowski on *Taxi*.

Seinfeld also drew on many traditional comic styles, combining Jerry's stand-up routines from real life (dropped in the final seasons, although Jerry continued to insert stand-up material into conversation) with other ensemble forms. The bantering on the show harkens back to the conversational humor of George and Gracie (*The George Burns and Gracie Allen Show* [1950–58]) and movie screwball comedies. The language of *Seinfeld* was one of its most notable contributions to popular culture; if you missed an episode, you might be befuddled when a colleague called you "smoopie" ("The Soup Nazi," 7006) come Friday morning. In addition, the show included plenty of physical comedy from a tradition as old as Chaplin and Keaton passed down through the Three Stooges, Lucille Ball, and others. With his various entries into Jerry's apartment, Kramer is the most consistent source of sight gags, but Elaine's "little kicks" ("The Little Kicks," 8004), George's toupee, and Jerry's puffy shirt ("The Puffy Shirt," 5002) all add to the show's visual comedy. Again, this combination of styles is not unique. Almost every sitcom finds a combination of visual and verbal humor. Stand-up comics doing sitcoms and including parts of their routines in their shows was not new either. Jack Benny, Bill Cosby, and Tim Allen have turned their stand-up material into the basis for successful shows (*The Jack Benny Program* [1950–65], *The*

Cosby Show [1984–92], and *Home Improvement,* respectively). Bob Newhart incorporated phone conversations from his stand-up routines into his television comedy, while Gabe Kaplan told those horrid jokes on every episode of *Welcome Back, Kotter* (1975–79). I would argue, however, that *Seinfeld* used the familiar and typical precisely to draw attention to the points at which it was neither, and to foreground those very conventions we take for granted. In doing so, it found a source of critical humor in the dissonance between the expected and the new.

For while *Seinfeld* contained numerous familiar elements, the creators combined those elements in original ways. The setting seemed typical—the city, jobs, families, etc.—yet *Seinfeld* was the first show to have as its central situation four unrelated characters on the streets and in the buildings of New York City. Traditionally, sitcom characters are more inter-related, usually either as a family unit (*The Adventures of Ozzie and Harriet* [1952–66], *The Brady Bunch* [1969–74], *Family Ties* [1982–89], *Mad About You* [1992–99]); as students and teachers (*Pearl* [1996–97], *Room 222* [1969–74], *Head of the Class* [1986–91]); or as coworkers (*M*A*S*H* [1972–83], *WKRP in Cincinnati* [1978–82], *Newsradio* [1995]). Some shows have thrown unrelated people together, such as *I Dream of Jeanie* (1965–70), *Mork and Mindy* (1978–82), or *Gilligan's Island* (1964–67), but these have tended to include outrageous situations or fantastic characters. *Seinfeld* stuck to a realistic setting and people without magical powers. While the locations were standard from week to week—Jerry's apartment, Monk's coffee shop—Elaine, Kramer, and George don't know each other at the beginning of the series. They meet each other through Jerry and, for the most part, relate through him. An episode entitled "The Dog" (3004) highlights this at first tentative connection, as George and Elaine find the only subject of conversation they have when Jerry's not around is Jerry; they are completely uncomfortable when left together without him. Such a configuration of characters, groups of *Friends,* as it were, was much copied: *Ellen* (1994–98) and *Friends* (1994–2004), in particular, followed *Seinfeld*'s lead. Like *Seinfeld,* they followed their component characters into both work and family, often finding humor in placing one of the friends in another's office or home.

In the world of *Seinfeld* everything came to seem familiar, especially as the series continued and the characters become an interrelated group. Even the differences in setting and situation described above become almost formulaic as the series wrapped numerous seasons and as other and newer shows started to emulate the *Seinfeld* formula. Yet the abundance of "everyday" things and people in traditional sitcom configurations (or in traditional *Seinfeld*ian configurations) only served to highlight the main difference between *Seinfeld* and other shows, the point at which it truly stood apart from other series: its almost hyperawareness of plotting and its consistent parody of its own genre. While longtime fans might predict what would happen once they see the first segment—was not an episode like "The Betrayal" intended to deliberately frustrate them?—the show's unique formula seemed at first unpredictable. By drawing attention to plot, the writers highlighted the way *Seinfeld* differed from other shows; by emphasizing plot over other elements, they created a show that critiqued other shows.[1]

This *Seinfeld*ian plot formula actually took several forms, all of which played with the traditional and expected story arc. The vast majority of sitcom episodes follow a problem/resolution format, with a secret/revelation being the most common variation. Richie (Ron Howard) has to learn to handle himself with bullies *(Happy Days)*, Hawkeye (Alan Alda) must decide whether to send an underage soldier back to the front lines *(M*A*S*H)*, or the leaky vase tells Mike (Robert Reed) and Carol (Florence Henderson) that the kids did indeed play ball in the house *(The Brady Bunch)*. In addition, episodes of typical shows are independent of each other in that they achieve closure thanks to the resolution or revelation. Yes, the characters are the same from week to week and some story lines or relationships may continue in other episodes, but a new viewer can start with any episode and not miss many of the jokes. Each episode is self-contained; each one has a similar pace. They cover the same amount of ground and usually take on the same plot structure: exposition, rising action, climax, falling action, conclusion. Because of their thirty-minute time frame, the climax is often very near the end of the episode, with a final comic moment following the last commercial (a new development in recent seasons, as networks try to discourage channel surfing).[2]

For example, in one episode of *Home Improvement*, Jill and Tim must convince Brad and Randy to stop picking on their little brother, Mark. The description of the problem by Mark at the beginning of the episode is the exposition; the rising action comes as Jill tries to talk some sense into her boys. The climax nears as Tim takes over, planning to turn the older boys' trick back onto them. They've told Mark that the family members are actually aliens and that the mother ship is coming back to Earth to get them that evening. In the climax to the episode, Brad and Randy arrive outside to razz Mark for waiting on the aliens, and Tim arrives in a bodysuit covered with lights as loud music and white light flood the backyard. After the final commercial break, we get the falling action/conclusion, with Jill and Tim dancing together in their alien costumes. The resolution comes with the solution of the problem, and the boys learn a moral lesson about dealing with their kid brother.

Though always inclined to play with viewer expectations, refusing to take such a generic plot for granted, *Seinfeld*'s writers nevertheless developed several standard ways to plot their episodes. I will look at four ways that *Seinfeld* consistently plays with traditional plotting: intersection, multiplicity, elongation, and continuation. In each of these, the writers depend upon our knowledge of the traditional sitcom episode, as they do with character and setting. They know that we know what they're toying with, and they use our awareness of the genre and their departures from it as the basis of their innovations.

Intersection. By "intersection" I mean the way subplots intersect the main plot and bring about resolution, or as much resolution as *Seinfeld* is willing to give. This is the plot formula that occurs most often in the series. Take, for example, "The Marine Biologist" (5014). In this episode, George meets up with an old college friend and, because of a lie on his behalf by Jerry, must convince her he is a marine biologist. He is, apparently, caught in the lie when they come across a beached whale while walking along the shore. A crowd gathers, and somebody calls for—you guessed it—a marine biologist. George rolls up his sleeves and heads towards the whale. Meanwhile, in a subplot that seems to be a throwaway, Kramer has been getting recovered golf balls from a source at the club. He goes out to the beach and hits them off into the ocean. In the end, George comes to the coffee shop and tells his friend how he saved the whale: when he climbed on top of it, he found a golf ball lodged in its blowhole. The subplot—noticeably smaller and, until the end, completely unrelated—has come to the forefront to resolve the main plot in an unexpected way: a hole in one.

This formulation creates unpredictability and denies viewer expectations precisely because it draws on and subsequently thwarts the characteristic plots of the genre, granting the subplot power over the main plot rather than using it as a mirror or contrast. In other words, if the theme of the main plot on *Home Improvement* is honesty—Tim lied to Jill and now they're arguing—then the subplot is likely to be a variation on that theme—Randy lied about his grades and has to learn to tell the truth right along with Dad. Or the subplot may provide comic relief from a serious main plot, as with so many Frank Burns escapades on *M*A*S*H*. The subplots are, therefore, subservient or secondary. Not so on *Seinfeld*, where, as we've seen, the "subplots"—and even that term must be called into question—can bring about the resolution in an unexpected manner. In another sitcom, everything in the episode contributes to the central idea of that week's show. *Seinfeld* spoofs that formulation implicitly, giving us seemingly unrelated subplots and tying them into the main plot in an arbitrary but humorous manner. As has often been noted, *Seinfeld* had as many as thirty scenes and customarily four plotlines per episode, while the standard sitcom averaged a dozen. (*The Simpsons* [1989–] tends to do the same thing in episodes that race up to a climax, seemingly irresolvable, and suddenly find a very contrived—and sometimes unbelievable—sense of closure, or at least a tongue-in-cheek moral from Lisa.)

Multiplicity. On *Seinfeld* subplots are sometimes all we have; I call this multiplicity. In most of the show's episodes, the different plots intersect at some point, as described above. But in some cases, there isn't a main plot to be intersected. Instead, the writers give us several separate plots. The best example of this is "The Subway" (3013), in which all four friends take the subway to separate destinations, seeing each other only in the beginning and ending scenes. Each one has an eventful ride, but we never even see them relate their adventures to the others. This kind of episode becomes a double thwarting of viewer expectations. "The Subway" draws attention to plot not only by refusing to have a main plot and a subplot, but also by refusing to follow even the formula of the typical *Seinfeld* episode by giving us the expected intersection. Multiplicity not only refuses to tie everything into one main idea, but it also frustrates the sitcom world expectation where everything concludes neatly at the end of the half hour.

Elongation. A third narrative structure, elongation, occurs when the writers take an event or situation that would, on another show, take up only part of the episode and allow it to expand over the entire thirty minutes. The most famous episode in this category is "The Chinese Restaurant" (2011), where George, Elaine, and Jerry spend the entire show waiting for a seat at a Chinese restaurant. Of course, we all identify with their plight, which is what makes the episode so funny. But *Seinfeld* was the first show to give an entire episode to this kind of humor. Similar episodes include the "The Parking Garage" (3006), in which the four spend the entire thirty minutes looking for their car in a mall garage. In these installments, the writers seem to critique those sitcoms with episodes on issues, morals (as in "The moral of the story is . . ."), or lessons. There will never be an advertisement for "a very special episode" of *Seinfeld,* for its humor is of a more practical and parodic nature.

Continuation. *Seinfeld* also exhibits what I will call continuation. Episodes of *Seinfeld* not only continue into the next half hour or weekly time slot, but they also draw on each other's language and characters in innovative ways, leaking into other shows and real life, breaking the traditional story arc completely. First there is the simple double episode, either an hour in length or a two-parter, which is a *Seinfeld* staple (though not original with the series). Most notable for *Seinfeld* is the sequence that begins with "The Keys" (3022), in which Jerry takes his spare house keys back from Kramer, and continues through "The Trip" (4001, 4002), a two-part episode that kicks off the subsequent season, in which George and Jerry go to L.A. to retrieve Kramer, who has run away because of his fight with Jerry in order to become an actor in Hollywood. But there have been several two-part or hour-long episodes.[3] A variation on this are "arced" seasons like four, which follows the development of the sitcom-within-a-sitcom *Jerry*, and seven, in which George is engaged to Susan in a story arc that continued from week to week.

In *Seinfeld* story lines continue past the end of the half hour in still other ways. Any sitcom has the same characters from week to week and a limited sense of history, and none of them reiterates character histories at the beginning of each episode; the viewer may be left with questions at the end of the episode. But a new viewer of *Seinfeld*, starting somewhere in the middle of the series' run, would find that there are recurring situations in *Seinfeld* that outnumber those found elsewhere, characters who don't show up for episodes at a time, only to surface unexpectedly—and unexplained. Crazy Joe Davola, for example, appears throughout Season Four, and each appearance is more humorous if the viewer has seen the others. Also, the internal allusions in *Seinfeld* often go unexplained, giving the consistent viewer a feeling of being in on the joke and enabling minor moments to have a life beyond their episode of origin. For example, in the episodes "The Opera" (4008) and "The Gymnast" (6006) we find out that Kramer is afraid of clowns. In an episode from the 1997–98 season ("The Gymnast," 6006), Elaine keeps Kramer from coming with her by telling him she's got to stop by the circus . . . where there are clowns. The moment is funny because of Kramer's physical reaction to the mention of clowns, but the allusion, if recognized, to the other episodes makes it that much more entertaining.

The sense of continuation in *Seinfeld* also comes from the fact that its episodes are often open-ended. Sometimes they lack a traditional resolution completely, as when the viewer is simply left with a final comic shot of a street hoodlum wrinkling his nose as he tries to steal "The Smelly Car" (4020). But the show is also open-ended in that it tends to leak out into the real world. I've already noted the vocabulary of *Seinfeld* that permeates our culture. (See the *Seinfeld* glossary.) *The Entertainment Weekly* Seinfeld *Companion*, which doubles as an episode guide for the first few seasons and a dictionary of terms, describes the language of the show this way:

> The *Seinfeld* devotee appreciates that no other sitcom in television history has made such inventive, idiosyncratic use of words, labels, brand names, and pop-culture references. No other TV comedy has experimented as daringly with the witty possibilities of language on a medium that traditionally relies heavily on physical action for easy laughs. On *Seinfeld*, open-ended conversation among characters who have nothing to gain in terms of plot development is its own reward.

The language of *Seinfeld* is certainly at the center of its appeal, and has given us wonderful new words to describe the annoying people around us (close talker) or things that drive us nutty (the drop-in). As one critic, contemplating the show's last season, comments: "The hard part will be coming up with The Catch Phrase. For nine years *Seinfeld* has been translating life's 'excruciating minutiae'—as cast member Julia Louis-Dreyfus once put it ("The Bizarro Jerry," 8003)—into an invaluable phrase book for our time: 'shrinkage' ("The Hamptons," 5021), 'Soup Nazi' ("The Soup Nazi," 7006), 'master of his domain' ("The Contest," 4010), 'low talker' ("The Puffy Shirt," 5002), 'close talker' ("The Raincoats," 5019), 'not that there's anything wrong with that' ("The Outing," 4016), 'yada yada yada' ("The Yada Yada," 8019). TV's biggest comedies are lucky to squeeze one slogan into popular parlance ('Sit on it!' 'Here come da judge!'). *Seinfeld*, way up there in the pantheon, knocks off winners almost every week" (Marin and Hammer 54).

Seinfeld regularly crosses over into the real world in yet another way; the appearance of actual people and the recognition of other television shows and movies in the series. Jerry appears on *The Today Show* (with a cameo by Bryant Gumbel) ("The Puffy Shirt," 5002), *The Tonight Show* (with a cameo by Jay Leno) ("The Trip, Part I," 4001), and *The Charles Grodin Show* ("The Doll," 7016). Kramer shows up on *Murphy Brown* ("The Keys," 3022), playing a bit part during his California sojourn, on *Live with Regis and Kathy Lee* ("The Opposite," 5022), and in a Woody Allen movie ("The Alternate Side," 3011). New York mayor Rudolf Giuliani ("The Non-Fat Yogurt," 5007), George Wendt and Corbin Bernsen (both in "The Trip, Part I," 4001), Geraldo Rivera ("Finale," 9021, 9022), Keith Hernandez ("The Boyfriend," 3017), Bette Midler ("The Understudy," 6022)—all play themselves. Kramer the tennis ball boy reinjures Monica Seles ("The Lip Reader," 5006). Elaine hates *The English Patient* ("The English Patient," 8017). George pursues Marisa Tomei in Season Seven. In all of these ways, *Seinfeld* rejects the tendency of sitcoms to be insular, allowing episodes to flow not only into each other but into our everyday lives.

Finally, I want to examine the connection between the structure and the content of *Seinfeld*, something I've mentioned all along as part of the show's parody of other series. I said earlier that the show's focus on nothing allows it a freedom to play with plot. Since the writers don't have to come to a lesson or a revelation at the end of every episode, they have more room to leave things open-ended or go for the surprising—and utterly comic—ending. But on *Seinfeld* the reverse is also true: *Seinfeld* has chosen to concentrate on plotting and defying expectations precisely so it can't have a resolution at the end.

The chicken and egg question of determining cause and effect in this case matters not. The writers plot a world where it's the little things that matter, but they also plot a world without closure or necessary solutions. This sitcosmos may be a backlash against innumerable shows that tell us problems can be solved inside of thirty minutes and the conventions of a genre that regurgitates the same themes, characters, and situations year after year. In this light, the meta-plotting of *Seinfeld* becomes not only entertainment—a joke for those familiar with the genre—but also a serious criticism of the form. I have pointed to this criticism of the genre's tendency to moralize as I described the various plot structures of the show. Of course *Seinfeld* is never overly serious, nor interested in issues, but at times, however, the series flies directly in the face of the moralizing we find in other series. As *TV Guide* says, with this series "Warm, fuzzy, moral lessons, lovable characters, the fake sanctimony of practically every sitcom in history went right out the window" (Appelo). In the world of *Seinfeld*, what goes around comes around, but consequences are practical and humorous, rather than ethical.

Case in point: the death of Susan ("The Invitations," 7022). After months of being engaged, George and Susan send out wedding invitations. By this point, George wants out of the relationship but can't extricate himself. He insists on purchasing cheap envelopes, being his typically frugal self, and Susan consequently dies from adhesive poisoning. At the hospital, there is neither grief nor remorse. Jerry, Elaine, and Kramer barely take note of her death, and the only consequences facing George come (in Season Eight) in his frustration from working with the foundation set up in Susan's name. The world of Jerry, Elaine, Kramer, and George has rules, both in the sense of manners and social interaction as well as an ironic view of action and reaction. The show has a definite sense of poetic justice; if you don't pass the toilet paper to the person in the stall next to you when she needs it, she might leave you without "a square" the next time around. But if the show has a "moral," it is simply that friends are as important as they are annoying. Because the writers are neither working with an ethical or moral view nor working to depict family values, warped or otherwise, they don't have to write toward a conclusion of reunion, retribution, or revelation. They can simply drive their plot—in whatever formulation they want to use—toward that last shot of Newman eating muffin stumps.

All of this is not to say that *Seinfeld* is the only show doing these things. *The Simpsons, Beavis and Butt-head* (1993–97), and *King of the Hill* (1997–) all parody the genre consistently (it is interesting to note the animated nature of these prime examples), and other shows have played with nonlinear narrative. For example, *Frasier's* 1997 Christmas episode had each character telling his or her version of the story. The tendency for sitcoms to have continuing story arcs (always an element of dramatic series, science fiction series, and soap operas, which also have multiple story lines) has been picked up in the post-*Seinfeld* era, most notably with shows like *Ellen*, with the story line in which Ellen sells the bookstore and buys a house, and *Friends,* with its saga of Ross and Rachel or the story of Phoebe's pregnancy. But *Seinfeld* is the only show with writers who make plot structure a primary source of humor and parody.

Seinfeld takes part in a long tradition of situation comedies, drawing on their characters and settings, playing with and critiquing their plot structures, and always depending on our knowledge of the formula to get the joke. Refusing to broadcast messages of political correctness, family values, or moral rectitude, *Seinfeld* instead takes as its subject matter itself and its genre, creating a sometimes biting parody of the very expectations and patterns on which it draws. Yet its criticism is candy-coated with remarkable verbal and visual humor and presented to us in the guise of four people who are comic exaggerations of ourselves . . . even if we don't want to admit it. Not that there's anything wrong with that.

Notes

1. Gerard Jones alludes to Seinfeld's ironic view of the sitcom form in his book *Honey, I'm Home! Sitcoms: Selling the American Dream.*

2. For a discussion of the narrative forms of sitcoms in the tradition of literature and literary theory, see Kolzloff, "Narrative Theory and Television." In addition, Grote describes the typical sitcom episode in his book *The End of Comedy: The Sit-Com and the Comedic Tradition.*

3. One-hour episodes include "The Boyfriend" (3017), "The Trip" (4001, 4002) "The Pitch"/"The Ticket" (4003), "The Pilot" (4022), "The Raincoats" (5019), "The Bottle Deposit" (7020), "The Cadillac" (7014), "Finale" (9021, 9022).

Many thanks to Bill Hagen, Renee Dechert, and Warren McWilliams for their help on this article.

III

"If I like their race, how can that be racist?" Gender, Generations, and Ethnicity

JOANNA L. DI MATTIA (Monash University)

Male Anxiety and the Buddy System on Seinfeld

An earlier version of this essay appeared in a special issue of *Michigan Feminist Studies* 14 (1999–2000) on "Masculinities" (59–81).

The "Something" That *Seinfeld* Is About?

In the several weeks preceding the very private nuptials of Jerry Seinfeld and Jessica Sklar, there was significant and curious speculation as to whether Jerry would actually say "I do."[1] Jerry on *Seinfeld* is the eternal bachelor, slipping easily in and out of relationships with no emotional attachment. It is not surprising then that many commentators, effortlessly traversing the seemingly thin line between *television Jerry* and *real Jerry*, wondered if life would end up imitating art. Would he break it off with Jessica if she ate her peas one at a time, or did housework naked, or accidentally dropped his toothbrush into the toilet? How had the relationship even reached the point of engagement?

A telling example of the slippage here between life and television comes from Tom Gliatto's *Who Weekly* report "Jerry Engaged? Get Out!"[2] From its opening lines, this article immediately implicates *Seinfeld* in real events.[3] Gliatto employs a number of *Seinfeld*-isms like "yada, yada, yada," interviews cast members to establish whether Jerry Seinfeld is really the marrying type, and suggests that being a fiancée is just another scripted role for Jerry to play. Gliatto compares the courtship of Jerry and Jessica to an episode of the show: "the relationship appears to have proceeded by fits and starts, like one of those *Seinfeld* romantic muddles" (69). It is fortunate, he exclaims, that she loves New York, too! The article is constructed around this self-conscious blurring of life and television, cautioning that Jerry's engagement may follow the fictional road. Because *Seinfeld* bears the name of its cocreator and star, Jerry Seinfeld, it has been difficult for viewers and commentators to separate his actual life from the homosocial environment depicted on television. Further, the other major characters—George Costanza,

Elaine Benes, and (Cosmo) Kramer—are all "versions" of people from Jerry Sein-feld's "real" life, collapsing the borders between diegetic and nondiegetic Seinfeld spaces. If *Seinfeld* is a chronicle of Jerry Seinfeld's everyday escapades, where does the real Jerry begin?

For nine seasons we watched a parade of relationship disasters on *Seinfeld*. In fact, the majority of the scripts of this fast-paced sitcom revolve around the ups and downs, errors and trials of the contemporary dating game for the insular "New York Four." We watched and wondered: what faults would Jerry find with his latest girlfriend? How would George squirm his way out of yet another embarrassing situation? Indeed, much of *Seinfeld* is about the fear and anxiety involved in men's encounters with women. In the shape of Jerry and George, *Seinfeld* presents its audience with two men incapable of committing to a serious, long-term relationship with a woman—men who prove themselves dependably childish and ineffectual as romantic partners, but amazingly loyal and resilient as friends. They work hard throughout the series to strengthen their exclusive bond against feminine invasion.

Despite its fixation with dating, *Seinfeld* never presents coupledom as an ideal state of living, instead preferring to make comedy out of the problems and bur-dens of relationships, the failures and defeats, many often bordering on disaster. The women in Jerry's and George's lives impinge upon their "buddy system" and threaten the insular homosocial order they work so hard to maintain. Theirs is a self-absorbed environment that keeps these men focused on their own problems and needs, hindering them from relating to women as adults. As a result, main-taining a romantic relationship is incompatible with their bond. Even for Elaine—the only regular female cast member—dating is a dilemma. At times she jealously longs for a perfect romance, yet settles for the imperfection of her male friends. The latter is simply presented as a much easier option.

If and when a couple *does* surface on *Seinfeld*, it is usually effortlessly dissolved before the next episode. If it miraculously survives longer than thirty minutes (including commercials), there is always a device in place to reduce that person to total insignificance, evacuating them completely from the narrative. In the case of Elaine's "long-term" boyfriend David Puddy, the perpetual insincerity and sil-liness of their relationship styles it as virtually nonexistent beyond the sexual. George and his long-suffering fiancée, Susan Ross, are stuck together until death, conveniently, parts them. Nothing, it would seem, can compare with the impene-trable cult of friendship these people have created around each other.

Geoffrey O'Brien, in "Sein of the Times," argues that *Seinfeld* breaks new ground in American television by avoiding social commentary (12–14). But his is a strangely decontextualized reading of the show. *Seinfeld* was not created within a vacuum and clearly comments on its social and cultural milieu. Bonnie Dow suggests that television is "simultaneously, a commodity, an art form, and an important ideological forum for public discourse about social issues and social change" (*Prime-Time Feminism* xi). For Lynne Joyrich, television is never a "neutral" instrument, but is "organized in particular ways, with particular intentions, and with particular effects" (30). By organizing its primary space as a homosocial, male-identified one, *Seinfeld,* I would argue, presents a point of view on how these male anxieties arise and how they may be negotiated. A decision regarding gender representation is made for every laugh.

It is my position that the male fear and anxiety central to *Seinfeld* collapses the commonly held idea, promoted by the show itself, that it is about nothing. *Seinfeld* satirically constructs images and narratives about *something*—it is aware of the wider cultural anxiety surrounding images of masculinity in the 1990s and comments on this. Self-consciously located within this discourse and a definable historical moment that it marks out, exposes, and ridicules, *Seinfeld* is a satirical social spectacle about *something more* than the exploits of four single New York friends—it is about the specific social and historical moment they live in and the responses it elicits from them. Behind the innovative humor and the satirical contempt it holds its own characters in, *Seinfeld* is aware that it enacts *something* representative of a very specific moment in American social history.

In "The Pilot" (4022) we can see that *Seinfeld* clearly knows the implications of what it presents under the guise of comedy. This incisive episode parodies *Seinfeld*'s own beginnings. After months of writing the pilot for their "show about nothing," entitled *Jerry,* Jerry and George have arrived at the time to cast and shoot it. This does not go as smoothly as either would hope, and the process of reconstructing their "show about nothing" within *the* "show about nothing" visualizes *Seinfeld*'s awareness of its own position as a contrived spectacle.

In this essay I read *Seinfeld* as a satirical template that comments on the anxiety about "men in crisis" that permeated American cultural discourse throughout the 1990s. I offer a feminist cultural studies perspective sensitive to the complex configurations and negotiations of hegemonic images of masculinity. The concept of homosociality is central to my reading of the organization of male relationships on the show. I argue that Jerry and George display an unwavering anxiety about being seen as "men," and that this is a constant theme throughout the show's nine seasons. I examine the connection here between the homosocial environment and how Jerry and George go about proving their manhood. With George at the helm as its most excessively anxious man, *Seinfeld* shows us the consequences of taking these anxieties to their most illogical conclusions. By presenting extreme scenarios in order to say *something* about them, *Seinfeld* offers a critical position on what is being satirized. Ridiculing male anxiety and fear through the sitcom's available conventions, therefore, functions as a form of social and cultural critique.

The Contemporary Crisis of Masculinity, or How to Be a Man

Seinfeld invites us into the world of the single American at the end of the twentieth century—a world in which friendship, not marriage, is the defining aspect of contemporary relationships. *Seinfeld*'s sitcosmos is peopled by predominantly white, heterosexual, middle-class New Yorkers. Jerry and his friends form among themselves a group of like-minded people whose individual goals reinforce those of the group as a whole. Theirs is an insular world largely intolerant of and indifferent to those whose characteristics fail to conform to their own. A number of recent American television programs testify to the primacy of friendship as a potent form of social organization, including *Friends, Queer as Folk,* and most successfully, *Sex and the City*. In a so-called postfeminist era, where an understanding of marriage as the fulfilling climax of a woman's (or man's) adult life is in steady decline, a strong network of friends has become an alternative and satisfying relationship model.[4] Friendships guard against social isolation. Sociologist Graham Allan points out that friendship can "help to provide us with our sense of identity" and "also confirms our social worth" (1, 48). Jerry and George, for example, have come together as friends through a definable social organization, a comforting sameness that includes the social markers of gender, race, and class.

Jerry and George participate in a mutual "homosocial enactment." This term is used by Michael Kimmel to explain the behavior of men seeking other men's approval (*Manhood in America* 7). It is a process of performative masculinity—visibly exhibiting so-called masculine codes and behavior in order to have manhood validated. Central to my discussion in this essay is the Season Seven episode "The Engagement" (7001), which offers an exemplary model of this homosocial enactment between Jerry and George. In this episode the buddies have a momentary awakening to the immaturity and monotony of their buddy routine and agree that the time has come for them to grow up and become men. The result is George's unexpected engagement to Susan, which he believes will prove to Jerry that he is a grown-up and, therefore, a man. George regrets his decision almost immediately when Jerry does not take action to "grow up" too. George is forever anxious about what is *actually* required of him to prove his manhood, and this dilemma triggers a series of absurd dating and relationship predicaments of which "The Engagement" is the most extreme.

Jerry and George struggle to attain the elusive standards of American manhood because what these standards currently are remains unclear to them. The ideals of white American manhood have historically been problematic to achieve because of their relationship to the promises of the American dream.[5] That dream—the belief that hard work in America can achieve anything—is part of a cultural mythology born in the earliest days of settlement and expansion for the primary benefit of white men. In the modern era it is thought to encompass the aspirations of *all* Americans. When first articulated, however, in the writings of Benjamin Franklin, settler narratives, and early literature, it shaped American culture and character as if absent of women and ethnicity.

The features of the American dream parallel the traditional tenets of white, heterosexual American masculinity, the particular model with which *Seinfeld* and this essay are concerned. Even today the American masculine ideal remains connected to this mythology, but what was once seen as a given for straight white men now seems an elusive mystery. Masculine ideals are incompatible with the conditions of contemporary America or, more importantly, the actual experiences of men's lives.[6] In *The United States of Anger*, Gavin Esler argues that "many of the country's citizens remain anxious or angry that the lives they lead fall short of the America of their dreams" (6). Cultural commentators, radio disc jockeys, and conservative politicians suggested throughout the 1990s that no citizen felt this anxiety and anger more acutely than the white, middle-class, heterosexual male.

In a nation still resonating with the significant social changes effected by second-wave feminism, the Vietnam War, and affirmative action policies, white heterosexual men feel themselves victims of transformations beyond their control, with a need to find scapegoats for their perceived losses. Responding most strongly, however, to the assertions of the women's movement, straight white men have been forced to reexamine the traditional meanings attached to masculinity. As Kimmel argues, crises and reconsiderations of the masculine role are most climactic when women have redefined their own role ("The Contemporary 'Crisis'" 124). The rules of American life and the foundations upon which it is built have profoundly changed, and American men are struggling to adapt. *Seinfeld* provides numerous examples of the ambiguous nature of male-female relationships in the wake of feminism—of men unsure how to behave or just what it is that they are measuring up to.

In the 1990s, these challenges launched a discourse of the white man as victim, or Angry White Male, besieged on all sides by those who want what he has always taken for granted. David Savran presents an interesting explanation of this discourse, arguing that it is a cultural fantasy perpetuated by white men to avoid economic and social responsibility for those they have oppressed.[7] As the traditional foundations for models of masculinity crumble, men no longer have practical, inherited symbols against which to measure their manhood. Feelings of victimization, I would argue, are primarily associated with this loss of power. To reclaim that power, Kimmel contends, men often go to any length to prove that they are indeed men. He likens this to a quest, making it clear that masculinity and manhood are not intrinsic to men but instead must be achieved and continuously tested (*Manhood in America* 4). The ideal American man—the self-made man—is *made*, not born, and therefore must participate in this quest.

Such crisis responses are not necessarily new or unique. At the turn of the twentieth century, amid rapid industrialization and the first wave of feminism, it was believed that American men were losing their manhood—becoming "feminized."[8] After second-wave feminism and the advent of the "new man," a feminization of American culture was believed to have occurred again (Kimmel, *Manhood* 141). And so, the Weekend Warrior was born, together with the New Age Man, whom the media told us was not afraid to cry, while others visited weekend retreats together to evoke the lost core of masculinity.[9] These crisis points force a redefinition of masculinity, often through a troubled and troubling reassertion of traditional "masculine" virtues such as violence, aggression, and separation from women. In 1910 it was the founding of the Boy Scouts of America, and in the mid-1980s, the response was evident in the abundance of macho Vietnam War films, "remasculinizing" feminized America from outside.[10]

Seinfeld exists as part of a social discourse on the changing male role in American society. It can be read as another axis of the contemporary response to pressures on the masculine role. As I have previously suggested, *Seinfeld* is a show about *something*. It is therefore necessary to examine the social structures that underpin the humor. Clearly, the point of view presented is motivated by male concerns. *Seinfeld* self-consciously locates itself within a particular historical discourse and comments upon its own construction. That is, *Seinfeld* is aware of its role in the discourse and *does* say something about it. If Jerry and George perceive themselves as victims struggling to prove they are men, *Seinfeld* suggests that there is something irrational about the manner in which they attempt to do this. We laugh at the plight of the nineties male because it is a recognizable plight—it says *something* to us about the society we live in.

Just Buddies?

The bonds between men are a significant feature of the Hollywood image machine in the postwar era, coming of age, as Cynthia Fuchs points out, in the

1960s in response to the cultural and political rise of sex and race issues. As she explains, these "buddy relationships . . . reconfirmed white male self-identity within radically shifting social and political frames; these men without women defined themselves in opposition to the (absented) other" (196). Buddy films, and the buddy system as a narrative strategy, aims to resurrect the white male hero, as his territory and identity are increasingly threatened, socially, psychically, and symbolically. While male bonding in film and television has been strategically employed as a cultural resource that reinforces traditional notions of the masculine in men, it never does this without first establishing and reinforcing difference. The buddy system is an insular construction. Importantly, women are usually introduced into the buddy system as a source of conflict between buddies, threatening to invade the masculine domain.

The institution of male friendship is central to *Seinfeld*, focusing the progression of the plot and instigating much of the humor. Jerry and George's buddy system is satirized in its insularity—when it comes down to it, they find the most fulfillment with each other. A suppressed homoerotic current, always quickly expelled, characterizes many moments in their relationship, and this, as I argue, is most explicitly suggested in both "The Outing" (4016) and "The Cartoon" (9013). Both their male friendships and random encounters with other male characters feature moments of homoeroticism, where the borders between the homosocial and homosexual temporarily blur. In "The Boyfriend" (3017), for example, Jerry finds himself relating to another man as if he were his boyfriend. In "The Outing" George visits his mother in the hospital to find himself distracted and aroused when he witnesses a male patient receiving a sponge bath in the adjoining bed.

Despite these transgressions, the central tenet of Jerry and George's friendship is a homosocial, not a homosexual, bond. Homosociality functions to reinforce manhood in men through the relationships they form with other men. As Eve Kosofsky Sedgwick defines it, the homosocial bond is distinct from homosexuality, and encompasses the qualities of "male friendship, mentorship, entitlement, rivalry"—qualities that mark male bonds as often insular and competitive (1). The homosocial order is a space defined by its traditional exclusivity to men, such as the workplace, the battlefield, and the sports arena, or any other space where men come together to reinforce their own interests. I would add that homosociality is predicated upon the repetition of "sameness"—the clear delineation and separation of that which is masculine and not masculine—and that it is fundamentally threatened by the presence of women.[11] Significantly, male bonding by its very nature undermines the omnipotence and stability of male identity.

In his analysis of the homosocial order in David Mamet's plays, David Radavich argues that male bonds are primarily about the pursuit of power between men (123). Women, as a sexual conquest, are often at the center of the competition in Mamet's world. Leslie Fiedler offers another view of homosociality, identifying the male bond as an "innocent," nonsexual substitute for marriage. Women, Fiedler argues, have no place in this Edenic mythology, and are "felt to be a feared and forbidden other" (348). The homosocial bond between Jerry and George ultimately informs the way they enter into relationships with women. It is a bond that requires the absence of women and the feminine, and it is this absence that plays a significant role in the articulation of masculine identity throughout the show.

Clearly, the presence of Elaine as a core member of the *Seinfeld* group problematizes our understanding of the insularity and restrictions of the homosocial order. If we acknowledge that the homosocial order requires a framework of sameness, Elaine's presence is not so threatening—the men see something akin to themselves in her character, something more masculine. She is both inside and outside the borders of the "buddy system," primarily welcome because of her past relationship with Jerry. Although George is a little afraid of her, Jerry's acceptance of her removes a certain amount of suspicion of the unknown from her feminine identity. Elaine is, as Sarah E. Worth argues, "one of the boys"—"a good friend whom Jerry can treat like he treats his other male friends" ("Elaine Benes: Feminist Icon" 29).[12] Indeed, in "The Pool Guy" (7008) Elaine engages in the following exchange with the ever-candid Kramer:

> Elaine: You know what—I don't have one female friend left.
> Kramer: Oh, no, of course you don't. You're a man's woman. You hate other
>   women, and they hate you.
> Elaine: Thank you.

Unlike Susan Ross, who ultimately embodies the restrictions of marriage for George and is therefore a real threat to the male friendships on the show, Elaine does not require that structures of homosociality change to accommodate conventional feminine codes. In contrast to Susan, Elaine might be called a "post-feminist" woman, freed from traditional constraints and possessing so-called masculine characteristics. She is just as weak and shallow as the men are and does not seem to care much about anyone. She can be aggressive and confrontational, and often challenges the male characters' sense of power and the stability of their identity. Despite the occasional sexual indiscretion with Jerry to save the friendship, she is mostly a nonsexual entity to the men,[13] acting within the satirical mode as an audience to their fears and anxieties. Within the homosocial order, Elaine functions as a foil to exaggerate the men's foolishness further. She illuminates the crisis of the contemporary man and the divide existing between him and this intimidating "new" woman.

Within the dictates of their homosocial setting, Jerry and George realize that to be a man, one must play at being a man and must be perceived by other men to possess an unquestionable manhood. In this sense, homosociality becomes an unstable dramatization of masculinity, performed over and over again. Women play an ancillary role in this performance. In "The Wink" (7004), Jerry is concerned that Elaine's cousin Holly, whom he is dating, may question his manhood because at lunch he has had a mere salad to her porterhouse steak, something he worries might be perceived "like a quiche thing." To stay in her favor, he fakes a love for mutton.

Jerry exaggerates this anxiety even further when proving his manhood to another man, as occurs in "The Wig Master" (7018). In this episode George discovers that the attendants of a cheap parking lot are using his car as a brothel, and Kramer, decked out resplendently and ridiculously in the title costume from *Joseph and the Amazing Technicolor Dreamcoat,* is arrested for being a pimp. Displays of sexuality and mistaken identity shape this episode. Jerry goes shopping for a crested blazer and, unsure whether to buy it, returns with Elaine, whom the salesman, Craig, asks out on a date. Jerry is distressed because Craig has presumed to know the nature of his relationship with Elaine. How did he know they were not dating? Jerry finds Craig's presumptuous labeling "very emasculating!" Later, this dismissal of Jerry as a "sexual partner" recurs, but with a significant twist: the dismissal occurs in a homosexual, rather than a heterosexual, context. Jerry is drinking champagne coulis with Ethan, the wig master for the Broadway production of *Joseph,* and another man asks Ethan out. Again, Jerry is perturbed: "How do you know he's not with me? . . . *It's very emasculating!*" Jerry is not concerned with being mistaken for a homosexual, but rather that he has not been seen as man enough to fit the role of Ethan's boyfriend. Jerry feels anxious about the perception of his manhood because he is separated from the reassurance of the homosocial order. In these scenarios Jerry's manhood is under scrutiny from other men who have seen him and found him lacking in some essential quality.

But whatever Jerry's concerns, George is the most insecure about his manhood, living in fear of it not being recognized and approved by other men. George's predicament, always extreme, is at the center of *Seinfeld*'s social critique. In "The Jimmy" (6017), a character's confusing references to himself in the third person lead to Elaine dating him without even knowing she is. She believes that when Jimmy refers to "Jimmy" he means another man from the gym, and that it is *this* man who is interested in her: "Jimmy likes Elaine." Typically, George does not assist in clarifying the confusion. Elaine asks him if he is familiar with a particularly good-looking man at their gym, the man she thinks is "Jimmy" but is really called Hank. George squirms under the weight of her question, and she remarks that "just admitting that another man is handsome doesn't necessarily make you a homosexual." George responds that "it doesn't help."

The suspicion that declaring this man is handsome will compromise his manhood is attached to George's fear of expulsion from a homosocial order defined by, and demanding, heterosexuality. Evaluating each other's attractiveness is not something George and Jerry do. This inclination toward the homoerotic and homosexual would weaken their buddy system, based on clearly delineated rules and behavior. These are best explained as those reinforcing and approving heterosexuality as the dominant and accepted model of masculinity in their world. If George were to admit, for example, that Jerry or Kramer was an attractive man (not necessarily that *he* is attracted to them), the world would collapse and need substantial rebuilding. He requires a world that reminds him, and anyone watching, that they are just good friends.

"The Free-Love Buffet": Love and Marriage, *Seinfeld*-Style

The seventh season episode "The Engagement" (7001) illustrates how to approach marriage with the most inappropriate partner, solely for the purpose of personal reinforcement. It takes a simple premise—an engagement—to a level that reveals it as a ludicrous expression of manhood. When George proposes marriage to Susan to prove to Jerry that he is a man, he does so to uphold his part in an informal "pact" with Jerry. But George ultimately finds himself stuck and feeling betrayed when Jerry refuses to uphold his end of the bargain. The episode's opening scene sets the tone for George's feelings of powerlessness and anxiety about his manhood. The scene also makes clear the extent to which the very idea of manhood is not intrinsic to men but rather something to be sought, *won* and preserved.

In "The Engagement" George is playing chess with a woman named Liz who defeats him after he criticizes her handling of her queen: "What do you think? She's one of these feminists looking to get out of the house? No, the queen is old-fashioned. . . . Likes to stay home. Cook. Take care of her man. Make sure he feels good." Significantly, the queen is the piece that defeats him, and George tells the woman that he cannot see her anymore. He later explains to Jerry that he has a problem sleeping with a woman who beats him at chess. With one word—*checkmate*—she has emasculated George, and the only way to immediately reassert his manhood is to remove this assertive and superior woman from his life. His manhood requires the absence of this model of femininity.

"The Engagement" suggests for the first time that the buddy routine Jerry and George repeatedly enact—hanging around the male space of Jerry's apartment, lunching at the coffee shop—might be losing its appeal. The next scene sees Jerry exhibiting his frustration at these rituals, wondering if there is anything better out there. He wonders just what they are doing with their lives. Jerry unknowingly critiques their homosocial union when he berates George for always seeking his approval. They agree that they are not men but immature children incapable of committing to adult relationships. George's speech about the queen is indicative of his own 1950s idealization of exaggerated femininity. These are the qualities he seeks, and neither he nor Jerry is willing to compromise this fantasy for the reality of the 1990s woman. Momentarily recognizing their ineptitude in contemporary relationships, they enter into a pact to become "new" men. This coffee-shop pact sees the buddies shake hands and vow to make some changes in their lives—to do what they believe will prove they are men, not boys, although neither of them can define what that is to the other. George, however, is the only one who takes the pact seriously.

A homosocial system of rejection and approval is being enacted here between Jerry and George. George wants Jerry to think he is a man, to see that, if *he* asks him to, he will change. Kramer, on the other hand, is outside the immediate affirmation of masculine values. His character challenges what is presented as the right thing to do. When Jerry tells him about his talk with George, Kramer informs him that change is useless, and that there is nothing more to life. His philosophy argues that the institutions of marriage and family are restrictive and deathly to the American man's freedom. They are, in effect, prisons in which *a man does time*. Kramer fears the disruption a wife would cause to his established routine and to his buddy system. She will want to talk to him and therefore end his fantasy life of eternal dinners in front of the television. In a typical satirical mode we are presented with another extreme position in Kramer's view. It is the threat of change presented by the feminine in his homosocial domain that convinces Jerry the coffee-shop pact is not for him.

George, on the other hand, takes it seriously and wants to take a blind leap into manhood and away from his life as Jerry's shadow. Equating manhood and adulthood with marriage, he runs off through a flock of seagulls—a motif of change recurring throughout the series—to ask former girlfriend (and former lesbian) Susan Ross to marry him. George eagerly wants to share with Jerry the news of his engagement. After all, he has only done this to prove to Jerry that he is *man enough,* believing that Jerry was doing the same. When he enters the homosocial space of Jerry's apartment and announces his distorted view of masculinity, the equation is clear: "I'm a man, Jerry. I'm a man!" The cycle of rejection and approval is in motion: George is reproached by Jerry for not being a man and doing his own thing and subsequently seeks affirmation by performing a manly act. George spends two hours convincing Susan to marry him, though he does not love her or want to spend the rest of his life, let alone the next episode, with her. Susan is an object in the competition between men to prove their manhood to each other. Susan is not George's prize; what he believes he has won is his manhood in the eyes of Jerry. George has seized the most extreme dramatization of masculinity for the benefit of other men, and Susan's eventual death in a later episode shows us the dangerous nature of his foolish behavior.

Immediately, George's world begins to collapse around him. Susan's presence disrupts the comfort and predictability of the homosocial order. The bond between Jerry and George can sustain girlfriends, but not future wives. By entering his life in the latter, incompatible role, Susan is asking George to remodel the homosocial order to encompass her, and what are presented as her very "female" needs. Susan believes in communicating with her fiancé, but George believes that some things are better not shared. This is evident in "The Secret Code" (7007), when he refuses to disclose his ATM number (it's "BOSCO") to his future wife because he fears he will lose his individuality.

A further example in "The Engagement" illustrates the extent to which the feminine threatens the familiar stability of the masculine world. Jerry asks George to see the latest blockbuster film, *Firestorm,* the kind of film all men are supposed to love. Susan, however, wants to see the latest Meryl Streep tearjerker, *The Muted Heart,* the kind of film, a "chick flick," all women are supposed to love. George goes to the movies with Susan and sees Jerry having a great time with someone else: his buddy has replaced him; he has been expelled from the buddy system. At home that night, George wants to watch the Yankees; Susan, an episode of *Mad About You.* As "The Engagement" closes with strains of the *Mad About You* theme song, Susan is content, blissful; George looks as if he has made the biggest mistake of his life. The irony, of course, is that George has invited her to do this through his own mistake. He does not see Susan as a real person, but simply as a vehicle through which he can achieve manhood.

Worlds collide, and Susan's presence throughout the duration of their engagement calls into question both George's idea of independent manhood and the sanctity of the homosocial environment at Jerry's. George feels the freedom of single life slipping away from him, fast. The homosocial order has been established so that the opposing worlds of friendship and love cannot coexist—worlds presented as masculine and feminine respectively, and requiring separation from one another in order to survive. In "The Pool Guy" (7008), George becomes concerned with the blossoming friendship between Susan and Elaine. In this episode Elaine feels momentarily restricted by her male friends and worries that she has no female friends left. When she invites Susan out and they begin spending time together, Kramer foresees that this will lead to the demise of George's sanctuary at Jerry's. George is divided in two between the worlds of homosocial friendship and imminent marriage, and he will do anything humanly possible to keep them separate. Maintaining the sanctity of the buddy system is the only way he knows how to be a man.

In a telling line to the pool guy, Jerry tells Ramone, who is attempting to insinuate himself into his world, "I actually only have three friends. I can't handle any more." Like George, Jerry's idea of himself cannot handle the changes required in adjusting the homosocial order. Both he and George have established a routine with which they are quite happy to continue. Later in the episode, George witnesses Susan sitting at *his* coffee shop, with *his* friends, and realizes just what he has lost by getting engaged. Symbolically, there is no space for him in the booth, and he goes across the street to sit alone at an alternate restaurant, Reggie's. His world is now unknown to him, and because he cannot face the changes around him, he removes himself from the scene. There are two Georges, Relationship George and Independent George, and the former is killing the latter. As he most dramatically exclaims: *"A George divided against itself cannot stand!"* Once the boundaries blur and the two worlds become one indefinable world, George's understanding of himself—and ultimately his manhood, no longer exclusively tied to the homosociality of his buddy relationship with Jerry—ceases to make sense. Susan has trespassed into a space never designed to sustain her presence, revealing it to be an inflexible entity. She has called the primacy of the homosocial order into question and with it the very foundation upon which George calls himself a man.

"Not that there's anything wrong with that!"

Seinfeld presents the perfect married couple—Jerry and George. Relationships do work on this show if they are between men. While the show appears to be, as Katherine Gantz explains, "a testament to heterosexuality," heterosexual unions are repeatedly frustrated by the primacy of the male bond (167). George discovers that he can never have with Susan what he has with Jerry. She only serves to heighten his masculine anxiety because she requires things to change. With Jerry, everything is already in place. To serve their own needs they have established the rules and borders of their buddy system and in doing so have created a homosocial order that ultimately prevents them from committing to, and maintaining, relationships with women. Most interesting is how *Seinfeld* exposes this bond as supporting adolescent and narrow ideas about contemporary women. That Jerry and George see women as disposable and are ultimately distressed by assertions of female sexuality is made evident by the presence of a new woman in nearly every episode. It is easier to find petty faults with these women and then break up than it is to reflect upon their own shortcomings, and as Gantz explains, "the feminine presence is often simply deleted for the sake of maintaining a stronger, more coherent male narrative" (171). Significantly, women are also presented as a means for personal gain—an object through which the men may better their own situation. In "The Boyfriend" (3017), for example, George dates his unemployment benefits officer's daughter to ensure that the benefits keep coming.

The very structure of the homosocial bond requires Jerry and George to view women as a disruptive force in their lives. "The Outing" (4016) is the episode that most explicitly suggests the ideal nature of Jerry and George's relationship and how it also appears as such to outsiders. Jerry, George, and Elaine are at the coffee shop. Jerry gets up to make a phone call to Sharon Leonard, a student reporter from NYU who is late for a scheduled interview with him. He returns to the booth, and Elaine points out to both he and George that the woman sitting behind them is listening to their conversation about who the ugliest world leader is. So Elaine decides to really give the woman something to listen to: "You know, just because you two are homosexuals, so what? I mean you should just come out of the closet and be openly gay already." George, curiously, is happy to play along: "You know you'll always be the only man I'll ever love." Jerry is a little less comfortable. This is too close to home for him. People often think he is gay, because he has three of the allegedly obvious signs: he is single, thin, and neat. Unknown to Jerry, the eavesdropper is Sharon; unknown to Sharon, one of these newly "outed" men is Jerry Seinfeld. She gets up and leaves Jerry a message, saying she got to the diner late and believes that she missed him and maybe they could catch up later.

Jerry and Sharon arrange another interview in the afternoon at his apartment. It is here that she realizes Jerry is the man whose conversation she overheard earlier and that he and George, who is staying for the interview, are a couple. In addition, and more significantly, her beliefs about Jerry's homosexuality are confirmed by the manner in which he and George interact. George becomes sensitive over Jerry's dislike of his new shirt. They argue over fruit. The connotations of this familiarity are magnified by a series of misunderstandings occurring while

Sharon is present. George tells Sharon, for example, that he and Jerry met in a gym locker room but fails to tell her that it was actually in high school. After Jerry and George realize that Sharon was the woman from the coffee shop and that she thinks they are gay—"not that there's anything wrong with that!"— Kramer makes it impossible for them to convince her otherwise, amplifying the likelihood of Sharon's misreading by announcing: "Let's go! I thought we were going to take a steam!"

The joke continues when Jerry receives two birthday presents that popularly signify gay culture—a ticket to see *Guys and Dolls,* "a lavish Broadway musical," and *The Collected Works of Bette Midler.* Meanwhile, Sharon is unconvinced of Jerry's heterosexuality and has played up that angle in her article. Worse still, her article is picked up by *The New York Post,* announcing to the world that "within the confines of his fastidious bachelor pad, Seinfeld and Costanza bicker over the cleanliness of a piece of fruit like an old married couple." George is referred to as Jerry's "longtime companion," and for all intents and purposes, Sharon could not be more correct. In all the episodes of *Seinfeld* we never see Jerry and George behaving as intimately and unself-consciously with a woman as they do when together. For them, this provocative interaction seems normal because it is the behavior they have approved for each other within their buddy system. When an outsider enters and witnesses it, as Sharon does here, it becomes something else—measured outside the rules of homosociality and heterosexuality, indicating how easily these borders can be transgressed when not rigorously policed. Richard Dyer explains that heterosexuality, "in its need to proclaim its own naturalness and normality, can only produce an anxiety at never actually being natural or normal" (271). The insularity of the codes of Jerry and George's bond are derided here to show the extent to which they have forgotten the signification of such behavior in the real world and the unstable and insecure nature of both gender and sexual borders and identities.

Jerry and George's inseparability is a manifestation of the comfort zone surrounding them in the absence of more complicated entanglements with women. It also illustrates their unwillingness to adapt to anything unknown. The narcissistic love promoted by the homosocial order frees them from the needs of the "new" woman and from ever having to relate to anyone not like them. This is further evident in "The Boyfriend" (3017), when Jerry becomes involved in an ambiguous attachment with real-life baseball legend Keith Hernandez. There is a homoerotic tone to this friendship—a friendship that begins in the homosocial space of the men's locker room—apparent when Jerry starts to think possessively of Keith as his "boyfriend." Jerry feels the same disappointment and confusion he would if Keith were a woman, declaring that he finds it "all very confusing." Jerry wonders if he is obliged to help Keith move house after only one "date" because this is the buddy equivalent of "going all the way." The episode is structured around the trials of heterosexual dating rituals and a love triangle (that keeps George out), with Jerry losing Keith to Elaine after the ballplayer breaks a date with Jerry to see her. "The Boyfriend" enacts some of the dilemmas men face in their relationships with women but does not have to offer solutions because Keith is a man. Perhaps Jerry assigns the role of boyfriend to Keith in the hope that it will be less complicated. It is a friendship that also indicates these men are finding something together, in the sameness of other men, that women cannot provide. These relationships, often based on sports or other manly events, affirm their manhood without compromising or reorganizing the homosocial order.[14]

These male substitutes for women reappear in later episodes such as "The Invitations" (7022) and "The Cartoon" (9013). "The Invitations" closes Season Seven with George's compulsion for cheapness killing his fiancée: he insists on the most frugal option for their wedding invitations, and the glue on the envelopes turns out to be toxic. This is the freedom George had been hoping for, and he is callously relieved. Jerry, however, by the end of this episode has fulfilled his part of the pact from the season opener, "The Engagement," and is engaged to Jeannie. Jeannie (played by comedienne Janeane Garafolo) is a female version of Jerry. They both love cereal; he reads *Superman*, she reads *Supergirl*. Jerry's attraction to Jeannie is based on sameness. He does not see her as a woman but as an unchallenging female version of everything he already knows. As he explains to Kramer: "I've been waiting for me to come along. And now I've swept myself off my feet!"

As he does with all women, however, Jerry begins to find faults with Jeannie and is in turn repulsed by how alike they really are. Caught within the conventions of male bonding, Jerry's "love" for Jeannie is satirized as a ridiculous fantasy, because he has fallen in love with himself. The sameness promised by this self-love is an effect of the fear and anxiety that compels most of Jerry's actions. On this occasion, however, his rejection of a woman is also a repudiation of what he finds lacking in himself, qualities appearing more unpleasant because they are removed from the homosocial sphere.

In "The Cartoon" George dates Janet, a woman with an uncanny resemblance to Jerry. At first George is not conscious of the likeness but is quickly troubled by the homoerotic implications of the relationship. Both he and Jerry are disturbed by Kramer's and Elaine's remarks, and they remind themselves that they are not gay. The anxiety initiated by "The Outing" returns, and this time George must attack the problem directly. What perturbs him most is that his relationship with Janet is not about anything except her "nice face," a face that everyone thinks looks like Jerry's. George recognizes Jerry in Janet and has assumed that this sameness will carry through to their relationship—he wonders to himself, can he have all he has with Jerry and sex too?

Similar to Jerry's attraction to Jeannie in "The Invitations," George has identified too closely with an image sustainable only within the bounds of homosociality. Janet is like Jerry, but in a form that George has never before encountered. Here, George has no established codes with which to relate to Janet, and she therefore becomes a problematic embodiment of his largely unacknowledged male fears and desires. As Kramer explains, George is "all mixed up in a perverse sexual amalgam of his best friend and girlfriend." Unknown to her, she has called his masculinity and heterosexuality into question. George needs a companion who affirms his masculinity and makes no demands on him to change. If only Janet could be more like Tony from "The Stall" (5012), an episode in which Jerry labels Elaine's boyfriend a "mimbo," the male equivalent of a bimbo, because of his classic good looks and insubstantial intellect. Tony excels at sports and outdoor activities, providing George, who finds he is drawn to Tony, with the ideal opportunity for masculine approval through sporting feats.

Seinfeld is not the kind of show to advocate character development or growth. Jerry and George do not move beyond their selfish and childish preoccupations. The show satirizes their peculiarities and succeeds in suggesting that as long as they continue returning to the homosocial bond the same inane behavior will continue.[15] *Seinfeld* does not promote homosociality as a solution to the masculinity crisis, nor does it advocate marriage as a solution to their form of adolescent manhood. Rather, it ultimately presents Jerry and George's buddy system as retarding their development as adults. They look to each other and seek a manhood based on isolating themselves from women. They are reluctant to adapt to whatever challenges women offer them, preferring insulation in the sameness of this routine. In satirizing this, *Seinfeld* suggests the folly in such an existence.

Conclusion: Jerry Seinfeld Becomes a Man

Wedding bells rang for Jerry and Jessica on December 25, 1999. Television Jerry never made a similar commitment. Again, reports brought life and television together, one headline exclaiming: "Thin, Neat—and Married" (*Who Weekly* 13). Is this reminder of "The Outing" suggesting that Jerry cannot find lasting happiness with a woman? Jerry took on the additional responsibilities of fatherhood with the birth of his first child in November 2000. A Jerry separated from his friends is hard to fathom. The blurring of the lines between life and television acknowledges the persistent primacy of the homosocial bond between Jerry and George. Its centrality to the show's satirical premise causes the fusion of *television* and *real* Jerry so that we come to understand the *Seinfeld* world as Jerry Seinfeld's reality, believing that he also lives within the homosocial order.

Seinfeld presents a "real" world—a reality exaggerated, yet recognizable as a vehicle for exploring the so-called crisis in American manhood. If we accept that *Seinfeld* satirizes a world in fact existing, it is also the world in which *the* Jerry Seinfeld, as an American man, lives. We have seen the anxieties bringing Jerry and George together, and perhaps cannot imagine the absence of these fears in Jerry's relationship with Jessica. But *Seinfeld* clearly does not advocate the restrictive codes of homosociality as an ideal solution to the crisis of masculinity. The course of a successful relationship is the script *Seinfeld* never had the chance to write. From somewhere in the middle, as Jerry and George negotiate their way through contemporary relationships, we see that they *cannot* be men or adults as long as they continue to insulate themselves from realistic interactions with women. *Seinfeld* makes explicit that an alternative to this bond is required—a manhood and masculine identity shaped, and capable of functioning, in a world where women inspire more than fear and anxiety.

Notes

1. Jerry and Jessica married on Christmas night, 1999.

2. *Who Weekly* is the Australian equivalent of North America's *People Weekly* magazine.

3. For a similar approach, see Michael Cameron (30).

4. For an early analysis of the "singles" phenomenon, see Simeauer and Carroll.

5. For early sociological analyses of the demands of American manhood, see Dubbert, Filene, and Pleck.

6. For an account of how the American dream has failed Americans in the 1990s see Esler and Samuelson.

7. See also Esler, who notes the irony of this discourse of white male victimization: "The idea is that black people, the real victims of generations of racial injustice, are now victimizing white folks" (82).

8. See Ann Douglas.

9. See Robert Bly as an example of the tone of this New Man. Much of the writing on the men's movement has been dismissed for being antiwoman, heterocentric, and predominantly white. It is also perceived to promote divisive gender relations.

10. See especially the writing of Susan Jeffords in this area.

11. Sedgwick notes that "no element of the pattern can be understood outside of its relations to women and the gender system as a whole" (1).

12. See Irwin, ed., *Seinfeld and Philosophy*, 27–37.

13. Exceptions exist, of course. After she leaves a steamy message on Jerry's tape recorder ("The Tape," 3008) or exposes a nipple ("The Pick," 4012) or cleavage ("The Shoes," 4015; "The Gum," 7010), Elaine does become momentarily sexualized.

14. As Gantz argues with reference to "The Pilot" (4022), the bond between men is so privileged on this show that "the feminine presence is often simply deleted for the sake of maintaining a stronger, more coherent male narrative" (171).

15. Gantz's queer reading of "The Contest" (4010) explores the eternal return to a union between Jerry and George when "the viewer is left with the suggestion that they have satisfied their sexual frustrations together" and "the duo's inability to sustain a romantic relationship with a woman leaves them again alone with each other" (186).

MATTHEW BOND

"Do you think they're having babies just so people will visit them?"

Parents and Children on *Seinfeld*

Unlike most Americans in their mid-to-late 30s, the characters of *Seinfeld*—Elaine Benes, George Costanza, Cosmo Kramer, and Jerry Seinfeld—are single and childless, reflecting the real Seinfeld and his creative partner, Larry David, who were single, childless, and approaching or passing the age of 40 during the years of *Seinfeld*.[1]

These characteristics, singleness and childlessness, are unusual for a situation comedy. Sitcoms have traditionally been about families, with settings of either homeplace or workplace. Sitcoms began in the homeplace: *I Love Lucy* (1951–57), *The Adventures of Ozzie and Harriet* (1952–66), *Leave It to Beaver* (1957–63). In the 1960s, they ventured out. *The Dick Van Dyke Show* (1961–66) revolutionized the sitcom by showing work as equal to home, creating an extended family of coworkers, wife, son, and neighbors. The occasional sitcom chose an outlandish site: *Gilligan's Island* (1964–67), but it was simply a re-creation of home and family (a slightly perverse and incestuous family, granted, but TV is nothing if not titillation). Choosing homeplace or workplace or fusing the two, à la *The Andy Griffith Show* (1960–68) or *M*A*S*H* (1972–83), and providing the hero with an actual family or a proxy family of coworkers have remained the sitcom's models and methods.

Seinfeld revamped that model. The homeplace dwindled to Jerry's one-bedroom Manhattan apartment and Monk's diner. We saw Jerry cook and serve food at his apartment only once. (Significantly, when Kramer accidentally gets a traditional job, and Jerry becomes his sulking, neglected "wife.") Otherwise, at home he eats cereal. As for workplace, Jerry is Seinfeld the comic, and though we see him at work, he is still just performing, doing Seinfeld's act for us and the audience in the club. We do see George and Elaine at their workplaces (at Yankee Stadium or Kruger Industrial Smoothing; at Pendant Publishing, with Mr. Pitt, or at J. Peterman's), but *Seinfeld* breaks another sitcom custom by having characters change jobs often over the course of the show's 180 episodes, as if these jobs were extraneous to our heroes' "real" lives.

No family, no homeplace to speak of, no workplace: *Seinfeld* has dispensed with the sitcom's paradigmatic setting and social dynamic, replacing them with a sitcom about grown-up children. It is *Big* (the 1988 movie starring Tom Hanks) writ large, but without the winsomeness and sentimentality. Jerry Seinfeld is Peter Pan. His apartment: Never-Never Land, the Island of Lost Boys (and one girl), the clubhouse, the tree house. These characters are adolescents: Their only familial relationship is with their parents: George's and Jerry's parents appear frequently, but even Kramer's mother makes an appearance and Elaine's father likewise.

Jerry makes this point himself in the opening monologue to "The Heart Attack" (2008):

> I gotta say that I'm enjoying adulthood. And I'll tell you reason number one: as an adult, if I want a cookie, I have a cookie, okay? I have three cookies or four cookies or eleven cookies if I want. Many times I will intentionally ruin my entire appetite. Just ruin it. And then I call my mother up right after to tell her that I did it. "Hello, Mom. Yeah, I just ruined my entire appetite . . . Cookies."

Seinfeld and Larry David, his *Seinfeld* cocreator, developed a fantasy land for their hero: a new beautiful woman each episode, plenty of money without any visible means of support, and never having to cook or clean. This is not an adult's fantasy but an adolescent's. It is a fantasy if you think that not growing up is the ideal way to live, and spoiling your appetite with cookies and then calling your mother to tell her what you've done is a blatant admission that you have not grown up.

Tempering this male adolescent fantasy world is Elaine, who was created by fiat of NBC. After the tepid response to *Seinfeld*'s first episode, the network committed itself to four more as long as a woman was brought in. Seinfeld and David, true to their Peter Pan (or Tubby's Playhouse) "No girls allowed" foundation, resisted, but the network was adamant (Tracy 90). Elaine is loosely modeled on Carol Leifer, a comic, former girlfriend, and friend of Seinfeld's, who was also one of the show's writers and occasional performers ("The Kiss Hello," 6015) (Tracy 103).

The introduction of Elaine in "The Stakeout" (1002), provides more evidence of the *Seinfeld*ian permanent adolescence and how the characters still feel oppressed by their parents. "The Stakeout" opens with Jerry and Elaine browsing in a video store. They pick up two videos. First, *Cocoon II: The Return* (1988), the sequel to a baby boomer fantasy of sending one's parents to another planet where they will "live useful lives" and live forever but far away. Second, a pornographic video. Their first thought?

> Elaine: What do you think their parents think?
> Jerry: "So, what's your son doing now, Dr. Stevens?" "Oh, he's a public fornicator. Yes, he's a fine boy."

Although Jerry and Elaine are supposed adults, their first thoughts are of parents. First, speculating why the old folks of *Cocoon* return, they conclude it must be how annoying and demanding parents are ("Maureen Stapleton [is] . . . probably screaming at those aliens, 'I've gotta have a lo mein.'"). Second, their own actions are still circumscribed by "What will our parents think?" They still seek parental approval. They haven't grown up yet.

George, who fantasizes about being a porn actor ("The Outing," 4016), is, naturally, the most dominated by parents. His are the only parents who live in New York. After losing his job, he must move back in with them for almost all of the fifth season. This emphasizes his place in the group as the loser and reinforces his inherent immaturity. Significantly, to the adolescent Oedipal nature of the series, George's first job interview after moving back home is to be a bra salesman ("The Sniffing Accountant," 5004): his father arranges it for him, and as he and his parents discuss it over supper, his father insists that his mother bring down a bra so that they can prepare George for the interview. The bra is tossed over the food as cup sizes are discussed.

Indeed, it is in the famous "Contest" episode (4010) that George's mother is introduced. Here we see George's character in essence and in relation to the others. George tells the others how his mother caught him masturbating, in his parents' house, with her copy of *Glamour*. Then George must sit with her by her hospital bed, where he has sexual fantasies about the woman getting a sponge bath in the next bed. Moreover, it was George who lost a job because he had sex atop his desk with the cleaning woman. The cleaning woman, needless to say, reminded him of his mother, the only woman "worse looking than Hazel" ("The Subway," 3013), the famous television maid (*Hazel* [1961–66]).

George's unrestrained Oedipus complex is obvious here. Oedipus runs rampant, though not blindly, throughout the series. As noted above: Jerry first mentions parents in relation to sex, the pornographic video, and this sexual aspect is compounded by the introduction of Elaine, a previous lover, and her immediate invitation to Jerry to join her at the birthday party of a friend, where Jerry will meet another woman to whom he is attracted ("The Stakeout," 1002). In the middle of this episode, he walks in on his parents in bed, his sofa bed, in the living room, and proceeds to discuss his love life. Later in the episode, Jerry and his mother play Scrabble, and his mother, at Kramer's instigation, lays down the supposed word "quone." This echoes, again, the Oedipal Peter Pan aspects of the series: "Quone" can equal "queer" plus "clone." As Kramer uses it, "To quone something," i.e., a perverse cloning, which is what incest would be: the taboo attempt to redo oneself, to replicate as closely as possible one's genetic arrangement.

Finally, when *Seinfeld* introduces Kramer's mother, Babs, in "The Switch" (6011), the episode ends with Kramer and Jerry finding her in a carnal embrace with Newman, the show's most repugnant recurring character. In horror, she calls out Kramer's first name, "Cosmo!," which becomes the actual punch line, rather than the sex. The series names Kramer via the comic horror of the Oedipal crisis.

Elaine, being female, is given no mother, but a father, the hard-boiled writer Alton Benes (Lawrence Tierney), who dominates an early episode ("The Jacket," 2003). Paralleling the sexual introductions of the men's mothers, Elaine's father shows not only how immature George and Jerry are, but also how easily a man can emasculate them. They are completely intimidated by this man who drinks Scotch and looks scornful when Jerry and George order cranberry juice and club soda respectively. At the episode's opening, Jerry buys the titular jacket: a beautiful, very expensive, very soft suede one, with a lining, however, of a loud candy stripe. When Alton Benes insists that Jerry not wear candy stripes out when they must walk through the falling snow. It is thus ruined by the "real man's" prohibition. (A delightful pun in the title: Jerry is straitjacketed by this interaction with a "man's man.") In the same episode, George has a song from *Les Miserables* stuck in his head.[2] Benes eventually says, "Pipe down, chorus boy," a remark that is driven home in the next scene, after the dinner, when Elaine announces, "Dad thinks George is gay." When Jerry surmises, "Because of all that singing," Elaine replies, "No, he pretty much thinks everyone is gay." (Thus, Benes's forbidding the candy stripe.) Oedipal (Electra) sexuality does rear its head just a bit: Benes greets his daughter with "Hello, dear. Who's the lipstick for?"—implying that he wants the lipstick to be for him, the guardian, the last bastion of straight male sexuality.

At the end of the fifth season, George escapes his parents by behaving contrary to his inclinations and instincts ("The Opposite," 5022). He tells George Steinbrenner what an awful job he's done with the Yankees, and so Steinbrenner hires him: approval from the father by standing up to the father, which, of course, George cannot do with his real father.

George and his parents go through many trials through the rest of the series. His parents separate, and his father moves in with George, which is, of course, torture. George must spend time with each of them separately, which doubles the torture. Lunching with George, his mother, Estelle, announces that she's "out there" now that she's separated ("The Fusilli Jerry," 6019). George insists that that cannot happen; there is no room for mother and son in the same world, unless permitted by the son.

> Estelle: Well, I'm out there, George.
> George: No, you're not out there.
> Estelle: I am, too!
> George: You're not out there! You can't be, because I am out there. And if I see you out there, there's not enough voltage in this world to electroshock me back into coherence!

His parents do reunite, and George has some moments of relief. They move temporarily to Florida, where Jerry's parents live and from where Jerry finds them oppressive, but to George, his parents' move is wonderful; he is "basking in the buffer zone" ("The Money," 8012).

Seinfeld's characters' relations to parents and (as we shall see) to children also speak to their roles within the group. That George and Jerry have the parents we frequently see signals their core position. Seinfeld described it:

> If we had been a troupe of acrobats, Jason [Alexander, playing George] and I would have been the two guys at the bottom of the pyramid who hold everybody else up. Nine years after the pilot, we were still setting the whole thing in motion. (Seinfeld 63)

A center is essential to the sitcom group dynamic. This does not mean that there must be one dull or flat or reliably sensible character in the show, just that someone must appear less eccentric than the others. On *The Dick Van Dyke Show*, it was, often alternately, Rob and Laura Petrie (Dick Van Dyke and Mary Tyler Moore). On *I Love Lucy*, it was Ricky (Desi Arnaz). On *Everybody Loves Raymond* (1996–2005), it is Raymond's wife, Deborah (Patricia Heaton). On *Barney Miller* (1975–82), it was Barney Miller (Hal Linden). *The Cosby Show* (1984–92) resembled *The Dick Van Dyke Show*, again sharing the center between husband and wife, although *The Cosby Show* really looked more like *The Honeymooners* (1952–57, 1966–70), where the wife, Claire (Phylicia Rashad), is truly the sensible center. In *Seinfeld*, it is Jerry. In the case of *Seinfeld*, however, this is done by making the other characters more strange—more estranged from the center.

Kramer lives a fantasy life that makes Jerry's look normal by contrast: the hot tub, the replacing all furniture with levels, the having no job. George, on the other hand, begins the series actually smarter and more sensible than Jerry. He advises Jerry, fairly competently, throughout the pilot episode, and in the show's first dialogue, when Jerry remarks that the second button on George's shirt is too high and that "the second button literally makes or breaks the shirt," George doesn't consider it an important topic: "Are you through? . . . [The shirt] was purple, I liked it. I don't recall considering the button."

Throughout the show's first years, George becomes progressively less competent and less stable, more intense, more neurotic, more paranoid. He rashly quits his job in Season Two ("The Revenge," 2007) and shows that he has no grasp of what getting another job entails. Immediately following his sudden unemployment, the show reinforces his decline and his permanent adolescence. George thinks he's having a heart attack, which would be a true sign of adulthood, but instead his tonsils have regrown (he's still a boy) and he must, again, have them removed ("The Heart Attack," 2008). What does everyone say to this grown man to console him? "Well, at least you'll get ice cream." What makes George bitter? That he didn't get ice cream when he first had his tonsils out, twenty years earlier.

Elaine is not as estranged from the center. She and Jerry do reflect each other, but her position as the only female—but not "the wife"—prevents her from possibly being the center. Also, like George, she goes through something of a decline during the series. Like George with Susan Ross (his fiancée in Season Seven), Elaine maintains a continuing relationship over several seasons with David Puddy, but again, like George, it exhibits more torment than love. Each of them repeatedly dumps the other. So, although Elaine seems to be the female Jerry, it becomes apparent as the series continues that she is the female George, which explains how Jerry and Elaine could hardly stay lovers but could become friends. By the time of "The Opposite" (5022), this equation is crystallized: As George's fortunes improve, hers decline, until she screams in horror, "I'm George! I've become George!"

Of all the characters in the show, George and Elaine go through the most changes.[3] Elaine and George have multiple jobs and different places to live, two violations of the sitcom paradigm, which usually considers the movement of any character to be quite a wrench. For a permanent adolescent, Elaine, however, is blessedly free from parental control (though, being female, she is the only member of the quartet badgered by friends who want her to become a parent herself). In the episode with her father, described above, Elaine is the last to arrive and is the least dominated by dear old dad.

Although *Seinfeld* pretends to be something new in sitcoms (Seinfeld and David's motto was "no hugging, no learning," i.e., none of the sentimentality and the "learning of lessons" that ends so many TV shows), it subscribed to the same old sitcom values: only marriage and family evince maturity—though all their contemporaries who have married or procreated are losers, creators of monsters ("Some ugly baby, huh?" Elaine murmurs to the obstetrician in "The Hamptons" [5021]). The show announces that these four have not grown up, yet it shows no "grown-ups" positively. The four *Seinfeld* characters are immature and selfish: Elaine dumps a "perfect" man because they differ on the use of exclamation points ("The Sniffing Accountant," 5004). This constant dumping of boyfriends and girlfriends, particularly by Jerry and Elaine, shows the naiveté of youth: presuming an infinite supply of mates and expecting perfection, any disagreement means doom to the relationship; they feel no need to grow old with someone, because growing old is for others. Peter Pan, meet Dorian Gray.

Unlike Jerry and Elaine, George rarely breaks up with his girlfriends; they usually break up with him. As in his oppressive relationship with his in-town parents, we see his impotent status in the group. To prevent his girlfriends from leaving him, he tries all kind of futile, immature tricks. In "The Susie" (8015), for example, he avoids answering the telephone so that his girlfriend cannot leave him before they go to a formal ball. Since she is "the kind of woman who makes a great entrance," he values her for a superficial, dandyish reason.

Fittingly, the Peter Pans of this series view all other children as competition and those who have children—i.e., their peers who are parents—as fools. In "The Parking Garage" (3006), George intervenes when a mother hits her son; the mother tells him to mind his own business. When George asserts that it is his business, the son tells George that he's ugly. In "The Bris" (5005), Jerry and Elaine are very reluctant godparents, and the high-strung *mohel* slices Jerry's finger when he flinches while holding the baby: Our heroes are not old enough for any responsibility. In "The Non-Fat Yogurt" (5007), Jerry swears in front of a mother and son, who then begins swearing. Jerry is powerless to correct him, and the mother blames Jerry vociferously. In "The Van Buren Boys" (8014), George is menaced by a gang of teenagers. In "The Blood" (9004), Elaine and, later, George babysit a boy who pours juice in her purse and kicks him in the shin.

Children, normally portrayed on television as either adorable, preternaturally smart (and smart-alecky), or purely innocent, are none of the above for *Seinfeld*. They are obnoxious, needless freaks of nature. Desirable women are not interested in getting pregnant. In "The Soul Mate" (8002), Elaine is badgered by her female friends and by Jerry to get pregnant. She then meets a new man who hears

her claim that she doesn't want children. They begin dating, and he spontane-
ously gets a vasectomy to demonstrate his commitment to her. Before the episode's end, Jerry, Kramer, and Newman will be lining up for vasectomies in order
to impress the women they love.

Also, in "The Fix-Up" (3016) and "The Chinese Woman" (6004), women are
not happy to have been possibly impregnated by George and Kramer, respectively. The first woman is just dismayed until she discovers that her period is
merely late. The second woman, Noreen, is about to jump off a bridge at the
thought of carrying Kramer's child.

Jerry never impregnates a woman. He is too neat, too sterile, too impervious,
too much the star. It is his extreme friends who cannot keep their sperm in control. Kramer, whose whole body is always on the verge of flying out of control,
certainly can't control his sperm.[4] George, who can do nothing right (in "The
Revenge" [2007], for example, George quits and then gets dismissed twice from
the same job, all in the same half hour), can almost get a woman pregnant but
not quite.

Jerry Seinfeld, though, stays Peter Pan, the boy-man with all the immaculate
girlfriends and all the immaculate sneakers, who is at utter ease and, thus, excessively irritated by the tiniest imperfection of the world and the neuroses and
pathologies of others. Peter Pan cannot sire chilren. Indeed, if one wants to retain
one's favored status, then "real" children become the competition. No wonder
their friends have "some ugly baby." In the *Seinfeld* world, others are unwelcome;
parents are oppressive; friends married or with children are buffoons; children are
monsters. Why *should* Jerry and Our Gang grow up?

Notes

1. Nomenclature note: Kramer, unlike the other characters, is almost always addressed
by his last name. Also, for the purpose of this paper, "Jerry" will refer to the character,
Jerry Seinfeld, and "Seinfeld" will refer to the actual Jerry Seinfeld, comic, creator, and
producer of the television show, *Seinfeld*.

2. The song is "Master of the House"; foreshadowing "The Contest" (4010), with its
"Master of Your Domain" theme. These phrases cut several ways. When Benes tells
George to "pipe down," he informs George who *is* "master of the house." Further, the
contest begins when George is discovered masturbating by his mother, in her house, dem-
onstrating that he's not master there, and of course, there's the interesting "master"/"masturbating" pun in which one achieves masterhood by *not* masturbating—*not* eating all the
cookies, in other words. The notion that masturbation is juvenile is accepted tacitly by all
the characters. In George's mother's first speech, she says, "I find my son treating his body
as an amusement park," i.e., where children would play, which adults (implicitly) should
grow out of.

3. Jerry is pretty much the same in the last episode as he was in the first. As Kramer tells him in "The Opposite" (5022), "You're even-Steven." After finally settling into his "hipster doofus" ("The Handicap Spot," 4021) persona around Season Three, Kramer, too, remains pretty much the same; after all, as Jerry tells him in "The Apartment" (2005), "You're not normal. You're a great guy, I love you, but you're a pod."

4. As Jerry says to Kramer in "The Contest" (4010), "You'll be out [i.e., will have masturbated] before we leave the coffee shop."

JON STRATTON (Curtin University of Technology)

Seinfeld *Is a Jewish Sitcom, Isn't It? Ethnicity and Assimilation in 1990s American Television*

This essay was originally published in *Coming Out Jewish: Constructing Ambivalent Identities*. New York: Routledge, 2000. 282–314.

The pilot episode of *Seinfeld*, "The Seinfeld Chronicles," went to air on July 5, 1989. At this point, the main characters were Jerry, George and the person who became Kramer. "The Seinfeld Chronicles" was received poorly and NBC ordered only four episodes of the show, which were shown in May and June 1990. In early 1993, *Seinfeld* started to be broadcast immediately after the high-rating *Cheers* and rapidly became one of the most popular shows on American television, coming in third in the overall Nielsen ratings for the 1993–1994 season (Marc xiv). By the time the final episode of *Seinfeld* was shown in the first half of 1998, there were, in total, 180 episodes, including a one-hour retrospective of clips. Some idea of the popularity of the series can be gained from knowing that, in 1997, *Business Week* estimated that Jerry Seinfeld was paid $22 million for the new series as an actor, writer, and producer. At the same time, the other three main actors negotiated a new pay deal giving them $600,000 each an episode. The extent to which the show has become a part of American cultural life is signaled by Greg Gattuso, who notes that "in addition to the catchphrases ('shrinkage,' 'slip one past the goalie,' 'puffy shirt,' 'Soup Nazi,' 'Get out!'), parroted throughout the day by fans, the show was having more lasting effects, inspiring everything from the coffee shop banter in Quentin Tarantino's film *Pulp Fiction* to a knock-off porno film, *Hindfeld*" (31). There has also been a wide range of *Seinfeld* merchandise.

It is clear that *Seinfeld* struck a chord in American life in particular, but Western life more generally in the 1990s. Here, I want to think through some of the conditions for its popularity. The underlying narrative issue of *Seinfeld* is, I will argue, intrinsically Yiddish, though ultimately a function of the experience of

many other migrant groups and their descendants in the United States. This issue
is usually addressed by describing *Seinfeld* as "a show about nothing." As *Seinfeld*
fans will know, this is the description George provides of the show that he and
Jerry pitch to NBC executives in "The Pitch" and "The Ticket" (4003):

> George: An idea for a show.
> Jerry: I still don't know what the idea is.
> George: It's about nothing.
> Jerry: Right. (Gattuso 63)

But what does this mean? In an interview with the *Hollywood Reporter*, Jerry
Seinfeld remarked that "nothing and everything are the same thing" and went on
to explain that the premise of the show involved looking at "the mini-events of
life—the kind of things that comprise most of life for most people. . . . I call it
micro-comedy" (Wild 30). Distinguishing between etiquette and civility and
arguing that civility is a description of the basis of interaction in that phenomenon of modernity, *society*, I will argue that *this* is what *Seinfeld* is about. Not a
comedy of manners, as such, it is a comedy about the experience of civility. In
this it is typical of the structure of American Yiddish humor.

However, what complicates matters is how elements of *Yiddishkeit* (Yiddish
culture) humor have, themselves, become naturalized as aspects of American cultural life. In this regard I will discuss the *schlemiel* and the *schlimazel* as Yiddish
concepts that evolved as aspects of a distinct, subaltern and oppressed culture but
which have now become accepted as part of the dominant Anglo-American culture, and which have been transformed in the process. In short, I will argue that
Seinfeld is ambivalently Jewish, that it is the most sophisticated example of the
surfacing of American Jewish identity as an ethnic identity in the entertainment
sector of the American public sphere in the 1990s, and that it evinces a preoccupation with what has always been the Yiddish dynamic with modernity, the problem of becoming civilized, in the most fundamental sense. However, as an
"American" program rather than a Jewish, or Yiddish, program, *Seinfeld* was able
to take advantage of its interrogation of the issue of civility to address topics that
would often have been thought of as improper—inappropriate for public discussion—by the dominant Anglo-American culture, and to do this in ways with
which very large numbers of Americans, not just the descendants of Yiddish and
other migrants from outside of the wellsprings of modern social life, could identify and find humorous.[1]

John Murray Cuddihy has commented that "differentiation is the cutting edge
of the modernization process, sundering cruelly what tradition had joined" (Cuddihy 10), and one area of life where this is most obvious is in the distinguishing

of religion from lived culture. It is, indeed, this distinction, and in a secular context the expression of morality and ethics as identifiable areas of knowledge, that allows for the description of society as being founded on shared moral assumptions. Cuddihy writes about what he calls the Protestant etiquette: "those expressive and situational norms ubiquitously if informally institutionalized in the social interaction ritual of our modern Western societies" (4). It is, then, this reification of religion that has provided the basis for the modern production of societies based on shared moral norms rather than shared cultural practices. Here, we are approaching the understanding of civility as the characteristic modern way of living. Kenneth Boulding has associated civility with civilization and described how the latter is "characterized by the elaborate systems of religion, politeness, morals, and manners" (Cuddihy 12). Civility is the typical organizing practice for interaction in the modern state. What makes the United States the most modern of states is that it is founded on a shared moral order rather than a shared culture (Stratton and Ang 124–138). This has made civility even more important as the shared basis for acceptable social interaction.

Cuddihy has argued that "Civility is not merely regulative of social behavior; it is an order of appearance constitutive of that behavior" (14). In this context, he reworks the experience of Jews in Western modernity as that of a colonized people, as a struggle simultaneously to retain their culture and to adapt to the civil way that underlies modern life. At the least, Cuddihy writes, civility requires "the bifurcation of private affect from public demeanor" (13). Where this modernizing was difficult for the long-resident Ashkenazi and Sephardi Jews of Western Europe, the problem was more traumatizing still for the Eastern European Jews steeped in *Yiddishkeit* who had not grown up with the experience of modernization but who confronted it as a result of migration. This describes well the situation in which the migrating Jews of Eastern Europe found themselves in the United States around the beginning of the twentieth century.

Jews and American Sitcoms

When *Seinfeld* went to air at the turn of the 1990s, it did so in an America that was emphasizing the importance of culture and asserting connections between cultural difference, race, and ethnicity. It was also in the context of a new multicultural Jewish visibility that was being made by choice (Stratton, "Not Really White—Again," 142–166). Nevertheless, the Jewish visibility of the show still had to be negotiated. Brandon Tartikoff, then president of NBC, had commented that the show was "too New York" and "too Jewish" (Wild 25). As a result, Jerry's neighbor Kessler (in "The Seinfeld Chronicles" pilot) had his name changed to the less Jewish-sounding Kramer and was subsequently given the un-Jewish forename of Cosmo. As we will see, there is a fundamental ambivalence about which characters in the show might be Jewish. One of the reasons why this ambivalence has become acceptable is because "Jewish" here refers primarily to culture; that is to say, the program is made and watched in a cultural context where the essentialist problem of who is or is not a Jew is of less importance to the majority of viewers than the representation of elements of Jewish culture. This may be because of the American tendency in multiculturalist thinking to think of Jews as an ethnic group within the white race. Where *Seinfeld* pioneered, other sitcoms have followed. *Mad About You,* with the ambivalently Jewish Paul Buchman married to the *shiksa,* Jamie, began in 1992; *The Nanny,* in which Fran Drescher plays Fran Fine, a Jewish nanny, started in 1993; and *Friends,* in which at least two of the main characters, a brother and a sister, Ross and Monica, are Jewish (another one is of Italian background), began in 1994. However, as the anonymous author of the article "Jewish Family Values" notes, "while certain Jewish values may be present [in *Friends*], the Jewish identities of Ross and Monica are all but invisible." This is because in the 1990s there has tended to be an emergence of Jewish culture rather than Jewish characters. *The Nanny* is the exception here. Dresher's character is represented as being unremittingly Yiddish-background and upper-working-class. I will discuss below why it is that while male characters can present as only partially Jewish, that is to say, can exhibit Jewish cultural aspects, female characters are either not Jewish at all, or, like Drescher's Fran Fine, are shown as unequivocally Jews.

The idea that ethnicity is cultural and can, therefore, be chosen is taken to its humorous limit in the sitcom *3rd Rock from the Sun.* Here, aliens assume human bodies in order to engage in participant observation of American culture. They set themselves up as a family, taking the name Solomon, we discover, from a removal van. In "Dick Like Me" (Episode 115, first screened in 1996), Tommy finds that in order to fit in at school he needs an ethnicity. In this takeoff on multicultural identity politics, the Solomons' neighbor Mrs. Dubcek, who once had a Jewish husband, helps the family to understand that, given their name, they must be Jewish. That the Solomons are really aliens provides an ironic reworking of the modern idea of the Jew as the stranger who comes to stay. Likewise, that the aliens take their name from a removal van humorously uses the idea of the Jews as being displaced, of being thought of in the modern world as being in diaspora.

In the 1940s and 1950s ethnic diversity was portrayed in working-class sitcoms such as the Yiddish American *The Goldbergs* (1948–54), the Norwegian American

Mama (1949–56), and the Italian American *Life with Luigi* (1952). In the late 1950s and 1960s sitcoms, such as *Father Knows Best* and *Leave It to Beaver*, portrayed middle-class Anglo-American values. Starting, perhaps, with *Who's the Boss* in 1984, through the 1990s, with the emphasis on multiculturalism, the ethnically diverse white characters of shows such as *Seinfeld*, *Mad About You*, and *Friends*, mostly Jewish and Italian, are now, themselves, second and third generation and, reflecting the ideal of upward social mobility, middle-class.

The problem these shows confront is how to represent white ethnic diversity without showing middle-class ethnic families. Were such families to be shown as working-class ethnic families were shown in the 1940s and 1950s, it would put into question the apparent Anglo-conformist white civil order over which is laid a variety of cultural identity inflections signifying "Jewishness" or "Italianness." The nuclear family, after all, is thought of as the point of imbrication of civil and cultural codes of behavior. It is not surprising, then, that familial diversity has been represented by showing Anglo white working-class families rather than non-Anglo ethnic middle-class families. *Married . . . with Children* (1987) was the seminal show here. Along with *The Simpsons*, which started in 1990, these two shows helped to establish the dysfunctional working-class Anglo family as the basis for the critique of the utopian suburban fantasy presented in 1950s sitcoms.

Given that the wife/mother was presented through the 1950s and 1960s as the site of reproduction of the civil and cultural codes, we have one answer to the question of why there are so few white ethnic female characterizations in present-day American sitcoms. Susan Kray writes that "Jewish women, like other minority women (except some blacks) do not get through the [gate-keepers onto television]" (353). In the rare cases where female Jewish characters do appear, they are usually presented as even more Anglo than their male counterparts. A very good example here is Courtney Cox's character, Monica, as the Jewish sister to David Schwimmer's much more obviously Jewish character, Ross, on *Friends*.

The virtual absence of a female Jewishness on 1990s American television is matched by the number of male Jewish-identified characters who have relationships with Anglo women. Jerry, on *Seinfeld*, with his parade of Anglo girlfriends, is the classic example here. Paul Buchman on *Mad About You* is another example. Often, this is accounted for from within the Jewish community as a reflection of the very high rate of marrying-out by Jewish men in the United States. This is a realist argument. Coupled with this argument is the claim of "shiksappeal," that Jewish men find Gentile women in some way exotic, fascinating, and attractive. There is even a *Seinfeld* episode, "The Serenity Now" (9003), that plays with this idea. Elaine, identified here as a Gentile, finds herself the source of attraction for both a rabbi and a Bar Mitzvah boy.

However, there is a more structural answer. Representations of Jewish men with Anglo-American women are reassuringly assimilatory for the dominant culture. When the women are middle-class, as they always are, these relationships are also reassuring for Americanizing Jewish men. A good example of this occurs in the film *There's Something About Mary* (1998). Jewish-identified women, having relationships with either Anglo-American men or Jewish-identified men, are more threatening. Aside from the *halachkic* consequences that the children of such a mixed relationship would be identified within the Jewish community as Jewish, there is the cultural assumption that the children, and maybe even the husband, would become more culturally Jewish. In other words, where Jewish men dating and marrying out connotes an increasing social cohesion by reconfirming the Anglo-American cultural dominance, Jewish women, whether marrying in or out, are more threatening to that hegemony. In *The Nanny*, Fran Drescher's response to this limitation on the female Jewish presence was to assert her character as unequivocally a Jew.

Lenny Bruce, Woody Allen, and Yiddish American Humour

While Jews, and Yiddishness, were repressed from middle-class American sitcom reality in the 1960s and 1970s in favor of portrayals of normative Anglo-American life, stand-up comedians such as Lenny Bruce and Woody Allen, most prominently after he started directing his own films—*Take the Money and Run* (1969) was the first—worked as Jews generalizing Yiddish humor. They used their position as simultaneously insider and outsider in the dominant culture to offer a critical take on American society while being somewhat aided by the cultural shift to an emphasis on culture. We can, then, make a distinction between the sitcom in the 1960s as, ideologically speaking, claiming to be representational and being preoccupied with naturalizing the dominant culture's view of the United States as white and Anglo-conformist, and the Jewish stand-up comic, though not of course all comedians, as critical cultural commentators.

At the same time, two further processes have been at work. One is the civilizing of the Yiddish Jews, and the other the Yiddishification of American culture. Bruce and Allen have generalized Yiddish culture by simultaneously teaching the *goyim* about the Yiddish outlook on life and reworking that subaltern outlook as an individual experience of modernity. David Biale has argued that:

> Bruce saw his role as liberating American culture from the sexual repression of its Puritan heritage. Bruce's comedy was specifically aimed at the intersection between

sexual and political hypocrisy in American culture. To "talk dirty" was to outrage convention, but it was also doing publicly what everyone was already doing privately. (Biale 216)

Bruce's critique was, in the first place, of an Anglo-American civility that distinguished what was appropriate in public from what was appropriate in private, a distinction he saw as being deceitful and self-serving.

Bruce also used the Yiddish lack of civility as a tactic to publicly discuss issues that Anglo-Americans would only normally talk about in private. These included things to do with race, drugs, and sex. In actual fact, in a rather less confrontational way, *Seinfeld* does exactly the same thing. One of the best examples is the episode called "The Contest" (4010), which involves George being caught masturbating by his mother and is built around a competition between Jerry, George, Kramer, and Elaine to see who can go the longest without masturbating. In another episode, "The Cigar Store Indian" (5010), Jerry has racial slur problems, managing to offend both the Chinese mailman and a Native American friend of Elaine's. Part of the pleasure of *Seinfeld* is being able to watch one's most personal foibles and faux pas being paraded as comedy in public. This is a far cry from the middle-class, nuclear family sitcoms of the 1960s, the didactic purpose of which was to teach people how to be civil even in the privacy of the family home.

Annette Wernblad has suggested a way that Woody Allen's and Lenny Bruce's humor can be differentiated:

The Allen persona . . . offends and deflates the people he does not like, and his verbal triumphs and revenge are transferred to the audience in the form of relief. Bruce, in contrast, . . . ridicules even the people with whom he sympathizes and identifies, and consequently he offends and deflates himself. (24)

Bruce always positioned himself as the outsider, and in an American individualism where there was no longer a clearly bounded Yiddish community to speak from, and where he did not want to identify with the Jewish community, Bruce's Jewish *schtik* even made fun of its own Jewishness. Perhaps the character of Bruce's that is closest to describing him is his Yiddish Lone Ranger, about whom he comments in his act: "You see, you and J. Edgar Hoover and Lenny Bruce and Jonas Salk thrive upon unrest, violence, and disease" (Cohen 31). Both the Lone Ranger and Lenny Bruce expect no thanks, the one for solving America's problems, the other for exposing them. Both remain outsiders.

Bruce generalized Jewishness through American culture. In one of his most well-known monologues, he divided American culture into Jewish and *goyish*. In his words:

> Now I neologize Jewish and *goyish*. Dig: I'm Jewish. Count Basie's Jewish. Ray Charles is Jewish. Eddie Cantor's *goyish*. B'Nai Brith is *goyish*; Haddasah, Jewish. Marine corps—heavy *goyim*, dangerous. Koolaid is *goyish*. All Drake's cakes are *goyish*. Pumpernickel is Jewish. . . . (Cohen 56)

Italians, he goes on to say, are Jewish, but Greeks are *goyish*. Broadly speaking, this binary system distinguishes that which is, in Bruce's opinion, uncivil, emotionally charged, lacking in respectability, that which has *chutzpah* as compared to superficial style, from all that is civil, merely well-mannered, disciplined. In his autobiography, *How to Talk Dirty and Influence People*, Bruce added to his distinctions:

> To me, if you live in New York or any other big city, you are Jewish. . . . If you live in Butte, Montana, you're going to be goyish even if you're Jewish. . . . (Biale 216)

Here the urban/suburban divide is expressed by Bruce in Jewish/*goyish* terms.

Allen's humor attempts to establish a complicity with his audience. While Allen also comments on issues, such as sex and death, that polite American society considers improper, he does so in a way that produces a new temporary subaltern group, as, in fact, does *Seinfeld*, which is why, even though it was the most popular show on American television, it is still talked about as a cult program. The source of Allen's humor lies not so much in a critique of civility but in a productive transgression of civility's rules. Allen is the "real Jew"—the phrase belongs to Diane Keaton's Annie Hall character in the 1977 eponymous film—who seeks to generalize his neuroses and anxieties to the Gentile population.

While his humor functions by means of a transgression of civility, when Allen made his first serious film, *Interiors* (1978), it was premised on the politeness of civility. There is a scene in *Annie Hall* where Annie takes Alvy (Allen) to meet her very civil, very *goy* Wisconsin family. At the dinner table, that most politely civilized of private sites, Alvy is unable to take part in the social conversation. His contribution is limited to humorous responses that fall on ears unable to comprehend them. *Interiors* is an expansion of this scene without the Yiddish uncivil transgression, and therefore without the humor.

Focusing on sexual behavior in Allen's films, Biale argues that:

> In some of Allen's movies the Jew's sexual ambivalence inflects the gentile women and turns them into mirror images of himself: even gentile Americans become "Jewish." The hidden agenda is to identify America with Jewish culture by generalizing Jewish sexuality and creating a safe, unthreatening space for the schlemiel as American anti-hero. (207)

Allen's own characters, we can note in passing, are all victims of *shiksappeal*. For Allen, being Jewish is not a cultural mode limited to Jews. More generally, as elements of Jewish culture become integrated into American culture, Gentile characters have begun to take on Jewish characteristics.

In this context we can utilize Alexander Doty's theorization of "queer moments" (Doty 3) and begin to think in terms of "Jewish moments." As aspects of Jewish, but perhaps I mean Yiddish, culture become pervasive in American culture, while also many characters like those of *Seinfeld*, as we shall see, are portrayed only as ambivalently Jewish, the idea of Jewish moments becomes an increasingly useful analytical tool. Doty writes that "unless the text is *about* queers. . . . the queerness of most mass culture texts is less an essential, waiting-to-be-discovered property than the result of acts of production and reception" (xi). Here, we can substitute "Jews" and "Jewishness" for "queers" and "queerness." From this point of view, Jewishness can be understood as a variable textual attribute not necessarily tied to characters identified as Jews, and any reader with varying degrees of knowledge of Jewish/Yiddish religion and culture may experience a Jewish moment, that is, recognize a Jewish characteristic in the text they are watching.

Biale claims that the direction of Allen's films is to generalize Jewish—actually Yiddish—male sexuality as American and, as a consequence, naturalize the *schlemiel* as an American antihero. Now, such a naturalization, "creating a safe, unthreatening space," would transform the *schlemiel* from a construction of a subaltern group, expressing the fears and survival tactics of that group, to membership of the dominant cultural order. In fact, this has been what has been happening to the *schlemiel*, but not as a consequence of Allen's films. Rather, these films have been one element in the long-term process of the naturalization of the *schlemiel* as an aspect of the Yiddishification of American culture. Thus, in many areas of American life these days, and in many popular cultural texts, one can experience a Jewish moment while identifying a *schlemiel*.

The *Schlemiel*, The *Schlimazel*, and American Culture

The problem with defining a *schlemiel* is a consequence of the transformation the term has undergone in its mainstreaming from subaltern, Yiddish culture to dominant, white Anglo-American culture and thence to becoming a part of general American culture. Ruth Wisse, whose quarter-of-a-century-old book, *The Schlemiel as Modern Hero* remains the authoritative work on the history of the *schlemiel*, argues that he—and the traditional *schlemiel* was always male—evolved out of the medieval European fool. In being taken up by a subaltern group, the fool was gradually transformed from the idiot savant: "Since Jewry's attitudes towards its own frailty were complex and contradictory, the *schlemiel* was sometimes berated for his foolish weakness, and elsewhere exalted for his hard inner strength" (Wisse 5). As Yiddish culture evolved, so the *schlemiel* became one of the characteristic figures of the predicament of the community. In Wisse's words: "At its best, the finished irony [of the *schlemiel*] holds both the contempt of the strong for the weak and the contempt of the weak for the strong, with the latter winning the upper hand" (6).

Within the Yiddish community the term could simply describe a stupid, if at times funny, loser, but the full complexity only appears when the term is applied to a Jew in interaction with the dominant culture. In this context, the stupid Jew is transformed into a naive innocent, a man imposed upon by the unreasonable and threatening forces of the dominant culture. While he may not be able to win, the *schlemiel* is able to provide insights into the condition of the community. As a character in a joke, the *schlemiel* provides the community with an opportunity to laugh at its own circumstance and at the dominant society that has placed it in this circumstance.

Writing about the eighteenth century renovation of the *schlemiel*, Sander Gilman argues that the character "is the Jewish enlightener's attempt to use satire to cajole the reader into not being a fool" (112). A fool, here, is a Jew who continues to follow traditional ways rather than involving himself in the Haskelah (the Jewish version of the Enlightenment). Clearly, Gilman arrives at his rather more negative definition of the *schlemiel* because of the character's polemical and political usage by those urging Jewish engagement with modern society: You will, they suggest, be a fool, and be taken advantage of, if you do not make the commitment. The engagement, it turns out, is fundamentally with civility. Almost two hundred years later, comics such as Lenny Bruce and Woody Allen reverse this use of the *schlemiel* and, in a more traditional usage, use it as a vehicle to comment on American, and more generally modern, society. Importantly, for Bruce and Allen, the *schlemiel* was no longer embedded in a community, and in particular a subaltern Yiddish community. I have already discussed how Bruce was speaking as an individualized Yiddish American, the Jewish Lone Ranger, and how Allen produced a community of complicity with his audience. In these examples we see the *schlemiel* losing his status as expressing the ambivalences of feeling of a subordinate group as Jewish attributes become Americanized.

What happens to the *schlemiel* as the character becomes a part of the dominant American culture? Most typically, the *schlemiel* is returned to being a version of the fool. Coupled with the American ideology of success, the *schlemiel* becomes the naive who succeeds in spite of himself and, in the process, provides moral insights for the audience. The high-water mark in the Americanization of the *schlemiel* has been the very popular film *Forrest Gump* (1994), in which Tom Hanks plays the intellectually subnormal Gump, who becomes a star footballer, is awarded a medal for bravery in the Vietnam War, represents the United States at table tennis, meets two presidents, and becomes enormously rich before finally finding love with his childhood sweetheart, who is dying of cancer. Without his legitimating in a subaltern community, the *schlemiel* becomes most straightforwardly a loser. In *Forrest Gump* the ambivalence of the Yiddish *schlemiel* is reworked in the American cultural context in a tension between what Gump, by all expectations, should be, a loser, and what he becomes, an overwhelming success. This is, if not a Yiddish moment, a Jewish American moment.

At this point we must return to *Seinfeld*. There has been much discussion about George as a *schlemiel*. The most detailed of these is by Carla Johnson, who argues that within the ensemble of characters, George plays the *schlemiel* to Jerry's *schlimazel* (116–124). For Wisse, this binary pairing is American. Of all the Yiddish character-types it is these two that have flourished in the American cultural context. Wisse writes that:

> The schlemiel is the active disseminator of bad luck, and the schlimazl its passive victim. Or, more sharply defined, the schlimazl happens upon mischance. . . . The schlemiel's misfortune is his character. (14)

In an important discussion of the *schlimazel*, Jay Boyer writes:

> Possessing a keener, more rational mind [than the *schlemiel*] the *schlimazl* tries to integrate more information than he should. Try as he might to hold one set of beliefs fixed in his mind, try as he might to maintain one logical superstructure, new information bombards him. He cannot revise quickly enough to keep up with events. (6)

This constant inadequacy to changing circumstances is a very good general description of Jerry's way of living in the world, and a very good way of understanding why he always seems so immobilized, able to comment as a comedian but not able to transform his situation. Outside of the *shtetl* the *schlimazel* has merged with the English music hall and American vaudeville role of the comic's offsider, the butt of the jokes. In short, in Gentile humor the *schlimazel* has been transformed into the fall guy (Boyer 6).

George's character is descended from Woody Allen's *schlemiel*. As Jason Alexander, who plays George, has admitted: "If you go back and look at [George's] early episodes, you're seeing a guy do a really blatant Woody Allen imitation" (quoted in Gattuso 8). However, as the character developed, George became much more self-serving and machinating, and much less self-aware, and yet stymied by his own self-awareness, than Allen's characters. Wild has insightfully noted that "Sergeant Bilko was a manipulative and self-serving liar decades before George Costanza made a veritable art form of such bad behavior" (17). Sergeant Bilko, from the sitcom of the same name, which ran from 1955 to 1959, starred Phil Silvers, a Yiddish-background comic who, in this show, played a *schlemiel* who, not surprisingly given the era, was never identified as Jewish.[2] In this revision of the *schlemiel*, the inability to take control of one's destiny because of the power and oppression of the dominant group is reworked as lucklessness and alternatively figured in terms of individualist ideology as a character defect. Bilko's shonky moneymaking schemes always ended in failure, suggesting a comparison with George, who is always the agent of his own failure whether it be with women or jobs or anything else. In the process, George's failure often impacts Jerry. We can say, then, that George in particular, but also Jerry, behave as Americanized versions of Yiddish character types.

Seinfeld and the Representation of Ethnicity

As I have remarked, the representation of some overt Jewishness, if not of Jews, is an aspect of the cultural turn, as epitomized in American multiculturalism, from the 1980s onward. To ask whether the main characters on *Seinfeld* are Jews is both foolish and instructive. It is foolish because it appeals to a reductionist and simplistic understanding of who is a Jew, but it is instructive because it enables us to appreciate just how blurred the category has become: the show is "Jewish" even when the characters are not designated as Jews. When we work back from the characters in the ensemble—that is, Jerry, George, Elaine, and Kramer—to the people on whom they are based, we find that all of those people are Jews. The same is probably true of the actors who play those characters, though there is no public evidence about Michael Richards, who plays Kramer. The blurring takes place in the characters themselves. Now, to some extent this is obviously an effect of production decisions and is a part of the history that repressed the presence of identifying Jews and overt Jewish culture in the middle-class family sitcoms of the 1950s and 1960s. I have noted Tartikoff's comment that *Seinfeld* was "too Jewish" and that Kramer's name was changed from Kessler.

The textual evidence for the show is confusing, indeed contradictory. An article in the *Jewish News of Greater Phoenix,* published on the Web, notes the reluctance of the show's publicists to provide the characters' religious identities and goes on to cite an episode ("The Fatigues," 8006) in which Kramer:

plans a Jewish singles function with authentic ethnic foods. He wants Jerry and Elaine to attend, and Elaine says, "Well, I'm not Jewish!" To which Kramer replies, "Neither am I."

In the same show, Kramer holds the function at the Knights of Columbus Hall, courtesy of George's dad's membership. Knights of Columbus is a Catholic organization.

An alternative point of view has been put forward by Michael Elkin in an article entitled "What's with Jerry and the Jews" at the Jewish Communication Network's Web site. Elkin writes:

> TV's "Seinfeld" offers multiple signs that the characters are Jewish—the pervasive smell of kasha in Frank and Estelle's [George's parents'] apartment, the Costanzas rye-bread rip-off, Jerry's mention of Jerusalem in the "Yadda Yadda Yadda" episode. Certainly the mohel episode was a tip-off that these neurotic New Yorkers knew their rites from their wrongs.

He goes on to itemize the counterevidence. It should be pointed out that, amid all this ambivalence about the characters being Jews, there is much less ambiguity in the case of Elaine. The show gives a clearer impression that she is a Gentile, bearing out the point about the absence of Jewish women on television. The irony being, as I have already noted, that Elaine is played by Julia Louis-Dreyfus, who is a Jew. To the extent that the audience knows this, and to the extent that she might be recognized as appearing Jewish, a tension is set up, one that comes to the fore in the *shiksappeal* episode mentioned earlier.

People do not seem worried by the inconsistencies. Even with the significant amount of overt Jewish references on the show, it can still be read as Gentile. Elkin notes that some of his midwestern colleagues do not think of the characters in terms of being Jews at all; the show's Jewishness is not apparent to them. He quotes one Michigan writer musing: "I think of them as New Yorkers." Here, the binary system I delineated earlier seems to be in operation. The ensemble are thought of as single city folk, and any unusual references or incomprehensible behavior is put down to this: they are New Yorkers. (Some would argue, and I think Lenny Bruce would be one, that New York is Jewish.) Joyce Millman, in "Cheerio, *Seinfeld*" cuts to the chase after noting the ambiguities attending the question of whether or not the characters are Jews. She writes: "Still, *Seinfeld* was the most successful Jewish-centric sitcom ever seen in prime time." In multicultural America, *Seinfeld* was allowed to be more or less overtly Jewish, while the characters were only ambiguously Jews. Nevertheless, reading it clearly remains a question of identifying Jewish moments.

There is another, more structural way of thinking about the status of the *Seinfeld* characters as Jews. At the core of the show are George, Jerry, and Elaine. Jerry is the most clearly Jewish of the three. George is Jerry's best friend from high school days. In American thinking there is a similarity of positioning of Jews and Italians: both have been perceived as not-quite-white while being granted the social status of white. It should therefore be no surprise to remember that George's family name is Costanza and he is portrayed as of Italian background when he is not Yiddish. (His background really cannot be identified as Jewish Italian, and he is certainly of Yiddish background rather than Sephardi, which is the background of the majority of Italian Jews.) Elaine and Jerry used to go out together. Focusing on these three, and their ambiguously Jewish behavior, the show "normalizes" them. Kramer is, here, the liminal character. He is Jerry's neighbor who has become largely incorporated into the group. His liminal status is regularly reinforced by the way he bursts explosively and unexpectedly into Jerry's apartment through the unlocked front door. In modern Western society it has been the Jew who has been thought of as the stranger in the nation-state, the stranger whose fantasy it is to be accepted (Bauman). Kramer, the stranger with the relatively non-Jewish name, certainly as compared to Jerry Seinfeld's name, can be read as the Gentile whose stranger status is a part of the "normal" Gentile nation-state/"stranger" Jew system.

Such a reading is reinforced by the difference in world experience between Jerry and George, and Kramer. As *schlimazel* and *schlemiel* respectively, Jerry and George are luckless, a negative representation of the powerlessness of the subaltern in Yiddish culture, but here normalized as the dominant experience of the world. Kramer, however, is lucky. As Johnson notes: "The contrast between Kramer, whose uncanny good luck relieves him of fate and control, and the luckless sidekicks creates one of the show's most powerful ironies" (119). At the same time, reflecting the ambivalence over the Jewish status of the other characters, Kramer's Gentile status is offset by his behavior. Where George, Jerry, and Elaine interact with presentations of self that are calm and polite—the content of their interaction is another matter—Kramer behaves like an uncivil Yiddisher. He is loud, brash, indiscreet, has little sense of any division between the private and the public, and tends to cause trouble as a result. These are the same qualities that Cuddihy explains are a threat to the fragile solidarity of civility. Thus, Kramer, too, is ambivalently Jewish, but structurally opposed to George, Jerry, and Elaine.

While being friends with the trio, Kramer is also friendly with Newman. In this system the "Jews" are known by their given names and the "Gentiles" by their family names. While Kramer is known by his family name, there was much fascination by the trio with his given name until it was revealed by his mother. Even when they find out his name is Cosmo ("The Switch," 6011), which is certainly not a Jewish name, everybody continues to call him Kramer.

Unlike the ambiguous status of the trio and the more borderline Kramer, Newman is clearly positioned. He is Gentile and Anglo-American. He is also, as he likes to say, in a position of power. When first introduced, in "The Suicide" (3015), Newman is the son of the owner of the building in which Jerry and Kramer have apartments. Later it turns out that he is a postal worker, and in a joke on his sense of self-importance and power he says, "When you control the mail, you control information" ("The Lip Reader," 5006). Newman is manipulative, treacherous, and utterly self-interested. Unlike the ensemble, including Kramer, he is also threatening and aggressive. Wayne Knight, who plays Newman, has explained that "There's a sense of blind aggression out of Newman, and it's kind of like you know you can venture to the dark side" (quoted in Gattuso 155). Jerry has described Newman as "pure evil" (quoted in Gattuso 18). Clearly, Newman is not just a Gentile; he takes on many threatening qualities that Yiddish Jews attributed to the Gentiles in the world around them, and also many of the negative qualities. Millman has summed him up as "a hilarious all-purpose nemesis for Jerry: equal parts empty bluster, sinister greed and sniveling cowardice." In this structural order, Newman gives subaltern meaning to George and Jerry's *schlemiel* and *schlimazel* while reinforcing the trio's position as Jews through a recognizable Jew/Gentile "Western" relation.

Such a perception is ratcheted up a notch by Newman's Aryan connotations. First, and most obviously, there is his name. "Newman" suggests the Nazi ideology of remaking the Germans as the master race, with the further connotation of an intertextual and superficial echo of Nietzsche's idea of the *Übermensch*. Second, there is the "Soup Nazi" episode (7006). Here, the main plot involves a temperamental and authoritarian soup chef whom the trio dub the Soup Nazi. As Millman notes, Newman "sucked up to the take-out food despot and proved to be the perfect collaborator." Third, there is the *Schindler's List* incident. Jerry and his new Jewish girlfriend, Rachel[3] (opportunely, a likely Jewish name), are spotted by Newman making out at the film. He tells both sets of parents ("The Raincoats," 5019). Jerry's Jewish parents are outraged. Newman, then, also embodies elements of post-Holocaust Jewish anxiety.

The construction of Newman in this way serves to anchor the show in a Yiddish experience of reality. By realizing Anglo-America through a Yiddish prism, but also placing Newman as a marginal though powerful character (at least in his own mind)—the first idea of making him the landlord's son suggests strongly the national metaphor in which Jerry, and indeed Kramer, rent rather than own their apartments in a white American-owned block, here connoting national territory in which the renters are (like) modern Jews, strangers or guests with limited rights—the show naturalizes the trio's way of life as the dominant culture. However, Newman's certainty indicates that the trio are not members of the dominant social group. Their ambiguous status as Jews is reworked diegetically in the show's ambivalent Jewishness, its Jewish moments.

Civility and *Seinfeld*

As I have already indicated, what is central to *Seinfeld* is not that its characters are, or are not, Jews, but its content, its Jewishness in the sense of the show's utilization of the Yiddish problem with understanding and learning that definitionally modern, and bourgeois, way of living, civility. Cuddihy writes that:

> The differentiations most foreign to the *shtetl* subculture of *Yiddishkeit* were those of public from private behavior and of manners from morals. Jews were being asked, in effect, to become bourgeois, and to become bourgeois very quickly. The problem of behavior, then, became strategic to the whole problematic of "assimilation." (12–13)

A surprisingly large amount of the time of each episode of *Seinfeld* is taken up by George, Jerry, and Elaine discussing not what is proper and improper behavior, that is to say not etiquette, but what certain forms of behavior are, what they involve, and how to decipher what other people mean when they act in particular ways or say particular things. Peter Mehlman, a writer-producer on the show, has remarked that "as urban and sophisticated as Jerry and George seem, they're so in the dark about so many things" (quoted in Gattuso 5). In this way Jerry and George, and to a much lesser extent Elaine, behave like nonmodern, indeed Yiddish, immigrants while at the same time appearing to be knowledgeable urbanites.

Etiquette is the conventionalized system in which civility is practiced, and that varies from one modern society to another. Gattuso notes that "Ironically, the zany one tends to be the group's etiquette watchdog. 'Without rules, there's chaos,' Kramer declares at one point" ("The Big Salad," 6002) (15). At this moment, Kramer is the white American bourgeois. He has grown up naturalizing the conventions of etiquette. In "The Face Painter" (6021), he tells Jerry that "good manners are the glue of society" and goes on: "If you don't want to be a part of society, Jerry, why don't you get in your car and move to the East Side!?!" The joke, and it is a rather complicated one given the structural inversion I have been describing, is that the East Side is WASP New York. Society, here, then, is the Jewish West Side. Knowledgeable audience members will appreciate that Kramer is suggesting an extraordinary reversal, one that parallels the normalizing of Jerry and his friends' uncivil behavior.

The problem of civility is most clearly identified in the finale to the entire show. In this one-hour episode, NBC decides to make the series called *Jerry,* which George suggested should be "about nothing," like *Seinfeld.* NBC offers George and Jerry a private plane for a trip to anywhere they would like to go. Taking along Elaine and Kramer, the four head to Paris. However, after a near accident, the plane makes an emergency landing in the white American heartland, in a small town called Latham, Massachusetts. The four are now in suburban, nuclear family land—the land of late 1950s and 1960s sitcoms, where civility is the foundation of society. In town, the four witness a robbery and carjacking. Rather than aiding the victim, they make comments to each other poking fun at him, and Kramer videotapes the event. The four then find themselves arrested for not helping under a new law, recently introduced in Latham, known as the Good Samaritan Law, which, as the four are told by the arresting officer, "requires you to help or assist anyone in danger so long as it is reasonable to do so."[4] The "New York Four" are no longer in a world where their problematically uncivil behavior is the norm. Rather, they are now a minority group in a society of white bourgeoisie and Anglo-American culture. This, of course, is the way it really is in the United States, at least ideologically.

That the moral obligation to help a person in trouble has had to be legislated suggests that there is a certain breakdown of civility, but as a narrative ploy, it enables the social sanctioning of the four's self-centered behavior, unmodified as it is by any acceptance of a civil moral order that imposes social obligations of aid on its members. As George remarks when they are in the lockup: "Why would we want to help somebody? That's what nuns and Red Cross workers are for." George completely fails to grasp that helping someone could be a social responsibility. He can only think of help as a function of specialized institutions.

If the town is almost entirely represented as white, Anglo-American (here, this does not include Yiddishers), and bourgeois, and the New York Four are now positioned as Yiddishers, albeit selfish and self-centered ones—this, for me, is definitely a Jewish moment—then it is not surprising that their lawyer is African-American. Moreover, Jackie Chiles (who first appeared in "The Maestro" [7003]) is also a New Yorker and does not speak in the modulated and measured tones of the civil white bourgeoisie, but rants and alliterates in a highly verbal, street rap African-American working-class style. Jackie may be a lawyer, but he, too, in spite of being able to tell the four what they should wear to evoke the jury's sympathy, is ultimately uncivil. The times we meet him in earlier episodes he is attempting to make dubious liability claims on behalf of members of the four. He also lacks the appropriate etiquette.

There is another point to make about Jackie Chiles. He was practically the only significant African-American character to appear on *Seinfeld*. American ideas of race are founded on the black-white binary. *Seinfeld*'s New York remains reassuringly white, even taking into account the "Cigar Store Indian" episode (5010). One other exception is "The Diplomat Club (6020), when George has to find himself an African-American friend and tries to befriend Jerry's flea exterminator. That the show can utilize George's lack of African-American acquaintances for humor actually reinforces the whiteness/Jewishness of its environments. *Seinfeld*'s concern with race is limited to ethnicity and the ambivalent status of Jewishness. Hence, Chiles's presence is a shock and a threatening, deconstructive moment of the same order as the appearance of Mary's African-American stepfather in *There's Something About Mary*.

The prosecution, having established its case and made certain of it by playing Kramer's video, goes on to confirm that this was not an isolated incident by bringing in witnesses who have previously fallen foul of the four's selfish and anti-social behavior. These include Mabel Choate, from whom Jerry stole a loaf of marble rye in "The Rye" (7011); Marla the Virgin, who was deeply shocked at the masturbation competition ("The Contest," 4010); the bubble boy whose antiviral protective bubble was punctured in an argument with George ("The Bubble Boy," 4006); and Sidra, whose breasts Jerry gets Elaine to investigate to check if they are real ("The Implant," 4018). As the television audience, "we" watch this train of witness accounts, we are repositioned. Where, first time around, we were complicit with the four as they acted out our own personal fantasies, failings, and foibles, now we are positioned with the white bourgeoisie, being asked to appreciate just how improper, transgressive of both etiquette and, finally, civility, the four's behavior has been. In the end the shocked judge sentences them to one year in jail.

Seinfeld can, itself, be described as a Jewish moment, as well as offering viewers Jewish moments, in that it is always already ambivalent about its Jewishness. It has, and yet has not, characters that are Jews—and at the same time, we are now living in a period when who is a Jew is itself problematic and sometimes overridden by the idea of Jewish culture. The program certainly manifests Yiddish cultural aspects, such as the types of the *schlemiel* and *schlimazel*, but in forms that are quite Americanized and, clearly, given the show's immense popularity, do not seem alien to Americans or others unversed in Yiddish culture. Yet, as I have argued, American society has also been, in certain ways, Yiddishized.

The very preoccupation of the show, its humorous disquisition on civility, is fundamentally Yiddish, but the accommodation with civility is, itself, a part of the history of all those who have had European bourgeois culture forced on them, from the working class to those peripherally European, and non-European, who have been colonized. In the United States, this most importantly includes African-Americans. For those who have internalized civility, *Seinfeld* provided an opportunity for them to laugh at the most private, and embarrassing, areas of life. These are areas that, normally, are not portrayed in the public sphere. On *Seinfeld*, the acceptance is made possible by way of four of the most selfish, self-centered, and yet naive, characters that have been envisaged for American television. In this, as I have noted, they follow in the footsteps of that earlier ambivalently Jewish character Sergeant Bilko.

When the moment of Jewish otherness and commentary is not recognized, the humor of the show is enabled by the excruciating failure of etiquette in characters who either simply do not understand it or, in the main, view etiquette at best as something to be disregarded or else utilized as a tactic for personal gain. In other words, the narrative reason for the humorous failure of etiquette, and the showing up of the problem of civility, can be alternatively identified in terms of Yiddish humor or a comedy of manners. *Seinfeld*, then, is typically modern in the way that it displaces the Jewish circumstance into an apparently universal possibility of modern identification.[5] However, it does this while simultaneously, ambivalently offering itself as, ambiguously, a Jewish program in an era of ethnic identification.

Notes

1. In England *Seinfeld* was shown on BBC2 in a late evening slot. It never achieved a comparable popularity to what it attained in the U.S.A. One possible reason for this is that English people are bound together by culture, rather than civility. English sitcom humor is very often class-based and concerned with etiquette.

2. Silvers's parents migrated from a *shtetl* called Kamenets Podolsk, near the Polish border around the turn of the century. Silvers's autobiography (with Robert Saffron) is *The Laugh Is On Me*.

3. Although not immediately identified as Jewish, in "The Hamptons" (5021) we later learn she is kosher and doesn't eat lobster.

4. Good Samaritan laws are common in the United States, but their purpose is quite different. They aim to protect people, such as doctors, who go to help a person, from being sued.

5. Of course, the more pragmatic reason is network television's attempt to garner the largest possible audience. There are a couple of things to say about this. First, we need to note the impact of cable television and the trend of network free-to-air broadcasting to become a residual category in an era of narrow casting and niche programming. Second, in the rare instances when ratings are broken down by race, it seems that *Seinfeld*'s audience is predominantly white, including, needless to say, Jewish. To put it another way, it seems that African-Americans do not tend to watch the program.

IV

"It is so sad. All your knowledge of high culture comes from Bugs Bunny cartoons" Cultural, Pop Cultural, and Media Matters

GEOFFREY O'BRIEN

The Republic of Seinfeld

This essay originally appeared as "Sein of the Times." *The New York Review of Books*, August 12, 1997: 12–14. It was republished as "The Republic of *Seinfeld*" in O'Brien's *Castaways of the Image Planet: Movies, Show Business, Public Spectacle*. Washington: Counterpoint, 2002: 162–72.

It is just another day in the Republic of Entertainment, and as always, a major story is taking shape. "DANGER SEIN," reads the headline of the *Daily News* for May 8, 1997, over a photograph of the stars of NBC's phenomenally popular sitcom *Seinfeld:* Jerry Seinfeld, Julia Louis-Dreyfus, Jason Alexander, and Michael Richards. They are clearly out of character, huddling cozily together and beaming with an appearance of warm feeling entirely inappropriate to the needling and conniving personae they embody on TV. The issue in the story is money, specifically the $1 million per episode that each of Jerry Seinfeld's costars is demanding for the impending ninth season of what the *News* reporter describes as "television's first billion-dollar sitcom." "THREE STARS HOLD OUT IN HIGH-STAKES BATTLE OVER NBC MEGAHIT": only the language of hostage-taking (the actors "imperil" the series with their "hard-line demands" and "it is essential that the impasse be resolved soon") can do justice to the drama of the event. (The impasse was resolved a few days later for roughly $600,000 per episode.)

A few days later a counterattack of sorts takes place, in the form of a *New York Times* Op-Ed piece in which Maureen Dowd professes shock at the "breathtaking" salaries demanded by the "surreally greedy" actors and proceeds to a ringing denunciation of the "ever more self-referential and self-regarding" *Seinfeld*. "The show is our Dorian Gray portrait, a reflection of the what's-in-it-for-me times that allowed Dick Morris and Bill Clinton to triumph." For backup she sites Leon Wieseltier of *The New Republic*, who describes the show as "the worst last gasp of Reaganite, grasping, materialistic narcissistic, banal self-absorption." (Neither addresses the question of why it is greedy for veteran actors who are indispensable to the most successful show on television—and who cannot reasonably expect another comparable windfall—to insist on a fair chunk of the money that would otherwise flow into the NBC kitty.)

In any event the diatribe scarcely registers, crowded out by celebrity cover stories in *TV Guide* ("Michael Richards: Still Kramer After All These Years. . . .
Seinfeld's slapstick sidekick strikes it rich!"); *Business Week* ("*Seinfeld:* The Economics of a TV Supershow and What It Means for NBC and the Industry");
and an encyclopedic special issue of *Entertainment Weekly*—*The Ultimate Seinfeld
Viewers' Guide*—including a plot summary of the series' 148 episodes to date (an
admirably meticulous piece of scholarship, by the way).

The ramifications extend: a franchising company will turn a soup restaurant
called Soup Nutsy, inspired by the *Seinfeld* episode about the Soup Nazi, itself
inspired by the allegedly intimidating proprietor of Soup Kitchen International
on West 55th Street) into a name-brand chain, that is if it is not outflanked by
another chain, Soup Man Enterprises, which (according to another story) has
struck a deal with the man from Soup Kitchen International (although the latter
is duly appalled by "the hateful name" he'd been given on *Seinfeld*); *The New York
Times* interviews Canadian comic Mike Myers about *Seinfeld* as an emblem of
American comedic values ("that observational comedy—observing the everyday
minutiae and creating a glossary of terms"); the *New York Post* reports that a
Miller Brewing Company manager has been fired for talking in the office about
a *Seinfeld* episode (the one about the woman whose name rhymes with a female
body part ["The Junior Mint," 4019])—"SEINFELD RHYME IS REASON BEER EXEC
GOT CANNED"—and the ensuing trial is covered by Court TV, in *Vanity Fair, The
New Yorker,* and elsewhere. Jerry Seinfeld himself poses with shoe polisher, gold-
fish bowl, and boxes of cereal as an advertising representative for the American
Express Card; a discussion in *New York* about the erosion of Jewish identity cites
Seinfeld as a supreme and troubling example of the assimilation of Jewish cultural
style into the mainstream; and *TV Guide* enshrines two *Seinfeld* episodes in its
special issue of the "100 Greatest Episodes of All Time" (an issue produced in
conjunction with the cable channel Nickelodeon order to promote, in turn, a
spin-off channel called TV Land, which is lobbying to be added to the roster of
Time Warner's Manhattan cable).

In exposure it doesn't get any better in this republic, all to make people even
more conscious of a show they would probably have been watching anyway, since,
quite aside from the hype, it happens to be inventive and suggestive and con-
sciously funny in ways that television seldom permits. How weirdly, in fact, the
speed and rigor of the show contrast with the elephantine and intrinsically
humorless mechanisms of publicity and subsidiary marketing that accrue around
it. My feelings about *Seinfeld*—a show I had long ago since gotten into the habit
of watching in reruns as a welcome respite from the execrable local news at
eleven—might have been different had I known I was watching (in the words of

a spokesman for what *Business Week* calls a "top media buyer") not merely a funny show but "one of the most important shows in history."

Once there wasn't anything that seemed quite so overpoweringly important, at least not anything short of World War II or space travel. I can remember, barely, what it was like when television was still a distinctive and somewhat raggedy presence in a world to which it was foreign. The memories have a pastoral quality, mixing in bushes from the other side of the window, perhaps, or a vase of flowers adjacent to the TV cabinet. Into that world of rich colors and complex textures emanated—from the squat monolithic box in the corner—a vague and grayish mass of moving figures, characters in a story line that often (given the vagaries of reception, the inadequacy of early TV amplification, and the clatter of household interruptions that people had not yet learned to tune out) had to be deduced from partial evidence.

The memories are imbued as well with a flavor of voluptuous indolence—an indolence associated with sofas, pillows, bowls of candy or popcorn, and apparently endless stretches of disposable time—that only at later ages would come to seem more like the flavor of weakness or compulsion or simple lack of anything better to do. (It took about a generation for the culture to acquire the absolute sense of the TV watcher's ennui that provides a major subtext for *Seinfeld,* which often ends as the characters are just clicking the set on as if in resignation to their fate.)

It didn't seem to matter particularly what programs were on. Between the ages of five and ten, for instance, I absorbed any number of installments of a stream of television comedies, including *The Abbott and Costello Show, Amos 'n Andy, You Bet Your Life, The Jack Benny Program, Private Secretary, Mr. Peepers, The George Burns and Gracie Allen Show, Make Room for Daddy, My Little Margie, The Adventures of Ozzie and Harriet, The Life of Riley, Ethel and Albert, Father Knows Best, December Bride, Mama, The Bob Cummins Show,* and *Bachelor Father.* Of all these, barely a single specific episode has engraved itself in my memory, although each left behind a vivid impressionism of its essential nature, a sort of Platonic episode embodying all possible variants. The plots, as I recall, tended to revolve around failed practical jokes, embarrassing household mishaps, doomed get-rich-quick schemes, ceaseless unsuccessful attempts to get the better of one's next-door neighbor, misinterpreted telephone calls, misdirected packages. A well-meaning husband would sell his wife's heirloom to the junkman by mistake, or invest his savings in a con man's Florida real-estate scam; a household pet would knock Aunt Flora's elderberry wine into the punch bowl; Junior would go to elaborate lengths to lie about the window he knocked out playing softball; a secretary would mix up the dunning letters and the party invitations, or uproariously blow off her boss's toupee by turning up the air conditioner full blast.

There were other and better comedies—*The Phil Silvers Show, The Honeymooners, I Love Lucy*—of which, with the reinforcement of endless reruns, I retain a much sharper recollection. But the overall effect was of an ill-defined, continually shifting flow not altogether unlike the movement of fish in an aquarium, soothing, diverting, and (with the exception of certain programs—such as *The Web* or *Danger*—given over to tales of the eerie and uncanny) incapable of causing upset. It was stuff that danced before one's eyes and then never came back—that was its charm and its limitation.

The sheer quantity of programming was already impressive in the fifties. In retrospect—as I scan complete schedules of network shows and realize just how many of them I watched—it seems unaccountable that there was ever time for other important cultural activities like going to the movies, reading comic books, listening to LPs of Broadway show tunes, collecting bubble gum cards, or studying with the utmost seriousness each new issue of *Life* and *Children's Digest* and, of course, *TV Guide*. Yet the evidence is inescapable as my eye runs down the listings and recognizes one forgotten companion after another, *The Court of Last Resort, The Millionaire, Mark Saber of London, Sergeant Preston of the Yukon, Name That Tune, To Tell the Truth*, not to mention *Schlitz Playhouse* and *The Gisele MacKenzie Show*.

Of course nothing was ever as unconscious as early television programming appears in hindsight. In fact, we thought television was a big deal then too; we just didn't have any idea what "big deal" really meant. Only by comparison with the present day do those rudimentary efforts take on the improvisational air of a reign of accident, where words and images washed up—anything to fill ten minutes here, twenty minutes there—as if their purveyors had given only the faintest glimmer of a thought to the overall design they formed.

The big deal that is *Seinfeld* is also just a quick little thing, a concentrated dose of farcical invention that seems to be watched by just about everybody. People watch it for reasons as varied as its uncannily precise analysis of miserable but inescapable relationships, its evocation of the bizarre randomness of urban life, its pratfalls and grimaces, its original contributions to the language (the "glossary of terms" to which Mike Meyers refers, evolving out of an almost Elizabethan fondness for protracted quibbles), its affinity with the fantastically mutating formalism of Edmund Spenser, or the platform it provides for the fantastically mutating eyes and eyebrows and mouth of Julia Louis-Dreyfus. It is a brief and reliable pleasure.

The most obvious source for this pleasure is a cast capable of unusual refinements of ensemble playing. Seinfeld himself (originally a stand-up comic whose routines revolved around rather mild evocations of life's absurdities) is the indispensable straight man, the perfect stand-in for anybody, just a guy in sneakers who lives alone on the Upper West Side of Manhattan, watches television, hangs out with his friends, and only gradually reveals himself as the *homme moyen obsessionel,* whose mania for neatness keeps incipient panic at bay. Seinfeld's manner, so understated as to make his lines seem thrown away, works beautifully against the relentlessly goading, operatically whining style of Jason Alexander's George (a character apparently modeled on the series' cocreator, Larry David), in whom the classic Woody Allen neurotic persona is cranked to a far more grating level of cringing self-abasement and equally monstrous self-serving. Alexander is the real workhorse of the series and inhabits the role so thoroughly that he can get away, for instance, with an episode in which he knocks over small children in an effort to escape from a smoke-filled building ("The Fire," 5020).

The blank zone inhabited by Jerry and George—their trademark ennui punctuated by ricocheting gags—is made richer and stranger by Julia Louis-Dreyfus as Jerry's ex girlfriend Elaine and Michael Richards as the perpetually mooching across-the-hall neighbor Kramer. Less striking in the earliest episodes, Louis-Dreyfus's brand of facial comedy has evolved into a distinct art form. Analyzed in slow motion, her shifts of expression are revealed in a complex ballet in which eyes, nose, mouth, neck, and shoulder negotiate hairpin turns or spiral into free fall. The smirk, the self-satisfied grin, the effusion of faked warmth, the grimace of barely concealed revulsion: each is delineated with razor precision before it slides into a slightly different shading.

As for Richards's Kramer, it seems hardly necessary at this point to praise what has become probably the most familiar comic turn in recent memory. Kramer as a character embodies all the expansive and ecstatic impulses that are severely curtailed in the others, creating an opportunity for the mercurial transformations in which Richards adopts by rapid turns the masks of Machiavellian intrigue, righteous anger, infant rapture, jaded worldliness, Buddhistic detachment, downhome bonhomie. Richards practices a refinement of the school of manic roleshifting of which Robin Williams and Michael Keaton were earlier exemplars, and seals his performance with pratfalls that by now are legendary.

Seinfeld's singular intensity has everything to do with its brevity, the twenty-two minutes of programming paid for by eight minutes of commercials. (In this case it works out to more than a million dollars a minute.) By straining at the limits of what can fit into a twenty-two-minute slot (rather than visibly struggling to fill it, like most shows), *Seinfeld* distends time. Its best episodes feel like feature films, and indeed have busier narratives than most features. (The periodic one-hour episodes, by contrast, sometimes go weirdly slack.) There is no padding; plot exposition is relayed in telegraphic jolts. An episode normally encompasses three separate plots that must converge in some fashion at the end, and the management of these crisscrossing story lines, the elisions and internal rhymes and abrupt interlacements, is one of the show's delights.

The sheer quantity of matter to be wrapped up enforces an exhilarating narrative shorthand. Comic opportunities that most shows would milk are tossed off in a line or two. The tension and destiny of working against the time constraint is a reminder of how fruitful such constraints can be. If Count Basie had not been limited by the duration of a 78-rpm record, would we have the astonishing compression of "Every Tub" (three minutes, fourteen seconds) or "Jumpin' at the Woodside" (three minutes, eight seconds).

The enormous budget, of course, makes possible frequent and elaborate scene changes that would be prohibitive for most shows. (It also makes possible a brilliant and constantly shifting supporting cast of taxi drivers, doormen, liquor store owners, television executives, German tourists, midwestern neo-Nazis, and hundreds more.) We are far from the primal simplicity of *The Honeymooners*, whose aura owed much to the rudimentary and unchanging space of Ralph and Alice Kramden's impoverished kitchen. *Seinfeld*—despite the recurrent settings of Jerry's apartment and Monk's café—is not about space in the same way, only about the psychic space of the characters and the catchphrases and body language that translate it. They carry their world with them into elevators and waiting rooms, gyms and airplanes and Chinese restaurants.

It is a world in sharp focus (rendered with an obsessive concern for surface realism of speech and clothing and furniture), in which everyone, friend and stranger alike, undergoes permanent uncomfortable scrutiny. The prevailing mood of *Seinfeld*'s protagonists is hypercritical irritation. Deeply annoyed by others most of the time, the four leads are only erratically conscious of how much annoyance they generate in turn. The spectrum of self-awareness ranges from George's abject self-loathing ("People like me shouldn't be allowed to live!" ["The Phone Message," 2004]) to the blissed-out self-approbation of Kramer, with a special place reserved for the scene where subtitles translate the comments of the Korean manicurists on whom Elaine is bestowing what she imagines to be a friendly smile while she waits impatiently to have her nails done: "Princess wants a manicure. . . . Mustn't keep Princess waiting" ("The Understudy," 6022).

The mutual kvetching of Jerry and George—of which we're given just enough to know how unbearable continuous exposure would be—serves as the ground bass over which Kramer, Elaine, and the expanding circle of subsidiary characters weaves endless comic variations. The relationship of Jerry and George is much like that of talk show host and sidekick, marked by constant obligatory banter indistinguishable from nagging. In short, a comfortable level of hostility and mistrust is maintained, upheld by everyone's fundamental desire not to get too closely involved with other people.

Seinfeld is defined by a series of refusals. Romantic love is not even a possibility, although deceptive or obsessive forms of it occasionally surface. Sex figures merely as a relentless necessity and an endless source of complications, and the intrigues that surround it have a detached, businesslike tone. (*Seinfeld* succeeds in making a joke not only out of sex but, more scandalously, out of sexual attractiveness, the "telegenic" currency of the medium.) Nor does the show succumb to the feel-good impulses that are the last resort of American movies and TV shows; it remains blessedly free of the simulation of human warmth evident in everything from weather reports to commercials for investment banking. There is a tacit contract that at no point will Seinfeld and friends break down and testify to how much they really like one another. It's clear that each thinks he really could have done better in the way of friends, but happens to be stuck with these ones and can't imagine how to survive without them.

The emotional tone is a throwback to the frank mutual aggressiveness of Laurel and Hardy or Abbott and Costello (the latter frequently acknowledged by Seinfeld as a prime influence), who never made the error of thinking their characters lovable. *Seinfeld* likewise keeps in sight the comic importance of subjecting its characters to cruelty and humiliation, of forcing them constantly to squirm and lie and accept disgrace before disappearing into the ether until next week. (The humiliations in question are often physical: the show has tirelessly enlisted body parts, bodily fluids, disgusting personal habits, diseases, and medical operations into its scenarios, as if the comedy of the lower body were necessary to keep in balance all that disembodied verbal riffing.)

What relief to encounter comedy that does not mistake itself for anything else. Its characters are free to start from zero each time, free to indulge the marvelous shallowness that is the privilege of the creatures of farce. Nothing counts here, nothing has consequences: as one of the show's writers (Larry Charles in *Entertainment Weekly*) has observed, the crucial guideline is that the characters do not learn from experience and never move beyond what they intrinsically and eternally are.

They cannot better themselves: a condition with positively subversive implications in a culture of self-help and self-aggrandizement, where has-beens no longer attempt comebacks but rather "reinvent themselves" and where a manual for would-be best-selling autobiographers advises how to "turn your memories into memoirs." There is a wonderful moment in "The Couch" (6005) when Kramer, swelling with indignation at some petty trespass of Jerry's, asks him, "What kind of person are you?" and he replies in squeaky desperation, "I don't know." The characters can only play at self-knowledge; any real consciousness of who they are—unless in some alternate world, along the lines of the celebrated "Bizarro Jerry" episode (8003), in which the leads are stalked by uncanny near-copies of themselves—would be like the cartoon moment when Bugs Bunny looks down and realizes he's walking on air.

Although they cannot evolve, they do change form ceaselessly. The fact of not really being people gives an ideal flexibility. If Kramer is convinced in one episode that Jerry has been a secret Nazi all along, or if sexual abstinence enables George to become an absurd polymath effortlessly soaking up Portuguese and advanced physics, it will have no aftertaste the next time around.

If *Seinfeld* is indeed, in the words of *Entertainment Weekly*, "the defining sitcom of our age" (one wonders how many such ages, each defined by its own sitcom, have already elapsed), the question remains what exactly it defines. Deliberate satire is alien to the spirit of the enterprise. *Seinfeld* has perfected a form in which anything can be invoked—masturbation, Jon Voight, death, kasha, deafness, faked orgasms, Salman Rushdie, Pez dispensers—without assuming the burden of saying anything about it (thereby avoiding the "social message" trap of programs like Norman Lear's *All in the Family* [1971–79] or *Maude* [1972–78]).

The show does not comment on anything except, famously, itself, in the series of episodes where Jerry and George create a pilot for a sitcom "about nothing," a sitcom identical to the one we are watching. This ploy—which ultimately necessitates a whole set of look-alikes to impersonate the cast of the show-within-a-show *Jerry*—ties in with the recursive, alternate-universe mode of such comedies as *The Purple Rose of Cairo* (Woody Allen, 1985) and *Groundhog Day* (Harold Ramis, 1993), while holding back just this side of the paranormal. If conspiracy theories surface from time to time, it is purely for amusement value, as in the episode ("The Boyfriend," 3017) where a spitting incident at the ballpark becomes the occasion for an elaborate parody—complete with a Zapruder-like home movie—of the "single bullet theory" (figuring in this context as the ultimate joke on the idea of explanation).

The result is a vastly entertaining mosaic of observed bits and traits and frames. Imagine some future researcher trying to annotate any one of these episodes, like a Shakespearean scholar dutifully noting that "tapsters were proverbially good at arithmetic." It would not merely be a matter of explaining jokes and cultural references and curt showbiz locutions—"He does fifteen minutes on

Ovaltine" ("The Fatigues," 8006) or "They canceled Rick James" ("The Abstinence," 8009)—but of explicating (always assuming that they were detected in the first place) each shrug and curtailed expostulation and deftly averted glance.

Where it might once have been asked if *Seinfeld* was a commentary on society, the question now should probably be whether society has not been reconfigured as a milieu for commenting on *Seinfeld*. If the craziness enacted on the show is nothing more than the usual business of comedy, the craziness that swirls around it in the outside world is of a less hilarious order. Comedy and money have always been around, but not always in such intimate linkage, and certainly not on so grandiose a scale. In the fifteenth century, the fate of Tudor commerce was not perceived to hinge on the traveling English players who wowed audiences as far afield as Denmark.

The information-age money culture for which *Seinfeld* is only another, fatter, bargaining chip clearly lost its sense of humor a long time ago, a fact that becomes ever more apparent as we move into an economy where sitcoms replace iron and steel as principle products, and where fun is not merely big business but seemingly the only business. The once endearing razzmatazz of showbiz hype warps into a perceptible desperation that registers all too plainly how much is at stake for merchandisers. One becomes uncomfortably aware of them looming behind the audience, running electronic analyses of the giggles and nervously watching for the dreaded moment when the laughter begins to dry up. It all begins to seem too much like work even for the audience, who may well begin to wonder why they should be expected to care about precisely how much their amusement is worth to the ticket sellers.

As for the actual creators of the fun, I would imagine that—allowing for differences of scale and pressure—they go about their work pretty much the same way regardless of the going price for a good laugh. Some years ago, in a dusty corner of Languedoc, I watched a dented circus truck pull up unannounced along the roadside. The family of performers who clambered out proceeded to set up a makeshift stage, which in a few hours was ready for their show: a display of tumbling and magic that could have been presented without significant difference in the fifteenth century. After two hours of sublime entertainment, they passed the hat around and drove away toward the next bend in the road. It is strange to think of the fate of empires, even entertainment empires, hinging on such things.

SARA LEWIS DUNNE (Middle Tennessee State University)

$Seinfood$: Purity, Danger, and Food Codes on Seinfeld

An earlier version of this essay was previously published in *Studies in Popular Culture* 18.2 (1996): 35–41.

In 1995 *Seinfeld* celebrated its one-hundredth episode with a summary show of the previous ninety-nine episodes. This milestone show begins with George and Jerry sitting in Monk's coffee shop discussing the condiments on the table. After a silly discussion about salsa, George says, referring to his proposed sitcom, "This should be the show." This is the show. This brief comic bit, chosen as the opener for an important episode, provides a clue to the importance of food in every episode of *Seinfeld* from its beginnings in 1989 to its ending episode four years later. In the hour-long one-hundredth-episode show, there are more than thirty food references, deemed memorable enough—and comic enough—to be included in this celebration. The entire nine-season span of shows has myriad food and eating references, as this partial list of titles reveals: "The Chinese Restaurant" (2011), "The Busboy" (2012), "The Café" (3007), "The Pez Dispenser" (3014), "The Junior Mint" (4019), "The Mango" (5001), "The Nonfat Yogurt" (5007), "The Dinner Party" (5013), "The Pie" (5015), "The Big Salad" (6002), "The Soup" (6007), "The Fusilli Jerry" (6019), "The Rye" (7011), "The Chicken Roaster" (8008), "The Muffin Tops" (8021), "The Wink" (7004—about George's eye irritation caused by a juicy grapefruit), "The Soup Nazi" (7006), "The Gum" (7010), "The Calzone" (7019), "The Bottle Deposit" (7020), "The Butter Shave" (9001), and "The Slicer" (9007). One *Seinfeld* Web site, http://wave.prohosting.com/tnguym/foods2.html, has divided the food references in the show into thirteen categories, with individual foods linked to their episodes. Here we can count up, as a case in point, twenty-five mentions of chicken or poultry being consumed or mentioned in the nine seasons of *Seinfeld*. Unsurprisingly, since few of the characters cook, the majority of the show's interior shots are either in a booth in Monk's coffee shop, in front of Jerry's refrigerator, or in front of his kitchen shelf filled with cereal boxes; many of the exterior shots are of a street in front of a produce market early in the series' run, and more often the "Restaurant/Restaurant" sign outside Monk's coffee shop.

Food, obviously, is a major thematic thread of *Seinfeld* and often serves as badge of identity for the show's regulars. In addition, food provides a vehicle for metaphors for some other concerns, sometimes serious, sometimes not. Food also acts as a signifier of social contracts or rules for social behavior, but most significantly, food on *Seinfeld* reveals a comically rigid set of rules about what should or should not, can or cannot be consumed safely. The danger is seldom physical, most often coming in the form of possible judgment and rejection by the small society of the show's regular characters or the show's larger social setting of peripheral characters who come and go with each episode. *Seinfeld* satirizes many aspects of modern urban life in the 1990s—O. J. Simpson's low-speed chase and the Tonya Harding-Nancy Kerrigan feud, for instance—but the show's most consistent target is modern urban America's obsession with food and food rules, a concept neatly conveyed in an early 1995 season episode called "The Soup Nazi" (7006).

Foods on *Seinfeld* serve first of all as identifiers for the characters. For example, Elaine, a self-styled vegetarian, often orders a "big salad" and it becomes a dish identified only with her. When the characters switch coffee shops temporarily from Monk's to Reggie's, their snippy waitress refuses to serve Elaine a "big salad" and sneeringly offers her two small salads instead ("The Soup," 6007). Elaine is also identified with a candy, Jujyfruits, which she stops to buy on the way to the hospital to visit her injured boyfriend, Jake Jarmel. He is offended that she has not rushed over to see him after his car wreck and that he plays second fiddle to her Jujyfruits, and their breakup is later referred to as the "Jujyfruit breakup." Elaine's continued indulgence in a mouthful of this gummy candy will cause her company, Pendant Publishing, to fold, when she is unable to tell her boss, Lippman, that he has forgotten his handkerchief, and he cannot shake hands with their prospective Japanese buyers because he's just sneezed into his hand; their reaction to this perceived offense queers the deal ("The Opposite," 5022). Elaine's other food identifier is muffins. In "The Showerhead" (7015), she fails her drug test because her consumption of poppy-seed muffins causes her to test positive for heroin, and in a later episode, she gives her former Pendant Publishing boss—Mr. Lippman again—her idea for a new business, muffin tops, because, to Elaine, the tops are the only good part of muffins ("The Muffin Tops," 8021). The "Chunky" Newman will be called upon to "clean up" the unwanted muffin stumps at the end of this episode. Elaine also identifies at least one other minor character, a fellow airline passenger, by his food—"vegetable lasagna" ("The Butter Shave," 9001).

George's identifying foods are varied, but it is Kramer, who often reveals a keen grasp of character, who correctly identifies George as a devotee of "the dark master, the cocoa bean" ("The Secret Code," 7007). George, like Newman, is connected with chocolate in three episodes, two of them with Bosco, and one with Twix candy bars. In "The Baby Shower" (2010), George confronts a woman who, years before, ruined one of his shirts when her "performance art" caused her to splash him with Bosco, and in this episode she accidentally smears chocolate cake and frosting on the same stained shirt. Five seasons later we learn that "BOSCO" is George's ATM password, which he refuses to share with even his closest friends, but he does blab to Peterman's dying mother, who emerges from her coma long enough to blurt out "Bosco!" as her dying utterance. Peterman is, of course, mystified by his mother's last words and wonders if her secret lover might have been named Bosco ("The Secret Code," 7007). Jason Alexander, who plays George Costanza, is a talented actor who has filled a broad range of dramatic and comedic roles, but in *Seinfeld*, his finest moments occur when his character gives vent to his ample supply of rage. The final-season episode "The Dealership" (9011) provides a showcase for Alexander's fine display of outrage when George is trying to buy a Twix candy bar from a car dealership's vending machine. He is frustrated at every turn, beginning with a Twix that refuses to fall from its visible perch inside the machine, and ending with the dealership's office, service, and sales staff eating his "candy lineup" of Twix bars. George's other food identity occurs when he tries to get his fellow workers and his boss to call him T-Bone, a name with more soul than George will ever have, and more cache as well. Instead, he is dubbed Koko, after the famous communicating monkey, when Kruger, his boss, sees him gesticulating through a window. By the episode's end, "Koko the monkey" is replaced by Gammy, a small boy's pet name for his late grandmother ("The Maid," 9019). George's various food identifiers probably are meant to emphasize his childish ineffectuality, or, in Kramer's words, that he is a "weak, spineless, a man of temptations"; Bosco is, after all, a drink usually consumed by children, and only a very childish man would carry on so intensely about a Twix bar or use such broad, simian hand gestures and body language.

Jerry's food identity is no less childish than George's: breakfast cereal. His open kitchen shelves sport a wide variety of dried, ready-to-eat cereal boxes, neatly lined up, and he is often seen snacking on cereal at times other than breakfast. When he meets a woman who seems to be his perfect soul mate (played by Janeane Garofolo), she shares his passion for cereal, eating it three times in one day ("The Invitations," 7022). In the series finale, Jerry's mother, Helen Seinfeld, packs a suitcase filled with full-sized cereal boxes to take to his trial in Latham, Massachusetts, because "he likes it. He says he misses that more that anything."

To no avail, Morty Seinfeld suggests that she take the smaller snackpacks ("Finale," 9022). Jerry, like George, also connects with a chocolate drink, Ovaltine, when he makes lame jokes about it and gives the jokes to his rival comedian, Kenny Bania, who "kills" with "Why do they call it 'Ovaltine' when it's round? They should call it 'Roundtine'" ("The Fatigues," 8006).

Kramer is identified with Mackinaw peaches, and when he temporarily loses his sense of taste, he is disappointed because the Mackinaw peaches have just come in at the market and he cannot taste them. At show's end, the gluttonous, gloating Newman—whose telephone is shaped like a hot dog in a bun, complete with mustard zigzag—usually (and appropriately) identified with his favorite chocolate candy, Chunky, eats the season's last remaining Mackinaw as the drooling Kramer, who has now regained his sense of taste, looks on ("The Doodle," 6018). One of Kramer's other food identities is connected to his abortive movie career when he muffs his one line, "These pretzels are making me thirsty!" in a Woody Allen movie ("The Alternate Side," 3011). The line has become one of those tag lines—like "Mulva" or "puffy shirt"—for *Seinfeld* fans. Kramer later becomes part of a continuing story line when he sneaks a hot cup of coffee into a movie theater and is burned. His lawyer, Jackie Chiles, is on the verge of a large settlement, when Kramer blurts out that he will take his settlement in free coffee ("The Maestro," 7003). He drinks so much free coffee that his behavior becomes even more manic. In Season Eight, Kramer, along with his fat buddy Newman, becomes addicted to Kenny Rogers's roasted chicken, a business that opens across the street from his apartment and whose red light wreaks havoc with, first, Kramer, and later Jerry, who has temporarily traded apartments and personalities with Kramer ("The Chicken Roaster," 8008). The series' final season opens with an episode in which Kramer decides that butter gives a better shave than shaving cream and that it is the perfect tanning cream as well. Smelling the hot butter sends Newman into a salivating hallucination of Kramer as a roasted turkey. Before this episode ends, Kramer is covered with oregano and parmesan, which, of course, stick to the butter on his face, and the scene ends with Newman about to bite into him ("The Butter Shave," 9001).

Perhaps the show's silliest instances of food-as-identity are the pasta figurines Kramer makes and gives to his friends. In explaining his "art," Kramer says, "The hard part is to find the pasta that fits the person." He makes a "fusilli Jerry" and explains the medium's appropriateness to Jerry: "Because you're silly." He promises to make George a "ravioli George" but does not explain why ravioli is an appropriate medium—perhaps because of its cheesy middle. Later in that episode, George's father falls on "fusilli Jerry" and the figurine must be removed by the proctologist who ordered the "ASSMAN" license plates Kramer was given by mistake ("The Fusilli Jerry," 6019). In a later episode when Kramer visits Bette Midler, a star he idolizes, after she has been injured by George in a softball game, he brings her a "macaroni Midler." Midler makes little comment and continues to eat the turkey sandwich, coleslaw, and black-and-white cookie—a pastry which made Jerry ill in an earlier show—that Kramer has ordered for her. The subtexts of the earlier food episodes, however, are essential to the humor of this scene ("The Understudy," 6022).

If food identities reveal character, obviously the *Seinfeld* people eat—and often behave—like children. Anyone who has fed children knows how unreasonably some children might insist that two small salads don't equal a "big salad," or that "only the tops of muffins are worth eating," or that cereal is always appropriate, any time of day or night. Possibly the most childish eater here is George, who in "The Dinner Party" (5013) wonders why he can't take a large bottle of Pepsi to his hostess instead of a bottle of wine and rhetorically whines, "Who says wine is better than Pepsi?" It takes an adult male could carry off the nickname T-Bone. Kramer's food identity, we might arguably conclude, is not quite so childish as that of the other characters, but it does show what M. M. Bakhtin would call the carnivalesque nature of his character, crossing food and social boundaries. Kramer turns food into art, himself into food, and his art enters the grotesque body in the least orthodox—and most painful—manner. All of these factors are consistent with the way he slides, falls, skids, leaps, and careens across the threshold into Jerry's apartment. We will return to Kramer's carnivalesque grotesquerie shortly.

In addition to food's power as an identity badge, the *Seinfeld* characters speak to one another in food metaphors. George, for example, calls Seattle "the pesto of cities" because, according to the *Entertainment Weekly Seinfeld Companion,* he "resents the sudden trendiness of both the basil sauce and the Northwest city" (62) ("The Busboy," 2012). Jerry explains in the famous "master of your domain" show that the sex drives of men and women are different, like "apples and oranges" ("The Contest," 4010). In a different show, Jerry calls Newman, whom he despises, "a mystery wrapped in a Twinkie," ("The Foundation," 8001), and George describes the sea as "angry, my friends, angry as an old man trying to send back soup in a deli" ("The Marine Biologist," 5014). Jerry and George remember that their old gym teacher's teeth are like "little baked beans" ("The Library," 3005). In a more complex metaphor, Kramer explains Marxism to his dwarf friend, Mickey, who has asked, "Suppose I want to open a deli?" in a Communist country. Kramer says, "You can't, because meats are divided up into a class system. You got pastrami in one class and salami and baloney in another.

That's not right." Mickey asks, "So you can't get corned beef?" To which Kramer replies, "Well, if you're in the politburo, maybe" ("The Race," 6010).

Food is employed in some more serious metaphors as well. The previously mentioned black-and-white cookie, identified with both Jerry and Bette Midler, serves as the vehicle for an extended metaphor about racial tolerance, delivered by Jerry, who has eaten the cookie while he and Elaine wait their turn in a bakery. Jerry ends his speech about the cookie and racial harmony by shouting, "Look to the cookie!" Shortly after his diatribe about tolerance, he begins to feel ill and suspects that the cookie's black and white halves are fighting inside him. He becomes ill and vomits—off camera—because of the failed metaphor and ends a fourteen-year record of healthy digestion, since June 29, 1980—"Fourteen years down the drain!" he says ("The Dinner Party," 5013). The cookie metaphor reveals, if nothing else, that racial problems are far too complex to be explained in such simplistic terms as cookies.

A similarly serious issue, abortion, is discussed in terms of a food metaphor, pizza ("The Couch," 6005). It is established early in the show that Elaine will not buy pizza from "Pequino's pizza" because of the owner's antichoice stand on abortion. In the same show Kramer and a peripheral character, Poppy, who owns a restaurant, try out a joint business venture, a restaurant where each customer may make his own pizza. However, when Kramer wants to put cucumbers on his pizza, Poppy says, "People can't choose whatever they want on a pizza," to which Kramer replies, "It's not a pizza yet." Poppy rejoinders with, "Yes it is. It's a pizza the minute you think of it," that is to say, the minute it is conceived. The issue is not resolved on the show, but the presence of the embryo/pizza metaphor, as well as the racial harmony/cookie metaphor, underscores the characters' use of food not only as identity but as language. To use a favorite term of Roland Barthes, the French structuralist critic who decoded the language of food in *Elements of Semiology*, the food metaphors on *Seinfeld* form an "alimentary rhetoric," (28) or a kind of language we might call "Seinfood," if you will, understood by the characters, but easily decoded by the viewers as well. In fact, Jerry Seinfeld's own book, published in 1995, is entitled *SeinLanguage*, his own recognition of the irresistible pun on his name.

Just as critics and grammarians arbitrate the rules of language, the *Seinfeld* characters are experts on the rules of food consumption in social contexts. One minor example of violating a food rule is provided in "The Wife" (5017), when Jerry and his "pretend wife," played by Courtney Cox, take Jerry's own bottle of syrup to Monk's because the syrup at Monk's is inferior. Monk himself, acting much like a school principal, says to them, "Uh, we don't allow any outside syrups, jams, or condiments in the restaurant. And if I catch you in here with that again . . . I will confiscate it." Jerry, responding the way a rule-breaking twelve-year-old might, blames this violation on his "wife." In "The Soup" (6007), Jerry is given an Armani suit by a fellow comedian, Kenny Bania, someone Jerry does not like much. The gift of the suit, which Bania has outgrown because he's been working out with weights, incurs an obligation, so Jerry agrees to buy Bania a meal. They go to a restaurant, Mendy's, but Bania orders only a bowl of soup and tells Jerry, "Soup's not a meal. You're supposed to buy me a meal." Jerry is appalled at the idea of another dinner with the obnoxious Bania and tries to get his friends to agree that soup is a meal. Elaine asks, "What kind of soup?" and the answer is "Consommé." Elaine clarifies the ruling by saying, "That's not a meal. If he had ordered chicken gumbo, matzo ball, even mushroom barley, then I would agree with you. Those are very hearty soups." Jerry counters with, "The act of sitting down is a meal," but Elaine, who seems to know more about food rules in this episode, asks, "Was it a cup or a bowl? Did he crumble any crackers in it?" and concludes, "That could be a meal." Jerry ends this hairsplitting session by commenting, "It's like I'm talking to my Aunt Sylvia here." Perhaps "Aunt Sylvia" is a similar expert on what is and is not a meal—an arbiter of food rules, like the stereotypical Jewish mother made so famous by Philip Roth in *Portnoy's Complaint*.

Dinner party "rules" seem to baffle all the regular characters on *Seinfeld*. As mentioned earlier, George deeply resents having to present his hostess with a bottle of wine in "The Dinner Party," and the loaf of Schnitzer's marble rye bread in "The Rye" (7011) provides a similar plot driver. The Costanzas present their hosts and George's prospective in-laws, the Rosses, with a marble rye at an ill-fated dinner party, and in this episode we see a peculiarly New York culture clash between the schlubby Costanzas and the ritzy Rosses. Much has been written about whether the Costanzas, whose name "sounds" Italian, are really Jewish, with George, according to both Carla Johnson and Jon Stratton (in this volume), as the ultimate schlemiel. A food called Schnitzer's Marble Rye certainly would seem to fit into the ethnic tradition that would offer it as a dinner-party gift, and its rejection by the Rosses seems an affront, which could easily be read as an ethnic affront, to Frank Costanza. When I first saw this episode, I (and probably many other viewers as well) was reminded of Jackie Mason's summation of the difference between Jews and Gentiles: Jews eat and Gentiles drink, and the Rosses are usually seen with a drink in their hands. Frank and Estelle Costanza are not only affronted by the Rosses' casual treatment of the marble rye ("People take buses to get that rye!") but at their failure to offer even a slice of cake for dessert. Frank Costanza steals back the marble rye, and when George finds that out, he feels compelled to cover for his father's breach of etiquette. His plan to return the rye bread and pretend it had been overlooked involves a hilarious convergence of plot elements and the street theft of the elderly Mabel Choate's marble rye, but we see again that in urban life, especially the culturally diverse urban life of New York City, rules rule.

There are other food rules in "The Wink" and, of course, in "The Soup Nazi." In "The Wink" (7004) Jerry treads a fine line between healthy eating and becoming "one of those," presumably a vegetarian health nut. Either way, he is trying to abide by both a set of health guidelines and a set of unwritten social customs. A bit of pulp from his healthy grapefruit breakfast squirts across the table into George's eye, causing him to undermine every utterance for the rest of the day with a wink. More than that, Jerry realizes that "Women don't respect salad eaters," to which Elaine replies, "You got that right." In order to gain the respect of his prospective girlfriend Holly, Jerry pretends to like the mutton she serves, secreting it in a napkin and then in his jacket pockets. Believing that he loves her mutton, Holly shows up at Jerry's apartment, ready to cook up a batch of pork chops. She soon discovers that Jerry doesn't much care for such a meaty diet, and, as we have come to expect, another relationship is lost, even though Jerry is trying to adhere to the "rules" of masculinity by eating meat. Two episodes later, "The Soup Nazi" shows all the characters trying, each in his or her own way, to deal with the "rules" by which the *soupier* does business. Oddly enough, Kramer understands the rules best, and Elaine is the least willing to comply with the soup seller's rigid ordering procedure, described here by George and Jerry: "So, you hold out your money, speak your soup in a loud, clear voice, step to the left and receive"; "No extraneous comments. No questions. No compliments" (7006). The Soup Nazi's response to Elaine's dithering and online chatter is a year's banishment, but she, by a twist, has her revenge when she finds his secret recipes in an old armoire. Sometimes Elaine gets to make her own rules.

Another brief example of an extraneous character who can make his own food rules involves a scene with George in Havana recruiting Cuban ballplayers for the Yankees. Fidel Castro invites George to a party and says, as many New Yorkers might, "The problem with parties is you have to eat standing up. Once at a party, I put my plate on someone's piano. I assure you if I had not been the dictator, I could not have gotten away with that one." New York rules of etiquette are apparently no different from Cuban rules ("The Race," 6010).

One final example is, probably, the most absurd—and therefore the most comical—rule about food as part of social life on *Seinfeld*: eating finger foods with eating utensils rather than with fingers. It begins with Elaine's boss, Mr. Pitt, eating a Snickers Bar with a knife and fork because of his rigidly upper-class upbringing. Elaine, astounded, tells George, and at a Yankees' staff meeting the neurotic George decides to emulate Mr. Pitt's supposedly aristocratic table manners. One of the executives follows suit, as does a minor and unrelated character, Noreen, who feels she must eat cookies that way. Yankees outfielder Danny Tartabull picks up on this odd practice and eats a doughnut with a knife and fork, and before the show is over, we see a man forking an Almond Joy and Jerry sees another character eat M&Ms with a spoon. The show satirizes the characters' need for rules even over the most minor points of their lives and their neurotic need to garner the approval even of strangers by imitating what they believe to be aristocratic manners ("The Pledge Drive," 6003).

Rules about how food is eaten with others on the *Seinfeld* show are intimately related to rules about what foods are safe to eat—alone or with others—and these rules reveal some important cultural assumptions about what is "pure" and what is "dangerous," to use the binary code of anthropologist Mary Tew Douglas. To the *Seinfeld* characters, food presents a more immediate danger than some of the actual dangers they might face in Manhattan: robbery, rape, death or dismemberment by automobile, permanent job loss, random street violence, or AIDS or STDs from some of their numerous sexual encounters. In the previously mentioned "black-and-white cookie" episode, a number of examples of food pollution are present. Jerry eats the cookie in the bakery while waiting with Elaine to return a babka with a hair on it, which revolts not only Elaine but Jerry as well, who remembers finding a hair in his farina as a child. As if these pollutants were not enough, the counter worker has a hacking cough. A similar instance of food pollution occurs when Jerry dates Audrey, daughter of the earlier restaurateur Poppy. Jerry offers Audrey a bite of his pie and is offended when she simply shakes her head in declining and refuses to explain why. Later they eat at Poppy's restaurant. Jerry and Poppy use the men's room at the same time, and Jerry notices Poppy touching his hair, his face, and patting his fly, but not washing his hands before he goes in to prepare a special pizza for Jerry and Audrey. Jerry, as Audrey had done earlier, refuses to eat the pizza and refuses to explain why, only shaking his head. In the same show George has a job interview/lunch and discovers the chef is someone he tricked out of a sale suit. Suspecting that the dessert will be poisoned, George, like Jerry and Audrey, refuses the pie and does not get the job because his refusal is interpreted as his unwillingness to be a "team player." However, George is the only luncher who is not ill as a result of poisoned food ("The Pie," 5015).

George is the prime offender in a similar show when he is caught by his girlfriend's horrified mother eating an éclair—a chocolate one, naturally—that he finds at the top of her garbage can. He defensively explains to Jerry, "It was above the rim; it was hovering like an angel" ("The Gymnast," 6006). Because he is the show's most neurotic and obsessive character, George is the most chagrined at being caught in breaking a food taboo, but George is also a rule keeper in another episode. In the show about the Mackinaw peaches, George's date picks up a peach pit George has discarded and she puts it in her mouth, much to George's extreme disgust. The fact that George has already had a sexual relation with this woman in no way lessens his disgust at her eating his discarded peach pit, a fact which might suggest that to George sexual intimacy is less intense—and less important—than food intimacy. In the world of the *Seinfeld* characters, violation of a food conduct code is a more serious social infringement than violation of a sexual conduct code, but the two codes collide in what is perhaps George's most serious breach of food rules. In "The Hamptons" (5021) George knowingly serves scrambled eggs with lobster to a kosher guest who got a fast look at his penis, shrunken by swimming in cold water. Here we see that for George, revenge trumps religion, and a food violation trumps a sexual one.

Another episode where food pollution is a concern for the Costanzas occurs in Season Eight in "The Fatigues" (8006), in which Kramer enlists Frank Costanza to cook for a "Jewish singles" night he is sponsoring. Frank, we know from earlier episodes, is a Korean War veteran and had a Korean mistress, as well, when he traveled there selling his "religious tchochkes." That he is also a cook is a well-suppressed fact because of his painful memories of the accidental food poisoning his food inflicted on the young soldiers. He reluctantly returns to cooking and, while things seem to be going well at this event, when Frank sees someone choking, he is sure that once again the food he has cooked is tainted. In character, he stops the diners and overturns the tables full of knishes and latkes. Food, like so many other substances, can provoke the Costanza family rage.

Even the eccentric Kramer, one of the characters least bound by social codes, is sometimes aware of the rules of food purity and food danger, such as when he decides to get rid of his refrigerator and eat only fresh food. He explains to Jerry, "After that kidney stone I only want fresh food. It's gotta be fresh. No more stored food. Fresh fish, fresh fowl, fresh fruit. I buy it, I eat it" ("The Soup," 6007). Kramer and Jerry also violate food purity rules when they accidentally drop a Junior Mint into a patient undergoing a surgery they are observing. Miraculously, the patient survives the Junior Mint. Kramer's "grotesque body" is more than once the subject of his part of the plot, and he is twice made ill by consuming spoiled foods. In "The Pitch" (4003) he drinks spoiled milk from Jerry's refrigerator and vomits on Susan, who will later become George's fiancée, and in "The Gum" (7010) he eats a hot dog that's been in the movie theater's display case "since the silent era" and he is later sick on the sidewalk outside. While hawking his coffee-table book on *Live with Regis and Kathie Lee,* he spits hot coffee all over Kathie Lee ("The Opposite," 5022). Because boundaries have so little meaning to Kramer, his body similarly seems, even more than the fat Newman's, to exceed its own margins—his passing of kidney stones at Madison Square Garden causes a tightrope walker to fall ("The Gymnast," 6006)—or to have those margins invaded ("The Big E" in "The Pilot," 4022). Kramer illustrates perhaps most of all—albeit comically—the basic premise that pollution, in food scholar Margaret Visser's words, is "matter out of place" (301).

Pollution is a socially designed and socially administered concept, and the more rigidly structured a society is, the more rules there are about purity and danger. To quote Mary Douglas again, "Pollution is a type of danger which is not likely to occur except where the lines of structure, cosmic or social, are clearly defined" (113). Margaret Visser contends that for all societies, "Food is sacred, and must also be pure, clean, and undefiled" (171). She goes on to say that cleanliness has become such a modern obsession that, "If we are not very careful, cleanliness rules can matter more to us than morality" (355). *Seinfeld* seems to have justified Visser's warning, comically exposing many Americans' obsessions with food rules, food dangers, food signs.

One need not look far for at least a rudimentary explanation for the show's insistent connection between food and laughter. Jerry Seinfeld, writer, star, and subject for the show, admits that comedy and food are inseparable to him. On the Sony *Seinfeld* page of the World Wide Web, Jerry Seinfeld says, "I knew I was going to be a comedian at a very young age. I remember one time I made a friend laugh so hard that he sprayed a mouthful of cookies and milk all over me. And I liked it. That was the beginning." He goes on to say, "Everyone's looking for good sex, good food, and a good laugh. They're little islands of relief in what's often a painful existence." More recently, James Kaplan's *New Yorker* piece about Larry David, the show's cocreator and, for many seasons, its cowriter, contains this tidbit of information: "One night in late November, Seinfeld and David were going to share a cab back to the West Side from Catch a Rising Star but decided to stop and pick up some groceries first. 'It was a Korean deli, and we were waiting to pay, and we started making fun of the products they kept by the register,' Seinfeld says. 'You know, those fig bars in cellophane, without a label, that look like somebody made them in their basement?'" At that point David, as George will later reiterate, says, "'This is what the show should be—this is the kind of dialogue that we should do on the show'" (69). Furthermore, the last episode's last words are uttered by Jerry, in prison: "Seeya in the cafeteria!"

Seinfeld is called a show about nothing, a phrase George uses in the self-referential "show about the show" that he pitches to NBC. I contend that it's not a show about nothing. It is a show about food, or, in the language of postmodern critical punsters, it is a show about "Seinfood."

ELEANOR HERSEY (Fresno Pacific University)

"It'll always be Burma to me"

J. Peterman on *Seinfeld*

This essay first appeared in *Studies in Popular Culture* 22.3 (2000):
11–24.

The appearance of J. Peterman on *Seinfeld* in May 1995 ("The Under-study," 6022) marks the convergence of two significant 1990s media phe-nomena: the clothing company that redefined the rhetorical conventions of the mail-order catalog and the television series that redefined the plot conven-tions of the situation comedy. The influence of these phenomena on one another is striking: while *Seinfeld* writers predicted and possibly contributed to the real J. Peterman Company's collapse, the presence of Peterman stretched the limits of *Seinfeld*'s status as a show "about nothing." Although J. Peterman catalogs have inspired many satirical commentaries, the foppish character played by John O'Hurley may have had the greatest impact on the real J. Peterman's image as an icon of rugged masculinity and world conquest. At the same time, Peterman's character compelled *Seinfeld* writers to address issues of colonialism and racial stereotypes that the series had avoided in its attempt to maintain a generally "lib-eral" but largely apolitical status. As a parody of the J. Peterman phenomenon, *Seinfeld* critiques the catalog's manipulation of native peoples while participating in its reduction of colonial history to entertainment. When Elaine and Peterman travel to Myanmar in "The Foundation" (8001) and "The Chicken Roaster" (8008), *Seinfeld* writers Alec Berg and Jeff Schaffer demonstrate the ways in which parodies of imperialist texts may contribute to the exploitation of the Third World.

With the character of J. Peterman, *Seinfeld* combines two of its most successful conventions: the gratuitous reference to real-life products (including Junior Mints, Snapple, and Drake's Coffee Cake) and the placement of Elaine in the power of an eccentric male boss, exemplified by her former position as executive assistant to Mr. Pitt. The series also capitalized on the J. Peterman catalog's increasing popularity with consumers in the early 1990s. According to Gail Buchalter of *Forbes*, John Peterman began the catalog in 1988 after selling thousands of duster coats by placing advertisements in magazines like *The New Yorker* (224). The catalog was distinguished by its heavy, high-quality paper, watercolor illustrations, and flowery prose, much of it devoted to tales of J. Peterman's adventures around the world. A description of the women's Balinese Mandarin Collar Tee on jpeterman.com represents the colonial nostalgia evoked by the catalog: "Ocean Pearl. Bali. Balmy beaches. Velvet green valleys, fragrant temples. Have you noticed that the open, friendly people of Bali always seem to be celebrating? Cause for you to celebrate: This wonderfully versatile tee based on a traditional Balinese design. (Their arms, bare. Ours, long-sleeved for less temperate climates.)" A description of the Vintage Seersucker Shirt on the same Web site evokes the past lives of J. Peterman's American male consumers: "What you used to wear steaming up to Luxor with your daguerreotype camera, attending get-togethers of the Soerabaja Planters Association or coffee auctions in New Orleans, circa 1850." Although the prices are steep ($38 for the Balinese tee, $54 for the seersucker shirt), the romantic prose seduced thousands of consumers, allowing John Peterman to begin a new catalog entitled *Booty, Spoils, and Plunder* and to open a chain of retail stores.

When the catalog gained a large circulation and significant consumer following, many journalists praised its lyrical prose and visual appeal, while others criticized its conservative race, class, and gender politics. In a 1991 article in *Gentlemen's Quarterly*, Hilary Sterne claims that J. Peterman is "a catalogue even a tree spiker could love," its copy "wry and rugged and clean as a dry martini" (78). In a 1994 article in the teen magazine *Sassy*, Marjorie Ingall calls the catalog "a veritable fork plunged into my neurons," filled with clothes "that wear their overblown, race-obsessed, imperialist male fantasies on their creamy white, starched linen sleeves" (80). Writing for *The New York Times Magazine* in 1993, Holly Brubach describes her own ambivalent reaction to the catalog: "Of all the catalogs I have come to know, this one is by far the most personal—a direct reflection of an individual who comes off as charismatic. It is also, in many respects, the most perplexing, inspiring not only fascination and even fondness but also irritation and exasperation" (59). This combination of fondness and exasperation suggests the opportunities for parody that the character of Peterman presents, as well as the public's tendency to collapse the real John Peterman with his persona, the "individual who comes off as charismatic." This tendency persists despite the reports in *Forbes* and *People Weekly* that the catalog copy was written by John Peterman's colleague Donald Staley (Buchalter 224) and that John Peterman has not traveled to many of the exotic places that the catalog describes (Sporkin and Shaw 128).

Although these articles describe the real John Peterman as a down-to-earth, middle-class salesman with a family, *Seinfeld*'s reinvention of the character as an eccentric, single New York City executive was so influential that journalists began to conflate the real man, the catalog persona, and the television character into a single cultural icon. In *People Weekly*, Michael A. Lipton and John Griffiths challenge the reader, "Spend a morning at home with John O'Hurley, and you would swear you'd stepped right into the pages of the chic, deliciously overwritten J. Peterman catalog" (115). Although the writers assert that the television character is "a dashing, slightly daft mail-order king very much unlike the real J. Peterman," they also claim that O'Hurley's speech falls "naturally into sonorous Petermanese" and include a photograph of John Peterman and John O'Hurley together on FOX's *After Breakfast*. O'Hurley also states that fans beg him to sign their J. Peterman catalogs, reflecting the quasi-literary status of the catalogs as well as the shifting identity of their author-figure (116). This article demonstrates the success of the *Seinfeld* character in making Peterman more likable and more laughable than he appears to be in the catalogs, both increasing J. Peterman's sales and potentially undercutting his colonial mystique. Peterman's appearances during the final three seasons of *Seinfeld* also emphasize the relationship between truth and fiction (Kramer sells his life stories to Elaine for Peterman's autobiography ["The Van Buren Boys," 8014] and then begins a Peterman Reality Tour ["The Muffin Tops," 8021]), as well as the relationship between colonial nostalgia and consumerism (Peterman threatens to fire Elaine because she does not like *The English Patient;* Elaine eats a piece of King Edward and Wallis Simpson's wedding cake that Peterman buys at auction).

In "The Foundation" (8001) and "The Chicken Roaster," (8008) both aired during *Seinfeld*'s eighth season in 1996, Elaine's attempt to run the company in Peterman's absence highlights the roles of gender, race, and colonial nostalgia in the series' J. Peterman parody. In "The Foundation," Peterman puts Elaine in charge of the company when he travels to Myanmar to find new products and to recover from his executive stress. Although Elaine fears that she is not qualified for the position, Kramer inspires her to find strength in her *katra*, or inner spirit, a concept that he adapts from *Star Trek* movies and his karate classes. Filled with false confidence, Elaine begins smoking cigars and shouting orders to her staff, but her Urban Sombrero is an aesthetic and financial disaster. In "The Chicken Roaster," Elaine travels to Myanmar to seek the advice of Peterman, who responds to her catalog cover with the words of Joseph Conrad's Kurtz: "The horror!" While these episodes explicitly parody the imperialist politics of the J. Peterman catalog, they also affirm the superiority of white masculinity in the business world by ridiculing Elaine's attempts to assume power through ethnic borrowing and gender performance.

An early scene in "The Foundation" both affirms and destabilizes Peterman's authority as salesman and symbolic colonizer of the world. Five copywriters (two white women, one black woman, and two white men) sit around Peterman's desk, reading the product ideas inspired by their recent trips to various Third World countries:

> Copywriter: "So I pressed through the rushes, and there, below me, the shimmering waters of Lake Victoria . . ."
> Peterman: Oh, for the love of God, man! Just tell me what the product is!
> Copywriter: It's a washcloth.

This exchange can be read as a joke on the white male copywriter who is trying to sell a washcloth by evoking the colonial trope of the white man's gaze at the landscape from a position of godlike authority. Yet this is also a joke on Peterman, whose stories sell insignificant items at high prices. As Elaine later claims, "I've watched Peterman run the company. I know how to do it. Pair of pants, stupid story, a huge markup." While the copywriter's first-person narrative suggests that Peterman's catalog persona is formed by a set of genre conventions employed by others, the "real" Peterman is divided against himself, split between nostalgia for colonialism and frustration with colonial rhetoric. Although this scene mocks Peterman's politics, the copywriter's failure to replicate Peterman's style establishes Peterman's superiority over imitators and predicts Elaine's failure to represent her boss.

Later in this scene, Elaine presents her idea for the Urban Sombrero, a fictional J. Peterman catalog item that reveals the racial and gender stereotyping in this episode:

> Elaine: Well, Mr. Peterman, I've got a really good idea for a hat. It combines the spirit of Old Mexico with a little big-city panache. I like to call it the Urban Sombrero.
> Peterman: Oh, my neck is one gargantuan monkey fist.
> Elaine: Are you OK, Mr. Peterman?
> Peterman: [Walking to the door.] Go on, go on, go on.
> Elaine: Well, see, it's businessmen taking siestas, you know, it's the Urban Sombrero. [Peterman leaves.] Mr. Peterman?

Like the copywriter's description of a washcloth, this passage mocks Elaine's attempt to replicate Peterman's combination of First and Third World styles. Yet the humorous nature of the Urban Sombrero depends on the type of racial stereo-typing with which Peterman is so often associated. In this passage, Berg and Schaffer juxtapose Peterman's executive stress with the image of the Mexican siesta, evoking a racist distinction between an American work ethic and Mexican laziness. Blurring the boundaries between city and country, First and Third World spaces, wealth and poverty, the Urban Sombrero is doomed as a Peterman product because it fails to maintain the subtle ideological and stylistic distinctions upon which *Seinfeld* and the catalog depend. According to these writers, American men who are struggling to maintain their position in the business world cannot wear a hat that is associated with laziness and with an immigrant drain on the American economy.

Soon after she proposes the Urban Sombrero as a catalog item, Elaine receives a phone call from Peterman asking her to take over the company:

> Elaine: Mr. Peterman, you can't leave.
> Peterman: I've already left, Elaine. I'm in Burma.
> Elaine: Burma?
> Peterman: You'll most likely know it as Myanmar, but it'll always be Burma to me.
>   . . . You there, on the motorbike! Sell me one of your belts!

Although Elaine is initially reluctant to take on Peterman's role as an icon of white masculine world conquest, she is inspired by Kramer's pep talk about *katra,* the "spirit, being, part of you that says 'yes, I can.'" When Jerry jokes that "Sammy Davis had it," he pokes fun at Kramer's attempt to find himself through ethnic borrowing, especially the children's karate classes where he poses in front of a poster of Bruce Lee. If the episode represents Kramer's Orientalism as mis-guided and childish, however, the stakes for Elaine are much higher. Kramer may suffer the ridicule of his friends and the hatred of his karate classmates, but the lesson for Elaine seems clear: as a woman, she is incapable of assuming Peterman's masculine role, however ridiculous and ineffectual he may appear.

As a symbol of Elaine's failure to assume Peterman's authority, the Urban Sombrero reveals the gender differences that are reinforced by the J. Peterman catalog and *Seinfeld.* Whereas the women's clothing in J. Peterman catalogs often combines First and Third World styles (like the Balinese Tee or the Power Caf-tan), the men's clothing is much more traditional than the advertising copy suggests: polo shirts, cotton twill pants, crewneck sweaters, leather jackets. In keeping with the disassociation of straight men from fashion in contemporary America, the catalog goes to great lengths to affirm Peterman's own machismo: an ordinary plaid shirt is "rugged (made for businessmen and warriors)," and it "makes your shoulders look broader." Following the same conventions, *Seinfeld* writers often use the limitations of male fashion as a source of humor. When Elaine dons the Urban Sombrero in Jerry's apartment in order to demonstrate her failure as president of the company, she parodies the moments in which Jerry's straight masculinity is threatened by an unusual or flamboyant piece of clothing: the puffy shirt ("The Puffy Shirt," 5002), the leather jacket with pink-and-white-striped lining ("The Jacket," 2003), the man-fur and the European carryall ("The Reverse Peephole," 9012). Whereas these fashion-related episodes affirm Jerry's straight male identity by mocking the unusual clothes, Lisa Schwarzbaum notes that the costumes in episodes like "The Foundation" emphasize Elaine's femininity: "[Elaine] looks really stylish, really tough, and (in more body-hugging styles) really sexy behind Peterman's desk" (35). These distinctions between male and female style suggest that the Urban Sombrero is ridiculous, and even dangerous, since it associates straight American men with Mexican men and with fashion itself.

The significance of the Urban Sombrero as a dangerous, border-crossing symbol is reflected in the final scene of the episode. Riding on the subway, Elaine overhears a white businessman claim that he woke up from his office nap to find his walking papers pinned to the brim of his Urban Sombrero: "I never thought a hat would destroy my life." Reflecting the limits of male style in the workplace, this anecdote reinforces the racial stereotyping that makes Elaine's fantasy of "businessmen taking siestas" ideologically impossible: in order to distinguish themselves from the immigrant workers who are perceived as threats to white job security, white men cannot nap. Of course, this anecdote is most explicitly a joke on Elaine, whose use of the term "big-city panache" suggests her failure to recognize the dress codes that disassociate white businessmen from ornament or flamboyance. The fact that the businessman's *wife* bought the Urban Sombrero for him reinforces the idea that women's misunderstanding of the male business world is destructive as well as ridiculous.

In the opening scenes of "The Chicken Roaster," Elaine's authority is further compromised by a stereotypically feminine vice, irresponsible shopping, that clarifies her position in the J. Peterman Company's hierarchy. Her reckless spending of company funds gets Elaine into trouble with Ipswich, a J. Peterman accountant who reminds her that she is still subject to orders from above:

> Ipswich: Nothing short of the approval of Peterman himself will save you this time.
> Elaine: But . . . but he's in the Burmese jungle.
> Ipswich: And quite mad, too, from what I hear.
> Elaine: Wait a minute, wait a minute. Can I fire you?
> Ipswich: No.

Despite the fact that Elaine has been named president of the company, she is s̶
subject to the rules of the absent Peterman, the male accountant, and the boa
of directors. While Peterman avoids feminization because his shopping is assoc
ated with world conquest, Elaine's shopping is stigmatized by her feminine irre
sponsibility. Her need for Peterman's approval suggests that her rationality is stil
inferior to his insanity. The fact that Ipswich is African-American complicates
this exchange further, suggesting an affirmative action context underlying
Elaine's inability to fire him. Kramer's offhand comment "You should sleep with
him" is also a bit surprising, considering the lack of racial difference on *Seinfeld*
in general, and among Elaine's many sexual partners in particular; even a boyfriend of ambiguous racial identity in "The Wizard" (9015, aired in 1998) turns
out to be white after all. The suggestion that Elaine may have to sleep with her
inferior in order to keep her job suggests her vulnerable position as a woman in
a man's world, while the threat of interracial sexual activity marks the perverse-
ness of Elaine's presidency according to *Seinfeld*'s conservative racial codes.

Marked by the image of a map of Myanmar and a riff of Oriental-sounding
music, Elaine's trip to find Peterman exemplifies the complex ideological work
performed by *Seinfeld*'s parody of J. Peterman's imperialism. The *Seinfeld* writers'
choice of Myanmar as the site of Peterman's Heart of Darkness is most likely
related to its relatively low-profile status in contemporary American discourses of
postcolonialism, both academic and popular. Yet Peterman's statement that "It'll
always be Burma to me" and Kramer's failure to recognize the name *Myanmar*
allude to a painful history of British colonialism and nationalist, religious, ethnic,
and economic struggle. In his *Historical Dictionary of Myanmar,* Jan Becka claims
that the Third Myanmar Empire was conquered by Britain between 1824 and
1885, when it "became known as Burma and was made a province of British India"
(4). Resistance movements began immediately, but the nation did not declare full
independence until 1948. Originally known as the Union of Burma, the nation's
name was changed in 1989, when the State Law and Order Restoration Council
"issued a ruling whereby the official name of the country in English—Burma—
was altered to Myanmar, which is the transcription of the official name of the
country in the Myanmar language used since independence in 1948" (vii). The
name Myanmar therefore represents national, economic, and religious independence, as well as the affirmation of a native language.

These historical contexts suggest that *Seinfeld*'s humorous representation of
Myanmar as the American man's retreat, the Buddhist temple in the midst of the
jungle, denies the political realities of one of the world's poorest nations. Peterman's insistence on calling the country Burma clearly reflects his nostalgia for the
British empire and his refusal to acknowledge the political victory symbolized by

the name Myanmar. Once again, however, this joke on Peterman is matched by a *Seinfeld* joke that replicates Peterman's dismissive attitude toward national independence. When Kramer asks if Myanmar is "the new discount pharmacy," he demonstrates American ignorance of international politics and the conception of the Third World as a source of cheap products for Western consumption.

Elaine's conversation with the mentally unstable Peterman in the shadowy Myanmar temple affirms the concept of the white man's burden while it mocks Peterman's assumption of power. When Peterman scares a native boy away with a stream of foreign-sounding words, Elaine asks, "You speak Burmese?"

> Peterman: Oh, Elaine. That was gibberish. So did you have any trouble finding the place?
> Elaine: Well, you're the only white poet warlord in the neighborhood.
> Peterman: Are you an assassin?
> Elaine: I . . . I work for your mail-order catalog.
> Peterman: You're an errand girl sent by grocery clerks to collect a bill.

While Peterman's unshaven, sweaty appearance and Elaine's position kneeling at his side evoke images of white colonizers driven insane by the horrors of the jungle, it is Peterman who speaks "gibberish" in this scene, rather than the native people. Peterman's status as "white poet warlord" is also ambiguous: is this Elaine's term, that of the locals, or that of Peterman himself? Satirizing the images of Peterman as warrior in the real-life catalog, this term and the dialogue that follows it link consumerism to violence, as Peterman confuses his copywriter with an assassin.

These lines also allude to Francis Ford Coppola's *Apocalypse Now* (1979) and Joseph Conrad's *Heart of Darkness* (1902), intertextual connections that are reinforced by the last words of the episode: "The horror! The horror!" The phrase *white poet warlord* links Peterman to Coppola's Colonel Kurtz, the former military hero who has isolated himself in an estate in Vietnam, where he is rumored to commit acts of violence against the American government. Although the military sends an American soldier named Willard to kill Colonel Kurtz, a sympathetic photojournalist describes him as "a poet warrior in the classic sense." This connection between Peterman and Kurtz reinforces Peterman's ambiguous relationship to colonialism and his simultaneously admirable and offensive character. In "'Left Alone with America: The Absence of Empire in the Study of American Culture,'" Amy Kaplan suggests that *Apocalypse Now* exemplifies the ambiguities of American imperial texts. Although the film critiques America's actions in Vietnam and links them to British colonialism, Eleanor Coppola's documentary on the making of the film in the Philippines "refuses recognition of the film's complicity with the imperial context that enables its production" (18). While Elaine's presence distinguishes "The Chicken Roaster" (8008) from the virtually all-male world of *Apocalypse Now*, the episode emphasizes her powerlessness and inferiority to men. While Coppola's Willard seeks Kurtz in order to confront and kill him, Elaine seeks Peterman's approval, only to become the object of the episode's final joke: Peterman looks at her Urban Sombrero catalog cover, and gasps "The horror!"

For *Seinfeld* viewers who are familiar with Joseph Conrad's *Heart of Darkness*, one of the best-known texts of British colonial literature, another layer of meaning is added to this scene. The allusion to Conrad's Kurtz, a white man living in the African jungle who manipulates the natives and is worshipped by them, has serious implications for *Seinfeld*'s critique of Peterman's politics. For example, Conrad's description of Kurtz's report to the International Society for the Suppression of Savage Customs resembles many descriptions of the J. Peterman catalog: "This was the unbounded power of eloquence—of words—of burning noble words. There were no practical hints to interrupt the magic current of phrases . . ." (123). This connection suggests that Peterman's eloquent prose may contain the same basic message as Kurtz's report: " 'Exterminate all the brutes!' " (Conrad 123). The last words of this episode, directed simultaneously at Elaine, at Peterman himself, and at the colonial legacy represented by Conrad, suggest that America's love/hate relationship with Peterman places us all in the position of Conrad's Marlowe, the white man whose awareness of colonial exploitation does not mitigate his own fascination with the racial Other.

These connections between *Seinfeld* and *Heart of Darkness* challenge many reviewers' claims that the series successfully avoids racial stereotyping. For example, Jill Rachlin in *Ladies' Home Journal*, claims that "Unlike many comics who poke fun at race, religion, or gender, Seinfeld tries to do upbeat comedy" (68). Comparing Seinfeld to fellow Jewish comedian Howard Stern, who makes explicitly racist jokes, James Wolcott of *The New Yorker* claims suggestively that "*Seinfeld* is a show that could play in a dark room without much being missed" (107), and argues that "the reluctance of the *Seinfeld* team to tackle racial tension until they have the tone right shows tact. Just because some part of the American psyche is gunning for a race war is no reason to rouse more rabble" (109). "The Foundation" (8001) and "The Chicken Roaster" (8008) suggest, however, that *Seinfeld*'s silence about racial issues constitutes a political statement, as does its rewriting of colonial texts as parodies of consumerism and bad taste. When Jerry teases Elaine about going to Mexico for six weeks when she could have been equally inspired by eating a bag of Doritos, he demonstrates what Kaplan calls

"Empire as a Way of Life," making a joke of the cultural difference and long history of political struggle between the United States and Mexico. Although Elaine seems genuinely concerned to expand her cultural horizons and those of her catalog audience, her plea for respect goes unheeded, and Jerry's adolescent humor prevails.

The ending of the *Seinfeld* series in May 1998 and John Peterman's bankruptcy in February 1999 both attracted a great deal of media attention. Ironically, however, the television show that was famous for its sarcasm and emotional detachment ended in a blaze of nostalgia and regret, whereas the demise of the highly nostalgic J. Peterman catalog met with satire and journalistic glee. While a *New Yorker* satire featured Peterman-like copy for the company's wastebaskets, paper, and toner (Kenney 33), a *USA Today* article began with a Peterman-like description of Chapter 11 filing: "He took the hand-rolled linen papers from the weathered goatskin carryall obtained on the last trek to Nepal. As he submitted them to the grub-stained clerk, he solaced himself as he gazed at the verdant Kentucky hills, thinking of little else but happier times with his long-lost Himalayan love" (Strauss, "J. Peterman's Travails" 1B). Several articles in *USA Today* invoked the rhetoric of the Western and the romance novel: "End of the trail at nostalgic retailer J. Peterman" (Strauss, *Seinfeld* 1B), "The Kentucky-based retailer . . . failed to find . . . a white knight" (Strauss, "One Mistake" 2B), "J. Peterman is preparing to ride off into the sunset" ("J. Peterman's Travails" 1B). While the finale of *Seinfeld* was called the end of an era and John Peterman's bankruptcy was regarded as poetic justice, America's fascination with the character of J. Peterman draws attention to the acceptance of First World power that continues to influence the most celebrated popular texts.

ELKE VAN CASSEL (Radboud University Nijmegen)

Getting the Joke, Even If It Is About Nothing

Seinfeld from a European Perspective

Although Jerry, George, Kramer and Elaine never ventured far from New York, and never actually made it to Europe—which is where they were headed in that very last episode—European audiences have been watching *Seinfeld* for some years now. But is the show, which is so typically New York, and so typically American on so many different levels, hitting home with European viewers?

It is beyond a doubt that *Seinfeld* was the most popular American sitcom of the 1990s, an era that it epitomized in many ways, and one of the most successful series in American television history. The show won a great number of awards, and during its final season it was the highest-rated show on American TV. It was also the first TV series to command more than $1 million for a minute of advertising and a record $1.7 million for a 30-second spot during the finale.

The immense popularity of the show is best characterized by the reactions to its conclusion. When Jerry Seinfeld announced that the 1997–1998 season would be the final one, *People* ran a cover story with the following headline: "Say it ain't so! A stunned nation prepares for life without *Seinfeld*."[1] By the time the final episode aired on May 14, 1998, so many articles had been written about the show that the *San Francisco Chronicle* ran a story with the heading "Enough already! In the end, *Seinfeld* was just a TV show." In the article, author John Carman argued that "if this whole *Seinfeld* phenomenon were a woman Jerry would stop dating her. 'It's not that she's so horrible,' he'd whine to George, 'it's just that she won't leave me alone. She's everywhere I go. She's driving me crazy.'"

How very different was the show's reception in the Netherlands. *Seinfeld*— which has been broadcast on Dutch TV since 1994—has received very little attention in the Dutch press. Between 1994 and 1998 only a handful of articles mentioned *Seinfeld*, most of which dealt with the media phenomenon *Seinfeld* had become in the U.S. during its final season rather than the show itself or its reception in the Netherlands. In more recent years, the arrival of Larry David's new show *Curb Your Enthusiasm,* which was broadcast briefly on Dutch TV, generated some publicity for *Seinfeld,* as did the recent release of the first season on DVD.

Stuck away in a very late-night time slot, *Seinfeld* has never really caught on in the Netherlands. After eight years of being broadcast on Dutch television *Seinfeld* has built a loyal audience among Dutch viewers, but the show has never seen high ratings. While *Seinfeld*'s American ratings were record-breaking—*Seinfeld* topped the ratings during both the 1994–1995 and 1997–1998 seasons, and the show's finale had a 41.3 percent rating and 58 percent market share, drawing an estimated 108 million viewers—in the Netherlands the show never reached more than a 1.4 percent rating and 10.2 percent market share in its 11:30 p.m. time slot, an average of 178,052 viewers. The fact that the show also failed to catch on in both Belgium and Germany—where it was broadcast at a similarly late hour—makes one wonder whether *Seinfeld* is perhaps too American for European tastes.

Surrounding *Seinfeld*

There are a number of explanations for the show's failure to catch on with European audiences. First of all, there is the fact that in both the Netherlands and Germany, *Seinfeld* has been moved around the TV schedule too often to secure a sizable audience. In addition to being moved to different time slots and days of the week, the show also changed networks with a frequency impossible for the average viewer to keep up with. In the Netherlands, *Seinfeld* has been broadcast on three different networks, with frequency of broadcast changing from once a week to every day, and a time slot that kept changing from 8 p.m. to 10:30 p.m., to 11:30 p.m., to 11:50 p.m., and finally back to 8 p.m. In Germany, the show was canceled altogether during its first season, after having been moved from a 6:50 p.m. to a 5:45 a.m., and then 11 p.m. time slot. Two years later, in 1998, the show was given a second chance, first at 1:10 a.m., then at 6 p.m., and most recently at 11:45 p.m. (Kracke).

This indecisiveness among European television programmers—who apparently found it difficult to place *Seinfeld*—has certainly not helped increase the show's popularity, but their indecision seems to be more of a consequence than a cause of the lack of interest displayed by the viewers. Both Dutch and German networks did try broadcasting *Seinfeld* at prime time at least once, but apparently the ratings did not increase.

In addition to the frequent changes of time slot and day of broadcast, it is important to note that when broadcast on Dutch television, *Seinfeld* is placed in completely different surroundings. During its first-run broadcasts in the U.S., *Seinfeld* was the headliner of NBC's Thursday night, surrounded by other sitcoms. When first broadcast on Dutch television, *Seinfeld* was surrounded by two action series: *The Sentinel* and *Riptide*.

As part of the research for my 1998 master's thesis—"*Seinfeld* & TV Flow: A Cross-Cultural Exploration of the Workings of TV Flow and Viewers' Perception of *Seinfeld*," I interviewed a number of American and Dutch *Seinfeld* fans. The main goal of my research was to find out what European viewers—watching the show from a perspective so very different from that of their American counterparts—see in *Seinfeld*.[2] In my focus groups, there was a distinct difference in viewing behavior between the Dutch and the American participants. While some of the American participants regularly watched the shows surrounding *Seinfeld*—in one case even starting with *Jeopardy* at 7 p.m. and leaving the TV on until the end of *The Tonight Show* with Jay Leno at 12:30 a.m.—none of the Dutch participants did so. The explanation for this particular difference in viewing behavior lies in the time of broadcast, in the content and genre of the shows surrounding *Seinfeld,* as well as in the placement of commercial breaks, previews, and program segments; in other words, TV flow.

In his 1974 book, *Television: Technology and Cultural Form,* Raymond Williams argued that "flow" is the defining characteristic of the experience of watching TV. What distinguishes TV from other media, Williams argued, is that it is not a discrete event—like a book or a play—or even a sequence of discrete events. Even though a TV schedule is made up of a series of timed units, of discrete events, that is not the way we experience it when we watch TV, and that is not the way the programmers see it when they plan an evening of TV. Williams argued that we experience TV programming as a flow, which is why we talk about watching TV, instead of watching the news or a specific program on TV. This is also why, Williams argued, "many of us find TV very difficult to switch off . . . again and again, even when we have switched on for a particular 'programme,' we find ourselves watching the one after it and the one after that" (88). Williams maintained that commercials, trailers, news flashes and such should not be seen as interruptions of a program, but as part of the whole of the flow that we are watching, because that is the way viewers experience them. Our perception of what we are watching is automatically influenced by what precedes, follows, and "interrupts" the program we are watching.[3]

Williams argued that the flow became more pronounced "when it became important to broadcasting planners to retain viewers—or as they put it, to 'capture' them—for a whole evening's sequence" (85). Trailers are an important aid in keeping people on the same channel for the whole evening's flow. So the more intense the competition with other channels, the more frequent the trailers for the programs that will come on later on in the evening. The flow is built into the television programs themselves as well: "There is a characteristic kind of opening sequence, meant to excite interest, which is in effect a kind of trailer for itself. In American TV, after two or three minutes, this is succeeded by commercials" (86). The impact of this opening sequence has to be strong—an attention grabber—because of the commercial break that follows it.

NBC's Thursday night of "Must-See-TV" is a good example of the programmers' objective to keep the audience tuned in throughout the entire evening. Until the 1998 season, this night was built around the headliners *Friends* and *Seinfeld*. The former aired at 8 p.m., followed by another, less popular sitcom. Then *Seinfeld* aired at 9 p.m., followed by yet another sitcom.

Williams—an Englishman—coined the term "TV flow" after being confronted with American television for the first time, arguing that the different levels of flow manifest in the British and American broadcasting systems corresponded with a difference in the stage of development of the respective television systems, and a difference in the way the function of television is defined in the respective cultures. Whereas in most European countries, television has traditionally been perceived as a public service medium, in the U.S. television is seen primarily as a means to sell products to consumers and consumers to advertisers. This latter interpretation leads to a highly developed ratings system and a high level of TV flow, because the function of TV flow is to make people stay tuned in order to obtain high ratings, which in turn drive up the prices of commercials.

Differences in the historical development of the Dutch and American broadcasting systems have resulted in different levels of TV flow. The main difference between Dutch and American broadcasting systems lies in the manner in which these systems address their viewers. The American system is first and foremost a commercial system, addressing its viewers as consumers living in markets. The Dutch system, like many other European broadcasting systems, addresses its viewers first and foremost as citizens living in communities.[4]

As a result of the different levels of TV flow, Dutch people who visit the U.S. are often shocked by the fast pace of American television broadcasts and the many interruptions of the main program. Americans, on the other hand, may find Dutch television—especially the noncommercial channels—very slow-paced. They may in fact get restless watching an entire movie without commercial interruptions, or they may find it peculiar that the mini-climaxes that usually precede a commercial break (zoom-ins and music building to a crescendo on soap operas and scene changes on sitcoms) are succeeded by the next scene of the program. In the Netherlands, both public and commercial television channels include American programs in their schedules. *Seinfeld* has been broadcast on several different commercial channels since 1994.

To confront the participants with the difference between Dutch and American TV flow and assess their reactions, I showed the Dutch focus groups an episode of *Seinfeld* as broadcast on American television—including American commercial breaks, trailers, news flashes, and parts of the programs preceding and following the show—and I showed the American participants an episode as broadcast on Dutch television.

The American participants noticed right away that on Dutch TV *Seinfeld* was not part of a sitcom lineup but was surrounded by programs of a completely different nature. Not only were they both action series, but *Riptide* was a much older series as well, having been originally broadcast in the 1980s.[5] Some of the American participants noted that this combination of old and new programs looked strange. NBC's Thursday night lineup, they noted, was much more homogeneous in format, the shows being almost interchangeable, not just because they were all sitcoms but also because the situations on which they were based were all similar to each other and because they all looked alike. One of the American participants in fact argued that the look and feel of these different sitcoms—the clothes the characters wear, the colors used on the sets—were very similar. Even the characters were interchangeable, or at least moved back and forth between the different shows; there were guest stars from *Friends* on *Seinfeld* (Courtney Cox), guest stars from *Mad About You* on *Friends* (Helen Hunt), and guest stars from *Friends* and *Seinfeld* on *Mad About You* (Lisa Kudrow and Michael Richards).

The Dutch participants also noticed the difference between the programs surrounding *Seinfeld* on Dutch and on American television, and they all agreed that if the programs surrounding the show on Dutch television were sitcoms instead of action series, they would be more likely to stay tuned.

The lack of coherence of Dutch programming—different types of shows often follow one another seemingly at random—and the fact that time slots and days of broadcast change frequently make Dutch viewers very dependent on the TV listings. The American participants in my focus groups were much better informed about what was on, on which channel, at what time, even though they hardly ever used the TV listings. As one of the Dutch participants noted, on Dutch television, you never know what is coming, because there are hardly any previews or trailers.

Whereas it was almost impossible to escape the announcements for the show that would come on after *Seinfeld* in the American broadcast, the Dutch broadcast included only one announcement for *Riptide*. Dutch television stations usually put a preview for the program that will come on after the commercials right before a commercial break. So, for example, a voiceover tells the viewer that *Seinfeld* is coming on after the commercials; then a short clip from *Seinfeld* is shown, followed by commercials; and then, after the advertisements, *Seinfeld* starts all the way from the beginning, including the clip already seen. The American practice is to put not just a preview, but the first bit of the next program before the commercial break. In addition, the commercial breaks that come on during a certain program will also include trailers or announcements for the show that will follow. On Dutch television there either is no commercial break or, if there is, it will not necessarily include an announcement of the next program to come on.

It is important to note that, in the Dutch broadcast, *Seinfeld* included only one commercial break, while in the American broadcast it included three. In addition, on Dutch television the beginning and end of a commercial break is announced by a very short trailer. One of the American participants noted that this announcement seemed to frame the show more: "This is the beginning of the show, this is the end of the show, you have now watched the show. If you want to watch something else, you can switch channels now. Normally [on American television] there is even a commercial break between the last scene and the credits, so you're not quite sure whether that was really the last scene or not sometimes." This clear separation between the commercial breaks and the show proper indicates a lower level of TV flow.

Dutch viewers, on the other hand, were annoyed by the fact that in the American broadcast commercial breaks came on unannounced, which not only startled them, but also made it difficult to distinguish the program segments from the commercials. Both the American and the Dutch participants agreed that the American broadcast was much more manipulative and geared toward keeping the viewer tuned in. One of the American participants noted: "With American TV, I think that one of the reasons that it does suck you in more is because it is broken up into so many more segments, that when the commercials come on, you're just like: Okay, this is just another set of commercials. While on Dutch TV, because there's not so many of them, when the commercials come on, you're like: Now it's over. You know that the show is over." This is the point where Dutch viewers either switch channels or turn off the TV, whereas American participants admitted they regularly let themselves get sucked in by the next show on NBC.

It seems that by showcasing a program on "Must-See-TV," as part of a sequence of similar programs, by running plenty of trailers, and by "sucking" the viewers in through the manipulative mechanisms of TV flow, American programmers can make almost any show a success. There is, of course, still a certain risk of failure, but it is much smaller than in the Dutch system, where programs are broadcast seemingly at random, the use of trailers is much less aggressive, and viewers have to work hard to find out when and where new shows are being broadcast. In addition, the clear division between program content and commercial breaks make it easier to turn off the TV or switch channels after a program has ended, which means it is much more difficult to introduce Dutch viewers to new programs. This difference in the level of flow, combined with the tendency of the media to pay more attention to new Dutch programs than to new American programs, make it difficult to create hype around a new American show, as so often happens in the U.S. This is, of course, not just true of *Seinfeld*; it is true of any new American show that wants to have a chance of success in the Netherlands.

Cultural Context

The real reason for *Seinfeld*'s failure to succeed in Europe, however, may lie in the different way in which American and European viewers perceive the show. In their study *The Export of Meaning: Cross-Cultural Readings of Dallas* (1990), Tamar Liebes and Elihu Katz note that "media professionals, including researchers," are often "mesmerized by the pervasiveness of American television programs" and "assume blithely that everybody understands them in the same way" (3). Although a number of important cross-cultural comparisons have been published, relatively little is known about the way foreign viewers consume television programs originally designed for an American audience.[6]

In each of my focus groups I asked the participants to describe the plotlines of the episode I showed them, and from their descriptions it was clear that the Dutch participants did not have any trouble understanding the main plot and identifying the show's main themes. But although both Dutch and American participants in my focus groups pointed to trivial everyday problems and relationships as *Seinfeld*'s two central themes, their perception and interpretation of these central themes differed considerably.

"*Seinfeld* is a show about reality," said one of the American participants. The show, she pointed out, is about "nothing in particular, but it's everything about what we deal with every day." These are very accurate descriptions of the show, but it should be noted that reality as portrayed on *Seinfeld* is essentially American. As another of the American participants pointed out, the show's humor is about "the little things people never talk about, but everybody knows about" and the "tacit assumptions about the way people are supposed to act." This participant also wondered "whether an audience from another culture would . . . get some of the jokes. They might, but I could see how specific jokes about breeches in etiquette would be American sort of jokes, things that Americans usually do or take for granted. Maybe in other cultures they don't understand why that's so funny." Another American participant pointed out that *Seinfeld* says a lot about the American character: "I really believe that humor is indicative of social values, what we perceive as funny, what we perceive as being immoral."

Social etiquette, or rather, breeches of social etiquette, social faux pas, are scattered throughout every episode. Striking examples include "The Pick" (4012), which includes both public nose picking and the accidental display of a nipple on a seasons-greeting card; "The Junior Mint" (4019), in which Jerry cannot remember the name of the woman he is dating; and "The Lip Reader" (5006), in which Elaine feigns deafness to avoid having to converse with a cab driver.

Coming to the show from a very different background and with a very different frame of reference than American viewers, Dutch viewers, it seems, do not always comprehend these culturally defined rules regarding social conduct. While American participants stressed their recognition of trivial everyday annoyances and situations, breeches of social etiquette, and dating rules portrayed on the show, Dutch participants emphasized that on *Seinfeld* everything is blown out of proportion, and the humor is often over-the-top.

American participants stressed that *Seinfeld* is not necessarily typically American, but that it might be hard for non-Americans to understand the show's humor. The language barrier could be one of the reasons for this lack of understanding. Some jokes, word jokes and puns especially, are hard to translate, and viewers who have to go by the subtitles will therefore miss out on these kinds of jokes. Some Dutch participants admitted that they missed some of the words and expressions that were not translated in the subtitles. Sometimes, one of the participants pointed out, the laugh track would come on, leaving him to ponder what the joke had been. While in the Netherlands viewers are at least given a chance to listen to the original English dialogue in addition to reading the subtitles, in Germany, France, and many other European nations, where dubbing is common practice, even more of the show's humor is lost in translation.

But the language barrier is only one of the reasons why non-American viewers may not always get the joke. Culture-specific jokes can also be problematic. Foreign viewers who have never been to the U.S., and whose image of the U.S. is for the most part shaped by the media, do not have any practical experience of what life in the U.S., and more specifically in New York, is like. They may view a culture-specific situation, such as trying to order coffee at Starbucks, or culture-specific behavior, such as dating, as funny, but they will not recognize it as part of their own culture.

"I don't think it's as funny if you don't understand the humor," one of the American participants said, "and I think it's definitely American humor." She explained that she had watched the show with a group of French exchange students who had laughed, but mainly because they found the characters funny, not because they really understood what was going on. Another American participant made a similar comment about his parents, who are from India: "I've seen it with my parents and they laugh nonstop at it, but . . . it's external to them." The Dutch participants in my focus groups who had visited the U.S. told me they found *Seinfeld* especially funny because the characters reminded them of Americans they had met. While American viewers seem to recognize themselves in the show and its characters, which they perceive as exaggerated versions of themselves, Dutch viewers perceive both the characters and the situations they get themselves into as innately foreign. Since recognition of the situations and identification with the characters play an important role in viewer understanding and enjoyment of any TV show, it is clear that *Seinfeld*'s potential audience is many times larger in the U.S. than it is in the Netherlands.

The main characters' dating behavior also proved to be especially difficult for Dutch viewers to understand. In the Dutch focus group fervent discussion of the term "dating" and what it entails transpired. Several Dutch participants noted that there is no proper Dutch translation for the term, and some even asked me how it works. "How often do you have to go out with a girl before you have a relationship?" one of them wondered. Another participant said: "You can date for a year and a half, and then you still don't really have a relationship, so I don't really get it." After one such discussion of dating behavior, one of the participants concluded: "It is somewhere in between a conventional relationship, where, after a very short while, you are already seeing a lot of each other, and a one-night stand. It's somewhere in between, so you don't know exactly what to do with it."

The fact that there is no proper Dutch translation for the term "dating" is telling. Dating behavior seems to be very culture-specific and representative of a completely different attitude toward relationships. All of the Dutch participants agreed that the way the characters deal with relationships is typically American. In the Netherlands, several participants pointed out, people do not have casual relationships like they do on *Seinfeld*. "Every episode they have a new one," one participant noted, "and the Dutch audience may not think that is very credible."

Another participant argued that this aspect of the show was really blown out of proportion: "The humor elements are so extreme, that you have a new girlfriend every week, so casual." It is, of course, true that Jerry, George, Elaine, and Kramer frequently dump their dates for very silly reasons, but their dating behavior itself is not as far-fetched as it may seem.

That the fall 1995 issue of the Dutch magazine *Amerika* (1993–2000)—a glossy quarterly with articles about American history, national parks, American cities, and other American phenomena—included a special "Need to Know" section devoted to matters of social etiquette underscores that the Dutch are essentially unfamiliar with many American rules for social behavior. The "Need to Know" section in *Amerika* included such topics as how to behave when Americans invite you to their home, how to do business in the U.S, what not to say in American company, and, of course, dating. Among other things, the section on dating explained the difference between a lunch date and a dinner date, and the possibility of dating more than one person at a time (Goudappel).

Recognition Is Part of the Fun

In *Seinfeld*, as in many other sitcoms, recognition is part of the fun. In laughing at Jerry, George, and Elaine (Kramer, being the odd one out, does not really seem suited for recognition), and the absurd situations they get themselves into, viewers are also laughing at the recognition of these situations, and at the recognition of parts of themselves in the characters. Viewers who do not recognize part of themselves in the characters, their behavior, and the situations they deal with can still enjoy the show but do so on a different level.

Although the Dutch and American participants all recognized relationships as one of *Seinfeld*'s central themes, the Dutch participants did not seem to recognize themselves in the characters' behavior, while the American participants—the women in particular—did. They especially recognized themselves in the hyperanalytical behavior surrounding male/female relationships.

In "The Wife" (5017), one of the episodes I showed my focus groups, Elaine obsesses over the mixed signals she is getting from a guy at the gym, especially after he gives her an inappropriate "open-lip kiss." In the episode, Elaine and Jerry thoroughly dissect the kiss's dynamics and implications:

Elaine: This guy gave me an open-lip kiss.
Jerry: So?

Elaine: So?! We've always just kind of pecked. This one had a totally different dynamic.

Jerry: Really?

Elaine: Yeah. I mean, his upper lip landed flush on my upper lip, but his lower lip landed well below my rim.

Jerry: Ahah . . . Moisture?

Elaine: Yeah, definite moisture.

Jerry: That's an open-lip kiss alright.

Elaine: I think he's giving me a big signal. Maybe he wants to change our relationship?

In response to my questions about this episode, one of the female American participants pointed out: "It's very indicative of how women think. . . . We always do that. Like, he shared his cereal with me, or he bought me a beer. . . . Those are things that will make us think: 'Oh, he must like me.' But of course we're always wrong. I am, anyway."

As we have seen, many of the jokes on *Seinfeld* are culture-specific. One of the American participants in fact pointed out that "maybe there could be a *Seinfeld* in every country. But it would be different for each one because you transfer little idiosyncrasies that fit each individual culture." Another American participant pointed out that a lot of the jokes are about American culture, giving the example of Jerry's opening stand-up comedy bit in "The Wife," in which he talks about Americans fervently obeying dry-cleaning tags, but not paying attention to government warnings. Yet another American participant noted that there are a lot of in-jokes in American sitcoms in general, jokes that are only funny if you know what they are all about. To get these jokes, viewers have to have an understanding not only of the historical, political, and cultural background of the United States; they also have to be aware of many current issues.

Since *Seinfeld* was not picked up by Dutch programmers until 1994, four years after the show started on NBC, the episodes appearing on Dutch television were always a couple of years old. This means that any jokes about current events lost part of their impact and meaning. This is, of course, also true for reruns on American television, but it can be assumed that American viewers will either have seen the episode before or will remember the current event in question more vividly, because it took place closer to home. The fact that episodes which are playful commentary on current affairs in the U.S. are not broadcast until years later explains why non-American viewers miss out on some of the humor of the show, and, therefore, on several of the different levels of meaning of which the show is comprised. For example, in 1997 I watched a rerun of the episode "The Understudy" (6022). This episode initially aired in 1995 and includes a spoof on Tonya

Harding. Jerry's girlfriend, the understudy for Better Midler, exclaims: "Look at my shoelace. I can't do it like this. Please let me start it over!" I have to say that in 1997, the Tonya Harding–Nancy Kerrigan saga, which took place in 1994, was not freshly on my mind. Which is why my American roommate had to explain the joke to me.

Every episode of *Seinfeld* consists of multiple layers of humor. In addition to the most obvious forms of humor, slapstick and visual jokes, there are jokes about social etiquette, political correctness, and the awkward and embarrassing situations the characters get themselves into. There are also funny comments about trivialities and the stuff of everyday life, witticisms about social relationships and dating, sarcasm and self-mockery. In addition, there are jokes that are funny because they are recurrent—"Hello, Newman . . ."; references to current events and pop culture; taboo-breaking comedy ("The Contest," 4010), for example; underlying layers of satire and social criticism; and finally, one-liners, word jokes, and puns. All of these layers are part of the *Seinfeld* experience, but, as my research shows, not all of them are perceived by a foreign audience.

Seinfeld's Peculiar Style of Humor

Why did *Seinfeld* fail to become a hit in Europe, even though other American shows did? Dutch television features a long list of American sitcoms and drama series, and despite the fact that Dutch programs usually take precedence over foreign programs in prime-time slots, shows like *Dallas, Cheers, The Cosby Show,* and *Roseanne* did acquire a permanent place in the prime-time schedule.

It has to be noted that all of these examples were broadcast at a time when Dutch television included only a few different channels—two at the time *Dallas* was first broadcast, and three by the time *Roseanne* appeared on Dutch television in 1989. Because of the limited number of channels, and because Dutch production companies did not have the money or the expertise to equal the high quality of American productions, American sitcoms, soaps, and drama series found a keen audience in the Netherlands. I remember watching *The Cosby Show* with the entire family on Saturday nights. Nowadays, with more than twelve Dutch channels to choose from, and production companies that not only produce their own versions of American genres such as soaps, sitcoms, and drama series, but also come up with completely new concepts, such as *Big Brother,* it is much more difficult to attract a large audience-share.

Friends is a more recent example of an American show that has caught on in a big way in the Netherlands, as it has in many other parts of the world. *Friends,* which owes its universal appeal to its recognizable and lovable characters, its main themes of friendship and relationships, and its well-written jokes, which can be wacky but are never too far-out, resembles a traditional sitcom much more than *Seinfeld* does. It can be argued that the emptiness of modern existence forms the main theme of both series, but where *Friends* tries to convince us that emptiness can be filled with love and friendship, *Seinfeld* exposes the emptiness such relationships themselves can embody. Despite being inspired by *Seinfeld*'s substitute family, a group of single New York friends, *Friends* certainly did not try to emulate the show's motto of "no hugging, no learning."

In addition to this different approach to morals and messages, there is also a great difference between the format of *Seinfeld* and more traditional sitcoms. *Seinfeld* changed the sitcom genre itself, breaking away from the conventional structure of TV sitcoms, which traditionally had no more than seven scenes and one or two plotlines per episode. *Seinfeld* jammed as many as thirty scenes and four plotlines into its 22-minute time slot. Both the show's fast-paced format and its humor, with its focus on trivial everyday problems, little annoyances, and small breeches of social etiquette, blown out of proportion but still very recognizable to an American audience, were derived from Jerry's stand-up comedy routines.

As several participants in my focus groups pointed out, *Seinfeld* has a very specific style of humor that is, in many ways, very American. One of the American participants defined American humor as follows: "Sarcasm has a lot to do with American humor. Puns, plays on words, and then just that sort of humor about everyday kind of things." This participant also felt that humor about trivial, superficial things, humor grounded in stand-up comedy, is very American. As we have already seen, the trivialities of everyday American life are less recognizable to a European audience. In addition, stand-up comedy itself, as a genre, and the type of humor it represents was, until recently, unfamiliar to most Europeans.

It is telling that in Germany, where the show was canceled after its first season in 1996 and was given a second chance in 1998, it was broadcast without Jerry's stand-up bit at the beginning and the end. The programmers decided that the German audience was not prepared for stand-up comedy.[7]

In the Netherlands, stand-up comedy was introduced a little over a decade ago, but has only recently experienced a real breakthrough.[8] Dutch stand-up comedy has now become a performance genre in its own right, inspired by both the American tradition and the Dutch heritage of cabaret, which in turn has received a new impulse from stand-up comedy.[9] Despite this recent success, it is quite clear that at the time when *Seinfeld* was first broadcast in the Netherlands in 1994, not many Dutch people had heard of stand-up comedy, or recognized the format. This is yet another reason why the show failed to attract a sizable audience in the Netherlands.[10]

No Longer Unfamiliar

As we have seen, other American shows have been successful on Dutch television, and there are certain reasons why *Seinfeld* specifically has not caught on. Certain forms of behavior and specific situations portrayed on the show are unfamiliar to European viewers, and so is the type of humor on which the show is based. The many different levels of humor also make it difficult for Dutch viewers to grasp the full meaning of the show, and, as we have seen, they do not tend to recognize themselves in the show's main characters, as American viewers do. Although none of this means they cannot still enjoy the show, it does make it harder for them to become as closely involved with the show as American viewers do.

This was all very true in 1998, when *Seinfeld* came to an end in the U.S., but in just four years, many things have changed. It should be noted, for example, that most of the illustrations of culture-specific situations and behavior that made it difficult for Dutch viewers to recognize themselves in the main characters are no longer valid. Due to recent socioeconomic trends, dating has become much more common in the Netherlands. Women have only recently begun to enter the job market in great numbers, and the difficulty of highly educated women to find a partner is, therefore, only a relatively recent development. During the last couple of years, singles have become a much more visible group, and television series such as *Sex and the City* and *Ally McBeal* have not only familiarized Dutch viewers with American dating behavior but also struck a sympathetic chord. Ordering coffee at Starbucks, another culture-specific situation I used as an example earlier, has not yet become an everyday reality in the Netherlands, but recent years have seen an incursion of Starbucks-like coffee places in the larger Dutch cities. As I have already pointed out, stand-up comedy has become a big success in the Netherlands during the last couple of years and is no longer a form of humor unfamiliar to Dutch viewers.

In addition, Raymond Williams's assertion that the level of TV flow is linked to the development stage of a particular broadcasting system is substantiated by recent developments in the Netherlands. Since the introduction of the dual broadcasting system in 1995, eight new commercial channels have appeared on Dutch television, and mergers as well as divisions are still the order of the day. The recent upsurge of digital television has given viewers even more choice. Among the new commercial channels, competition is fierce, and, for the first time in Dutch broadcast history, the public channels are being scrutinized for disregarding the ratings as well. The public channels have lost so many viewers to the commercial channels that their composition and function have come under attack. These recent developments have led to a higher level of TV flow on both the commercial and public channels. Programmers are more aware of the need to suck viewers in and bind them to one channel for more than one program. As a result, the number of trailers has increased, and so has the coherence of programming. One of the commercial channels has had great success with a special women's night cantered around such shows as *Ally McBeal, Sex and the City, Desperate Housewives, Gilmore Girls,* and *Will & Grace.*

It seems fair to conclude that in many ways, and especially where socioeconomic developments are concerned, Dutch society is some years behind the U.S., but may be developing in a similar direction. Had *Seinfeld* been introduced in the Netherlands only recently, instead of in 1994, it may have had a much better chance at success, hitting home with programmers as well as the Dutch viewing public.[11]

Notes

1. *People Weekly* (January 12, 1998).

2. Although my research method was qualitative rather than quantitative—I worked with a small group of interviewees and my findings are certainly not representative of the American or the Dutch population at large—I do feel that individual viewers' experiences can provide some interesting insights into the perception of *Seinfeld* from a European perspective. All of the participants were between 18 and 30 years of age. As a group, the American participants were slightly younger than the Dutch participants. The division of male and female participants was 60/40 for both the American and Dutch focus groups. On average, the Dutch participants had been watching *Seinfeld* for three years, while the American participants had been watching the show an average of five years. *Seinfeld* was first broadcast on Dutch television in 1994. During the 1997–1998 season, the Dutch participants watched the show an average of once a month, while the American participants watched the show an average of once a week.

3. Some of Williams's assertions have been called into question, or adapted by subsequent researchers. See specifically the following articles: Rick Altman, "Television/ Sound"; Klaus Bruhn Jensen, "Reception as Flow: The 'New Television Viewer' Revisited"; Tania Modleski, "The Rhythms of Reception: Daytime Television and Women's Work." Williams did not, for example, take into consideration the fact that viewers switch channels, or tape their favorite shows, fast-forwarding through the commercials; in other words, the relative power of television and its viewers was reconsidered. Despite these questions and doubts, however, Williams's basic concept of TV as flow still stands.

4. Despite numerous initiatives to introduce commercial channels to supplement the noncommercial public channels—Dutch television started out with one public channel in

1951, a second one was added in 1964, and a third one in 1988—it was not until 1995 that the singular public broadcasting system was replaced by a dual system consisting of both public and commercial channels. To clarify, Dutch public television includes commercials broadcast by an organization that is separate from the organization responsible for the actual programming. The commercials finance the programming but are not aimed at making a profit. The revenues from the commercials go to the government, which in turn subsidizes the public channels. The commercial channels, on the other hand, do strive to make a profit from the commercials they broadcast. For these commercial channels, high ratings are an important objective, because high ratings sell advertising time.

5. *Riptide* aired from 1984 till 1986, and *The Sentinel* aired from 1996 till 1999.

6. Although not complete, the following list includes a significant sample: Ang, *Watching Dallas: Soap Opera and the Melodramatic Imagination* and "(Not) Coming to Terms with *Dallas*"; Liebes and Katz, *The Export of Meaning: Cross-Cultural Readings of Dallas*; Payne and Peake, "Cultural Diffusion: The Role of U.S. TV in Iceland"; Pingree et al., "Television Structures and Adolescent Viewing Patterns: A Swedish-American Comparison"; Weimann, "Images of Life in America: The Impact of American TV in Israel"; Wilhoit and de Bock, *Archie Bunker Goes to Holland: Selective Exposure and Perception in the Dutch Television Audience*.

7. In order to prevent the show from failing a second time, the programmers also decided not to broadcast a number of episodes that they considered too "*Seinfeldtypisch*." They wanted the audience to get used to the show's characters and humor first, before exposing them to anything too strange and unfamiliar, because, they pointed out, "German humor is very different from American humor." The result, however, was that many of the recurrent jokes and references to earlier episodes were lost to the viewers, because the episodes were not broadcast in the original order. Torsten Kracke, "Seinfeld," *epguides.de*, 2002, http://www.epguides.de/seinfeld.htm, December 18, 2002.

8. In 1990, Raoul Heertje introduced stand-up comedy in the Netherlands. He gathered a group of performers around him, and together they formed the Comedytrain. This group tried to fuse stand-up comedy with the more traditional Dutch genre of cabaret. The Netherlands has a long tradition of cabaret, a form of theatrical performance that has its origin in the French *cabaret artistique*, which originated in Paris at the beginning of the twentieth century. The original French form included songs about social abuses and everyday life, which in the Dutch variation were combined with sketches and spoken word. The biggest difference between stand-up comedy and Dutch cabaret lies in the fact that whereas stand-up comedians perform mainly in bars and clubs, thrive on interaction with their audience, and try to stay as close to their own everyday experience as possible, in modern Dutch cabaret satirical jokes and social criticism are embedded in a dramatic performance with a clear moral and working toward a climax. The performance takes place in a theater, where the audience is largely passive, and the performers characters and songs to convey their message, which is often based on social criticism (Schumacher).

9. The fact that stand-up comedy has now truly caught on in the Netherlands is best illustrated by the fact that in 2002 the theatrical production *Lenny Bruce*—a play about the life of stand-up comedian Lenny Bruce, performed by Holland's first and most acclaimed stand-up comedian, Raoul Heertje—drew full houses all over the country, and received very good reviews as well. In addition, more and more stand-up comedians are appearing

on Dutch television, not yet with their own sitcoms, but in satirical shows on current events.

10. Although Dutch television features a long list of American sitcoms and drama series, success is never a given, not even for top-of-the-bill series. *The West Wing*, for example, was canceled completely after the first two seasons failed to attract a sizable audience, and although it has recently been given a second chance on a different channel, the day and time of broadcast—Sunday at 12:15 a.m.—will surely keep its audience small. *The Sopranos* was also canceled after its first two seasons failed to produce good ratings. It did, however, attract media attention and was granted a restart on a different network, where it acquired a cult following. *The West Wing* is a good example of a series that is too American for European tastes, both in content and appeal. Dutch viewers would need an extensive manual just to understand the characters' job descriptions and motivations. Both *The West Wing* and *The Sopranos* owe their critical acclaim largely to their subtlety and complexity, qualities that make their potential Dutch audience too much of a niche for programmers to consider profitable.

11. Since March 3, 2003, one of the smaller Dutch commercial television channels has been broadcasting *Seinfeld* at 8 p.m. every workday. The show is once again preceded by such action series as *The Sentinel* or *The Pretender* and is usually followed by a movie (mainly older action movies). The show does not, however, usually draw a big audience. The average rating during the first two weeks of March 2003 was 0.9 percent, equaling 131,310 actual viewers. As could be expected, the ratings were highest for 20-to-34-year old men, 1.75 percent, which equals 28,595 actual viewers (Source for these figures: *Stichting Kijkonderzoek*. www.kijkonderzoek.nl, March 14, 2003). In this early evening slot on one of the smallest Dutch commercial channels, *Seinfeld* is actually reaching fewer viewers than it was in its late-night time slot a couple of years earlier. This seems to be due in part to the fact that in this particular time slot the show is in direct competition with the evening news. The most important complicating factor, however, lies in the fact that *Seinfeld* is no longer a new show. There are no new episodes being produced. Therefore, *Seinfeld* no longer generates news, and the Dutch media no longer deem the show worthy of extensive coverage.

MICHAEL M. EPSTEIN (Southwestern University School of Law)
MARK C. ROGERS (Walsh University)
JIMMIE L. REEVES (Texas Tech University)

From Must-See-TV to Branded Counterprogramming: Seinfeld and Syndication

Television's capacity to make its history and evolution continuously available (even to younger members of its universal audience) is surely without precedent, for the system of reruns has now reached the point of transforming television into a continuous, living museum which displays for daily or weekly consumption texts from every stage of the medium's past.

—David Thorburn (602)

Thorburn's words, embedded in one of the most influential academic essays ever written about popular television, serve as inspiration for our investigation of *Seinfeld* in syndication.[1] When Thorburn wrote these words in the mid-1970s, Ted Turner was still waiting on the FCC to approve his superstation concept, and the launching of Nick-at-Nite was a decade in the future. If anything, then, Thorburn's insights about "television's capacity to make its history and evolution continuously available" are even more relevant today. Thorburn reminds us that grasping the cultural and historical significance of a benchmark series like *Seinfeld* means appreciating its place in "television's continuous, living museum." Though *Seinfeld*'s novelty value as the stuff fueling Friday-morning watercooler conversation may, indeed, have been depleted by its initial prime-time run on NBC, its worth as both communication and commodity is far from exhausted. In television's "system of reruns" (Thorburn), *Seinfeld* still generates big ratings numbers (Galloway). But, as we hope to demonstrate, in moving from network prime time to "off-network syndication," *Seinfeld*'s commodity value has experienced radical transformations. No longer a tent pole for NBC's "Must-See-TV" franchise, *Seinfeld* in syndication has become branded counterprogramming. Ironically, as such, *Seinfeld* would eventually undermine the very network that once gave it such a prominent place in its prime-time schedule.

By the time *Seinfeld* entered into negotiations for its first cycle of syndication licenses in 1993, the off-network syndication marketplace, which had once been a revenue backwater, had grown into a tidal wave of profitability for the television industry. As a hostile alternative to networking, syndication—in the years before the consolidation mania instigated by the FCC's deregulatory agenda in the late 1990s—involved the licensing of programs to individual stations (or cable channels) for a limited time. Where networks provided their far-flung affiliate stations with an entire schedule of programs, anti-consolidation syndicators dealt with their client stations/channels on a program-by-program basis. The financial arrangements in networking and syndication were also significantly different. Traditional broadcast networks paid their affiliates "compensation" to carry the schedule of programs. In addition to compensation, affiliate stations were also provided spots within the network schedule (called adjacencies) that could then be sold to local or national advertisers. Syndicators, in stark contrast, required compensation from their client stations for the right to carry the programming. This compensation took two forms: cash and barter (airing advertising spots embedded in the program that have been pre-sold by the syndicator) (De Moraes; Walley).

Since the 1950s, syndication has been the final resting ground for movies. After all the other revenue streams for a movie have dried up, the movie will, typically, be bundled with others and sold in a package to a cable channel or broadcast station. In addition to movies, two other forms of syndicated programming have appeared. The first is original programming produced exclusively for the syndicated market. Game shows like *Jeopardy!* and *Wheel of Fortune,* talk shows as different as *The Oprah Winfrey Show* and *The Jerry Springer Show,* and magazine shows such as *Entertainment Tonight* and *Access Hollywood* are the most common types of first-run syndicated programming. First-run series are generally stripped (that is, run every weekday in the same time slot). Since the success of the syndicated *Star Trek: The Next Generation* in the late 1980s and early 1990s, weekly original programming, particularly of science fiction or fantasy-oriented dramas, has become more prevalent ("Getting the Picture"). *Seinfeld* is an example of another type of syndication: off-network syndicated programming. Series popular enough to have relatively long lives on network TV achieve a second life as syndicated reruns. Usually, a show needs to accumulate at least 100 episodes or four full seasons before entering off-network syndication. Situation comedies generally do better than dramas in this market, as they tend to be more episodic and less serial. They can be run in any order, and do not require regular viewing (Garron).

Early Television Syndication

In the 1950s and early 1960s, networks primarily focused on a show's network run because, with more than 90 percent of the television audience watching ABC, CBS, and NBC, the initial airings generated the big advertising revenue. In most cases, the shows with the best brand identification, including genre-defining programs such as *I Love Lucy* (1951–57), *Bonanza* (1959–73), and *Perry Mason* (1957–66), became icons of popular culture through hugely popular, long runs on the networks. Since networks largely controlled a show's popularity and lifespan, there was little incentive to promote off-net syndication on independent stations, at least through the early '60s. For one thing, independent stations did not have a lot of money for the same reason that the networks were flush: audiences were generally miniscule compared to network viewership, especially during early fringe, prime time, and late night (Garron; "Getting the Picture"). Moreover, the technology of distribution was not cost-effective in the early days of television. In order to syndicate a program in local markets, traveling salesmen needed to swing through hundreds of local stations, market by market, often with film stock in hand, in order to make their sales presentations. For the most part, networks could avoid this costly and cumbersome routine by offering their best shows to their own affiliates or selectively airing them out of prime time as reruns on their own schedules. Keeping these reruns within the family also helped prevent audience erosion from the local stations that formed the network (Epstein 42, 48).

Because networks were permitted to have ownership interests in their entertainment programming back then, the big three nets were able to use their economic clout to acquire equity and syndication rights in the shows they aired from independent creators and studios. A network could therefore require a producer to relinquish all or part of its financial and syndication interests to the network as a condition for placement on the national schedule. Studios and other independents had little option but to agree, since the only way to get national distribution for their programming was to get it placed on one of the three networks (Boliek).

In an effort to consolidate their power, the nets created subsidiaries that managed the syndication process, forcing independent creators to contract with these subsidiaries and stifling competition among syndicators allied either with a different network or independent of the nets altogether. The result of this effort was that networks exercised complete control over the branding of shows that aired nationally, not only choosing shows for their networks, but also exerting control over the show's production contracts, the length of a show's run, and whether a show would even be permitted to rerun in syndication. Networks could decide that a popular program no longer on the network would not be made available for syndication, a strategy that became known as warehousing, for reasons having nothing to do with that show's potential profitability in the marketplace, to the detriment of the interests of the studios and producers who created the content (Brennan).

By 1970, complaints by independent producers, coupled with a governmental concern that anticompetitive network conduct was harming programming diversity, prompted the Federal Communications Commission to promulgate new rules that prevented networks from syndicating shows to independent stations and prohibited the nets from having a financial stake in the entertainment shows they aired. Known as the Financial Interest and Syndication Rules, or "Fin-Syn," the new regulations effectively ended network participation in the syndication marketplace (FCC, Fin-Syn).[2] Networks were required to divest themselves of programs they owned and spun off their syndication subsidiaries, including CBS's successful syndication venture, which became known as Viacom in 1971 (McClintock). At the same time, the FCC issued the Primetime Access Rule (PTAR), forbidding networks from airing programming from 7 to 8 p.m. weeknights (FCC, Primetime Access Rule). While the rule was intended to promote local programming on network affiliates, PTAR effectively gave Viacom and its fledgling independent competitors an opportunity to sell syndicated programming during a lucrative day part—following nightly news—which had once been highly prized by network programmers (Brennan).

The Syndication Revolution

Although Fin-Syn and PTAR were part of an effort by the FCC to curb network dominance that had begun in the 1930s, they couldn't have come at a worse time for the big three networks. By the early 1970s, the seeds of economic change were already becoming apparent in the industry. CBS, no longer content to offer programs without regard to demographics, conducted what has since become known as its rural purge, canceling popular rural situation comedies such as *The Beverly Hillbillies* (1962–71), *Green Acres* (1965–71), and *Petticoat Junction* (1963–70) because not enough young people watched them, despite overall high ratings. While the nets briefly flirted with a largely unsuccessful effort to bring "social relevancy" to their prime-time schedules, the emergence of cable television as an alternative provider of content—symbolized by the birth of a small company known as Home Box Office in 1972, became an even bigger threat to network dominance. As cable grew more competitive in the 1970s, the combined network audience plummeted, a trend that continues to this day. By 1990, the big three networks attracted about 60 percent of the prime-time audience (Lowry). In 2003, fewer than 40 percent of American viewers watched network programming as once-loyal consumers turned to digital cable, satellite, and a maturing market for videos and DVDs.

Spurred on by the enormous success of *Star Trek* in the early 1970s, show creators, usually studios, and newly independent syndicators teamed up to offer off-net reruns to local independent stations that were beginning to attract larger audiences. The fact that Paramount's *Star Trek* (1966–69) and Fox's *M*A*S*H* (1972–83), which would later become the most popular off-network syndicated program of the decade, appealed to younger viewers only enhanced their profitability for both syndicators and the local stations, each of whom could sell their respective advertising time at premium rates. Indeed, with *M*A*S*H*, studio owners realized that they could rerun banked episodes of a long-running program even while new episodes were still being produced for the network, essentially cashing in on a show's continued popularity with network viewers and enjoying the benefits of network efforts to maintain audience interest through promotional efforts (Dempsey).

With the proliferation of new cable channels in the 1980s and 1990s, the syndication market matured into the television industry's most profitable sector. The annual convention of the National Association of Television Programming Executives (NATPE) became a showcase for every type of syndicated fare and would eventually rival the National Association of Broadcasters (NAB) as a mandatory industry gathering. However, ownership consolidation has had a devastating impact on NATPE; in an age when syndication decisions are made by large station groups, attendance at the annual NATPE convention is now only relevant to a rather small number of suits in upper levels of management comprising a shrinking number of big fish. Even so, prior to the age of consolidation, more channels in the marketplace meant greater competition—and higher licensing fees—for syndicated shows as cable channels and independent broadcasters turned to studios for content to fill their schedules. In addition to developing a burgeoning first-run syndication marketplace, studios continued to leverage the popularity of their shows' network runs both to command huge fees from the big stations and, at the same time, to sell national syndication rights to cable channels such as TNT and FX. More cable channels also increased the demand for older programs that had lost most of their syndication value through repetition or over-exposure, as channels such as Nick-at-Nite and TV Land began to air lesser-known programs like *The Donna Reed Show* (1958–66) and *Car 54, Where are You?* (1961–63), in addition to well-worn staples like *The Andy Griffith Show* (1960–68) and *Bewitched* (1964–72) (Robb 37).

So, in years prior to the end of Fin-Syn and the advent of consolidation, one major consequence of all these changes in the television industry was a hierarchy of brand building that was then controlled by the studios and producers who created programming content. While networks once controlled the branding of television shows, under Fin-Syn they had become merely a phase in the brand-building process, essentially an incubator for content owners to promote programs nationally and nurture audience interest so that a show would later succeed in syndication. When Fin-Syn was rescinded in the 1990s, allowing networks to compete with studios and syndicators, the FCC and the courts recognized what has become the new reality of the television marketplace: the future of television lies in syndication—and content providers are the new royalty in the thousand-channel universe (FCC, *Report*). This is still the case in our current age of consolidation, but networks, or the conglomerates that own them, now generally either insist on an equity interest from an independent creator or own the program outright.

Off-Network *Seinfeld*

Although *Seinfeld*'s experience in off-network syndication was unusual for a number of reasons, it still stands as a reminder of the way the television business operated in the late cable era (before consolidation would re-write the operating rules of the business). This case study, then, is meant to show how the syndication history of *Seinfeld* speaks not only to the way things were, but also, to the way things have become in the always changing business of television. Because it began as a mid-season replacement, the show was somewhat slow to reach 100 episodes. The pilot episode of the show (then called *The Seinfeld Chronicles*) aired as a summer replacement in 1989, and both its first and second seasons were short-run mid-season replacements, with four episodes airing in May and June 1990, and twelve airing from January to June 1991. *Seinfeld* was renewed for a full season for the 1991–1992 season. Because of its gradual introduction, the show did not reach 100 episodes until its sixth season in 1994–1995. The 110 episodes of *Seinfeld* produced by Castle Rock Entertainment were sold into syndication by syndicator Columbia TriStar Television Distribution beginning in fall 1995. In this first syndication window, Columbia TriStar and Castle Rock earned between $2.5 and $3 million per episode. While this was slightly below what rival Buena Vista Television's *Home Improvement* got ($3 million per episode), *Seinfeld* set a record by reaching 220 stations, covering 99 percent of the United States (Smith).

In addition to the massive cash payments, Columbia TriStar also received as much as an additional $1 million per episode in barter income. Under barter syndication, the syndicator retains the right to sell some of the advertising on a program on a national basis. In *Seinfeld*'s case the syndicated episodes contained five minutes of advertising for the local station to sell and one minute that was retained by the syndicator (Walley). As is customary, time was shaved off the original network *Seinfeld* episodes to make room for the barter advertising. Jerry Seinfeld himself supervised this trimming; most of the deleted sections came from the stand-up comedy interludes that opened or closed the show (Smith).

Seinfeld proved to be a rare commodity among network shows. Despite the fact that it was syndicated five days a week in most markets, ratings for the new network episodes did not decline substantially. A 1995 survey by BJK&E Media indicated that 82 percent of the off-network programs entering their first syndication window lost network viewers. For example, ABC's *Home Improvement*, which entered syndication at the same time as *Seinfeld*, saw its network ratings decline by about 15 percent. By contrast, *Seinfeld*'s 1995–1996 network ratings actually improved (Winship).

The second unusual aspect of *Seinfeld*'s syndication was its performance in its second syndication cycle. The initial window length was dependent on the longevity of the show's run on NBC. When it was announced that *Seinfeld* would end after the 1997–1998 season, the widespread interest in the series' finale put Columbia TriStar in a strong position to sell the show in a second syndication window beginning in spring 2001. By mid-1998, Columbia TriStar had locked up most of its renewals through 2006. While most programs have saturated the market somewhat by the time they reach their second syndication period, *Seinfeld*'s syndication fees actually rose in most markets, and Columbia Tri-Star's overall take rose to more than $4 million an episode with as much as an additional $1.5 million in barter income. The only show that had previously increased its revenue substantially in its second cycle was *M*A*S*H* (Dempsey and Littleton; Littleton).

Much of the increase in the license fee is attributable to competition among broadcast stations. In New York, for example, the Fox-owned and operated station WNYW paid a premium to steal the show away from rival WPIX. Its performance for WPIX had been extraordinary, allowing the Tribune Media–owned WB affiliate to beat out the three local newscasts in the 11 p.m. 1998 timeslot.

The new fee (between $250,000–300,000 per week) doubled what WPIX had been paying (Littleton).

The increased second cycle license fees are more surprising in light of the fact that the broadcast stations would have to share *Seinfeld* with a cable outlet. In September 1998, just a few months after *Seinfeld*'s ratings-bonanza finale, Columbia TriStar auctioned the rights to an exclusive four-year cable window. Castle Rock's sibling company, TBS, purchased the rights to the 180 episodes for $180 million; Columbia TriStar still retained one minute of barter time (Cooper).

In Los Angeles, the second cycle competition was even stranger. KCOP, a station owned by the Chris Craft/United group, outbid competitors KTLA (who had the show's first cycle rights) and KTTV, another Fox-owned and operated station. KCOP paid $315,000 per week, doubling what KTLA had paid. In addition, this broke what had been a virtual law at Chris Craft/United stations not to purchase any syndicated programming that would be simultaneously available on a cable outlet (Davies).

Seinfeld as Counterprogramming

As an offbeat example of how the series was deployed as counterprogramming, consider the case of *Seinfeld*'s first cycle in syndication in Lubbock, Texas. In 1995, the series was acquired by Lubbock's CBS affiliate, KLBK, which at that time was managed by Mr. Rick Lipps. Lipps scheduled *Seinfeld* for 4 p.m. weekdays. Sandwiched in the slot between Maury Povich's afternoon talkfest and *Jeopardy!*, *Seinfeld* seemed to stick out like a bagel on a plate of tacos. The scheduling was an incongruity that seemed to run counter to one of the key concepts of programming—control of flow. According to this concept, shows should be arranged on the schedule in an order that encourages what programmers term "flow through." This goal is usually achieved by putting together a sequence of shows with similar appeals that are aimed at roughly the same audience. Furthermore, scheduling *Seinfeld* at a time when so many adults were still at work seemed to violate a second cardinal concept of the programming game—that is, compatibility. Simply put, compatibility means conforming the schedule to the logic of the routines of everyday life. Lipps's decision to run the adult-oriented sitcom at 4 p.m. seemed, on the face of it, to be about as logical as scheduling *Sesame Street* at midnight. In fact, according to Nielsen's May 1996 *Report on Syndicated Programming*, of the 194 markets carrying *Seinfeld* in syndication, only two scheduled the program earlier than KLBK. Most of the other markets either put the show in the prime access slot (the thirty-minute period just before prime time) or aired it post–prime time (Lipps).

Although local general managers are usually not punished for the network's misfortunes and mistakes, they are held accountable for the profits and losses generated by the parts of the broadcast day that they schedule. In fact, syndication decisions can make or break a station manager. Lipps knew of several stations that had to be sold and people who lost their jobs because of a bad decision on syndicated programming. Because of the soaring costs of acquiring first-run and off-network syndicated programs, a mistake can mean the difference between a small market station showing a profit or a loss at the end of the fiscal year. In the Lubbock market, the cost of acquiring a quality off-network program like *Seinfeld* was between $75,000 and $100,000 per year. According to Lipps, the cost of syndicated programming accounted for well over 10 percent of KLBK's operating budget.

In fact, a local station manager's worst nightmare is to acquire a syndicated program that does not take off in the local market. This means that a manager may be forced to shelve the program—which means that although it is taken off the air, it is still part of the station's inventory and the station still pays the syndicator the price agreed upon in the contract as if it were still on the air. As Lipps puts it, "TV programs are inventory, and you have to have inventory control." Lipps gave several examples of shows that did not work in the Lubbock market and have cost local stations hundreds of thousands of dollars a year: *Married . . . with Children* (1987–97), *Roseanne* (1988–97), and *Empty Nest* (1988–95) (Lipps).

Lipps was initially attracted to *Seinfeld* because of David Letterman's horrendous showing in the Lubbock metro market. According to the Neilsen's February 1996 *Station Index*, Letterman ranked a dismal fourth place at 10:30 p.m. with a 7 rating and 15 share, trailing NBC's *The Tonight Show* (12 rating/27 share), off-network syndicated episodes of *M*A*S*H* (8 rating/19 share) on the ABC affiliate (KAMC), and *Cheers* (7 rating/16 share) on the Fox affiliate (KJTV). Lipps figured that *Seinfeld* would definitely do better than Letterman. But Lipps's scheme to push Letterman back and run *Seinfeld* at 10:30 p.m. was foiled by a set of events that were out of his control (Lipps).

Lipps started seriously considering acquiring the series in March, April, and May of '95 because it hadn't yet been cleared in the Lubbock market. Like Lipps, all of the other stations in the market considered *Seinfeld* to be a 10:30 p.m. show. The NBC affiliate couldn't schedule it at 10:30 p.m. because of *The Tonight Show*. The management of the Fox affiliate had too many shows on the shelf and was not convinced *Seinfeld* would work in Lubbock. The ABC affiliate had even worse inventory problems, and *M*A*S*H* had become something of a local institution in its 10:30 p.m. slot. According to Lipps, "Nobody wanted to commit to an earlier time slot. I just lucked out. I thought it was the perfect 10:30 show, and we got it for a decent price."

However, soon after Lipps acquired *Seinfeld,* the Bank of America sold KLBK to Petracom, which took over the station in August 1995. When the station changed hands, Petracom worked out a new affiliation agreement with CBS in which it was able to get an increase in network compensation (what the network paid KLBK for carrying CBS's commercials). But to Lipps's dismay, there was also a provision in the new agreement that required KLBK to continue running all network programming in their current time slots. Since KLBK was airing Letterman live, he was contractually prevented from scheduling *Seinfeld* in the 10:30 p.m. slot (Lipps).

This put Lipps in a terrific bind because of other contractual arrangements. Quoting Lipps:

> All of sudden with 30 or 45 days to go before the start of the season, we had to come up with a place for *Seinfeld.* It was too expensive to have on the shelf. I definitely hit the panic button. I have a contract until 2002 to run *Wheel of Fortune* at 6:30. And it's doing well in that time slot. And *Jeopardy!,* we just kind of piggybacked on the *Wheel of Fortune* contract because they're both sold by King World. It was at five o'clock. But I had a provision that if I ever started a five o'clock news, I could push *Jeopardy* back to 4:30. But that was it. The new ownership wanted a five o'clock news, as I did. So that dropped *Jeopardy!* to 4:30. I had *Maury Povich* 3 to 4. I was actually fortunate I had a half hour at 4. *Full House* was in that slot, but it had run its course. So we put *Seinfeld* in there and the national rep firm, the buyers, and everybody said, "Whoa!" Even my new owners said, "It's just gonna be a loss."

To everyone's surprise, *Seinfeld* was actually a success in the 4 p.m. slot. Winning its time slot, it took viewers away from *Oprah,* increased the ratings across demographic groups for the station, and, from Lipps's point of view, was much more valuable than *Povich* or *Jeopardy!*

According to Lipps, the unexpected success of *Seinfeld* at 4 p.m. was primarily attributable to the quality of the show. But he also argued that this success illustrated how conventional programming wisdom no longer applied in the age of "appointment TV":

> It used to be that what everybody preached in programming was flow, flow, flow. They used to say that you could break away from flow at 5 because there were so many new viewers or you could at 10:30, or maybe 3 in the afternoon because kids

were coming home. But other than that you needed flow. Now flow is not nearly as important. People still preach it, teach it, and talk about it, but I've seen it's not nearly as important. I mean how would going from a trash talk show, to a *Seinfeld*, to a 35-plus *Jeopardy!* to the news—how would all that work in terms of flow? And it does work . . . it has become appointment television. People watch *Seinfeld* at 4, then watch the last half hour of *Oprah* and then turn over to KCBD's news, then watch Peter Jennings on ABC, then come back to KLBK for *Wheel of Fortune* at 6:30, etc. With the remote control it's not the hassle of walking twelve feet to turn the channels. So, if you have a good show, people will put it in their mental appointment book, and they'll watch it.

In the second cycle of syndication, *Seinfeld* would move to the Fox affiliate in the Lubbock market and would be scheduled at 10 p.m., counterprogramming the late local newscasts on the major network affiliates.

Indeed, even after consolidation had become the watchword in the industry, *Seinfeld* continued to be used as an avatar of branded counterprogramming. Consider, for example, the programming patterns that emerged at the beginning of *Seinfeld*'s second syndication cycle, in 2002. In the top 25 markets nationally, *Seinfeld* did not appear on affiliates of any of the three traditional broadcast networks. Instead, *Seinfeld* appeared on fifteen Fox affiliates, five WB affiliates, four UPN affiliates, and two independent stations. The independents were WTBS (the original superstation) in Atlanta, and KDFI in Dallas–Fort Worth. KDFI shared the show with its sister station, KDFW. Although only KDFW was a Fox affiliate, both stations were owned and operated by Fox. On all of these stations, *Seinfeld* was stripped (shown every weekday). Many of the stations also had the right to air *Seinfeld* during the weekend. In every market, it appeared twice daily during the week. Usually the first episode was shown during the early fringe period (7–8 p.m. EST), where it competed with other syndicated programming or local news. The second episode was generally shown between 10 p.m. and midnight, where it competed against local news or network late-night programming.

Because the Fox network does not program from 10 to 11 p.m., most Fox stations run local news in that slot. Nine of the fifteen Fox stations ran *Seinfeld* opposite local CBS/ABC/NBC news at 11 p.m. The remaining stations mostly used the late airing to compete against the late-night talk shows of the three traditional networks. Most UPN and WB stations did not have local news; six of the nine stations from these netlets used *Seinfeld* against local Fox newscasts. An additional two of these stations ran *Seinfeld* opposite traditional local newscasts.

The situation of the independents varied. KDFI and KDFW were the only major market stations that ran *Seinfeld* only once a day, and they ran it twice daily between them. KDFW had the later episode, at 10:30 p.m. CST, which it used to compete against the traditional networks' late-night programming. KDFI showed *Seinfeld* at 6:30 p.m, the end of early fringe and a time when it didn't compete with the local news on KDFW.

The only station that didn't really conform to these counter-programming strategies was WTBS in Atlanta. The original superstation paid more than $180 million in 1998 for the right to be the exclusive cable outlet for *Seinfeld* for four years beginning in fall 2002. Because of its sizable investment in the show, WTBS used *Seinfeld* as part of its branding strategy. In 2002, *Seinfeld* anchored the TBS daily comedy block from 4:30 to 8 p.m. EST, appearing at 6:30 and 7:30 p.m (Dempsey and Littleton; Grego; Littleton).

Controlling the "Brand"

Some may take issue with our view that *Seinfeld* should be seen as a brand unto itself, since the popularity of the show helped NBC build its own "Must-See-TV" brand. Still, accepting this point is critical to understanding the economic reality of television in an era where syndication offers program owners the possibility of endless control and profitability. *Star Trek* is a prime example of this. Originally, it was a Desilu production, then became Paramount, and is still associated with the late Gene Roddenberry, the original creator. In fact, one might argue that Roddenberry himself—not unlike Walt Disney—has become a separate brand, as well as *Star Trek*—witness *Gene Roddenberry's Earth: Final Conflict* and *Gene Roddenberry's Andromeda*—even though Paramount/Viacom has nothing to do with either series. The point is that syndication profit potential has made the shows themselves the driving force—a brand unto itself, a brand that the networks, studios, and creators will tap into over the life of a series, which, in syndication, may indeed be forever.

In reflecting upon this branding analysis, we think it may be useful to make a distinction between "brand" and "brand equity." *Seinfeld*, like *Star Trek* or *I Love Lucy*, is a brand, but NBC has no brand equity in the series that aired on its network, unlike Paramount/Viacom, which acquired *Star Trek's* and *I Love Lucy's* brand equity when it purchased Desilu in 1966. NBC, of course, is a brand itself—as is "Must-See-TV." NBC, because it owns these brand names, controls the brand equity. NBC, for example, might be able to license "Must-See-TV: The Golden Years" to TV Land at some point in the future, or, for that matter, license the NBC logo—as it, in fact, does. The *Seinfeld* brand has helped NBC build brand equity in "Must-See-TV" and the NBC name, but since they don't own the brand equity of *Seinfeld*, the network (1) cannot continue to benefit directly from the brand behemoth that they helped build, and (2) will likely lose any indirect benefit—afterglow or aura—over time. Indeed, that process is well under way.

Another example of our point is the announcement, in April 2003, that HBO is rolling out a line of *The Sopranos* clothing for men and women (Tony ties will begin at $40) (DiPasquale). The branding of *The Sopranos* in the marketplace certainly will help HBO, but it will help *The Sopranos* more, even when it is no longer on HBO. Moreover, because HBO owns *The Sopranos*, it has more control in the way it uses the series to build the "It's not TV; It's HBO" brand, rerunning the series multiple times as a lead-in to new series or delaying the series for a season to fuel audience interest. HBO can tie its brand to *The Sopranos* even after the show has completed its run on HBO, issuing *The Sopranos* DVDs with HBO logos emblazoned on them so that viewers will continue to associate *The Sopranos* with HBO.

With *Seinfeld*, however, there is no similar long-term benefit for NBC. Because of the Fin-Syn rules, which were still in effect when the series first aired, NBC cannot exploit the *Seinfeld* brand after the series' first-run window has ended (except perhaps to say "from the network that brought you *Seinfeld*"). With no equity in the content, networks essentially became a stepping-stone for building a brand they would be able to tap into for a period of time, but that will ultimately benefit creators and studios with no permanent connection to the incubating network. Consider, for example, the Paul Henning rural comedies of the 1960s. Except for academics and industry insiders, few audiences will remember what network initially aired *The Beverly Hillbillies* and *Green Acres* or, for that matter, even more iconic shows such as *I Love Lucy* or *The Honeymooners* (1951–57). The shows themselves are the brand, and as such, they can be used to bring viewers and money to new channels such as TV Land and Nick-at-Nite, to be understood and consumed in a context completely different than when they originally aired nationally. Because it has created an environment where shows can be profitable and popular ad infinitum, syndication has revealed that shows can have lives of their own, radiating a brand afterglow that helps numerous players in television, including local stations, producers, creators, actors, studios, and now that the Fin-Syn rules have been repealed, networks. All of them benefit, variously, from a show that becomes a runaway hit in syndication, and today all of these players try to negotiate contracts that will give them access to the equity of a show. Brand benefits may also be less tangible for actors and others. Consider that the actors from *Friends* (1994–2004), for example, benefit when they are referred to as one of the "friends." Leonard Nimoy's continued identification with

Star Trek's Mr. Spock has landed him other acting and spokesperson jobs related to science and the supernatural. The fact that Larry David's *Curb Your Enthusiasm* can tout that it is "from one of the creators of *Seinfeld*" is also a helpful marketing tool for HBO's once-fledgling series.

In the world of tangible consumer products, many brands do not associate themselves with their corporate manufacturers. Few people know or care that General Foods or RCA no longer exists as a company or that Kraft Foods is owned by Altria, the former Phillip Morris. Consider also that many brands that were once trademarks became (or are in danger of becoming) generic terms that transcend the proprietary uses of the companies that controlled them, such as aspirin, cellophane, Kleenex, Band-Aid, Sanka, Kool-Aid, and Xerox. Brands are also bought and sold today—often without publicity—not because the brands will help companies build their reputations, but because the brands themselves will add to the corporation's bottom line. Entenmann's cookies became extremely profitable not because they are owned by a Canadian company, George Weston, Ltd., but because New Yorkers became aware that Entenmann's, when it was an independent bakery in Brooklyn, made great cookies. Consumers love Spaghetti-Os and Häagen-Dazs, but most have no idea who makes these products, nor do they really care.

The problem with calling *Seinfeld* a franchise is that, unlike franchises such as *Star Trek* and *Law & Order*, there has not been a proliferation of new versions with the same title and/or characters. NBC would have loved to make *Seinfeld* a franchise, but without the participation of the program's owners—the owners of the brand—they cannot. The best that NBC can claim is that it got the benefit of branding the product—building the *Seinfeld* brand into something that will be a flagship program for local stations and, in the future, for cable syndication recyclers like TV Land. NBC will get little benefit, if any, in the future for being the network that premiered *Seinfeld*. Again, a product-focused branding analogy may be of use. Tropicana orange juice, a leading brand, was for years made by a company called Beatrice. Beatrice even placed its name on cartons and in advertisements. Beatrice then sold the Tropicana brand to Seagram, who then developed the brand into a franchise, being careful not to have the product associated with the Seagram spirits line of brands. Seagram, in turn, sold off the Tropicana unit, including all the brand equity to PepsiCo.

The fact is, very few consumers have any idea who makes popular products. In many cases, all they care about is the brand itself. That's how we would characterize the relationship between *Seinfeld* and NBC. NBC had the opportunity to help build the brand and, in the process, exploit it. Unlike Seagram or Beatrice, however, the network could not control the brand, since they did not own it.

Seinfeld's owners, while they do control the program (at least during the term of copyright), continue to get some benefit from being associated with the brand, although that too will likely wane over time. The real beneficiaries of the *Seinfeld* brand will be those who license the show for their stations/channels in the future. These entities will continue to benefit from what NBC did, quite possibly, for decades to come, even though NBC's involvement may be long forgotten.

Those who control the *Seinfeld* brand are now essentially renting out their brand in syndication for local and cable channels to use. *Seinfeld* may build the local cachet of a little-watched independent station in Lubbock, but we would argue that the effects may be as temporary for these windows as it was for the network window. In the process of doling out the benefits of its brand equity to the highest bidders, *Seinfeld*'s owners will continue to build *Seinfeld*'s equity—which they own fully—and, unlike its syndication participants, can continue to exploit *Seinfeld* or invest in its brand. Thus, the owners of *Seinfeld*'s brand equity will be able to determine if they want a tenth cycle of syndication rights years from now, negotiate an exclusive national airing deal with one channel, or, as Sherwood Schwartz did some time ago with *The Brady Bunch,* decide to authorize a live stage show, or musical, with different actors playing the characters. For nine seasons, NBC both built and exploited *Seinfeld* as a brand. Now that that window has closed, the benefits of the *Seinfeld* brand to NBC are quickly diminishing. In a few more years, when people no longer associate the program with the network that first aired it, *Seinfeld* will indeed become a show that means nothing, at least as far as NBC is concerned.

Notes

1. Thorburn's essay originally appeared in the first edition of Newcomb's pathbreaking anthology published in 1976.

2. See also *Viacom Intern. Inc. v. F. C.* C. 672 F.2d 1034, 1037 (2nd Cir. 1982).

V
Afterword

DAVID LAVERY (Middle Tennessee State University) with
MARC LEVERETTE (Colorado State University)

Afterword

Rereading *Seinfeld* after *Curb Your Enthusiasm*

> Larry and Jerry handled the network restrictions brilliantly on *Seinfeld.*
> Those restrictions forced them to be really creative just to get around
> them. Look at what they got away with by using phrases like "Master
> of your domain" or "Not that there's anything wrong with that." But
> *Curb* is pure, undiluted Larry David.
>
> —Robert Wiede

S ix years after *Seinfeld* went off the air on the Peacock Network, its sitcosmos lives on.[1] At the time of writing, DVDs for Seasons One through
Four are available—among the best yet produced for any television series,
and *Sein*fans can watch their show just about any day of the week in syndication,
where, as Epstein, Rogers, and Reeves demonstrate in their essay in this volume,
the series continues to be a powerful commodity, a daily habit in millions of
households. (As we write, it is possible in middle Tennessee to watch no less than
four random episodes a day, two on Nashville's Fox affiliate, two on Ted Turner's
TBS superstation.) And subscribers to HBO are also able to periodically revisit
the *Seinfeld* sitcosmos: *Curb Your Enthusiasm*, the Emmy-award winning verité-
style comedy about the misadventures of *Seinfeld* cocreator Larry David, carries
on the tradition. Its next season will be its fifth.

Like *Seinfeld*, *Curb* concerns the life of a real comic—Larry David this time,
not Jerry Seinfeld—and his friends, which in *Curb* include both real (Richard
Lewis, Ted Danson, Mel Brooks) and imaginary characters. As in *Seinfeld*, in
each episode a series of seemingly unrelated situations (this time in the life of a
single individual), usually caused by David's utter lack of tact or complete unwillingness to compromise, customarily result in a final moment of sheer degradation

for its comic antihero. Unlike *Seinfeld*, however, it is not carefully scripted. Working from a scenario, its actors improvise each scene, resulting in the series' signature "fly on the wall" documentary feel.[2] Being on HBO, and offered in only ten installments a season, it may not be TV, and Jerry Seinfeld has had no hand in it, but the far more profane, far more ribald, far more adult, laugh-trackless *Curb* provides many of the same satisfactions as *Seinfeld*. *Curb* is certainly no spin-off; unless we count Larry David himself—the inspiration for George on *Seinfeld*—it has no recurring characters.[3] In *Curb*'s second season Jason Alexander and Julia Louis-Dreyfus do appear, but as themselves, and both of their careers are suffering from having been on *Seinfeld*. Alexander in particular is sick and tired of "the George thing"—of being mistaken for "the idiot, the schmuck" he once played—and lists some of the disgusting things he did on the show: stealing a tape from an answering machine ("The Phone Message," 2004), being part of a masturbation contest ("The Contest," 4010), eating an éclair out of a trash can ("The Gymnast," 6006). Larry David, taking the complaints personally, responds to each with the protestation "But I did that!" ("The Car Salesman," *Curb*, 2001).

In "The Grand Opening," the final episode of Season Three of *Curb*, the new restaurant in which Larry is an investor finally opens. All season long, the partners have had difficulty hiring a chef (one had been fired by the bald Larry for wearing a toupee) and have been forced at the last minute to hire a new one who, as they discover too late, suffers from Tourette's syndrome, spewing streams of profanity without provocation or warning. At the grand opening, all is going well when, as expected, the chef's extreme profanity shocks the packed house. Not knowing what to do, Larry improvises, responding with his own string of vulgarities. Others join in, even Larry's father-in-law, and the air is filled with the bleepable, and since this is not TV but HBO, the obscene chorus rings out loud and clear. As the episode and the season end, the camera pulls in for a close-up of a satisfied David, his arms folded confidently across his chest, an atypical look of triumph on his face. It is one of television's most magical moments, but it could never have happened on *Seinfeld*.[4] (In "The Shrimp Incident" [2004] from *Curb*'s second season, Julia Louis-Dreyfus, *Seinfeld*'s Elaine, announces her desire to appear on an HBO program so she can say the word "fuck," an expletive never uttered on NBC.)

The fourth-season *Curb* episode that aired while this afterword was being written ("The Weatherman," 4004) nevertheless exhibited multiple jokes and situations immediately recognizable as *Seinfeld*ian in origin. Larry injures his back while attempting to urinate sitting down in the middle of the night; on *Seinfeld* George is a "stall man," scared of urinals ("The Note," 3001—written by David). Larry has a suede jacket ruined by the adhesive on a name badge; on *Seinfeld*

Jerry's suede jacket is ruined by snow ("The Jacket," 2003—cowritten by David). Larry's reluctance to wear a name badge itself recalls Jerry's unwillingness to have his photo displayed in the lobby of his apartment building ("The Kiss Hello," 6015—cowritten by David), as well as Lloyd Braun's politically disastrous plan to have all New Yorkers wear name tags ("The Non-Fat Yogurt," 5007—written by David). Nearly every mercifully laugh-trackless *Curb* episode reminds the attentive viewer of *Seinfeld*'s ancestor text.

But the DVDs and *Curb Your Enthusiasm* do much more than perpetuate the *Seinfeld* legacy: they enable, even require, a rereading of *Seinfeld*, a wandering about in its seemingly familiar terrain already encouraged and facilitated by the accelerated revisiting of a series' text that syndication (and now DVDs) enables. We should not simply assume that *Seinfeld* in its original airing, *Seinfeld* in syndication, *Seinfeld* on DVD, and *Seinfeld* after *Curb* are the same series. In an important essay on "Audience-Oriented Criticism and Television," Robert C. Allen outlines the many ways in which the "reader-response criticism" of critics like Wolfgang Iser may be imported into the interpretation of TV texts. "[A]ny narrative form involves the reader's—or viewer's—movement through the text, from one sentence, shot, or scene to the next," Allen explains. "Because narratives unfold in time (reading time or screen time), as viewers or readers we are always poised between the *textual geography* we have already wandered across and that we have yet to cover." This wandering gives rise to a perpetual "tension between what we have learned from the text and what we anticipate finding." Questions are answered and new ones asked, Allen explains, by "[e]ach sentence of a literary narrative or each shot of a television narrative."

> Each new "block" of text we cover provides us with a new vantage point from which to regard the landscape of the text thus far, while at the same time it causes us to speculate as to what lies around the next textual corner. Hence our viewpoint constantly "wanders" backward and forward across the text. (105–106)

Exploring the "textual geography" of *Seinfeld* in the more random travel of syndication, or surveying via the much more systematic trek provided by DVDs, moving back and forth through episodes visited (and revisited and re-revisited . . .) at random, "*re*-connoitering" (if you will) the series, we see things differently.

Watching very early episodes, for example, we may be shocked to find Jerry, George, and Kramer (in particular) not themselves—out of character (Jerry too kind, George too confident, Kramer too doofus and not enough hipster). Such reconnoitering may well have begun with *Seinfeld*'s finale. Many *Seinfeld* veterans found themselves a bit taken aback by the David-authored one hour episode in which a Massachusetts jury sends the "New York Four" to prison for violating a Good Samaritan Law after listening to a chorus of accusers, from Babu Bhatt ("He's a very bad man!") to Mabel Choate (mugged by Jerry in order to steal a marble rye).[5] Somehow, the week after week laughter induced during *Seinfeld's* original run had mesmerized, making fans unwilling to realize what horrible people Jerry, George, Elaine, and Kramer really were. With the *Seinfeld* text now complete, it was time to begin rereading *Seinfeld.*

Rereading *Seinfeld* after *Curb* alters the original in additional ways. For example, its obnoxious laugh track (if *Seinfeld's* laugh track was one of Jerry's girl-friend's, he would have dumped it as more detested than "Elmer Fudd sitting on a juicer" ["The Bubble Boy," 4006]) becomes all the more intolerable once we have experienced the democratic humor of *Curb,* a series that allows us to decide for ourselves what is funny. And it is difficult not to conclude that Larry David's collaboration in the creation of the earlier program may have been underappreci-ated.[6] Post-*Curb Seinfeld* seems more scatalogical, more sex-obsessed, more con-cerned with race, more politically incorrect, more Davidesque.

Jerry Seinfeld's patented stand-up comedy, his "shallow, fairly obvious obser-vations" ("The Serenity Now," 9003) about everyday things, was famous for its uncharacteristic-for-its-time lack of profanity. (In the documentary *Comedian* [2002], which follows Seinfeld and a much younger comic as they struggle to make it—or remake it in Seinfeld's case—in the comedy clubs, he comes across as a modest, basically sweet guy—not surprising in a film he executive-produced—who swears only offstage.) In his best-selling *SeinLanguage* (1993), we even find him making the following endearing observation:

> Friends are the DNA of society. They are the basic building blocks of life. If you have a couple of good ones, treasure them like gold. There's nothing better. Ever look at that MCI ad they have, "Friends and Family"? Who do they mention first? Your friends help you carry the big weight in life. That big burden we've all got called, "What the hell am I doing?" (51)

It is impossible, is it not, to imagine Larry David saying any such thing, in or out of persona. Such an avowal might serve as the mission statement for *Seinfeld* imi-tator and heir *Friends,* which ended a ten-year run on NBC in the spring of 2004, but on neither *Seinfeld* or *Curb* could any character utter such platitudes with a straight face. Indeed, in "The Serenity Now" (9003) we are given an-under-the-spell-of-a-former girlfriend Jerry, encouraged to get in touch with his feelings, who temporarily believes such things, telling freaked-out George and oblivious-as-usual Kramer that he loves them and even proposing to Elaine, and all his friends, and the audience as well, immediately take him to have lost his mind.

The Improv in New York City, early seventies. A young stand-up comedian onstage, not telling any jokes. Silent, standing still, staring at the audience, scanning the group from left to right. After a few seconds of perusal, he shakes his head in a dismissive fashion and, just before he makes an abrupt exit, says, "Fuck you."[7]

Scores of anecdotes such as this one, some apocryphal, surround the early days of Larry David, whose pervasive neuroses became legendary in the comedy industry. His tacit rejection of the crowd as a stand-up comedian—"you people," he would say—often garnered feelings of embarrassment, nervousness, and anger from audience members. But not so with the in-crowd, the "Larry David cognoscenti . . . the other stand-ups who are sitting at the bar *plotzing,* tears streaming down their faces" (Oppenheimer 233). He was the guy to see, the ultimate comic's comic.[8]

Strange as his onstage behavior was, David's antics offstage were even more peculiar. Complimented three nights in a row by a fellow comedian, David's reaction was a searching glare and the question. "What's with all the nice-guy shit?" So insecure is David that, ultimately, life becomes an act. As he has said: "If [Nazi war criminal] Mengele gave me a compliment, we could've been friends. 'Larry, your hair looks very good today.' 'Oh, really? Thank you, Dr. Mengele!'" (Thompson 2).[9] We are unwelcome guests in David's world, a world where nothing is sacred, and if you can't take a joke, you can get the hell out.

Both Howard Gruber ("Breakaway Minds") and Nora John-Steiner have argued that the nature of collaboration may well be the final frontier in understanding creativity. These pages are not likely to contribute much to that important task, but reconnoitering *Seinfeld* after *Curb* we should be better able to render onto Jerry the things that are Jerry's and onto Larry the things that are Larry's.

Scatalogy, Sex, and the Bodily Canon

The humiliations in question are often physical: the show has tirelessly enlisted body parts, bodily fluids, disgusting personal habits, diseases, and medical operations into its scenarios, as if the comedy of the lower body were necessary to keep in balance all that disembodied verbal riffing.

—Geoffrey O'Brien, "The Republic of *Seinfeld*"

In a multi-episode development in Season Three of *Curb* ("Crazy Eyez Killa," "Mary, Joseph, and Larry" [3008, 3009]), Larry David gets a pubic hair stuck in his throat after performing cunnilingus on his wife. (It is finally dislodged after he gets in a fight with the man playing Joseph in a manger scene after Larry comments on how hot the Virgin Mary is.) In "The Doll" (2007) a small girl walks in on Larry while he is urinating. In "The Nanny" (3004), Larry inappropriately comments on the large penis of a young boy. In "The Weatherman" (4004), Larry may or may not have become aroused while a dog nuzzles his groin (in the subsequent episode ["The Five Wood," 4005], the dog bites his penis while he sits on the toilet). *Curb*'s notoriously edgy (perhaps over the edge?) humor often concerns bodily functions.

For most of its history television has been ruled by Mikhail Bakhtin's "bodily canon." "Wherever men laugh and curse, particularly in a familiar environment, their speech is filled with bodily images," Bakhtin insists in *Rabelais and His World*, but since the Renaissance a repressive, authoritarian "bodily canon" has censored the human body and its "grotesque expressiveness." The bodily canon, according to Bakhtin, has a not-so-hidden agenda. It demands that all bodily orifices must be closed, allows no mergers of the body with the external world, insists that all signs of inner life processes and bodily functions (farting, belching, vomiting) be hidden or repressed, finds evidence of fecundation and pregnancy suspect, seeks to eliminate all protrusions and deformities.[10]

Jack Paar momentarily quit *The Tonight Show* in the early sixties because he was not allowed to tell a joke about a toilet (delicately called a WC). When Archie Bunker merely flushed a toilet, off-screen but audibly, in an episode of *All in the Family* ("New Year's Wedding," aired on January 5, 1976), television history was made. Neither before nor since (with the exception of potty-mouthed cable shows like *Ren and Stimpy, Beavis and Butthead,* and *South Park*) has television been scatologically inclined, and though more prominent than the scatological, sexuality has not found all that much free expression on TV before the coming of cable.[11]

On *Seinfeld* the bodily canon is clearly a player. Has there ever been a more "anal" character than Jerry?[12] He gargles six times a day ("The Dog," 3004), is appalled when chef Poppie fails to wash his hands before fixing his meal ("The Pie," 5015), and is so grossed out by a girlfriend whose toothbrush has fallen in the toilet that he can no longer bring himself to kiss her ("The Pothole," 8016).[13] And yet the scatological on *Seinfeld* seems ever present; Bakhtin's grotesque body is always in danger of erupting.

George admits to fantasizing about having sex with a giant woman. It's his "life's ambition" ("The Boyfriend," 3017).

Vomit figures prominently: Jerry keeps track of his vomit streak (In "The Dinner Party" [5013] it ends after fourteen years [1980–94]); Kramer vomits all over Susan in "The Pitch" (4003) and again in "The Gum" (7010).

Elaine is grossly embarrassed by an exposed nipple on her Christmas card photo ("The Pick," 4012).

Calvin Klein finds Kramer's buttocks "sublime" ("The Pick," 4012).

Jerry loses a supermodel girlfriend when she thinks she sees him picking his nose, which leads to a spirited discussion with George as to what exactly constitutes nose picking ("The Pick," 4012).

Elaine meets an elderly woman (once Gandhi's mistress) with a huge goiter that looks like a "second head" ("The Old Man, 4017).

Jerry's car is attacked by "BBO" (Beyond Body Odor), "The Beast," a stench so bad he encourages, at episode's end, a thief to steal the car ("The Smelly Car," 4020).

Toilet paper is a recurring character: George discourses on it fatuously (it's one of his favorite subjects[14]), and Elaine can't convince a woman in an adjoining stall to "spare a square" ("The Stall," 5012).

A hair ruins a cinnamon babka ("The Dinner Party," 5013).

Cleavage is a dangerous thing. when George stares at NBC exec Russell Dalrymple's daughter's breasts, the result is termination of *The Jerry Show*; when Dalrymple, in turn, stares at Elaine's purposely displayed bosom, his obsession leads to his death at sea ("The Shoes," 4015; "The Pilot," 4022).

A woman has a name that rhymes with a female body part, but "Delores" ditches Jerry when he can't remember it ("The Junior Mint," 4019).

Bras figure prominently: George interviews for a job as a bra salesman (after receiving instruction from his father on cup sizes, construction, etc.) ("The Sniffing Accountant," 5004); the "braless wonder" Sue Ellen Mischke walks down the street wearing a bra as a top (and causing traffic accidents) ("The Caddy," 7012); Kramer and Frank Costanza develop a bra for "man boobs": "the Bro" or "the Manssiere" ("The Doorman," 6016).

Kramer stops wearing underwear so that his "boys" may be free and "out there" (and his sperm cell count will increase) ("The Chinese Woman," 6004). Jerry and Elaine recoil in horror at the thought that only a "thin layer of gabardine" separates them from Kramer's genitals.

Jerry is arrested for urinating in a parking garage at a shopping mall ("The Parking Garage," 3006); George gets in trouble for urinating in the shower at his health club ("The Wife" 5017); restaurateur Poppie twice ruins sofas due to incontinence ("The Couch," 6005; "The Doorman," 6016).

Jerry has to shave off his chest hair to satisfy a "hairless freak" girlfriend ("The Muffin Tops," 8021).

Not surprisingly for a show about four single, serial-dating New Yorkers, *Seinfeld*'s subject matter often involves sex, where its (bodily) function as both text and subtext made the series a prime candidate for the wrath of Religious Right media watchdogs.[15]

His privacy destroyed due to a parental visit ("The Raincoats," 5019), Jerry is desperate to have sex with his girlfriend Rachel because he is so "backed up" (this leads to their famous make-out session at *Schindler's List*).

When in "The Sponge" (7009), she learns that the Today sponge contraceptive has been discontinued, Elaine begins to fanatically horde them, buying out the entire stock of one pharmacy and making careful decisions about whether or not potential lovers are in fact "spongeworthy." One man who does pass her rigorous pre-sex interview is deemed not worthy of a repeat performance the following morning. In the same episode, we learn, though Jerry does not, that his altruistic girlfriend, whose goodness is a turnoff—"I mean, she's giving and caring and genuinely concerned about the welfare of others," Jerry confesses to George. "I can't be with someone like that! . . . You can't have sex with someone you admire."—is also hording the sponge.

In "The Fusilli Jerry" (6019) Jerry's patented sexual maneuver becomes a contested and much-sought technique when it is ripped off by Elaine's lover Puddy, and George seeks, with great difficulty, to master it as well. Before he resorts to crib notes written on his hand, George's girlfriend describes his modus operandi in one of the strangest, most disturbing lines ever uttered on network television: "It feels like aliens poking at my body."

In "The Blood" (9004), George, anxious to unite all the things he loves into one, combines "food and sex into one disgusting uncontrollable urge."

Appalled even at his own shallowness for dating a beautiful woman he despises, Jerry describes his dilemma as being "like my brain . . . facing my penis in a chess game. And I'm letting him win" ("The Nose Job," 3009), a face-off we get to see in a dream sequence.

Condoms have at least two cameos. The ubiquitous (but never seen) Bob Sacamano gives Kramer a defective case of them, which almost results in George's "boys" truly "swimming" ("The Fix-Up," 3016); George leaves a prophylactic wrapper on his parents' bed ("The Cigar Store Indian," 5010).

Pornography is frequently mentioned. Jerry and Elaine talk themselves into having sex again, combining "this" and "that," after watching the "naked channel" on TV; George has gone so far as to imagine a possible screen name: Buck

Naked ("The Outing," 4016), should he become a porn star; dentist Tim Whatley runs an adults-only office that features *Penthouse* as reading material in the waiting room ("The Jimmy," 6017); in "The Butter Shave" (9001) a mustachioed George admits to "feeling like an out-of-work porn star"; Jerry cruelly suggests that his nemesis Sally Weaver deserves a downward career spiral that entails "years of rejections and failures till she's spit out the bottom of the porn industry" ("The Cartoon," 9013); when George tries to convince Jerry of reasons to have a computer, porn comes to mind ("The Serenity Now," 9003).[16]

Masturbation plays an unprecedented role for a network television show. Inspired by a *Glamour* magazine, George gets caught masturbating by his mother, who ends up in the hospital ("The Contest," 4010), leading to the four engaging in an infamous contest to see who can be "master of [his/her] domain" and go the longest without "gratifying themselves" (facing certain death in the near plane crash of the series finale, George admits he cheated) ["Finale," 9021–9022]). As an aspiring hand model himself, George learns of a legendary figure in the field whose failure to master his domain ruined his career ("The Puffy Shirt," 5002). On *Seinfeld* even the animal world masturbates. When Kramer insults a chimpanzee, the zookeeper complains that it has "curtailed his autoerotic activities" ("The Face Painter," 6021).

And all this rampant mono- and hetero-sexuality is routinely subverted by prominent "homosociality," as Di Mattia (in this volume) and Gantz have so clearly demonstrated. But neither gives credit to the theory Jerry articulates in "The Beard" (6014) in order to explain why heterosexuals cannot convert members of the other team:

> Jerry: Not conversion. You're thinking conversion?
> Elaine: Well it did occur to me.
> Jerry: You think you can get him to just change teams? He's not going to suddenly switch sides. Forget about it.
> Elaine: Why? Is it irrevocable?
> Jerry: Because when you join that team it's not a whim. He likes his team. He's set with that team.
> Elaine: We've got a good team.
> Jerry: Yeah, we do. We do have a good team.
> Elaine: Why can't he play for us?
> Jerry: They're only comfortable with their equipment.

Although she temporarily proves Jerry's theory wrong, the conversion fails, and now Elaine is ready to theorize:

Jerry: He went back? What do you mean he went back?

Elaine: He went back.

Jerry: I don't understand it. You were having such a great time, the sex, the shopping.

Elaine: Well here's the thing. Being a woman, I only really have access to the, uh . . . equipment, what, thirty, forty-five minutes a week. And that's in a good week. How can I be expected to have the same expertise as people who own this equipment, and have access to it twenty-four hours a day, their entire lives?

Jerry: You can't. That's why they lose very few players.

Prior to the imposition of the bodily canon, Bakhtin was convinced, our species experienced embodiment as "a point of transition in a life eternally renewed, the inexhaustible vessel of death and conception" (335–36). Such a mindset—which Bakhtin calls "carnivalesque"—made the scatological celebratory. With its circus-evoking theme music and occasionally joyful profanity (in episodes like "The Grand Opening"), *Curb* sometimes seems Rabelaisian. Needless to say, we find little or no sign of the carnivalesque in "*Seinfeld*'s humor noir."[17]

Race

The thing about eating the black-and-white cookie, Elaine, is you want to get some black and some white in each bite. Nothing mixes better than vanilla and chocolate. And yet somehow racial harmony eludes us. If people would only look to the cookie, all our problems would be solved.

—Jerry in "The Dinner Party" (5013)

You my Caucasian?

—Crazy-Eyez Killah in "Crazy-Eyez Killah," *Curb Your Enthusiasm* (3007)

In "Affirmative Action" (*Curb Your Enthusiasm*, 1009), Larry David is walking with his friend Richard Lewis when an African American man runs by. When Lewis introduces the jogger as his dermatologist, Larry, "trying too hard to be affable," makes what he thinks is a joke, mock questioning Lewis's choice of doctors: "Even with the whole affirmative action thing?" The doctor is very insulted. "I tend to say stupid things to black people sometimes," Larry explains in defense after the doctor angrily departs. Later, on the way to the restroom in a restaurant, he runs into a drunken African American woman who he failed to hire for a part in David's post-*Seinfeld* movie *Sour Grapes*. She castigates "Mr. Larry David" for his racism. As proof of her charge she cites the complete absence of black people on *Seinfeld*. As luck (and *Curb*'s signature convoluted plotting) would have it, Larry is forced to take Cheryl to the dermatologist's house for urgent medical attention. Before a gathering of black people, he manages not to say anything stupid for a change and has won the group over with his apology, when out of the restroom appears the actress who had accosted Larry earlier. His cover is blown.

Larry's "Affirmative Action" nemesis's charges could not have been news to *Seinfeld*'s cocreator. During its original run and frequently since, *Seinfeld* was chided for its obliviousness to matters of race.[18] Rereading *Seinfeld*, however, the complaint seems less justifiable. Reconnoitering, we note that in fact, minor characters on *Seinfeld* represent a wide variety of minorities: Jackie Chiles, the ambulance-chasing lawyer who took on two of Kramer's litigation schemes (against big tobacco and big coffee), only to be frustrated, and who represents the New York Four in their finale trial (while sleeping with the enemy) is African American, as is George's front-office nemesis Morgan (the one who looks like Sugar Ray Leonard). So, too, are the exterminator who George tries to pass off as an old friend in order to impress Morgan ("The Diplomat Club," 6020); the NYU dean who takes away Kramerica Industries' intern ("The Voice," 9002); the family George imposes himself upon so he can see *Breakfast at Tiffany's* ("The Couch," 6005); the no-nonsense manager of Monk's, who threatens to confiscate Jerry's personal maple syrup ("The Wife", 5017) and promises to make George into his "own personal hand puppet" ("The Soup," 6007); the woman Kramer is dating and her family in "The Wife"; the tough custodial supervisor who bosses Elaine around during her flounder-acquiring sojourn in a broom closet ("The Pothole," 8016); the oddly named homeless shelter employee Rebecca DeMornay ("The Muffin Tops," 8021; "The Bookstore," 9017); the chairless security guard in a clothing store whom George insists on helping ("The Maestro," 7003). Many of these individuals—Morgan, Rebecca DeMornay, the NYU dean—are in positions of power over the gang. When Grandpa gets a look at black-faced Kramer (who fell asleep in the tanning parlor) in the closing shot of "The Wife," his concluding assessment is one almost all of *Seinfeld*'s African Americans seem justified in making about our four: "I see a damn fool!"

Seinfeld also gives us Hispanic busboys ("The Busboy," 2012); Chinese mailmen ("The Cigar Store Indian," 5010) and delivery boys ("The Tape," 3008; "The Virgin," 4009); a Native American ("The Cigar Store Indian," 5010); Dominicans who roll their blintzes too tight ("The English Patient," 8017); Cubans ("The Cheever Letters," 4007); Puerto Ricans ("The Soup Nazi," 7006; "The Puerto Rican Day," 9020); a Pakistani ("The Café," 3007; "The Visa," 4014"); Arabs ("The Smelly Car," 4020); and a Mexican ("The Little Jerry," 8011).

More than one episode foregrounds race as an issue. In "The Cigar Store Indian" (5010), for example, Jerry, interested in a Native American woman whom he offends when he gives Elaine a tasteless, racist present, finds himself unable to open his mouth without sounding like a racist. Needing directions to a Chinese restaurant, he asks a mailman who turns out to be Chinese and is offended:

> Jerry: Uh, excuse me, you must know where the Chinese restaurant is around here.
> Mailman: Why must I know? Because I'm Chinese? You think I know where all the Chinese restaurants are? Oh, ask honolable Chinaman for rocation of lestaulant.

Words and phrases like "reservation" and "Indian-giver" suddenly become problematic.

In "The Diplomat's Club" (6020) a conniving George, anxious to make himself look better at work, tries to convince Morgan not only that he is deeply concerned with minority issues but even that he has black friends.[19] Eating lunch with "The Exterminator," George shows he can at least talk the talk of "color blindness":

> Carl: Do I know you?
> George: Yeah, sure, we met at Jerry Seinfeld's apartment. When you fumigated for fleas over there.
> Carl: Seinfeld . . . Oh yeah, funny white guy, right?
> George: Jerry? Yes, I suppose he is white. You know, I never really thought about it. I don't see people in terms of color.

In an intriguing final season episode ("The Wizard," 9015), Jerry's suggestion that the guy Elaine is dating is black comes as a shock to her (and to George, who thinks he "looks Irish") and sets off a series of schemes in which she tries to determine his actual ethnicity (he is Caucasian).

We certainly do not mean to suggest *Seinfeld,* ever committed to the "marvelous shallowness" of farce (O'Brien), was interested in scoring points as an equal opportunity employer. Albert Auster's remark (see above) that "If the series did have one strong point in its dealings with race, it was with the embarrassment and uneasiness that middle-class whites often feel about the issue" seems quite accurate and perfectly in keeping with the thesis of Jeff Hitchcock in *Lifting the White Veil* that the typical American may not be racist so much as clueless when faced with issues of race. *Seinfeld* takes place in a predominantly white world in which its chief characters simply do not feel comfortable with race or know the proper way to behave in a multiracial society. A perfect example of the gang's awkwardness can be found in "The Wizard." When, following Jerry, George, and Elaine's initial discussion at Monk's of Darryl's race, a black waitress appears at their table, each fumbles to lay down a more generous than usual guilt-alleviating tip.

Jerry Seinfeld confessed in a *Playboy* interview that the series had always planned to do an episode in which Elaine finds herself lost in Harlem but abandoned the idea because they simply could not get the tone right (cited in Zurawik). *Seinfeld* may at times have pondered "look[ing] to the cookie," Jerry's exemplary baked good (see the epigraph to this section), but we would do well to remember that actually ingesting this symbol of racial harmony causes him to lose his cookies, putting to an end his much-bragged-about fourteen-year "vomit streak." "I think I got David Duke and Fahrikan down there," he admits to Elaine, his dream of just getting along upset.

Political Incorrectness and Irreverence

Like comedy through the ages, they say the unsayable, do the undoable, as they casually ignore sanctioned morality and recognized correctness.

—John Docker

In an interview with Ricky Gervais, star of the BBC America cult hit *The Office*, on National Public Radio's *Weekend Morning Edition*, the series' lead tells Lianne Hansen that his notoriously edgy show does have its limits. *The Office*, he insisted, would never go for laughs at the expense of the disabled. The same cannot be said of *Curb Your Enthusiasm*. "Everything is fair game for *Curb*," we read on the HBO Web site. In "The Group" (1010) Larry accompanies a friend to an incest survivors group and finds it laughable. In "The Special Section" (3006) Larry uses his mother's death as an all-purpose pity-inducing way to get what he wants (including sex with his wife, Cheryl). In "The Corpse-Sniffing Dog" (3007), Larry gets a young girl drunk (accidentally) in order to secure her agreement to give up her dog. In "The Five Wood" (4005), he steals his own golf club back from the coffin of a dead man at a funeral.

Long before *Curb*'s irreverence, *Seinfeld* was already triumphantly politically incorrect, playing all sorts of out-of-bounds subjects for a laugh. The elderly are depicted as mean and cantankerous ("The Old Man," 4017) or completely imbecilic ("The English Patient," 8017). Jerry hits on a beautiful woman whose husband has attempted suicide ("The Suicide," 3015).[20] George is concerned about his girlfriend's possible bulimia because he resents buying her expensive dinners that end up in the toilet ("The Switch," 6011). George pretends to be handicapped in order to have access to a special bathroom at his new employer's ("The

Voice," 9002) and even starts using a motorized wheelchair ("The Serenity Now," 9003). Under the influence of Novocain, Kramer is mistaken as mentally retarded and honored at a banquet, serenaded by the Velvet Fog ("The Jimmy," 6017). Elaine breaks up with a sexually attractive mover because he is opposed to abortion ("The Couch," 6005).

Several episodes are outright sacrilegious. In the final scene of "The Face Painter" (6021), Elaine is mistaken as the Virgin Mary by a deranged priest who earlier had thought New Jersey Devils' hockey fan Puddy was the devil. Jerry visits a confessional to complain about dentist Tim Whatley's conversion to Judaism so he can practice Jewish humor:

> Priest: And this offends you as a Jewish person.
> Jerry: No, it offends me as a comedian. ("The Yada Yada," 8019)

When "Triangle Boy" ("The Junior Mint," 4019) recovers from his surgery, even his doctor thinks it might have been the result of divine intervention ("I have no medical evidence to back me up, but something happened during the operation that staved off that infection. Something beyond science. Something perhaps from above . . ."), but it was in fact not God's work but a Junior Mint that Kramer accidentally dropped into the patient's open chest cavity while watching the surgery.

Finale

> We're people—real TV people.
>
> Jerry Seinfeld, introducing the
> 100-episode-clip show of *Seinfeld*

In a Season Five episode of *The Simpsons* called "Homer Loves Flanders," a series of circumstances lead to Homer becoming close friends with his pious nerd neighbor Ned Flanders. At the end of the episode, with typical *Simpsons* self-referentiality, Lisa and Bart argue about what this departure from the laws of the sitcosmos of the show (and the very genre itself) might mean for its future. As "real TV people" who watch the tube more than perhaps any characters before on the medium, the Simpson children well know that the sitcom formula dictates restoration of the status quo at the end of an episode:

> Bart: I don't get it, Lis. You said everything would be back to normal, but Homer and Flanders are still friends.
> Lisa: Yeah. Maybe this means the end of our wacky adventures.

As if on cue, Homer and Ned begin to fight. Relieved that order has been restored, Bart and Lisa breathe a sigh of relief, and the episode ends.

Seinfeld was never as self-aware as *The Simpsons,* TV's all-time most meta-series, but it had its moments. Consider, for example, Jerry Seinfeld's out-of-persona direct-address introduction of the clip show that preceded *Seinfeld's* final episode:

> Oh, hello. Nine years, seems like a long time doesn't it? It is, and we've packed a lot in, the four of us—it seems like every week a whole new set of problems would just crop up outta nowhere . . . except for summer, where nothing seemed to happen for months at a time. Anyway, the point is over the last nine years . . .

Now the problems are never-ending. Every weekday and Sundays too, at least ten weeks a year when *Curb* is in season, every night for those with the DVDs, *Seinfeld's* sitcosmos is open for exploration, ready for reconnoitering, and, part of popular culture and part of us, not likely to be exhausted any time soon.

Notes

1. Television series occasionally do have afterlives outside of syndication. When *Buffy the Vampire Slayer* ended in May of 2003, fans of the "Buffyverse" found some consolation in the renewal of *Buffy* spinoff *Angel* and were heartened to learn that one of *Buffy's* most loved characters, the vampire Spike (James Marsters), would become a recurring character on television's only remaining Joss Whedon series. The "Whedonverse" would live on, at least for another year.

2. For more on *Curb's* unusual shooting method, see the interviews with Robert Weide on the HBO Web site.

3. See Bill Wyman's comments on this exchange in his essay above.

4. Profanity did occasionally surface on *Seinfeld.* In "The Non-Fat Yogurt" (5007), recall, Jerry's swearing inspires a small boy to mimic him, but all the four-letter words are bleeped.

5. For an excellent analysis of the "cultural spectacle" of the *Seinfeld* finale, see Morreale.

6. By critical consensus, *Seinfeld* was in decline in its final two seasons—after, that is, Larry David left the show.

7. Alternate versions of this "myth" involve David simply walking offstage without ever having said a word, or simply shaking his head in utter disappointment (that the audience wasn't up to his standards) and saying "Never mind" upon leaving.

8. These descriptions are derived largely from Oppenheimer's unauthorized *Seinfeld* biography. However, a plethora of articles and interviews reveal the same information. Also see some of the opening interviews in *Larry David: Curb Your Enthusiasm,* Robert Weide's quasi-documentary, which served as the seed crystal for the HBO series.

9. This need for only complimentary criticism (even though that seems to freak him out a little), would make sense since David as a stand-up never dealt well with hecklers, or anyone not devoting their complete attention to his act. When people ordered drinks or went to the bathroom, he was often more comfortable yelling at them then simply ignoring them.

10. For another application of Bakhtin's concepts to the situation comedy, see Wexman in Morreale, ed., *Critiquing the Sitcom*.

11. See the chapter on "Sex" (27–45) in Schneider.

12. Our use of the term here is not strictly Freudian. We much prefer Ernest Becker's understanding of the term (in *Denial of Death*):

> To say someone is "anal" means that someone is trying extra-hard to protect himself against the accidents of life and the danger of death, trying to use the symbols of culture as a sure means of triumph over natural mystery, trying to pass himself off as anything but an animal.

13. Elaine is certain Jerry's reticence is a troubling sign:

> Elaine: Jerry, you have tendencies. They're always annoying, but they were just tendencies.
>   But now, if you can't kiss this girl, I'm afraid we're talking disorder.
> Jerry: Disorder?
> Elaine: And from disorder, you're a quirk or two away from full-on dementia.

14. Seeking to impress a new girlfriend in "The Face Painter" (6021), George holds forth: "Take toilet paper, for example. Do you realize that toilet paper has not changed in my lifetime? It's just paper on a cardboard roll, that's it. And in ten thousand years, it will still be exactly the same, because really, what else can they do?"

15. A search of L. Brent Bozell's Media Research Council Web site (http://www.mediaresearch.org) finds scores of references to *Seinfeld*, the epitome for Bozell not of "Must-See-TV" but of "Prurient Prime Time": a show that endorsed rampant sexuality, approved of lying, and discouraged marriage.

16. "Well," George explains, "I got just the thing to cheer you up. A computer! Huh? We can check porn and stock quotes."

17. This is the title of a somewhat valuable essay on *Seinfeld*'s dark humor by psychologists Irwin and Cara Hirsch. When the Hirsches take pity on the Bubble Boy—"George gets into a fight with the Bubble Boy, a child who lives in a sterile tent because of an immune disorder, and accidentally destroys his bubble, almost killing him" (123)—they seem oblivious, however, to the anti-PC, ironic humor of the episode (coauthored by Larry David and Larry Charles). In fact, the Bubble Boy is no child but a profane and crude adult who asks Susan Ross to take her top off.

18. Note Stratton's conclusion above: "*Seinfeld*'s concern with race is limited to ethnicity and the ambivalent status of Jewishness."

19. In a conversation with Jerry at Monk's, George reveals his deep concern for civil rights:

> George: So you really think Morgan thinks I have a racial bias?
> Jerry: Maybe.
> George: This is so unfair. I would've marched on Selma if it was on Long Island.
> Jerry: So you would've marched on Great Neck.
> George: Absolutely. I still might. I always hated those women. They would never date me.

20. In "The Suicide's" (3015) cruelly funny opening monologue, Jerry wonders how failed suicides deal with their disappointment:

> The thing I don't understand about the suicide person is the people who try and commit suicide, and for some reason they don't die and that's it. They stop trying. Why? Why don't they just keep trying? What has changed? Is their life any better now? No. In fact it's worse because now they've found out one more thing they stink at. Okay, that's why these people don't succeed in life to begin with. Because they give up too easy. I say, pills don't work, try a rope. Car won't start in the garage, get a tune up. You know what I mean? There's nothing more rewarding than reaching a goal you have set for yourself.

VI

"Get out!"
Back Pages

Glossary of Seinfeld*ian Terms*

Aggravation Installment Plan: Annoyance, "grief," dispensed (by parents and others) over time. ("The Parking Garage," 3006)

Anti-Dentite: A person who is opposed to dentists—the mass of dentists, dentists as a species. ("The Yada Yada," 8019)

Anti-Virgin: The condition of being opposed to virgins. A sexually promiscuous woman who speaks bluntly and salaciously about sex in the presence of a virgin, for example, may be accused of being *anti-virgin*. ("The Virgin," 4009)

Assman: A proctologist, a doctor of the ass. ("The Fusilli Jerry," 6019)

Backslide: See *Bump Into.* ("The Voice," 9002)

Baldist: A woman who is opposed to dating bald men. ("The Tape," 3008)

B.B.O: abbr., Beyond Body Odor. Supernaturally strong body odor. ("The Smelly Car," 4020)

Big Favor/Small Favor: A system of classification that allows one to predict the scope of an oncoming favor. A *small favor* is generally requested without hesitation. With a *big favor*, however, the question "Could you do me a favor?" is characteristically followed by a long pause and then by a statement of the favor being requested. ("The Stranded," 3010)

Bizarro: The antipodal version of oneself, who behaves by a system of opposites. A *Bizarro* character says "good-bye" when s/he arrives, and "hello" when s/he leaves. A schism in the school of *Bizarro* thought has emerged as a result of the debate over whether the *Bizarro* character would say "good-bye" or "bad-bye." ("The Bizarro Jerry," 8003)

B.O.: abbr., Body Odor. As a compound word, B.O. refers to the unpleasant odor emitted by a human body. The components can be referred to as separate entities, however—as the Body and the Odor, thus allowing for examination of the odor outside of its bodily context, for example: "When somebody has B.O., the 'O' usually stays with the 'B'. Once the 'B' leaves, the 'O' goes with it." ("The Smelly Car," 4020)

Body Odor Police: See *Smell Gestapo.* ("The Smelly Car," 4020)

Bombable: A person who is *bombable* is thought to be significant by virtue of being worthy of the time and efforts that are required to carry out this malicious act. Similarly, a person is said to be *stabworthy* if the malicious act is a stabbing. ("The Package," 8005)

Bottle Wipe: The act of wiping the mouth of a bottle of a shared beverage prior to drinking from it. Taken to be an indication of a lack of intimacy between the drinkers. ("The Wife," 5017)

Breakup by Association: The assumed dissociation of mutual friends brought forth by the end of a romantic relationship. Thus, if lover A initiates a breakup with lover B, the friends of lover A are automatically subject to a breakup of their friendship with lover B. ("The Deal," 2009)

Bro: An undergarment designed to support the weight of adipose tissue in the male breast, a symptom of obesity or gerontological processes. Also known as the *Mansierre*. ("The Doorman," 6016)

Bump Into: Following the breakup of a romantic relationship, ex-lovers who contemporaneously occur in a given location are said to have experienced a *bump into*. This may be followed by a *backslide*, which is a tentative resumption of sexual relations. ("The Voice," 9002)

Call-Waiting Face-Off: The conflict that arises from telephone call-waiting, which demands that a decision be made between two parties who are simultaneously seeking attention. ("Finale," 9022)

Cell-Phone Walk and Talk: A debauchery of telephone etiquette, in which a telephone call is made while the caller is busy engaging in other tasks. This is taken as a gesture of indifference and disinterest in the party being called. ("Finale," 9022)

Changing Teams: The conversion of a homosexual to heterosexuality, or vice versa. This is thought to be a fictional concept, invented by those who are hopeful of initiating a romance with someone of the opposite team. ("The Beard," 6014)

Close Talker: An aggressive vocalizer. A person who speaks at an uncomfortably close distance to his speaker. *Close talking* is unfavorably received as a violation of the listener's personal space, and further, often results in a perception of unpleasant oral odors and salivary ejaculations. ("The Raincoats," 5019)

Coma Etiquette: Ethical questions (or lack thereof) concerning what sort of behavior is appropriate in the presence of someone in a coma. ("The Suicide," 3015)

Conjugal Visit Sex: See *Fugitive Sex*. ("The Little Jerry," 8011)

Consolation Guy: The role that is taken on by a man in a casual dating relationship, who finds himself in a position of comforting a woman in a time of emotional hardship. The advantage of this position is thought to be an automatic acceleration of the intimacy process, i.e., *Instant Boyfriend Status*. ("The Implant," 4018)

Cop Slash Garbageman: A proposed fusion of the two occupations of *cop* and *garbageman* into a single occupation. The concept of *cop slash garbageman* is intended to achieve an optimal level of efficiency in allotting civic duties, and would require, simply, that cops begin to carry brooms on duty and clean when there are no criminal matters to attend to. ("The Chinese Restaurant," 2011)

Covenant of the Keys: A pact that is made between two friends, by exchanging a set of spare keys to their homes. When the pact is made between two males, they are said to be *key brothers*, and the agreement assumes no privileges or rights of entry, but rather is a precautionary measure for emergency situations. ("The Keys," 3022)

Crib Notes: A cheat sheet for an inadequate lover. An abridged manual for the sexual *schlimazel*. A set of instructions that can be written on, for example, the palm of the hand, for use by sexually inept persons as a guide to executing sexual procedures. The instructions may define a specific sexual maneuver, a trick-of-the-trade, such as the Pinch, the Knuckle, or the Clockwise Swirl. ("The Fusilli Jerry," 6019)

Dating Decathlon: When a date exceeds the conventional duration of a single evening, it can be called a *dating decathlon*. A dinner and movie can be classified as a date, but a road trip, for example, would fall under the category of a decathlon. ("The Stock Tip," 1005)

Deaf Date: A counterpart to the term "blind date," a *deaf date* is one in which neither party has heard the other's voice. ("The Wink," 7004)

Degifting: The act of giving a gift, and then asking to have it back. *Degifting* is generally allowed during the short grace period that follows the giving of the gift. ("The Label Maker," 6012)

Do Me a Solid: Performing a major favor for another. ("The Jacket," 2003)

Double Dipper: One who contaminates a shared supply of chip-dip via the following process: (1) the chip is dipped into the chip-dip; (2) the dipped portion of the chip is consumed; (3) the now-contaminated remaining portion—possibly polluted by the saliva and other oral slimes of the chip-dipper—is then redipped, causing a transference of contaminants into the chip-dip. ("The Implant," 4018)

Earth Suit: Proposed as a possible uniform to be worn by all inhabitants of the Earth. It is suggested that political candidates in the future will no longer need to present a platform or to engage in debates. Rather, they will be voted for according to the appeal of their *Earth Suits*. ("The Jacket," 2003)

Excuse Rolodex: An alphabetized catalog of excuses that may be utilized when one is repeatedly attempting to avoid meeting with another, or in other situations in which a single person is recurrently being presented with excuses. Implemented in order to escape redundancy and exposure. ("Male Unbonding," 1004)

Face-to-Face Breakup: An in-person, not over-the-phone, ending of a relationship, required after seven dates. ("The Alternate Side," 3011)

Festivus: A holiday that can be celebrated as an alternative to Christmas. The *Festivus* counterpart to the Christmas tree is an aluminum pole, and the holiday is celebrated with a ritual competition known as the *feats of strength*. The trademark slogan of *Festivus* is "Festivus for the Restivus!" ("The Strike," 9010)

Fiancée Time: The period of time, post engagement and prior to marriage, in which an engaged woman indulges in arousing the envy of her friends. ("The Little Jerry," 8011)

Flagged: In a bookstore, a book is said to be *flagged* once it has been taken into the restroom as a companion to excretory activities. The book cannot be reshelved but must be purchased by the reader. Further, the *flagged* status is immediately recorded into the store's computer systems and the book cannot be returned for a refund. ("The Bookstore," 9017)

Fornicating Gourmet: Sexual activity combining the pleasures of eating and fornication. Alternatively referred to as a *free love buffet*. ("The Blood," 9004)

Fugitive Sex: The optimum condition of sexual activity, in which one of the fornicators is a recently escaped fugitive. *Fugitive sex* is thought to surpass the conditions of *conjugal visit sex* and *make-up sex,* but the latter two are also embraced as highly desirable contexts for sex. ("The Little Jerry," 8011)

Germaphobe: One with an unreasonable fear of germs. A neurotic sanitarian. ("The Apology," 9009)

Hand Sandwich: See *Two-Hander.* ("Good News, Bad News," pilot episode)

Hard of Smelling: The smelling equivalent of deafness. ("The Smelly Car," 4020)

High Talker: A sopranic male. A man who speaks in a high-pitched voice and may thus be mistaken for a woman. ("The Pledge Drive," 6003)

Home Bed Advantage: The desirable position of hosting sexual activities at one's home as opposed to being a visiting fornicator. ("The Apartment," 2005)

"Hoochie Mama": A therapeutic expression used as a medium for rage. See also *"Serenity Now."* ("The Serenity Now," 9003)

I Love You **Return:** ("The Face Painter," 6021) The desired "I love you, too" response expected as a mutual return when expressing the words "I love you" for the first time. Alternatively, the first "I love you" can provoke a less favorable response, for example:

> **George:** I love you.
> **Siena:** You know, I'm hungry. Let's get something to eat.

Instant Boyfriend Status: See *Consolation Guy.* ("The Implant," 4018)

Intercourse Hello: See *Kiss Hello Program.* ("The Kiss Hello," 6015)

"It's Not You, It's Me" Routine: A generic script for ending a romantic relationship, intended to be as minimally offensive as possible. ("The Lip Reader," 5006)

Key Brother: See *Covenant of the Keys.* ("The Keys," 3022)

Kid Court-of-Law: ("The Robbery," 1003) A judicial system that settles disputes by the irrefutability of "calling it." For example:

> **Attorney:** Your Honor, my client did ask for the front seat.
> **Judge:** Did he call it?
> **Attorney:** Well, no, he didn't call it.
> **Judge:** Objection overruled. He has to call it. Case closed.

Kiss Hello Program: An expected system of greeting between two people, established out of habit, and characterized by an embrace and kiss on the cheek. Less tedious alternatives—for example, the *Touch a Breast Hello,* or the *Intercourse Hello*—have been proposed. ("The Kiss Hello," 6015)

Leave-Behind: A dating tactic that involves leaving personal items, such as keys and accessories, at the home of the dated individual. Consequently, a phone call is required in order to retrieve the items, and a resumption of dating activities is likely. ("The Chicken Roaster," 8008)

Level Jumping: Asking for a usually substantial favor (etc.) beyond what a relationship might permit. ("The Bris," 5005)

Little Man: The inner "wise" (in some idiotic) counselor that governs the self. ("The Pick," 4012)

Long Talker: An enthusiastic conversationalist. One who speaks excessively in situations where only a brief greeting is appropriate. ("The Chinese Woman," 6004)

Low Talker: One who speaks softly and is consequently misunderstood or unheard. ("The Puffy Shirt," 5002)

Make-Up Sex: Sex, much sought-after, following the reconciliation of a conflict between lovers. See also *Fugitive Sex*. ("The Postponement," 7002)

Mansierre: See *Bro*. ("The Doorman," 6016)

Mimbo: A male bimbo. A vacuous man, devoid of brain matter. ("The Stall," 5012)

Nice-Face Discount: A reduced price given to someone simply because the seller likes his or her attractive countenance. ("The Soup Nazi," 7006)

Nonvite: An invitation to an event, sent at such short notice that it may be assumed to be a formal gesture, but not a sincere invite. Alternatively known as an *unvitation*, a *nonvite* does not allow adequate time for the guest to prepare for the event or to resolve possible schedule conflicts. ("The Betrayal," 9008)

Phase Two: That second, more advanced, more intimate phase in a relationship that involves, among other things, "extra toothbrushes, increased call frequency, walking around naked." ("The Stock Tip," 1005)

Pick, The: In dating, *the pick* is a strategy that is employed when one no longer desires to be in the relationship: (1) the picker places a finger into a nostril, as if in an attempt to remove dried mucus deposits; (2) the picker is observed in this act by the unwanted dating partner, who is repulsed by the sight; (3) the relationship ends abruptly. ("The Pick," 4012)

Pig-Man: A mutant hybrid of pig and man. An unsightly species known to make pig noises. Speculations as to the origin of *pig-men* suggest government experiments to assemble an army of pig warriors. ("The Bris," 5005)

Pocket Diet: A self-imposed plan for eliminating the burdens of carrying unnecessary objects in one's pockets. Men on a *pocket diet* may cease to carry wallets and henceforth begin using a men's carryall, a European product that resembles a purse. ("The Reverse Peephole," 9012)

Pop-In: The spontaneous and uninvited appearance of a romantic partner into one's home. This can be avoided, for example, by engaging in long-distance relationships or by dating prison inmates. ("The Little Jerry," 8011)

Preemptive Breakup: Ending a relationship before (and in order to prevent) a suspected termination by the other. ("The Pez Dispenser," 3014)

Quone: A fabricated word, invented for use in the game of Scrabble. There is no precise meaning, but the following context is suggested: "When a patient gets unruly, you *quone* him." ("The Stakeout," 1002)

Rage-aholic: A person who is unharnessably temperamental. One who is perpetually pissed. ("The Apology," 9009)

Regifting: The process of recycling unwanted gifts by transferring them to a third party as supposedly new gifts. ("The Label Maker," 6012)

Riconic Relationship: The general linguistic framework that may be used by men who wish to name relationships after themselves. Just as a Platonic relationship refers to an asexual relationship between a man and woman, a *Riconic relationship* would refer, for example, to a relationship with a man named Rico, who may define this relationship as being free of formalities, emotions, and focused exclusively on sexual activities. ("The Stakeout," 1002)

Sentence Finisher: ("The Frogger," 9018) A human incarnation of Mad Libs. A person who interrupts a speaker, midsentence, in an attempt to predict and complete the execution of the sentence. Spoken, usually, with the intonations of a question, for example:

Jerry: I was thinking maybe we should—
Lisa (Sentence Finisher): Go for a hansom cab ride?
Jerry: Call it a night. I'll walk you home. Where do you live?

"Serenity Now": A therapeutic expression, articulated "Serenity, *now!*" intended to be a healthy projection of aggression. Alternatively: *"Hoochie Mama!"* ("The Serenity Now," 9003)

Sexual Camel: A person who is capable of abstaining from sex for long periods of time. When the *sexual camel* is a male, the portion of the brain normally devoted to sex is redirected toward more productive activities, achieving a condition of optimal intellectual functioning. ("The Abstinence," 8009)

Sexual Perjury: The act of faking an orgasm. ("The Mango," 5001)

Shiksappeal: The sexual attractiveness of a *shiksa*, a non-Jewish woman, to Jewish men. Presumably, the shiksa is appealing because she is unlike the mother of the interested Jewish man. ("The Serenity Now," 9003)

Shrinkage Factor: The phenomenon by which the size of the male genitalia decreases upon prolonged exposure to cold water. An inaccurate appraisal of the affected organ may result when the observer is a female unaware of the *shrinkage factor*. ("The Hamptons," 5021)

Shusher/Shushee: See *Unshushables*. ("The Apartment," 2005)

Smell Gestapo: Also known as *Body Odor Police*. This term refers to a proposed unit of patrolmen whose duties would consist of capturing and washing smelly individuals. The method of deodorizing might involve, for example, scrubbing the malodorous offenders with big soapy brushes. ("The Smelly Car," 4020)

Smoopie: Sweetie tweetie weetie weetie. A pretentiously affectionate term to refer to one's lover. ("The Soup Nazi," 7006)

Spare a Square: The act of generosity in which one gives a single unit of toilet paper to another who is toilet paper deficient. ("The Stall," 5012)

Spongeworthy: A male of a sexual caliber that merits the use of a contraceptive device *(sponge)* in a rare and limited supply. ("The Sponge," 7009)

Stabworthy: See *Bombable*. ("The Andrea Doria," 8010)

Step Skipper: A recovering addict or phobiac, such as a *rage-aholic* or a *germaphobe,* who intentionally neglects a formal step in the recovery program prescribed by a support group. ("The Apology," 9009)

Surprise-Blindfold Greeting: A method of greeting in which the initiator places each of two hands over the recipient's eyes, accompanied by a verbal *"Guess who?"* Reveals no conventional interpretation as to the level of affection or intimacy that is expressed. ("Good News, Bad News," pilot episode)

Switch, The: An impossible maneuver that involves, first, the termination of a relationship with a lover and, second, the establishment of a romantic relationship with the ex-lover's roommate. ("The Switch," 6011)

Tap, The: During oral sex, the less favorable of two conclusions. In the more favorable case, the activity ends when the woman reaches a climax. Alternatively, *the tap* may be given by the woman to her cunnilingually incompetent partner, signifying her loss of interest and the cunniliguist's lack of potential for producing the more favorable outcome. ("The Mango," 5001)

This, That: Friendship—social relations, as opposed to sex—intimate relations. ("The Deal," 2009)

To Turn the Key: In a romantic relationship, the mutual acceptance by both partners of a decision to end the relationship. For the relationship to be officially terminated, both partners must *turn the key.* ("The Strongbox," 9014)

Touch a Breast Hello: See *Kiss Hello Program.* ("The Kiss Hello," 6015)

Two-Face: A person whose appearance sporadically fluctuates between attractive and unattractive. ("The Strike," 9010)

Two-Hander: A *hand sandwich.* A handshake involving the use of two hands by the shake initiator. Thought to be a more intimate gesture than the single-handed shake but subject to interpretation according to the qualities of the hand sandwich and accompanying body language. ("Good News, Bad News," pilot episode)

Undateable: An unattractive person. Approximately 95 percent of the general population are *undateable* but are still able to engage in dating activities because of poor judgment resulting from alcohol intoxication. ("The Wink," 7004)

Unshushables: The group of patrons in a movie theater who are unresponsive to the *"shh."* The efforts of the *shushers* are thought to be futile, since the *shushees* are unsure of the source of the shush. ("The Apartment," 2005)

Unvitation: See *Nonvite.* ("The Betrayal," 9008)

Upper Hand: In a romantic relationship, the person who is the dominant recipient of affection—the one who is the *subject* of love more often than s/he is the *subjector.* The status can be achieved superficially, or automatically assumed by the partner who is, for example, wealthier, more intelligent, or more physically attractive. Also, the *upper hand* can belong to the partner who is more self-sufficient, that is, the partner who is the least emotionally attached and the least concerned with the romance. ("The Pez Dispenser," 3014)

Wait Out: Waiting for a separation, a severe dispute, or a divorce when the object of one's affection is married. If the *wait out* proves to be worthwhile, the opportunity calls for the following strategy to be employed: (1) the *waiter* calls the *waited out* and says, simply, "I'm there for you"; (2) The words "for you" are gradually removed; (3) The *waiter* is simply "there." ("The Wait Out," 7021)

Yada, Yada, Yada: Equivalent to "and so on," "etc., etc.," "blah, blah, blah"; often used when the abbreviated meaning cannot be clearly implied. For example: "I apologize for being late. I was in an accident, almost died, *yada, yada, yada.*" The listener is usually left with a sense of confusion, curiosity, and dissatisfaction. ("The Yada Yada," 8019)

"You're So Good-Looking: " An expression to be used, in response to a sneeze, as an alternative to "God bless you." Pronounced *"you're sooooooo good-lookin'!"*—with a sustained intonation of the word *so*. ("The Good Samaritan," 3019)

Seinfeld *Episode and Situation Guide*

Entries are organized by number, episode name, season number, and air date. The guide chronicles the writer(s) (**W**), director (**D**), Jerry's situation in the episode (**J**), George's situation (**G**), Elaine's situation (**E**), and Kramer's situation (**K**).

(01) **The Seinfeld Chronicles** (1001), July 5, 1989. **W:** Larry David/Jerry Seinfeld. **D:** Art Wolff; **J:** Preparing for a visit to NY by a woman he met on the road, wonders what the significance may be of her staying with him. **G:** Speculates with J about his upcoming visitor. **E:** Not yet a character. **K:** Appears in his bathrobe after knocking on the door (we learn he hasn't left the building in years).

(02) **The Stakeout** (1002), May 31, 1990. **W:** David / Seinfeld. **D:** Tom Cherones. **J:** Interested in a lawyer friend of his old girlfriend **E** but must stake out her office building to find her because he feels uncomfortable asking his ex for her phone number. **G:** Accompanies J on the stakeout. **E:** Invites J to accompany her to a party in return for him joining her at a wedding. **K:** Brief appearance playing Scrabble with J and his visiting parents.

(03) **The Robbery** (1003), June 7, 1990. **W:** Matt Goldman. **D:** Cherones. **J:** While J is on the road, thieves enter his open apartment and steal his stuff. **G:** Working as a real estate agent, finds a great apartment he offers to J and then comes to covet himself. **E:** Apartment-sits while J is away and covets J's apartment if he decides to move. **K:** Carelessly leaves J's door open during one of his habitual drop-ins.

(04) **Male Unbonding** (1004), June 14, 1990. **W:** David / Seinfeld. **D:** Cherones. **J:** Must break up with Joel, an old childhood friend who continues to annoy him. **G:** Advises J to break up with Joel. **E:** Helps J expand his "excuse Rolodex." **K:** Enamored with his idea to open a chain of make-your-own-pizza parlors.

(05) **The Stock Tip** (1005), June 21, 1990. **W:** David / Seinfeld. **D:** Cherones. **J:** Accompanies the woman from "The Stakeout" on a disastrous weekend in Vermont; loses money when he bales on a stock. **G:** Entices J to buy a stock, on which he ends up making money

after deciding to "go down with the ship." **E:** Dating a "normal guy" with cats but, bothered by her allergy to the pets, demands he choose between them or her . . . and loses. **K:** Develops an idea for a rollout tie dispenser.

(06) **The Ex-Girlfriend** (2001), January 23, 1991. **W:** David / Seinfeld. **D:** Cherones. **J:** Begins dating the woman **G** has just broken up with but is ditched by her because, after seeing his comedy routine, she can't continue to see anyone whose work she doesn't respect. **G:** Breaks up ("like a Band-Aid—one motion, right off") with a southern woman after he has already told her he loves her; pays a visit to **J**'s chiropractor. **E:** Puzzled why a man in her apartment building has stopped even acknowledging her. **K:** Seeks to return a bad cantaloupe to the market.

(07) **The Pony Remark** (2002), January 30, 1991. **W:** David / Seinfeld. **D:** Cherones. **J:** Offends an elderly aunt by his dinner table comment that he hates anyone with a pony and, when she dies, thinks she may have put a hex on him, affecting his play in a championship softball game. **G:** Plays softball with **J**; kibitzes on the goings-on [hereafter **KOG**]. **E:** Accompanies **J** to the dinner party; schemes to acquire the deceased aunt's apartment. **K:** Plans to redesign his apartment.

(08) **The Jacket** (2003), February 6, 1991. **W:** David / Seinfeld. **D:** Cherones. **J:** Buys an expensive suede jacket, which he wears to a dinner with **E**'s father and ruins in a snowstorm. **G:** Accompanies **J** to a very difficult dinner with Alton Benes; driven nuts by a song ("Master of the House" from *Les Misérables*). **E:** Working at Pendant Publishing; fails to show up for dinner with her father. **K:** Taking care of a magician friend's doves while he is on vacation.

(09) **The Phone Message** (2004), February 13, 1991. **W:** David / Seinfeld. **D:** Cherones. **J:** Breaks up with a woman because she likes a Dockers commercial he hates. **G:** Stupidly turns down an end-of-date invitation and then must retrieve an answering machine tape on which he left angry messages. **E:** KOG. **K:** KOG.

(10) **The Apartment** (2005), April 4, 1991. **W:** Peter Mehlman. **D:** Cherones. **J:** When he learns of an inexpensive apartment available in his building, he tells **E** about it and then immediately regrets the potential loss of privacy that will result if she moves in. **G:** Tries wearing a wedding ring because he has heard that it attracts women, and it does, though none will become involved because they think he is married. **E:** Excited by the prospect of moving into **J**'s apartment building but loses out on the bidding. **K:** With newly moussed hair, helps **J** sabotage **E**'s plans to move into their apartment building by finding someone who will pay $10,000 for the lease.

(11) **The Statue** (2006), April 11, 1991. **W:** Larry Charles. **D:** Cherones. **J:** Finds a longmissing statue given to him by his grandfather; when it disappears, he suspects the man he has hired to clean his apartment. **G:** Covets the statue, which reminds him of a traumatic childhood experience. **E:** Editing a book by a very difficult Finnish novelist at Pendant

(her husband steals the statue). **K:** Masquerading as a Joe Friday–ish cop, takes back the statue.

(12)   **The Revenge** (2007), April 18, 1991. **W:** David. **D:** Cherones. **J:** Convinced that the laundromat has stolen $1,500 he left in a laundry bag, enlists **K**'s aid in seeking revenge. **G:** Having quit his job too hastily with a real estate company, seeks to drug his old boss with a Mickey. **E:** Assists **G** in his revenge scheme. **K:** Assists **J** in his revenge scheme.

(13)   **The Heart Attack** (2008), April 25, 1991. **W:** Charles. **D:** Cherones. **J:** Accompanies **G** on his hypochondriacal adventures. **G:** Afraid he had a heart attack, seeks the help of an alternative health practitioner and ends up in the hospital—for a tonsillectomy. **E:** Starts seeing **G**'s doctor but finds his medical knowledge a turnoff. **K:** Sets **G** up with his holistic healer friend.

(14)   **The Deal** (2009), May 2, 1991. **W:** David. **D:** Cherones. **J:** Watching the "naked channel" on TV leads him and **E** to experiment with having sex ("that") while still maintaining their friendship ("this"). **G:** Initially fascinated when **E** and **J** start having sex again, later feels the effects of "breakup by association." **E:** Upset when **J** gives her money for her birthday. **K:** Gives **E** a birthday present that upstages **J**'s gift of money.

(15)   **The Baby Shower** (2010), May 16, 1991. **W:** Charles. **D:** Cherones. **J:** Agrees to **K**'s scheme to give him new television options. **G:** Shows up at the shower to confront the performance artist who once ruined a shirt of his with a can of chocolate syrup. **E:** Throws a baby shower at **J**'s apartment for a performance artist friend. **K:** Talks **J** into hiring his Russian friends to install illegal cable equipment.

(16)   **The Chinese Restaurant** (2011), May 23, 1991. **W:** David / Seinfeld. **D:** Cherones. Waiting on a table in a Chinese restaurant before attending a screening of "the worst movie ever made," *Plan 9 from Outer Space*, **J**, **E**, and **G** talk of many things: **J** offers **E** $50 to steal food; **J** worries Uncle Leo will learn he has stood him up; **G** argues over use of a pay phone—so he can call girlfriend Tatiana (**K** does not appear).

(17)   **The Busboy** (2012), June 26, 1991. **W:** David / Seinfeld. **D:** Cherones. **J:** KOG. **G:** Inadvertently gets a busboy fired in a restaurant and then compounds the problem by trying to make it up to him. **E:** Plays host to a guy from Seattle whom she hates and can't get rid of soon enough. **K:** Accompanies **G** on his ill-fated attempts to make amends.

(18)   **The Note** (3001), September 18, 1991. **W:** David. **D:** Cherones. **J:** With **G** schemes to get insurance to pay for a massage by getting a note from a dentist, but his unfortunate remarks lead his masseuse to think he's a child molester. **G:** Deeply troubled when "it" moves at the hands of a male masseuse. **E:** KOG. **K:** Convinced he has spotted Joe DiMaggio at Dinky Donuts.

(19)   **The Truth** (3002), September 25, 1991. **W:** Elaine Pope. **D:** David Steinberg. **J:** Facing a tax audit, his accountant ends up institutionalized. **G:** His brutally honest

breakup with a new girlfriend sends her to a mental institution. **E:** Must deal with her roommate's new date. **K:** Dating **E**'s roommate.

(20) **The Pen** (3003), October 2, 1991. **W:** David. **D:** Cherones. **J:** During a visit to his parents' condo in Florida, accepts Jack Klompus's insincere gift of an astronaut pen, with disastrous results. **G:** Does not appear. **E:** Accompanying **J** on his trip to Florida, seeks medical help (including painkillers) for back pain brought on by the sofa bed from hell. **K:** Does not appear.

(21) **The Dog** (3004), October 9, 1991. **W:** David. **D:** Cherones. **J:** Must look after a huge dog that belongs to his drunken seatmate on a plane flight. **G:** Driven from **J**'s dog-infested apartment, hangs out (awkwardly) with **E**. **K:** Has an on-again, off-again relationship with a woman the others don't like.

(22) **The Library** (3005), October 16, 1991. **W:** Charles. **D:** Joshua White. **J:** Pursued by a library cop who wants **J** to return a Henry Miller book he borrowed 20 years ago. **G:** Plots revenge against a high school gym teacher, now a bum, who gave him an "atomic wedgie" in high school. **E:** Puzzled by strange vibes at work. **K:** Dates a librarian.

(23) **The Parking Garage** (3006), October 30, 1991. **W:** David. **D:** Cherones. After a visit to a mall in New Jersey, misadventures (including **J**'s arrest for public urination) occur in a parking garage as **J**, **G**, **E**, and **K** try to find **K**'s car.

(24) **The Cafe** (3007), November 6, 1991. **W:** Tom Leopold. **D:** Cherones. **J**'s attempts to help restaurateur Babu Bhatt lead to disaster and his conviction that **J** is a "very bad man." **G**'s new girlfriend wants him to take an IQ test. **E:** Helps **G** by taking the IQ test for him. **K:** Struggles over possession of a lucky jacket left at his mother's house.

(25) **The Tape** (3008), November 13, 1991. **W:** David / Bob Shaw / Don McEnery. **D:** Steinberg. **J:** Discovers a Penthouse letter left (by **E**) on a tape recorder he used to capture his routine at the club. **G:** Tries out a Chinese treatment for baldness. **E:** Admits to **G** she did the porn tape but only later tells **J** (all the men see her in a new light as a result). **K:** Seeks to document **G**'s hair growth.

(26) **The Nose Job** (3009), November 20, 1991. **W:** Mehlman. **D:** Cherones. **J:** A beautiful but superficial woman he is dating makes him feel like "my brain is facing my penis in a chess match." **G:** Dating a woman with quite a large nose, who after one botched operation breaks up with him and, finally, returns, now a beauty, and **K**'s girlfriend. **E:** Assists **K** (in the guise of Prof. Van Nostrand) in a scheme to get back his lucky jacket. **K:** With his usual tactless candor, tells **G**'s new girlfriend she needs a nose job.

(27) **The Stranded** (3010), November 27, 1991. **W:** David / Seinfeld / Matt Goldman. **D:** Cherones. **J** and **E** go to a party with **G** at his coworker's house on Long Island but find it to be a bore; when **G** goes off with someone he meets at the party, **K** has to come rescue **J** and **E**. The party's host later appears in New York, causing problems for **J**.

(28) **The Alternate Side** (3011), December 4, 1991. **W:** David / Bill Masters. **D:** Cherones. **J's** car is stolen when the car mover leaves the keys in the ignition. **G:** Replaces the man who moves cars to the opposite side of the street. **E:** Is dating a 66-year-old man, who has a stroke. **K:** Gets a job in a Woody Allen film where he has only one line ("These pretzels are making me thirsty").

(29) **The Red Dot** (3012), December 11, 1991. **W:** David. **D:** Cherones. **J's** mistake at a party drives an alcoholic off the wagon. **G:** With **E's** help, begins work at Pendant Publishing (he thanks her with a deeply discounted flawed cashmere sweater), but is fired after having sex with the cleaning lady. **E:** Is dating coworker Dick, a recovering alcoholic. **K:** KOG.

(30) **The Subway** (3013), January 8, 1992. **W:** Charles. **D:** Cherones. **J:** On the subway, converses with a large naked man and accompanies him to Coney Island. **G:** Seduced by a woman who leaves him, sans clothes, handcuffed to a bed in a hotel. **E:** On her way to a lesbian wedding, has a terrible time on a stalled train. **K:** Pursues a racing tip.

(31) **The Pez Dispenser** (3014), January 15, 1992. **W:** David. **D:** Cherones. **J:** Reluctantly hosts a drug intervention for a comic acquaintance. **G:** Dating a pianist, with whom he attempts a "preemptive breakup." **E:** Breaks into laughter at a piano concert when **J** shows her a Tweety Bird Pez dispenser. **K:** Concocts a plan for a new cologne that smells like the beach.

(32) **The Suicide** (3015), January 29, 1992. **W:** Leopold. **D:** Cherones. **J:** Tempted by the wife of a dangerous neighbor who attempts suicide. **G:** Visits a chain-smoking pregnant psychic in the hope of discovering his destiny. **E:** Accompanies **G** on his visit to a psychic, but **E's** anger at her smoking habit gets them both expelled. **K:** Advises **J** in "coma etiquette."

(33) **The Fix-Up** (3016), February 5, 1992. **W:** Pope / Charles. **D:** Cherones. **J:** Helps **E** set up a blind date between her friend and **G**. **G:** Agrees to go on a blind date with a friend of **E's** and finds himself proud ("My boys can swim!") when she thinks she might be pregnant. **E:** Enlists **J's** aid in fixing up **G** with a bulimic friend who wants to meet a man who will appreciate her because he is desperate. **K:** Receives a gross of (defective) condoms thanks to Bob Sacamano.

(34) **The Boyfriend** (3017), February 12, 1992. **W:** David / Larry Levin. **D:** Cherones. **J:** Becomes pals with ex–Met First Baseman Keith Hernandez and becomes jealous when he starts dating **E**. **G:** Tries to pull the wool over the eyes of the unemployment office, including dating Mrs. Sokol's daughter. **E:** Steals Keith Hernandez away from **J**. **K:** With Newman, still angry at Hernandez because they believe he spit on them in 1987.

(35) **The Limo** (3018), February 26, 1992. **W:** Charles / Marc Jaffe. **D:** Cherones. **J:** With **G**, accepts a ride in a limo at the airport actually meant for a white supremacist leader and must masquerade as neo-Nazis "O'Brien and Murphy." **E** and **K:** Wait for "O'Brien and Murphy" to arrive at Madison Square Garden.

(36)   **The Good Samaritan** (3019), March 4, 1992. **W:** Mehlman. **D:** Jason Alexander. **J:** Follows a hit-and-run driver and ends up dating her. **G:** Accompanying **E** and friends to dinner, gets in trouble for an inappropriate "God bless you." **E:** Has to settle for **G** as her companion on a dinner date. **K:** The voice of Mary Hart causes him to have seizures.

(37)   **The Letter** (3020), March 25, 1992. **W:** David. **D:** Cherones. **J:** Dates a painter who may be plagiarizing her letters from Neil Simon. **G:** KOG. **E:** Wearing a Baltimore Orioles hat in the owners' box gets her thrown out of Yankee Stadium. **K:** **J**'s painter love interest does a portrait of him that is much talked about in the art world.

(38)   **The Parking Space** (3021), April 22, 1992. **W:** David / Greg Daniels. **D:** Cherones. While **J** and **K** (waiting for guests to arrive to watch a boxing match) bicker over the latter's busybodiness, **G** and **E** (in **J**'s damaged car) return from a flea market and **G** spends the entire day fighting with an acquaintance of **K**'s over who has the rights to the spot (the whole neighborhood becomes involved in the debate).

(39)   **The Keys** (3022), May 6, 1992. **W:** Charles. **D:** Cherones. **J:** Becomes angry at **K** for abusing his "Covenant of the Keys" and visiting his apartment too often. **G:** Must deal with the fallout from the end of **J** and **K**'s key agreement. **E:** Also deals with the fallout of the end of the Covenant and is revealed to be writing a script for *Murphy Brown*. **K:** Takes **J**'s anger over the Covenant as a sign he should head for California and become an actor.

(40)   **The Trip, Part I** (4001), August 12, 1992. **W:** Charles. **D:** Cherones. **J:** Gets booked on *The Tonight Show* and heads for California, accompanied by **G**, hoping to patch things up with **K**. **G:** Uses **J**'s free ticket to join in their California sojourn. **E:** Does not appear. **K:** In his new life in California must deal with an aging movie actress and being mistaken as the Smog Strangler.

(41)   **The Trip, Part II** (4002), August 19, 1992. **W:** Charles. **D:** Cherones. **J** and **G** try to clear **K**'s name. **E:** Does not appear. **K:** Finally acquitted of being a serial killer.

(42)   **The Pitch/The Ticket** (one hour) (4003), August 16, 1992. **W:** David. **D:** Cherones. **J:** NBC likes his stand-up and invites him to pitch an idea for a series, where he angers off-his-meds Crazy Joe Davola, who will later attack **K**. **G:** Comes up with the idea for a "show about nothing." **E:** On a European trip with her therapist, who forgets to prescribe medication for his patient Crazy Joe Davola. **K:** Doesn't like the idea of being a character in **J**'s new sitcom (unless he can play himself) and vomits (after drinking curdled milk from **J**'s fridge) all over Susan.

(43)   **The Wallet** (4004), August 23, 1992. **W:** David. **D:** Cherones. **J:** Asked to come back to talk to NBC, he offends Uncle Leo, causing a family crisis. **G:** Takes the lead in "negotiating" with NBC, telling Susan they will pass. **E:** Returns from Europe but wants to break up with her "Sven Jolly." **K:** Unstable from Joe Davola's kick to the head in the previous episode (he keeps saying "Yo Yo Ma" uncontrollably); acquiesces in Newman's scheme to get out of a speeding ticket.

(44) **The Watch** (4005), August 30, 1992. **W:** David. **D:** Cherones. **J:** Must explain why the watch his parents gave him (and that he threw in the trash) is missing; dating a woman with an annoying laugh. **G:** Succeeds in driving down NBC's offer. **E:** Still trying to extricate herself from her affair with her psychiatrist, she meets Crazy Joe Davola and flirts with him. **K:** Poses as E's boyfriend to help with her breakup with Dr. Reston.

(45) **The Bubble Boy** (4006), October 7, 1992. **W:** David / Charles. **D:** Cherones. **J:** Breaks up with the "Elmer Fudd sitting on juicer" woman, agrees to visit a boy (a fan) encased in a protective plastic bubble. **G:** With Susan, on the way to her parents' cabin, arrives at the Bubble Boy's, where an altercation over Trivial Pursuit nearly kills the BB. **E:** Accompanies J on the trip to meet the Bubble Boy. **K:** Joins "Elmer Fudd" on a trip to the Ross cabin, which burns down in a fire ignited by his cigar.

(46) **The Cheever Letters** (4007), October 28, 1992. **W:** David / Pope / Leopold. **D:** Cherones. **J:** While struggling with writer's block, dates E's former secretary, who he offends with a remark about panties. **G:** Discovers, in the aftermath of the fire at Susan's parents' cabin, that Mr. Ross and the bisexual writer John Cheever were lovers. **E:** Has major problems with her secretary at Pendant. **K:** Tries to secure more Cuban cigars by visiting the Cuban embassy.

(47) **The Opera** (4008), November 4, 1992. **W:** Charles. **D:** Cherones. The gang must deal with the threat of Crazy Joe Davola as they attend a performance of *I Pagliacci*. **E** discovers that her new boyfriend is, in fact, Davola; **K** and **G** try to scalp their tickets; while waiting in line, Davola attacks J and E.

(48) **The Virgin** (4009), November 11, 1992. **W:** Mehlman / Peter Farrelly / Bob Farrelly. **D:** Cherones. **J:** Is dating a woman who is still a virgin. **G:** Seeks to dump Susan. **E:** Is sued by Ping for causing a traffic accident by jaywalking. **K:** After giving his TV to **G**, becomes even more addicted to watching it—in J's apartment.

(49) **The Contest** (4010), November 18, 1992. **W:** David. **D:** Cherones. **J:** Becomes part of a contest to see who can last the longest without masturbating. **G**'s mother catches him masturbating and ends up in the hospital, where he must witness a sexy sponge bath jeopardizing his chances in the contest. **E:** Tempted by JFK, Jr., a new member of her health club. **K:** First to lose in the contest, thanks to a naked woman in the apartment across the street.

(50) **The Airport** (4011), November 25, 1992. **W:** Charles. **D:** Cherones. **J:** Returning from a gig in St. Louis, accompanied by **E**, he is offered an upgrade to first class, where he meets, and hits it off with, a fashion model. **G:** Accompanies **K** on what he hopes will be a perfect airport pickup and ends up locked in an airplane restroom with a serial killer. **E:** Suffers through a terrible flight back from St. Louis in coach. **K:** Drives **G** to the airport to pick up J and E, where he spots an old roommate who owes him money.

(51) **The Pick** (4012), December 16, 1992. **W:** David / Jaffe. **D:** Cherones. **J:** Loses his new model girlfriend after she thinks she sees him picking his nose. **G:** Blows hot and

cold about getting back together with Susan and then breaks up again by using the pick technique. **E:** Horribly embarrassed when the photograph (taken by **K**) on her Christmas card shows an exposed nipple. **K:** After accusing Calvin Klein in person of stealing his idea for a scent that smells like the beach, becomes an underwear model for CK (who finds his buttocks "sublime").

(52) **The Movie** (4013), January 6, 1993. **W:** Steve Skrovan / Bill Masters / Jon Hayman. **D:** Cherones. The four are to meet at a movie (they end up at *Rochelle, Rochelle: The Musical)* but each has problems getting there: **J** is double-booked at comedy clubs, **K** has a hot dog craving, **E** can't save seats, **G** clashes with an usher.

(53) **The Visa** (4014), January 27, 1993. **W:** Mehlman. **D:** Cherones. **J**'s failure to file Babu's visa renewal gets him deported. **G:** Afraid his new girlfriend will like **J** better and convinces him to be "dark and disturbed" instead of funny. **E:** Talks **G**'s new girlfriend into persuading her cousin Ping to (temporarily) drop his lawsuit against her. **K:** Returns from a fantasy baseball camp where he beaned Joe Pepitone and got in a fight with Mickey Mantle.

(54) **The Shoes** (4015), February 4, 1993. **W:** David / Seinfeld. **D:** Cherones. **J:** KOG. **G:** Caught by Russell Dalrymple looking at his daughter's cleavage and convinces **E** to help him get revenge by having him stare at hers. **E:** Puzzled why everyone is talking about the expensive shoes she bought. **K:** KOG.

(55) **The Outing** (4016), February 11, 1993. **W:** Charles. **D:** Cherones. **J:** Due to a joke by **E**, mistaken as gay (as is **G**) by an NYU student reporter ("not that there's anything wrong with that"). **G:** While news of his sexual preference alarms his parents, he attempts to use it to break up with his current girlfriend. **E:** KOG. **K:** KOG.

(56) **The Old Man** (4017), February 18, 1993. **W:** Charles / Bruce Kirschbaum. **D:** Cherones. **J:** The old man he volunteers to help is profane, racist, and mean. **G:** Fired when he tries to convince the 82-year-old he is helping he should be depressed over his imminent death but hooks up with **J**'s guy's Senegalese housekeeper. **E:** As a volunteer to help the elderly (which shames the others into doing the same), she meets a woman with a huge goiter, the former lover of Gandhi (who, we learn, shared a sexual fantasy with **G**). **K:** Partners with Newman to sell used records, including those they steal from the elderly man **J** is helping.

(57) **The Implant** (4018), February 25, 1993. **W:** Mehlman. **D:** Cherones. **J:** Plots to discover whether the breasts of his new girlfriend Sidra are real or fake. **G:** Accompanies a new girlfriend to a funeral, gets caught "double-dipping," and connives to get the airline bereavement discount. **E:** Recruited by **J** to find out whether Sidra's breasts are artificially enhanced. **K:** Convinced that he has seen Salman Rushdie at the health club.

(58) **The Junior Mint** (4019), March 18, 1993. **W:** Andy Robin. **D:** Cherones. **J:** Forced to masquerade as **E**'s boyfriend when she visits an old boyfriend in the hospital and is dating a woman whose name he can't remember (but rhymes with a female body part). **G:**

Watches *Home Alone* (and cries) and later, after being trapped into buying one of **E**'s friend's triangles, hopes the artist will die so he can make a profit on the purchase. **E:** Visits a former boyfriend (an artist who paints only triangles) in the hospital for surgery and finds him more attractive now that he has lost weight. **K:** While watching surgery on **E**'s artist friend, accidentally drops a Junior Mint into his open chest cavity.

(59) **The Smelly Car** (4020), April 15, 1993. **W:** David / Mehlman. **D:** Cherones. **J**'s car comes down with a terminal case of "BBO" (Beyond Body Odor) from a valet at a restaurant. **G:** Runs into Susan, now a lesbian, and becomes convinced he drove her away from heterosexuality. **E:** Finds herself unable to shake the stink she has picked up from **J**'s car. **K:** Steals away Susan's new (formerly lesbian) girlfriend.

(60) **The Handicap Spot** (4021), May 13, 1993. **W:** David. **D:** Cherones. The four stop at a mall on the way to the Drake's engagement party and must deal with an angry crowd after they park illegally in a handicap parking space (**G**'s father's car is trashed).

(61) **The Pilot** (one hour) (4022), May 20, 1993. **W:** David. **D:** Cherones. **J:** Works on the pilot for *Jerry*. **G:** Thinks he has cancer. **E:** Continues to deal with Dalrymple's obsession with her. **K:** Has a problem with constipation, which sinks his audition (as Martin Van Nostrand) to play himself on *Jerry*.

(62) **The Mango** (5001), September 16, 1993. **W:** Lawrence H. Levy / Buck Dancer. **D:** Cherones. **J:** Shocked to learn that E faked all of her orgasms with him when they were dating. **G:** Gets "the tap" from a new girlfriend who gets more of a sexual thrill from risotto than from his lovemaking. **E:** Almost ends her friendship with **J** after admitting her feigned sexual climaxes but finally offers to have sex once again "to save the friendship." **K:** Banned from his favorite fruit stand after complaining about the peaches.

(63) **The Puffy Shirt** (5002), September 23, 1993. **W:** David. **D:** Cherones. **J:** Without comprehending the request of **K**'s "low talker" girlfriend, agrees to wear a pirate-like puffy shirt on *The Today Show*. **G:** After suffering the ignominy of moving back home, becomes a briefly successful hand model. **E:** KOG. **K:** Dating a "low talker" clothes designer.

(64) **The Glasses** (5003), September 30, 1993. **W:** Tom Gammill / Max Pross. **D:** Cherones. **J:** Believes his new girlfriend may be having an affair with his cousin Jeffrey after a squinting, glassless **G** thinks he spots them in the park. **G:** After his glasses are "stolen" at the health club, seeks to save money (with **K**'s connections) on a new pair. **E:** Thinks she has rabies after being bitten by a dog. **K:** Gets **J** a new air conditioner—at a wholesale price.

(65) **The Sniffing Accountant** (5004), October 7, 1993. **W:** David / Seinfeld. **D:** Cherones. **J:** Is convinced his accountant has a drug problem. **G:** Almost gets a job as a bra salesman. **E:** Breaks up with Jake Jarmel because he is stingy with exclamation marks. **K:** Goes undercover in a bar to investigate the accountant's drug habit.

(66) **The Bris** (5005), October 14, 1993. **W:** Charles. **D:** Cherones. **J:** Asked to be a godfather and organize the bris for the new son of some friends. **G:** Proud of his great

parking spot at the hospital, his car is damaged by a suicide's leap. **E:** Asked to be a godmother and organize the bris for the new son of some friends. **K:** Thinks he sees a Pig-Man in the hospital.

(67)   **The Lip Reader** (5006), October 28, 1993. **W:** Carol Leifer. **D:** Cherones. **J:** Dating a deaf linesman he meets at the U.S. Open. **G:** Enlists J's deaf girlfriend to find out the truth about an ex. **E:** Angers a limo driver by pretending to be deaf so she won't have to talk to him. **K:** Aspires to become a ball boy at the Open.

(68)   **The Non-Fat Yogurt** (5007), November 4, 1993. **W:** David. **D:** Cherones. **J:** Obsessed—as are **E, K, G,** and Newman—with a new nonfat yogurt store but becomes convinced the product is a fraud when he begins to gain weight. **G:** After feigning a spastic movement of his arm in order not to lose face before long-time rival Lloyd Braun, is forced to continue to fake the ailment. **E:** Convinces Braun, an adviser to NYC mayor David Dinkins, to float her plan to have all New Yorkers wear nametags. **K**'s amorous activities with a chem lab attendant result in a false high cholesterol count for mayoral candidate Rudolph Giuliani.

(69)   **The Barber** (5008), November 11, 1993. **W:** Robin. **D:** Cherones. **J:** Disappointed with an older Italian barber forces him to be unfaithful with his *Edward Scissorhands*–loving nephew. **G:** Shows up for work after a job interview not certain whether he has been hired or not. **E:** Organizing a charity bachelor auction. **K:** Struts his stuff at a bachelor auction.

(70)   **The Masseuse** (5009), November 18, 1993. **W:** Mehlman. **D:** Cherones. J's new masseuse girlfriend won't give him a massage and dislikes **G** intensely. **G:** Reunites with the risotto woman ("The Mango") but loses her because of his obsession with J's girlfriend (who hates him). **E:** Dating a guy with the same name (Joel Rifkin) as a serial killer. **K:** Becomes addicted to J's girlfriend's massages.

(71)   **The Cigar Store Indian** (5010), December 9, 1993. **W:** Gammill / Pross. **D:** Cherones. **J:** Makes a bad impression on a Native American woman when he gives her a cigar store Indian as a present and continues to make remarks that suggest he is a racist. **G:** Must have a coffee table refinished before his parents' return and then leaves a prophylactic wrapper on his parents' bed. **E:** Pursued by a nerdish man she meets on the subway who is as obsessed by *TV Guide* as he is with **E** and is the object of Frank Costanza's ire for taking his copy. **K:** Hatches his scheme to create a coffee-table book about coffee tables and, when he sells the cigar store Indian to Mr. Lippman, finds a publisher.

(72)   **The Conversion** (5011), December 16, 1993. **W:** Kirschbaum. **D:** Cherones. **J:** Finds fungicide in his girlfriend's bathroom cabinet. **G:** Decides to convert in order to keep a Latvian Orthodox girlfriend (and cheats on the conversion exam). **E:** Dating a podiatrist who **J** insists does not count as a real doctor. **K:** Seduces (thanks to his powerful "Kevorka") a Latvian Orthodox nun but is convinced the power is actually a curse.

(73) **The Stall** (5012), January 6, 1994. **W:** Charles. **D:** Cherones. **J:** Dating a woman who, unbeknownst to **J**, works for a phone sex service. **G:** Has a man-crush on **E**'s "mimbo" boyfriend and (with **K**) sends him to the hospital after causing a mountain climbing accident. **E:** Becomes furious when the woman in the next toilet stall will not loan her much-needed toilet paper. **K:** Becomes obsessed with a phone sex service.

(74) **The Dinner Party** (5013), February 3, 1994. **W:** David. **D:** Cherones. On their way to a dinner party, major problems ensue when the four stop for a gift: the bakery is out of chocolate babka, **J**'s vomit streak ends (the cause a black-and-white cookie), **G** loses his GORE-TEX jacket, **K** gets parked-in by Saddam Hussein.

(75) **The Marine Biologist** (5014), February 10, 1994. **W:** Ron Hauge / Charlie Rubin. **D:** Cherones. **J:** After getting **E** in trouble with Yuri Testikov, must help her avoid a lawsuit; mourns the loss of Golden Boy. **G:** Must pretend he is a marine biologist to impress a woman from college and is called upon to save a beached whale. **E:** Has to deal with the very gruff visiting Russian writer Testikov. **K:** Gives **E** an organizer; hits a gross of golf balls into the ocean.

(76) **The Pie** (5015), February 17, 1994. **W:** Gammill / Pross. **D:** Cherones. **J:** Refuses to eat after Poppie prepares food with hands he failed to wash after going to the bathroom. **G:** Goes to great lengths to buy a one-of-a-kind suit for a job interview. **E:** Tries to get to the bottom of mannequins appearing around town that look just like her. **K:** Bothered by an itchy back, but finds a Monk's employee willing to scratch it.

(77) **The Stand-In** (5016), February 24, 1994. **W:** David. **D:** Cherones. **J:** Tries (and tries and tries) to make a sick acquaintance laugh. **G:** Insulted when his new girlfriend is warned not to get involved with him and vows not to break up with her (even though he wants to). **E:** Shocked when a guy **J** fixes her up with takes "it" out. **K:** With his dwarf friend Mickey, gets a job as a stand-in on *All My Children*.

(78) **The Wife** (5017), March 17, 1994. **W:** Mehlman. **D:** Cherones. **J:** Agrees to a "pretend marriage" in order to get a dry cleaning discount for his girlfriend but can't stand the pressure and becomes unfaithful. **G:** Caught urinating in the shower at the health club. **E:** Also at the health club, reads (and misreads) the signs that a guy may be smitten with her. **K:** Dating an African American woman but is rejected by her family after showing up as a blackface "damned fool" (severely burned in a tanning parlor).

(79) **The Raincoats** (one hour) (5018, 5019), April 28, 1994. **W:** Gammill / Pross / David / Seinfeld. **D:** Cherones. **J:** While his parents are shown a good time by **E**'s boyfriend, is forced to make out with Rachel during *Schindler's List*. **G:** Sells his father's Cabana clothes to a used-clothing store and reluctantly becomes a Big Brother. **E:** Dating a too-good-to-be-true "close talker" named Aaron, who shows more interest in **J**'s parents than in her. **K:** Schemes with Morty Seinfeld to sell the beltless raincoats he invented.

(80) **The Fire** (5020), May 5, 1994. **W:** Charles. **D:** Cherones. **J:** Seeks revenge against a coworker of **E**'s by coming to her office and heckling her, making him the new "Rosa

Parks" of comedians. **G:** Runs in terror from a small fire at a birthday party, knocking down women, children, and the elderly. **E:** Greatly annoyed by her Pendant coworker, the heavily caffeinated cackling Toby. **K:** Saves Toby's severed pinky toe by engineering a mad cross-city bus trip.

(81) **The Hamptons** (5021), May 12, 1994. **W:** Mehlman / Leifer. **D:** Cherones. **J:** Accompanied by Rachel, visits friends on Long Island in order to "see the baby." **G:** Distressed when the others get to see his girlfriend topless and embarrassed when Rachel inadvertently sees him (after swimming) with "significant shrinkage." **E:** Develops a crush on a pediatrician who calls her "breathtaking." **K:** Gets in trouble with police after stealing lobsters from a trap.

(82) **The Opposite** (5022), May 19, 1994. **W:** Andy Cowan / David / Seinfeld. **D:** Cherones. **J:** Becomes "Even Steven": losing one job, gaining another; losing one girlfriend, gaining another. **G:** At J's suggestion, begins, with miraculous results (including a job with the Yankees), to do the exact opposite of everything he would normally do. **E:** Breaks up with a serious boyfriend (Jake Jarmel) after stopping to buy Jujyfruits on the way to visit him after a bad traffic accident, only one of several negatives (including the demise of Pendant Publishing) as she fears she has become **G**. **K**'s book tour begins (and ends) with a disastrous appearance on *Regis and Kathy Lee*.

(83) **The Chaperone** (6001), September 22, 1994. **W:** David / Bill Masters / Shaw. **D:** Andy Ackerman. **J:** Dates Ms. Rhode Island (and her chaperone) and accidentally kills her doves (for her magic/talent act). **G:** Pushes for a Yankee uniform switch (to cotton, which "breathes"). **E:** Becomes the personal assistant to Mr. Pitt. **K:** Serves as chaperone and mentor to Ms. Rhode Island.

(84) **The Big Salad** (6002), September 29, 1994. **W:** David. **D:** Ackerman. **J:** Sickened to learn that his girlfriend used to date Newman until *he* ditched *her*. **G:** Upset when his new girlfriend takes credit for a big salad he bought for **E**. **E:** Hit on by a stationery store guy after she orders a special pen for Mr. Pitt. **K:** Plays golf with former baseball player Steve Gendason and infuriates him by penalizing him for cleaning his ball, after which he kills a dry cleaner and ends up in a slow speed chase (K as A. C. Cowlings).

(85) **The Pledge Drive** (6003), October 6, 1994. **W:** Gammill / Pross. **D:** Ackerman. **J:** Agrees to appear on a Public Television fundraiser, cashes his nana's old check, and is convinced **E**'s married friend is hitting on him. **G:** Convinced everyone is giving him the finger; after imitating Mr. Pitt's penchant for eating Snickers with a knife, it becomes a citywide fad. **E:** Mistakes her friend's "high talking" husband for her and reveals J's suspicion about her flirtation. **K:** Agrees to answer phones at the fundraiser, where he becomes convinced that the "high talker" is in love with J.

(86) **The Chinese Woman** (6004), October 13, 1994. **W:** Mehlman. **D:** Ackerman. **J:** Interested in a woman named Donna Chang but is disappointed to learn she is not Chinese. **G:** Concerned over his father's meeting with a mystery man in a cape, learns his

parents may be splitting up. **E:** Talks her friend into leaving the High Talker. **K:** Trying to improve his sperm count, switches to boxers and then, to J's and E's horror, to no underwear at all.

(87)   **The Couch** (6005), October 27, 1994. **W:** David. **D:** Ackerman. **J:** Gets a new sofa, soon to be ruined by Poppie. **G:** Invites himself over to a black family's apartment to watch *Breakfast at Tiffany's* so he won't have to read it. **E:** Falls for J's moving man until she discovers he is pro-life and anti-abortion. **K:** Goes into the pizza business with Poppie, who has strong anti-abortion (and anti-cucumber) views.

(88)   **The Gymnast** (6006), November 3, 1994. **W:** Alec Berg / Jeff Schaffer. **D:** Ackerman. **J:** Dating a Romanian gymnast (with fantasies about the sex), though they can find nothing to talk about. **G:** Crosses "the line from man into bum" by eating an éclair out of a trashcan. **E:** Becomes involved in the Morgan Creek/Poland Springs merger and ends up turning Mr. Pitt into Hitler. **K:** Has kidney stones.

(89)   **The Soup** (6007), November 10, 1994. **W:** Fred Stoller. **D:** Ackerman. **J:** Fellow (annoying) comic Kenny Bania gives him an Armani suit and expects a meal in return. **G:** Determined to find out why a date has ditched him. **E:** Suffers through a visit from a British "bounder." **K:** Decides to eat only fresh food.

(90)   **The Mom And Pop Store** (6008), November 17, 1994. **W:** Gammill / Pross. **D:** Ackerman. **J:** Doesn't know whether he has been invited to Tim Whatley's party or not; after **K** takes away all his shoes, is reduced to wearing cowboy boots. **G:** Buys a used Chrysler LeBaron thinking it belongs to Jon Voight. **E:** Wins a big-band trivia contest that gets Mr. Pitt a chance to steer a Woody Woodpecker balloon in the Macy's parade. **K:** Tries to help a mom-and-pop store's business by taking J's shoes to be cleaned (which leads to their going out of business); bitten by Jon Voight.

(91)   **The Secretary** (6009), December 8, 1994. **W:** Leifer / Marjorie Gross. **D:** David Owen Trainor. **J:** Thinks his dry cleaner may be secretly wearing his clothes. **G:** Passes over potential secretaries, purposely selects the plainest one, and then ends up having a torrid affair with her. **E:** Becomes convinced that the mirrors in a clothing store are "rigged." **K:** Has a chance to meet Uma Thurman.

(92)   **The Race** (6010), December 15, 1994. **W:** Gammill / Pross / David / Sam Kass. **D:** Ackerman. **J:** Meets an old nemesis from grade school he once beat in a race (though **J** may have cheated). **G:** Answers a personals ad in *The Daily Worker*, which leads to Steinbrenner thinking he's a Communist, sending him to Cuba (he meets with Castro) to recruit players for the Yankees. **E:** Dating a man who may be a Communist (he reads *The Daily Worker* and dresses drably), she gets both of them "blacklisted" at Hop Sing's. **K:** Becomes a Marxist department store Santa.

(93)   **The Switch** (6011), January 5, 1995. **W:** Kirschbaum / Kass. **D:** Ackerman. **J:** Dating a woman who seems impervious to his humor and hopes to trade her for her roommate (a ménage à trois is part of the scheme). **G:** Suspects that his model girlfriend is bulimic and

enlists **K**'s matron mother's help in proving it. **E:** Loans Mr. Pitt's expensive tennis racket to a potential employer at Doubleday and then has to scheme to get it back. **K**'s name (Cosmo) is revealed in his reunion with his mother.

(94)   **The Label Maker** (6012), January 19, 1995. **W:** Berg / Schaffer. **D:** Ackerman. **J:** Gives dentist Tim Whatley Super Bowl tickets and receives a "regifted" label maker in return. **G:** Perplexed by his girlfriend's male roommate (and gets trapped in a ménage à trois). **E:** Becomes interested in Tim Whatley. **K** and Newman are obsessed with playing Risk.

(95)   **The Scofflaw** (6013), January 26, 1995. **W:** Mehlman. **D:** Ackerman. **J:** Sworn to secrecy about Gary's cancer lie. **G:** Pretend cancer victim Gary puts toupee-wearing **G**'s status as a liar to a test. **E:** Breaks up (again) with Jake Jarmel but loses the upper hand. **K:** Learns that Newman's often-ticketed car is a kind of Moby-Dick to an eye-patch-wearing cop.

(96)   **The Beard** (6014), February 9, 1995. **W:** Leifer. **D:** Ackerman. **J:** Attracted to a female cop but must pass a polygraph test on whether his claim he never watched *Melrose Place* is true. **G:** On the prowl with his new toupee, makes a date with a bald woman and has his piece thrown out the window by **E**. **E:** Tries to get her gay friend to "play for her team." **K:** Earns money by appearing in police lineups.

(97)   **The Kiss Hello** (6015), February 16, 1995. **W:** David / Seinfeld. **D:** Ackerman. **J:** Annoyed by the kiss hello of a physical therapist friend of **E**; ostracized for not kissing hello in his apartment building. **G:** Infuriated when **E**'s physical therapist friend charges him for a missed appointment. **E:** After skiing with her physical therapist friend, needs help herself. **K:** Puts everyone's photo up in the lobby of their apartment building.

(98)   **The Doorman** (6016), February 23, 1995. **W:** Gammill / Pross. **D:** Ackerman. **J:** Clashes with a doorman at Mr. Pitt's building. **G:** Traumatized when he sees his father's "man breasts" ("my own personal *Crying Game*"). **E:** Accused of being involved in the theft of a couch. **K:** With Frank Costanza, develops a new undergarment for men: the Bro/Manssiere.

(99)   **The Jimmy** (6017), March 16, 1995. **W:** Gregg Kavet / Robin. **D:** Ackerman. **J:** Thinks something unseemly occurred in the dentist's chair while he was under anesthetic. **G:** Comes under suspicion of a theft at work because he is always sweating. **E:** Mistakenly agrees to date Jimmy, an obnoxious gym rat who talks in the third person. **K:** Still feeling the effects of Novocain, is mistaken as mentally retarded and becomes the guest of honor at a banquet.

(100)   **The Doodle** (6018), April 6, 1995. **W:** Berg / Schaffer. **D:** Ackerman. **J:** Has fleas and has to have his apartment fumigated (with **E**'s important manuscript inside). **G:** Troubled by his girlfriend's doodle of him. **E:** Loses a job when **J**'s parents, Uncle Leo, and nana run up a huge bill in a hotel room in her name. **K:** Enthused over the arrival of some special peaches.

(101)   **The Fusilli Jerry** (6019), April 27, 1995. **W:** Gross / Jonathan Gross / Ron Hauge / Charlie Rubin. **D:** Ackerman. **J:** In addition to dealing with car problems (after a breakup with Puddy), has a run-in with his former fellow sidewalk umbrella salesmen. **G:** Traumatized by his parents' separation (and his mother's appearance on the dating scene), must learn "The Move" from J and tries to apply it to his new girlfriend using crib notes. **E:** In order to get permission for Puddy to use "The Move" on her, must coerce information from him about J's car problems. **K:** Receives by mistake the vanity license plates ("ASS-MAN") of a proctologist.

(102)   **The Diplomat Club** (6020), May 4, 1995. **W:** Gammill / Pross. **D:** Ackerman. **J:** Flies to Ithaca, accompanied by his ultra-controlling manager, on what turns out to be a gig from hell. **G:** Seeking to get in good with an African American Sugar-Ray Leonard look-alike at work, pretends to have black friends. **E:** Plans to quit her job with Mr. Pitt until he announces his intent to put her in his will but ends up suspected of conspiring with J of trying to kill him. **K:** After taking J to the airport, K's gambling problem returns big-time as he makes bets on flight arrivals with a Texan at the gate.

(103)   **The Face Painter** (6021), May 11, 1995. **W:** David / Stoller. **D:** Ackerman. **J:** Given free tickets to a hockey play-off game but fails to properly thank the giver. **G:** Thinks he may have found the perfect woman (she lets him discourse about toilet paper) and decides to tell her he loves her. **E:** Appalled by Puddy's body paint in support of the New Jersey Devils hockey team, which leads to a traumatized priest and her being mistaken as the Madonna. **K:** Clashes with a chimpanzee on a zoo tour and is asked to apologize.

(104)   **The Understudy** (6022), May 18, 1995. **W:** Gross / Leifer. **D:** Ackerman. **J:** Dating the understudy to Bette Midler in the musical *Rochelle, Rochelle*, a woman who cries at everything. **G:** Puts Bette Midler in the hospital after running her over in a play at the plate in a softball game. **E:** Suspecting that her Korean manicurists are making fun of her, enlists the help of fluent-in-Korean Frank Costanza to understand what they are saying, and along the way meets J. Peterman for the first time. **K:** Nurses Bette Midler back to health after her collision with **G**.

(105)   **The Engagement** (7001), September 21, 1995. **W:** David. **D:** Ackerman. **J:** Agrees with **G** that neither is a man and makes a pact to change their lives (a promise he immediately breaks); breaks up with a woman because of the way she eats her peas. **G:** Disillusioned with his life, becomes engaged to Susan Ross. **E:** Kept awake by a neighbor's barking dog. **K:** Assists **E** (and Newman) in a plot against the dog.

(106)   **The Postponement** (7002), September 28, 1995. **W:** David. **D:** Ackerman. **J:** Finally goes to see *Plan 9 from Outer Space* with **K. G:** Breaks down in tears before Susan and gets her to agree to a postponement. **E:** Despondent that **G** is getting married and she is not, confides in a rabbi who lives in her building, who tells everyone what she said in confidence. **K:** After burning himself while smuggling a caffe latte into a movie, hires Jackie Chiles to sue Java World.

(107) **The Maestro** (7003), October 5, 1995. **W:** David. **D:** Ackerman. **J:** Determined to prove that there are houses to rent in Tuscany, journeys there with **K**. **G:** Tries to demonstrate his sensitivity by supplying a chair for the security guard in a clothing store. **E:** Dating a third-rate musician who insists upon being called "The Maestro" instead of Bob. **K:** Destroys his case when the Maestro's balm heals his coffee burns.

(108) **The Wink** (7004), October 12, 1995. **W:** Gammill / Pross. **D:** Ackerman. **J:** After going on a fruit diet, must demonstrate to his new girlfriend that he is a real man who loves meat. **G:** Suffering from an uncontrollable wink brought on by grapefruit juice, inadvertently gets Morgan fired and himself promoted. **E:** Begins dating a man who works for her wake-up service but is far too fond of dogs. **K:** Must get back a birthday card for Steinbrenner (signed by the entire Yankee organization) that he has sold to a sports memorabilia shop.

(109) **The Hot Tub** (7005), October 19, 1995. **W:** Kavet / Robin. **D:** Ackerman. **J:** Becomes obsessed with making certain a former Olympian wakes up in time to make his race. **G:** Meets with people from Houston to negotiate interleague play and begins to talk as profanely as they do. **E:** Plays host to a Trinidad-Tobegan who has come to run in the NY Marathon and struggles with "catalog writer's block." **K:** Installs a hot tub in his living room that leads to an electrical outage in the building.

(110) **The Soup Nazi** (7006), November 2, 1995. **W:** Spike Feresten. **D:** Ackerman. **J:** Obsessed with the "knee buckling" soup of a very difficult soup chef. **G:** Angry with **J**'s "smoopie" behavior with his new girlfriend, feigns lovey-dovey behavior with Susan. **E:** After being given (without his knowledge) an armoire by the Soup Nazi, steals his secret recipes. **K:** Left to protect an armoire **E** has received, has a scary encounter with a couple of gay men.

(111) **The Secret Code** (7007), November 9, 1995. **W:** Berg / Schaffer. **D:** Ackerman. **J**'s agreement to make commercials for Leapin' Larry's Appliance Store is handicapped by his foot falling asleep. **G:** Must have dinner with J. Peterman; unwilling to share his PIN number with Susan or anyone (even when it might save a life). **E:** Becomes convinced that she has lost her ability to make an impression on men. **K:** Seeks to make his childhood dream of becoming a fireman come true and finds himself driving a hook and ladder.

(112) **The Pool Guy** (7008), November 16, 1995. **W:** David Mandel. **D:** Ackerman. **J:** Menaced by a pool attendant from his athletic club who starts stalking him until he is crushed by a belly flopping Newman. **G:** Terrified that his "worlds" may collide and **G** as **J** knows him will be destroyed. **E:** Strikes up a friendship with Susan. **K:** When he gets a new phone number, is besieged by misdialed MovieFone calls and eventually starts pretending to be the automated voice.

(113) **The Sponge** (7009), December 7, 1995. **W:** Mehlman. **D:** Ackerman. **J:** Dates a woman whose phone number he found on an AIDS walk list but finds her hard to take. ("You can't have sex with someone you admire!") **G:** Plans for make-up sex with Susan

are thwarted by the disappearance of the Today Sponge and **E**'s unwillingness to surrender even one. **E:** When her favorite contraceptive sponge is discontinued, begins to horde them and is forced to determine whether potential lovers are "spongeworthy." **K:** Refuses to wear an AIDS ribbon in the charity event and gets beaten up by the armoire thief from "The Soup Nazi."

(114) **The Gum** (7010), December 14, 1995. **W:** Gammill / Pross. **D:** Ackerman. **J:** A series of missteps (including wearing a huge pair of myopic glasses to cover for an **E** lie) result in buying some costly Chinese gum from Lloyd Braun. **G:** An old high school friend convinces him he is headed for a crack-up, and everything he does seems to confirm she is right. **E:** While trying to avoid Braun, continues to flaunt her breasts at him. **K:** Befriends the recovering-from-a-nervous breakdown Braun and works to restore an old movie theater.

(115) **The Rye** (7011), January 4, 1996. **W:** Leifer. **D:** Ackerman. **J:** Must steal a loaf of marble rye from an old woman in order to maintain peace between the de-gifting Costanzas and the Rosses. **G:** Tries to maintain peace at the first meeting of his and his fiancée's parents. **E:** Ruins her new saxophonist boyfriend's technique by introducing him to oral sex. **K:** Moonlights as a handsome cabdriver, but feeding them Beefaroni causes the horses major flatulence.

(116) **The Caddy** (7012), January 25, 1996. **W:** Kavet / Robin. **D:** Ackerman. **J:** With **K** (and Jackie Chiles) sues Sue Ellen Mischke for causing a traffic accident by appearing in public wearing only a bra. **G:** After accidentally locking his keys in his car at work, the Yankee organization comes to believe he never stops working and, later, that he is dead. **E:** Buys her old nemesis Mischke a bra, which becomes a new J. Peterman item after she walks down the street wearing it (and only it) as a top. **K:** Finds his golf game improving with the help of a new caddy and joins **J** in a lawsuit against "the braless wonder."

(117) **The Seven** (7013), February 1, 1996. **W:** Berg / Schaffer. **D:** Ackerman. **J:** Dating a woman who appears to always wear the same black and white dress. **G:** Upset when Susan's cousins use his favorite name ("Seven"—Mickey Mantle's number) for their child. **E:** Injures her neck removing a bike from the wall and offers to give the bike to anyone who can fix her up. **K:** Decides to carefully account for everything he takes from **J**.

(118) **The Cadillac** (one hour) (7014), February 8, 1996. **W:** David / Seinfeld. **D:** Ackerman. **J:** Buys his father a Cadillac, which leads Jack Klompus to believe Mr. Seinfeld has been embezzling money from the condo association. **G:** Manages to get a date with fantasy woman Marisa Tomei. **E:** Shows a sudden new interest in the surprisingly wealthy **J**. **K:** Must hide out from the cable guy who wants to disconnect his premium services.

(119) **The Showerhead** (7015), February 15, 1996. **W:** Mehlman / Gross. **D:** Ackerman. **J:** Must deal with his parents' return to New York (they have moved in with Uncle Leo). **G:** Continues to obsess over Marisa Tomei, including annoying a hospitalized relative of **E**'s for her phone number. **E:** Fails a drug test at work (due to excessive poppy-seed muffin

eating) and is temporarily fired. **K:** With Newman, plots to use an illegal, higher-pressure shower nozzle.

(120)   **The Doll** (7016), February 22, 1996. **W:** Gammill / Pross. **D:** Ackerman. **J:** Returns from a gig in Memphis with a gift for Susan (from Sally Weaver) and a broken bottle of barbecue sauce. **G:** Deeply troubled by a doll that has an uncanny resemblance to his mother. **E:** Hopes to get the autograph of the "other guy" (from the Three Tenors) for the Maestro. **K:** Plays billiards on Frank Costanza's new table and become a whiz with the Maestro's baton.

(121)   **The Friars Club** (7017), March 7, 1996. **W:** Mandel. **D:** Ackerman. **J:** Hopes to become a member of the Friars Club. **G:** Enjoying a three-month delay in his upcoming wedding, tries to set up **J** with a friend of Susan's. **E:** Annoyed by a new deaf coworker who appears to be faking his disability. **K:** Inspired by Leonardo, experiments with not sleeping; plans a restaurant that serves only peanut butter and jelly.

(122)   **The Wig Master** (7018), April 4, 1996. **W:** Feresten. **D:** Ackerman. **J:** Feeling a bit emasculated, is offended when both gay and straight guys don't assume he is the boyfriend. **G:** Thinks the parking lot he uses may be a front for a prostitution ring. **E:** Dating a particularly difficult Brit (again). **K:** Strutting about in the coat from *Joseph and the Amazing Technicolor Dream Coat,* gets mistaken for a pimp.

(123)   **The Calzone** (7019), April 25, 1996. **W:** Berg / Schaffer. **D:** Ackerman. **J:** Becomes dependent on his new girlfriend's good looks in order to get what he wants (tickets for a sold-out movie, out of a speeding ticket). **G**'s own obsession with the calzones at a local pizzeria leads to Steinbrenner's addiction and big problems when he is suspected of stealing tips. **E**'s new man, Todd Gack, will not admit they are dating, even though he takes her home to meet his parents. **K:** Becomes addicted to hot clothes.

(124)   **The Bottle Deposit** (one hour) (7020), May 2, 1996. **W:** Kavet / Robin. **D:** Ackerman. **J:** A zealot mechanic abducts his car because he has not cared for it properly. **G:** Given an important assignment to complete for the Yankees but must go to great lengths to find out what it is; committed to a mental hospital by Steinbrenner. **E:** At Peterman's request, must outbid Sue Ellen Mischke at an auction for JFK's golf clubs, which are then stolen, along with **J**'s car. **K:** With Newman, finally acts on a scheme to make money by returning soda bottles (a whole postal truck load) in Michigan.

(125)   **The Wait Out** (7021), May 9, 1996. **W:** Mehlman / Matt Selman. **D:** Ackerman. **J:** After long waiting for the breakup of a couple's marriage, he moves in on the woman. **G:** Continues to seek a way to break up with his fiancée. **E:** After long waiting for the breakup of a couple's marriage, she moves in on the man. **K:** Has problems with a way-too-tight pair of jeans.

(126)   **The Invitations** (7022), May 16, 1996. **W:** David. **D:** Ackerman. **J:** Meets a woman named Jeannie who seems to be a female version of himself. **G:** Insists on using the cheapest (and poisonous) invitations available, which leads to Susan's death and his hitting on

Marisa Tomei. **E:** Irritated at not being included in **G**'s upcoming wedding. **K:** Schemes to get $100 from his bank, which promises the sum if any employee fails to say "hello."

(127) **The Foundation** (8001), September 19, 1996. **W:** Berg / Schaffer. **D:** Ackerman. **J:** Reunites with Mulva/Delores (from "The Junior Mints"). **G:** Done "grieving" for Susan, he serves on the board of the Susan Ross Foundation. **E:** Begins running J. Peterman while he seeks a rest cure in Burma. **K:** Takes up karate, joining a class meant for kids.

(128) **The Soul Mate** (8002), September 26, 1996. **W:** Mehlman. **D:** Ackerman. **J:** Semi-dating a woman who is also interested in **K**. **G:** Becomes convinced that the Susan Ross Foundation board thinks he killed Susan. **E:** Becomes interested in guy who shares her distaste for having children (and gets a vasectomy to prove it). **K:** Helped by Newman (in the Cyrano role), seeks to steal **J**'s new semi-girlfriend.

(129) **The Bizarro Jerry** (8003), October 3, 1996. **W:** Mandel. **D:** Ackerman. **J:** Dating a woman who has "man hands"; turns into an unhappy housewife, waiting for **K** to return from work. **G:** Tries to pick up women with sad tales (and fake photos) of his late fiancée. **E:** Switching allegiance, she begins to hang out with "Bizarro World" versions of **J**, **G**, and **K**. **K:** Begins working (without ever being hired) at an investment firm.

(130) **The Little Kicks** (8004), October 10, 1996. **W:** Feresten. **D:** Ackerman. **J:** Becomes a bootleg videotape auteur. **G:** Discovers that women find him attractive in the role of a bad boy. **E:** Loses all respect as boss at work after her "full-body dry heave set to music" dance at a party. **K:** Hanging out with a friend who makes bootleg videos in movie theaters.

(131) **The Package** (8005), October 17, 1996. **W:** Jennifer Crittenden. **D:** Ackerman. **J:** Charged with mail fraud when he acquiesces in **K**'s scheme to get his stereo repaired. **G:** Thinks the woman at the photomat is interested in him, so **K** suggests a risqué photo shoot. **E:** Must deal with a bad itch and being labeled difficult by the AMA. **K:** Talks **J** into a post office scam and becomes **G**'s cheesecake photographer.

(132) **The Fatigues** (8006), October 31, 1996. **W:** Kavet / Robin. **D:** Ackerman. **J:** After dating a woman with a mentor who is dating Kenny Bania, becomes Bania's mentor. **G:** Must present a talk on risk management (claimed on his résumé to be an area of expertise) at a Yankees meeting. **E:** Promotes the tough-guy mailroom manager to a position of leadership at J. Peterman. **K:** Plans a Jewish singles night but must talk Frank Costanza into putting his painful memories as a Korean War cook behind him in order to assist him.

(133) **The Checks** (8007), November 7, 1996. **W:** Steve O'Donnell / Gammill / Pross. **D:** Ackerman. **J:** Comes down with carpal tunnel syndrome from signing hundreds of small royalty checks from Japan. **G:** Excited by **K**'s idea to export *Jerry* to Japan, also seeks to expose a carpet-cleaning cult. **E:** Dating an obnoxious guy who thinks **J** is a complete loser and will not share his song—"Desperado"—with her. **K:** Becomes the financially disastrous tour guide for a group of Japanese tourists.

(134) **The Chicken Roaster** (8008), November 14, 1996. **W:** Berg / Schaffer. **D:** Ackerman. **J:** Turns into **K** after they switch apartments. **G:** Must get back a sable hat he left at
a girlfriend's apartment so she can't get rid of him. **E:** In trouble with accounting at J.
Peterman for impermissible purchases, including **G**'s horrid sable hat. **K:** Becomes (along
with Newman) obsessed with the chicken sold by the Kenny Rogers franchise across the
street.

(135) **The Abstinence** (8009), November 21, 1996. **W:** Steve Koren. **D:** Ackerman. **J:**
After being bumped as a Career Day speaker at his old junior high school, bombs at a full
assembly and is later rejected for a gig on *Letterman*. **G:** When his girlfriend comes down
with mono, lack of sex makes him a kind of idiot savant (and even helps him give hitting
instruction to the Yankees). **E:** Dating an intern who can't pass his medical exams and, in
her sex-denying obsession to help him study, becomes stupider and stupider. **K:** Opens a
smoker's lounge in his apartment, leading to such physical deterioration he hires Jackie
Chiles to sue the tobacco companies.

(136) **The Andrea Doria** (8010), December 19, 1996. **W:** Feresten. **D:** Ackerman. **J:**
Ends up delivering mail (badly) as Newman's substitute. **G:** Tries to beat out an *Andrea
Doria* survivor for a vacant apartment. **E:** Because of a boyfriend's comment, becomes
obsessed with her too big head. **K:** After seeking help from a veterinarian, starts exhibiting
doglike behavior.

(137) **The Little Jerry** (8011), January 9, 1997. **W:** Crittenden. **D:** Ackerman. **J:** Becomes
involved in cockfighting, rooting for the bird named for him. **G:** Seeking to live out his
dream of conjugal sex, starts dating an inmate. **E:** Dating a guy who may be going bald.
K: Gets involved in cockfighting and names his bird after J.

(138) **The Money** (8012), January 16, 1997. **W:** Mehlman. **D:** Ackerman. **J:** His parents
think he's broke and sell the Cadillac he gave them to Jack Klompus. **G:** Convinced his
parents are blowing his nest egg. **E:** Loses her job when Peterman returns. **K:** Can't get
any sleep because of his new girlfriend's "jimmy legs."

(139) **The Comeback** (8013), January 30, 1997. **W:** Kavet / Robin. **D:** Trainor. **J:** Discovers his Eastern European tennis pro is in fact a terrible player and then agrees to make
him look good so he can save face. **G:** After being insulted at work ("The ocean called,
and it's running out of shrimp"), schemes to get revenge with his own lame retort. **E:**
Becomes involved with a video store employee whose personal recommendations bring
her to tears. **K:** Decides to write a living will and is put in a coma by tennis balls.

(140) **The Van Buren Boys** (8014), February 6, 1997. **W:** Darin Henry. **D:** Ackerman. **J:**
Seeing a woman who seems to be without flaws, though her friends, and his, see her as a
loser (they part company when his parents find her perfect). **G:** Interviews high schoolers
for the Susan Ross Fellowship and picks a young man who reminds him of himself (he,
too, dreams of being an architect). **E:** Asked to ghostwrite J. Peterman's autobiography,
she discovers her boss's life is actually incredibly mundane. **K:** Falls in with the Van Buren

boys after inadvertently giving their secret sign; sells his stories to J. Peterman (for his autobiography).

(141) **The Susie** (8015), February 13, 1997. **W:** Mandel. **D:** Ackerman. **J:** A friend of K's thinks he is mafioso after crushing his hands in a car trunk. **G:** Takes K as his date to a Yankees gathering. **E:** Mistaken for a nonexistent Peterman employee named Susie. **K:** Anxious to establish his own daylight savings time, sets his watch behind one hour.

(142) **The Pothole** (8016), February 20, 1997. **W:** O'Donnell / Dan O'Keefe. **D:** Ackerman. **J:** Revolted by his new girlfriend after she uses a toothbrush that has fallen into the toilet. **G:** Having lost his keys (and a prized Phil Rizzuto key chain) in a pothole, must find a way to unearth them. **E:** Goes to elaborate lengths (including living in a janitor's closet) to secure Chinese food outside of the restaurant's delivery area. **K:** Adopts a section of highway and makes it distinctly his own (including narrowing four lanes into two).

(143) **The English Patient** (8017), March 13, 1997. **W:** Koren. **D:** Ackerman. **J:** In Florida, gets into a macho competition with elderly Izzy Mendelbaum. **G:** Meets a woman who claims her boyfriend looks just like him and becomes more interested in Neil than the woman. **E:** Her hatred for *The English Patient* leads to her near firing and being sent to Tunisia for reeducation by Peterman. **K:** Imports some Cubans (actually Dominicans) to make cigars, and they end up rolling (too tight) crepes instead.

(144) **The Nap** (8018), April 10, 1997. **W:** Kavet / Robin. **D:** Ackerman. **J:** Having his kitchen remodeled but is being driven nuts by a too passive carpenter. **G:** Has J's carpenter build a special hideout under his desk in Yankee Stadium so he can take secret naps. **E:** Her new boyfriend buys her an ergonomic mattress (from the Lumbar Yard) after only one date. **K:** Starts swimming in the East River and "funks up" E's new mattress.

(145) **The Yada Yada** (8019), April 24, 1997. **W:** Mehlman / Jill Franklyn. **D:** Ackerman. **J:** Upset by dentist Tim Whatley's conversion to Judaism so he can tell jokes. **G:** Bothered by a new girlfriend who uses the phrase "yada yada" constantly—even to describe sex. **E:** Sabotages a friend's planned adoption. **K:** Fights with Mickey on a double date.

(146) **The Millennium** (8020), May 1, 1997. **W:** Crittenden. **D:** Ackerman. **J:** His place on his new girlfriend's speed dial mirrors their relationship. **G:** Tries to get himself fired so he can take a job with the Mets but is traded to an Arkansas fast-food chain. **E:** Tries to drive a snooty clothing store that treated her rudely out of business. **K:** Must choose between J's and Newman's millennium parties; assists (with his pricing gun) E's scheme.

(147) **The Muffin Tops** (8021), May 8, 1997. **W:** Feresten. **D:** Ackerman. **J:** Has to shave his chest to please his "hairless freak" girlfriend. **G:** Dates a woman who thinks he is from out of town. **E:** With her old boss Lippman, opens a shop that sells only the tops of muffins and not the "stumps." **K:** Starts conducting Peterman Reality Tours.

(148) **The Summer Of George** (8022), May 15, 1997. **W:** Berg / Schaffer. **D:** Ackerman. **J:** Must deal with a high-maintenance girlfriend. **G:** Plans to make the most of the Yankees' severance package, which gives him the summer off. **E:** Stalked by a roommate who

calls her a shrew. **K:** Due to a series of mix-ups, must fire Raquel Welch as the star of a Broadway show.

(149)   **The Butter Shave** (9001), September 25, 1997. **W:** Berg / Mandel / Schaffer. **D:** Ackerman. **J:** Deliberately throws a comedy set in order to sabotage Bania. **G:** Hired by Play Now because they think he is handicapped. **E:** Endures a terrible flight home from Europe with Puddy. **K:** Unhappy with his shave cream, begins using butter instead.

(150)   **The Voice** (9002), October 2, 1997. **W:** Berg / Mandel / Schaffer. **D:** Ackerman. **J:** Forced to choose between his obsession with a silly imitation ("Hellooo!") and his new girlfriend. **G:** Shunned by his Play Now coworkers who see through his grift. **E:** Loses (and loses and loses) a bet with **J** that she will get back together with Puddy. **K:** Assigned an NYU intern to help him with Kramerica Industries.

(151)   **The Serenity Now** (9003), October 9, 1997. **W:** Koren. **D:** Ackerman. **J:** Gets in touch with his feelings (thanks to a new girlfriend). **G:** Reluctantly participates in his father's telemarketing scheme (to sell computers). **E:** Her "shiksappeal" attracts not only Lippman and his son but also the rabbi. **K:** Puts a screen door on his apartment.

(152)   **The Blood** (9004), October 16, 1997. **W:** O'Keefe. **D:** Ackerman. **J:** His parents hire Izzy Mandelbaum to whip him into shape. **G:** Becomes convinced he can combine all his interests—food, sex, TV—into one. **E:** Babysits for a friend. **K:** When the price for storing his blood goes up, begins keeping it in Newman's freezer.

(153)   **The Junk Mail** (9005), October 30, 1997. **W:** Feresten. **D:** Ackerman. **J:** Gets stuck with a van he doesn't want. **G:** So bothered that his parents have "cut him loose" he starts dating his cousin. **E:** Replaces Puddy with a guy who used to be an annoying TV pitchman. **K:** Sick of all the unwanted catalogs he is receiving, seeks to stop receiving mail altogether.

(154)   **The Merv Griffin Show** (9006), November 6, 1997. **W:** Bruce Eric Kaplan. **D:** Ackerman. **J:** After discovering his new girlfriend has a collection of vintage toys, begins drugging her so he can play with them. **G**'s animal-loving girlfriend has him taking care of an injured squirrel. **E:** Must deal with a new coworker who takes credit for her accomplishments. **K:** After finding the set of *The Merv Griffin Show* in a dumpster, begins hosting his own talk show.

(155)   **The Slicer** (9007), November 13, 1997. **W:** Henry / Kavet / Robin. **D:** Ackerman. **J:** Dating a dermatologist who he offends with a comment about aloe. **G:** In order to keep his new job with Kruger Industrial Smoothing, must doctor a photograph in his boss's office. **E:** Has a nightmare in which she sleeps with **J**, **G**, and **K**. **K:** Unhappy with the quality of NY deli meat, begins slicing his own and, in his white frock, is mistaken for a doctor.

(156)   **The Betrayal** (9008), November 20, 1997. **W:** Mandel / Mehlman. **D:** Ackerman. **J:** Accompanies **E** and **G** to an Indian wedding, but during the trip **E** spills the beans that

J once slept with **G**'s new amour. **G:** When **K** refuses to go to India, is able to invite his new girlfriend Nina. **E:** Attends Sue Ellen Mischke's wedding in India, where the revelation (by **G**) that she once slept with the groom brings the ceremony to a disastrous end. **K:** Cursed ("drop dead") by FDR and stays behind to remove the threat.

(157) **The Apology** (9009), December 11, 1997. **W:** Crittenden. **D:** Ackerman. **J:** His always naked girlfriend teaches him the meaning of "bad naked." **G:** Demands an apology from a guy (now at Step 9 of AA) who once told him he had a "big neck" and ends up being sent to a rage-aholics meeting himself. **E:** Bothered at work by a "germaphobe" and learns Puddy is a "recovering germaphobe." **K:** To save time, begins to do everything, including cooking, while in the shower (with Puddy's help, he even installs a garbage disposal).

(158) **The Strike** (9010), December 18, 1997. **W:** Berg / O'Keefe / Schaffer. **D:** Ackerman. **J**'s new girlfriend is beautiful one minute, ugly the next. **G:** Must again deal with his father's invention of the holiday of Festivus. **E:** Almost qualified for a free sub, she loses her card. **K:** When a strike of twelve years finally ends, returns to work at a bagel shop.

(159) **The Dealership** (9011), January 8, 1998. **W:** Koren. **D:** Ackerman. **J:** Hopes to get a deal on a new car from Puddy, who has become a car salesman. **G:** Spends most of the episode complaining about his loss of money and then a Twix bar in a vending machine. **E:** Her continuing perpetual breakup with Puddy imperils **J**'s good deal on a new car. **K:** Turns a test drive into a thrill ride by seeing how far he can go with the fuel gauge on empty.

(160) **The Reverse Peephole** (9012), January 15, 1998. **W:** Feresten. **D:** Ackerman. **J:** His "pocket diet" leads him to accept **E**'s offer of a European carry-all/"man purse." **G:** Refuses to trim his "morbidly obese" wallet. **E:** Grossed out by the "man fur" Puddy wears, she throws it out the window at a party. **K:** Along with Newman, reverses the peephole in his apartment door so outsiders have a fish-eye view of the odd goings-on inside.

(161) **The Cartoon** (9013), January 29, 1998. **W:** Kaplan. **D:** Ackerman. **J**'s harsh criticism of fellow comic Sally Weaver makes an enemy for life as she mounts a one-woman show called *Jerry Seinfeld Is the Devil*. **G:** Begins dating a girl who everyone thinks looks like **J**, which results in grave doubts about his own heterosexuality. **E:** Unable to get *New Yorker* cartoons, she becomes a cartoonist herself, but Peterman recognizes her first work as a "Ziggy" rip-off. **K:** Betrays **J** to his new arch enemy.

(162) **The Strong Box** (9014), February 5, 1998. **W:** O'Keefe / Kimball. **D:** Ackerman. **J:** Everything he does further alienates a parrot-loving neighbor. **G:** Tries to ditch an unwanted girlfriend by playing her off against another and makes them both more obsessed. **E:** Thinks her new boyfriend may be poor or married or both (he's both). **K:** His anxiety to hide the key to a strongbox containing his valuables leads to the death of a parrot.

(163) **The Wizard** (9015), February 26, 1998. **W:** Steve Lookner. **D:** Ackerman. **J:** Gives his father a Wizard organizer for his birthday. **G:** Caught in a lie (about owning property in the Hamptons) by Susan's parents. **E:** Wants to know if her new boyfriend is actually black. **K:** Flush after a contract for a movie based on his coffee-table book, retires to Florida.

(164) **The Burning** (9016), March 19, 1998. **W:** Crittenden. **D:** Ackerman. **J:** Learns the truth about his "It's me" girlfriend's tractor story. **G:** Tries to master the art of leaving on a high note, but it gets him extra work at Kruger. **E:** Discovers Puddy is religious but is upset he is not trying to save her from hell. **K:** Joins Mickey in acting out diseases at Mount Sinai.

(165) **The Bookstore** (9017), April 9, 1998. **W:** Feresten / Henry / Jaffe. **D:** Ackerman. **J:** Turns in Uncle Leo for shoplifting at Brentano's. **G:** Hanging out in bookstore in order to meet women, has to pay for an expensive art book he takes to the bathroom. **E:** Caught making out with a coworker, she tries to find a cover story for her behavior. **K:** With Newman, opens a rickshaw business employing the homeless.

(166) **The Frogger** (9018), April 23, 1998. **W:** Kavet / Koren / Robin / O'Keefe. **D:** Ackerman. **J:** Irritated at his new girlfriend for finishing his sentences. **G:** After discovering he still holds the high score on a Frogger at an old hangout, schemes to save the game. **E:** Boycotting the perpetual parties at J. Peterman, eats a $29,000 piece of the Duke and Duchess of Windsor's wedding cake. **K:** Advises **G** on his move of the Frogger.

(167) **The Maid** (9019), April 30, 1998. **W:** Berg / Mandel / Schaffer / Kit Boss / Mehlman. **D:** Ackerman. **J:** Starts having sex with his maid, who soon forgets all about housework, and when he refuses to pay her, her "pimp" pays him a call. **G:** Sick of his name, tries to come up with alternatives, but another man at Kruger beats him to his first choice, "T-Bone." **E:** Her new 646 area code leads to her feeling cut off from her friends. **K:** Depressed when his girlfriend moves downtown.

(168) **The Puerto Rican Day** (9020), May 7, 1998. **W:** Berg / Crittenden / Feresten / Kaplan / Koren / Mandel / O'Keefe / Robin / Schaffer. **D:** Ackerman. After getting stuck in traffic caused by Puerto Rican Day, each has a solo adventure: **G** takes in a movie (and must compete with a laser pointer); **E** catches a taxi, **K** (in the guise of A. G. Pennybacker) must find a bathroom, **J** must negotiate an apology to another driver.

(169–170) **Finale** (9021–9022), May 14, 1998. **W:** David. **D:** Ackerman. Given another chance to develop a sitcom for NBC, the four are given a free flight to Paris on the NBC jet. After a near crash, they witness (but do not interfere in) a carjacking and are charged with violating a Good Samaritan law. At their trial, scores of "character witnesses" testify to their previous crimes, and the "New York Four" are sentenced to prison.

Seinfeld *Intertexts and Allusions*

In *Derrida*, a 2002 documentary film by Kirby Dick and Amy Ziering Kofman, we hear the following exchange between a South African television interviewer and Jacques Derrida (1930–2004), the father of deconstruction:

Interviewer: "*Seinfeld*, which is America's most popular—ever—sitcom. . . . Jerry Seinfeld made this sitcom about a bunch of people living together. Everything is about irony and parody, and what you do with your kitchen cupboard is imbued with as much feeling or thought as whether someone believes in God or the like.

Derrida: Deconstruction, as I understand it, doesn't produce any sitcom. If sitcom is this and people who watch this think deconstruction is this, the only advice I have to give them is just stop watching sitcom, do your homework, and read.

If Derrida had bothered to actually watch the show he was so quick to denounce, he might have noticed that its creators were surprisingly culturally literate. Though *Seinfeld* may not have been grounded in the Great Books, it did demonstrate a high degree of cultural literacy. The follow is a partial list of intertexts and allusions, from both high and low culture, evoked on *Seinfeld*.

■ *9½ Weeks* ■ *90210* ■ *Alien Autopsy* ■ *Alive* ■ *All My Children* ■ Loni Anderson ■ Susan B. Anthony ■ Anti-Christ ■ *Apocalypse Now* ■ Aquaman ■ "Archie" ■ Clara Barton ■ *Basic Instinct* ■ Batman ■ *Beaches* ■ Bermuda Triangle ■ Corbin Bernsen ■ *The Blob* ■ Boggle ■ *The Bold and the Beautiful* ■ Book Depository ■ Bosco ■ Boutros Boutros-Ghali ■ *Breakfast at Tiffany's* ■ Alexander Brezhnev ■ Helen Gurley Brown ■ Lenny Bruce ■ Sandra Bullock ■ Caligula ■ *Cape Fear* ■ Truman Capote ■ Captain and Tennille ■ Thomas Carlyle ■ Nikolai Ceausescu ■ Neville Chamberlain ■ *Chapter Two* ■ John Cheever ■ Confucius ■ Ray Coniff ■ Joseph Cotton ■ Steve Croft ■ *A Cry in the Dark* ■ *The Crying Game* ■ C-Span ■ Ted Danson ■ Charles de Gaulle ■ "Desperado" ■ Dockers ■ *Edward Scissorhands* ■ *The Elephant Man* ■ Endora ■ *The English Patient* ■ *Fatal Vision* ■ *A Few Good Men* ■ *Fiddler on the Roof* ■ Diane Fossey ■ Elmer Fudd ■ Gandhi ■ *Ghostbusters* ■ Godzilla ■ *The Great Gatsby* ■ Green Lantern ■ Greenpeace ■ Charles

Grodin ▪ Bryant Gumbel ▪ *Guys and Dolls* ▪ Buddy Hackett ▪ Mary Hart ▪ *Hazel* ▪ Hezbolla ▪ Don Ho ▪ Abbie Hoffman ▪ Dustin Hoffman ▪ *Holocaust* ▪ Lena Horne ▪ John Housman ▪ L. Ron Hubbard ▪ Saddam Hussein ▪ The Incredible Hulk ▪ Rick James ▪ Peter Jennings ▪ *JFK* ▪ Lyndon Baines Johnson ▪ Jor-El ▪ John Fitzgerald Kennedy ▪ John F. Kennedy Jr. ▪ Dr. Kevorkian ▪ Kix ▪ Kool-Aid ▪ C. Everett Koop ▪ Stanley Kowalski ▪ *Last Tango in Paris* ▪ Spike Lee ▪ Sugar Ray Leonard ▪ *Lord of the Flies* ▪ Sophia Loren ▪ Peter Lorre ▪ *The Machado* ▪ *Mad About You* ▪ Jayne Mansfield ▪ Don Mattingly ▪ "MacArthur Park" ▪ Elle MacPherson ▪ Golda Meir ▪ *Melrose Place* ▪ Sergio Mendes ▪ *The Merv Griffin Show* ▪ Russ Meyer ▪ Bette Midler ▪ *Midnight Cowboy* ▪ minimalism ▪ *Moby-Dick* ▪ Claude Monet ▪ *Murphy Brown* ▪ Edward R. Murrow ▪ *Naked Gun* ▪ Nedda ▪ Liam Neeson ▪ Ozzie Nelson ▪ *The Net* ▪ *New Yorker* ▪ Nick at Nite ▪ Florence Nightingale ▪ Paul O'Neil ▪ Lee Harvey Oswald ▪ *Outlaw Josey Wales* ▪ Al Pacino ▪ *Pagliacci* ▪ Pandora's Box ▪ *The Paper Chase* ▪ Rosa Parks ▪ *Patty Duke Show* ▪ *Penthouse* ▪ Peter Pan ▪ Harold Pinter ▪ *Plan 9 from Outer Space* ▪ *The Planet of the Apes* ▪ Ponce de Leon ▪ Pottery Barn ▪ *The Private Life of Henry VIII* ▪ *Punky Brewster* ▪ *Regis and Kathy Lee* ▪ Chita Rivera ▪ Geraldo Rivera ▪ Al Roker ▪ *Runaway Train* ▪ Salman Rushdie ▪ William Safire ▪ Fred Savage ▪ *Scent of a Woman* ▪ *Schindler's List* ▪ Scientology ▪ Seals & Croft ▪ Monica Seles ▪ Selma ▪ *Shaft* ▪ Buck Showalter ▪ Neil Simon ▪ Skinheads ▪ *Spartacus* ▪ Spider-Man ▪ Joseph Stalin ▪ *Star Trek* ▪ *Star Wars* ▪ Steel Cage Death Match ▪ Stella ▪ Meryl Streep ▪ *Sunset Boulevard* ▪ Superman ▪ Svengali ▪ Clarence Thomas ▪ Three Stooges ▪ The Three Tenors ▪ *Today Show* ▪ Leo Tolstoy ▪ *Tonight Show* ▪ Mel Torme ▪ *Tropic of Cancer* ▪ *Tropic of Capricorn* ▪ Tupperware ▪ *TV Guide* ▪ Tweetie Bird ▪ *The Twilight Zone* ▪ Two-Face ▪ Utopian ▪ Jerry Vale ▪ Jon Voight ▪ *War and Peace* ▪ "War, What Is It Good For?" ▪ George Wendt ▪ George Will ▪ Winnie the Pooh ▪ "Witchy Woman" ▪ Woody Woodpecker ▪ Yo-Yo Ma ▪ "Ziggy"

List of Contributors

Matthew Bond is a doctoral student at Middle Tennessee State University.

Barbara Ching is an associate professor of English and director of the Humanities Center at the University of Memphis. She is the author of *Wrong's What I Do Best: Hard Country Music and Contemporary Culture* (Oxford University Press).

Joanna L. Di Mattia was awarded her Ph.D. in 2005, *yada yada yada*. She is currently an assistant lecturer at the Centre for Women's Studies and Gender Research at Monash University in Melbourne, Australia, where her primary teaching area is in feminist cultural studies. Recent publications include chapters in *Reading* Sex and the City (I.B. Tauris: 2004) and *Reading* Six Feet Under: *TV to Die For* (I.B. Tauris: 2005). She will never tire of watching *Seinfeld* re-runs . . . and she likes fruit.

Michael Dunne is a professor of English at Middle Tennessee State University, where he teaches courses in American literature, Hawthorne, criticism, film, narratology, Calvinist humor, and popular culture. He is the author of three books: *Metapop: Self-Referentiality in Contemporary American Pop Culture* (1992), *Hawthorne's Narrative Strategies* (1995), and *Intertextual Encounters in American Fiction, Film, and Popular Culture* (2001). With Dr. Sara Dunne, he edits *Studies in Popular Culture*.

Sara Lewis Dunne is a professor of English at Middle Tennessee State University. She is the coeditor of the journal *Studies in Popular Culture*.

Michael M. Epstein is an associate professor at the Southwestern University School of Law, where he teaches courses on media and entertainment law.

Dennis Hall is a professor of English at the University of Louisville. He is the coeditor, with M. Thomas Inge, of *The Greenwood Guide to American Popular Culture* and is coediting, with Susan Grove Hall, a collection of essays for Greenwood on American cultural icons, which should appear in 2006.

Eleanor Hersey teaches at Fresno Pacific University. She has published essays on *The X-Files* and on television movie versions of novels by L. M. Montgomery, Willa Cather, and Edith Wharton.

David Lavery is a professor of English at Middle Tennessee State University. He is the author of more than forty essays and the author/editor/coeditor of *Late for the Sky: The Mentality of the Space Age* (1992), *Full of Secrets: Critical Approaches to Twin Peaks* (1994), *"Deny All Knowledge": Reading* The X-Files (1996), *Fighting the Forces: What's at Stake* *in* Buffy the Vampire Slayer (2002), *Teleparody: Predicting/Preventing the TV Discourse of Tomorrow* (2002), and *This Thing of Ours: Investigating* The Sopranos.

Betty Lee made her concert debut as a pianist at the age of nine and has won more than thirty piano competitions around the world. She is currently studying microbiology at the University of Florida and continues to appear as a soloist on concert stages across the United States, Europe, and Asia.

Marc Leverette is an assistant professor of media studies in the department of speech communication at Colorado State University. His books include *Professional Wrestling, the Myth, the Mat, and American Popular Culture; Understanding McLuhan* (forthcoming); and *Zombie Culture: Studies of the Monster That Won't Go Away* (coedited with Shawn McIntosh). His articles have appeared in such journals as *Image & Narrative* and *Studies in Popular Culture*.

David Marc is a visiting professor of television, radio, and film at the Newhouse School of Syracuse University. He is the author of such books as *Demographic Vistas; Comic Visions; Bonfire of the Humanities: Television, Subliteracy, and Long-Term Memory Loss;* and is the coauthor, with Robert J. Thompson, of a forthcoming history of television, to be published by Blackwell.

Amy McWilliams is a doctoral candidate in English at Texas A&M University. Her academic interests include the mid-Victorian novel, gender studies, popular culture, narrative structures, representations of the family, and narrative uses of illness. She currently works as an editor.

Geoffrey O'Brien is the author of *Phantom Empire, Sonata for Jukebox: An Autobiography of My Ears,* and *Castaways of the Image Planet: Movies, Show Business, Public Spectacle.* He is editor in chief of the Library of America.

Jimmie L. Reeves is associate professor of mass communication at Texas Tech University. In addition to articles on subjects ranging from Mr. T to *The X-Files,* he is the coauthor of *Cracked Coverage: Television News, the Anti-Cocaine Crusade, and the Reagan Legacy* (1994).

Mark C. Rogers is an assistant professor of communication at Walsh University. His previous publications include collaborative pieces on *Twin Peaks, The X-Files,* and *The Sopranos.*

Jon Stratton is a professor of cultural studies at Curtin University of Technology in Perth, Australia. He is the author of *Coming Out Jewish, The Desirable Body: Cultural Fetishism and the Erotics of Consumption,* and other books.

Elke van Cassel is currently completing her doctoral dissertation, an examination of the impact and influence of *The Reporter*—a public-interest magazine published from 1949 to 1968—on American political, social, and cultural life, at Radboud University Nijmegen, the Netherlands.

Bill Wyman, formerly the arts and entertainment editor of Salon.com, is an assistant managing editor of National Public Radio. He lives in Washington, D.C.

Bibliography

Allan, Graham. *Friendship: Developing a Sociological Perspective.* Hertfordshire, England: Harvester Wheatsheaf, 1989.

"Alec Berg & Jeff Schaffer." *So Long,* Seinfeld. 83.

Allen, Woody. *Four Films of Woody Allen: Annie Hall, Interiors, Manhattan, Stardust Memories.* New York: Random House, 1982.

Altman, Rick. "Television/Sound." *Studies in Entertainment: Critical Approaches to Mass Culture.* Edited by Tania Modleski. Bloomington, Indiana: Indiana University Press, 1986: 39–54.

"Andy Ackerman." *So Long,* Seinfeld. 57.

Ang, Ien, "(Not) Coming to Terms With *Dallas.*" *Global Television.* New York: Wedge Press, 1991. 69–77.

———. *Watching Dallas: Soap Opera and the Melodramatic Imagination.* Translated by Della Couling. New York: Methuen, 1985.

Appelo, Tim. "10 Reasons We Already Miss *Seinfeld.*" *TV Guide,* January 17, 1998: 36–39.

Austen, Jane. *Emma* (1815). Edited by David Lodge. London: Oxford University Press, 1971.

Bakhtin, Mikhail. *Rabelais and His World.* Translated by Helen Iswolsky. Bloomington, Indiana: Indiana University Press, 1968.

Barthes, Roland. *Elements of Semiology.* Translated by Annette Lavers and Colin Smith. New York: Hill and Wang, 1967.

Bauman, Zygmunt. *Modernity and Ambivalence.* Cambridge, England: Polity, 1991.

Becka, Jan. *Historical Dictionary of Myanmar.* Asian Historical Dictionaries Series, no. 15. Metuchen, New Jersey: Scarecrow Press, 1995.

Becker, Ernest. *The Denial of Death.* New York: Free Press, 1973.

Biale, David. *Eros and the Jews: From Biblical Israel to Contemporary America.* Berkeley: California University Press, 1997.

Bly, Robert. *Iron John: A Book About Men.* Brisbane, Australia: Element Books, 1990.

Boliek, Brooks. "Cap Conundrum." *Hollywood Reporter,* January 22, 1999. *Westlaw.* 1999 WLNR 5380286.

Boyer, Jay. "The *Schlemiel:* Black Humor and the *Shtetl* Tradition." *Semites and Stereotypes: Characteristics of Jewish Humor.* Edited by Avner Zvi and Anat Zajdman. Westport, Connecticut: Greenwood Press, 1993.

Brennan, Steve. "Yuks and Bucks: Some Buyers Are 'Willing to Walk Over Glass' to Secure the Biggest Off-Net Sitcoms." *Hollywood Reporter,* January 19, 1996: S15.

Brod, Harry. "The New Men's Studies: From Feminist Theory to Gender Scholarship." *Hypatia* 2.1 (1987). 179–196.

———, ed. *The Making of Masculinities: The New Men's Studies.* Boston: Allen & Unwin, 1987.

Brook, Vincent. "From the Cozy to the Carceral: Trans-Formations of Ethnic Space in *The Goldbergs* and *Seinfeld." Velvet Light Trap* 44 (fall 1999). 54–67.

Brown, Julia Prewitt. "Civilization and the Contentment of *Emma." Modern Critical Interpretations of Jane Austen's Emma.* Edited by Harold Bloom. New York: Chelsea House Publishers, 1987. 45–66.

Brubach, Holly. "Mail-Order America." *The New York Times Magazine,* November 21, 1993. 54–70.

Buchalter, Gail. "Posters from France, Motorcycles from China." *Forbes,* October 26, 1992. 222–25.

Butler, Jeremy G. *Television: Critical Methods and Applications.* 2nd edition. Mahwah, New Jersey: Lawrence Erlbaum Associates, 2002.

"Bye, for Now: Before It's All Over, Warm-Up Comedian Jeff Bye Takes a Minute to Answer Your Questions." Seinfeld *Forever.* 65.

Cameron, Michael. "Seinfeld to Tie the Knot." *Herald Sun,* November 10, 1999. 30.

Carman, John. "Enough Already! In the end, *Seinfeld* was just a TV show." *San Francisco Chronicle,* May 14, 1998. E1, 7.

"Carol Leifer." *So Long,* Seinfeld. 37.

Caws, Peter. "Flaubert's Laughter." *Philosophy and Literature* 8, no. 2 October 1984. 167–180

Chase, Jon. "The Utility Players." *So Long,* Seinfeld. 40.

Cohen, John, ed. *The Essential Lenny Bruce.* London: Open Gate, 1973.

Conrad, Joseph. *Heart of Darkness* and *The Secret Sharer.* New York: Signet Classic, 1983.

Cooper, Jim. "Cable TV: Big Money for Nothing." *Mediaweek,* September 21, 1998. Lexis-Nexis, June 2005.

Cuddihy, John Murray. *The Ordeal of Civility: Freud, Marx, Lévi-Strauss and the Jewish Struggle with Modernity.* New York: Basic, 1974.

Dateline, NBC." Seinfeld *Forever.* 52–55.

Davies, Jonathan. "KCOP Pays Big for 'Seinfeld'." *Hollywood Reporter,* May 18, 1998. *West-law.* 1998 WLNR 5393503.

De Moraes, Lisa. "Station Identity Key for New UPN, Salhany." *Hollywood Reporter,* January 9, 1995. *Westlaw.* 1995 WLNR 3767994.

Dempsey, John. "It's a Fuzzy Future for Offnet Laffers." *Variety,* January 13, 1997–January 19, 1997, news, Natpe 1997. 1.

——— and Cynthia Littleton. "Billion-Buck Bonanza." *Variety,* March 23, 1998–March 29, 1998, news. 1+.

Di Mattia, Joanna L. "The Show About Something: Male Anxiety & The Buddy System on *Seinfeld." Michigan Feminist Studies* 14 (1999–2000). 59–81.

Dipasquale, Cara, ed. "HBO Seeks Hit with 'Sopranos' Wear." *Chicago Tribune,* April 17, 2003, red-eye edition. 27.

Doherty, Thomas. "DVD Comentary Tracks: Listening to the Auteurs." *Cineaste* 26 (2001). 78–80.

Doty, Alexander. *Making Things Perfectly Queer: Interpreting Mass Culture*. Minneapolis: University of Minnesota Press, 1993.

Douglas, Ann. *The Feminization of American Culture*. New York: Avon Books, 1977.

Douglas, Mary Tew. *Purity and Danger*. New York: Praeger, 1966.

Dow, Bonnie J. *Prime-Time Feminism: Television, Media Culture, and the Women's Movement Since 1970*. Philadelphia: University of Pennsylvania Press, 1996.

Dubbert, Joe L. *A Man's Place: Masculinity in Transition*. Englewood, New Jersey: Prentice Hall, 1979.

"Dumping Grounds." *So Long*, Seinfeld. 29.

Dunne, Michael. *Intertextual Encounters in American Fiction, Film, and Popular Culture*. Bowling Green, Kentucky: Bowling Green State University Popular Press, 2001.

Dunne, Sara Lewis. "Seinfood." *Studies in Popular Culture* 18.2 (1996). 35–41.

Dyer, Richard. "Heterosexuality." *Lesbian and Gay Studies: A Critical Introduction*. Edited by Andy Medhurst and Sally R. Munt. London and Washington, D.C.: Cassell, 1997. 261–273.

Eco, Umberto. "Innovation and Repetition: Between Modern and Post-Modern Aesthetics." *Daedalus* 114, 4 (fall 1985). 161–184.

Elkin, Michael. "What's with Jerry and the Jews: Getting Ready to Part Company with His Funniness" at http://www.jcn.

Entertainment Weekly, Inc. *The Entertainment Weekley Seinfeld Companion*. New York: Warner Books, 1993.

Epstein, Michael M. "Go Westinghouse, Young Man" (interview with Joel Chaseman). *Television Quarterly* 31.1 (spring 2000). 41–49.

Esler, Gavin. *The United States of Anger: The People and the American Dream*. New York: Penguin, 1997.

"Fascinatin' Rhythm: Composer Jonathan Wolf Gets Toes Tapping with His Finger-Snapping Theme Song." Seinfeld *Forever*. 89.

FCC Financial Interest and Syndication Rules, 47 C.F.R. 73.658 (j)(1)(ii) (1984).

———. Primetime Access Rule, 47 C.F.R. 73.658 (k) (1994).

———. *Report and Order: In Re Review of the Syndication and Financial Interest Rules, Sections 73.659–73.663 of the Commission's Rules*. 10 F.C.C.R. 12,165 (1995).

"Fear and Loathing in New York: Larry David Helped Put the Fun in Dysfunctional." Seinfeld *Forever*. 45.

Fiedler, Leslie. *Love and Death in the American Novel*. 2nd edition. Normal, Illinois: Dalkey Press, 1997.

Filene, Peter G. *Him/Her/Self: Sex Roles in Modern America*. 2nd edition. Baltimore: Johns Hopkins University Press, 1986.

Flaherty, Mike. "Introduction" to "The Seinfeld Chronicles." *So Long*, Seinfeld. 18–20.

———. "The Older, the Bitter." *So Long*, Seinfeld. 92–95.

Folio Society advertisement. *The New York Times Book Review*, February 18, 1996. 5.

Fretts, Bruce. "Cruelly, Madly, Cheaply." *So Long*, Seinfeld. 44

———. *The Entertainment Weekly Seinfeld Companion*. Edited by Jeannie Park. New York: Warner, 1993.

Frye, Northrop. *Anatomy of Criticism: Four Essays.* Princeton, New Jersey: Princeton University Press, 1957.

Fuchs, Cynthia J. "The Buddy Politic." *Screening the Male: Exploring Masculinities in Hollywood Cinema.* Edited by Steven Cohan and Ina Rae Hark. London and New York: Routledge, 1993. 194–210.

Galloway, Stephen. "Money Matters: When It Comes to Media Buys, Overall Spending Is Down—But Niche Dollars Are Eating a Bigger Portion of the Pie." *Hollywood Reporter,* May 10, 2005. *Westlaw.* 2005 WLNR 8983120.

Gans, Eric. "The End of *Seinfeld.*" *Chronicles of Love and Resentment.* January 10, 1998. http://www.anthropoetics.ucla.edu/views/vw121.htm.

Gantz, Katherine. "'Not That There's Anything Wrong With That': Reading the Queer in *Seinfeld.*" Edited by Thomas, in *Straight with a Twist.* 165–190.

Garron, Barry. "Laugh Factory." *Hollywood Reporter,* January 22, 1999. *Westlaw.* 1999 WLNR 5379942.

Gattuso, Greg. Seinfeld *Universe: An Unauthorized Fan's-Eye View of the Entire Domain.* Secaucus, New Jersey: Carol Pub, 1996.

"Getting the Picture: TV Takes the Stage (Supplement: Broadcasting—The First Sixty Years)." *Broadcasting & Cable,* December 9, 1991. S29 + . *Lexis-Nexis,* June 2005.

Gilman, Sander. *Jewish Self-Hatred: Anti-Semitism and the Hidden Language of the Jews.* Baltimore: Johns Hopkins University Press, 1986.

Gliatto, Tom. "Jerry Engaged? Get Out!" *Who Weekly* November 22, 1999. 66–72.

"Glossary: Cosmo Kramer." *So Long,* Seinfeld. 38–39.

"Glossary: Elaine Marie Benes." *So Long,* Seinfeld. 32–33.

"Glossary: George Louis Costanza." *So Long,* Seinfeld. 58–59.

"Glossary: Jerry Seinfeld." *So Long,* Seinfeld. 23.

"Glossary: Newman." *So Long,* Seinfeld. 73.

"The Gotham Guide to Good Manners." Seinfeld *Forever.* 33.

Goudappel, Annerieke. "Need to Know. The Rules of the Game: Dating in Amerika." *Amerika,* fall 1995. 52–53.

"Gregg Kavet & Andy Robin." *So Long,* Seinfeld. 72.

Grego, Melissa. "TV Does Du-Op Bop." *Daily Variety,* August 7, 2002, news. 1.

Grote, David. *The End of Comedy: The Sit-Com and the Comedic Tradition.* Hamden, Connecticut: Archon Books, 1983.

Gruber, Howard E. "Breakaway Minds" (interview with Howard Gardner). *Psychology Today,* July 1981. 68–73.

Hague, Angela and David Lavery, eds. *Teleparody: Predicting/Preventing the TV Discourse of Tomorrow.* London: Wallflower, 2002.

Hall, Dennis. "1996 [Kentucky Philological Association] Presidential Address: Why Jane Austen? Why Now?" *Kentucky Philological Review* 11 (1996). 1–4.

Harmon, William, and C. Hugh Holman. *A Handbook to Literature.* 7th edition. Upper Saddle River, New Jersey: Prentice Hall, 1996.

Harvey, David. *The Condition of Postmodernity.* Cambridge, Massachusetts: Basil Blackwell, 1990.

"Head Case." *So Long,* Seinfeld. 63.

Hellman, John. *American Myth and the Legacy of Vietnam.* New York: Columbia University Press, 1986.

Hersey, Eleanor. "'It'll Always Be Burma to Me': J. Peterman on *Seinfeld*." *Studies in Popular Culture* 22.3 (2000). 11–24.

Hibbs, Thomas S. *Shows about Nothing: Nihilism in Popular Culture from the Exorcist to Seinfeld*. Dallas: Spence Publishing, 1999.

Hills, Matt. *Fan Cultures*. London: Routledge, 2002.

Hine, Thomas. "Notable Quotables: Why Images Become Icons." *The New York Times* February 18, 1996. 37.

Hirsch, Irwin and Cara Hirsch. "A Look at Our Dark Side: *Seinfeld*'s Humor Noir." *Journal of Popular Film and Television* 28:3 (fall 2000). 116–23.

Hitchcock, Jeff. *Lifting the White Veil: An Exploration of White American Culture in a Multiracial Context*. Roselle, New Jersey: Crandall, Dostie & Douglass Books, Inc., 2002.

Hutcheon, Linda. *A Poetics of Postmodernism: History, Theory, Fiction*. New York: Routledge, 1988.

Ingall, Marjorie. "The J. Peterman Catalog." *Sassy*, October 1994. 80.

Irwin, William, ed. *Seinfeld and Philosophy: A Book About Everything and Nothing*. Chicago: Open Court, 2000.

"J. Peterman's Fate." *USA Today*, February 23, 1999. 1B.

"The J. Seinfeld Catalog." Seinfeld *Forever*. 72–73.

Jacobs, A. J. "Larry David." *So Long*, Seinfeld. 27.

———. "Mr. Seinfeld's Neighborhood." *So Long*, Seinfeld. 49–51.

———. "*Seinfeld*: A Show About Nothing? Now That Was Something!" *The 100 Greatest TV Shows of All Time*. New York: Entertainment Weekly Books, 1998. 10–11.

———. "You've Been a Great Audience! Good Night!" *So Long*, Seinfeld. 4–9.

James, Caryn. "'Seinfeld' Goes Out in Self-Referential Style." *The New York Times*, May 15, 1998. Section B, Column 2, page 1.

Jameson, Fredric. *Postmodernism, or, The Logic of late Capitalism*. Durham, North Carolina: Duke University Press, 1991.

Jeffords, Susan. *Hard Bodies: Hollywood Masculinity in the Reagan Era*. New Brunswick, New Jersey: Rutgers University Press, 1994.

———. *The Remasculinization of America: Gender and the Vietnam War*. Bloomington: Indiana University Press, 1989.

"Jennifer Crittenden." Seinfeld *Forever*. 77.

Jensen, Klaus Bruhn. "Reception as Flow: The 'New Television Viewer' Revisited." *Cultural Studies* 8 (1994). 293–305.

"Jewish Family Values," http://jewishfamily.com/Features/996/tvjews2.htm.

Johnson, Carla. "Luckless in New York: The Schlemiel and the Schlimazel in *Seinfeld*." *Journal of Popular Film and Television* 22.3 (1994). 116–124.

John-Steiner, Nora. *Creative Collaboration*. New York: Oxford University Press, 2000.

Jones, Gerard. *Honey, I'm Home! Sitcoms: Selling the American Dream*. New York: Grove Weidenfeld, 1992.

Joyrich, Lynne. *Re-Visioning Reception: Television, Gender, and Postmodern Culture*. Bloomington: Indiana University Press, 1996.

Kant, Immanuel. *Critique of Judgment*, part I, book II, chapter 54.

Kaplan, Amy. "'Left Alone with America': The Absence of Empire in the Study of American Culture." *Cultures of United States Imperialism*. Edited by Kaplan and Donald E. Pease. Durham, North Carolina: Duke University Press, 1993. 3–21.

Kaplan, James. "Angry Middle-Aged Man." *The New Yorker*, January 19, 2004. 66–73.

Kenney, John B. "The Last Catalogue." *The New Yorker*, February 8, 1999. 33.

Kimmel, Michael, ed. "The Contemporary 'Crisis' of Masculinity in Historical Perspective." In Brod, *The Making of Masculinities*. 121–153.

———. *Manhood in America: A Cultural History*. New York: Free Press, 1997.

Kozloff, Sarah. "Narrative Theory and Television." *Channels of Discourse Reassembled: Television and Contemporary Criticism*, edited by Robert Clyde Allen. Chapel Hill, North Carolina: University of North Carolina Press, 1992.

Kracke, Torsten. "Seinfeld," *epguides.de*, 2002, http://www.epguides.de/seinfeld.htm, December 18, 2002.

"Kramer vs. Kramer." *So Long*, Seinfeld. 79.

"Kramer's Big Ideas." *So Long*, Seinfeld. 53.

"Kramer's Hair-Brained Ideas." Seinfeld *Forever*. 85.

Kray, Susan, "Orientalization of an 'Almost White' Woman: The Interlocking Effects of Race, Class, Gender, and Ethnicity in American Mass Media." *Critical Studies in Mass Communication* 10 (1993). 349–366.

"Larry Charles." *So Long*, Seinfeld. 42.

Liebes, Tamar, and Elihu Katz. *The Export of Meaning: Cross-Cultural Readings of Dallas*. New York: Oxford University Press, 1990.

Lipps, Rick. Personal interview. 1997.

Lipton, Michael A. and John Griffiths. "Catalog Card." *People Weekly*, January 27, 1997. 115+.

Littleton, Cynthia. "WNYW Nabs Rerun Rights to 'Seinfeld'." *Daily Variety*, March 18, 1998, news. 1.

Long, Rob. "Jerry Built: The Success of *Seinfeld* Was an Implicit Rebuke to PC Pieties— and a Confirmation of America's Unpredictable Spirit." *National Review* February 9, 1998. 32, 34.

"A Lot of *Seinfeld* Lists." <http://wave.prohosting.com/tnguym/foods2.html> February 10, 2004.

"Love on the Rocks." Seinfeld *Forever*. 60.

Lowry, Brian. "B'cast TV's Long Fall; Big 3 Fail to Stem Erosion; Fox Builds." *Daily Variety*, December 29, 1994, news. 1.

"The Lyin' King." Seinfeld *Forever*. 80.

Marc, David. *Comic Visions: Television Comedy & American Culture*. 2nd edition. Malden, Massachusetts: Blackwell, 1999.

"Marc Hirschfeld." *So Long*, Seinfeld. 67.

Marin, Cheech and Joshua Hammer. "Jerry Seins Off." *Newsweek*, January 12, 1998. 54–57.

McClintock, Pamela. "Viacom Asks That Eye Ban Be Vacated." *Daily Variety*, September 3, 2002. 5.

McConnell, Frank. "How *Seinfeld* was Born." *Commonweal* 9, February 1996. 19.

———. "No Way to Exit?: *Seinfeld* as Sartre." *Commonweal*. June 5, 1998. 19–20.

McMahon, Jennifer. "*Seinfeld*, Subjectivity, and Sartre." Irwin, 90–108.

McMaster, Juliet. "Love: Surface and Subsurface." *Modern Critical Interpretations of Jane Austen's Emma*. Edited by Harold Bloom. New York: Chelsea House Publishers, 1987. 37–44.

Millman, Joyce, "600,000 an Episode, and Worth Every Penny." *Salon*, May 16, 1997.

———. "Cheerio, *Seinfeld*," *Salon*, May 4, 1998.

Modleski, Tania. "The Rhythms of Reception: Daytime Television and Women's Work." *Regarding Television: Critical Approaches—An Anthology*. Edited by E. Ann Kaplan. Frederick, Maryland: University Publication of America, 1983. 67–75.

Morreale, Joanne, ed. *Critiquing the Sitcom: A Reader*. The Television Series. Syracuse: Syracuse University Press, 2003.

———. "Sitcoms Say Goodbye: The Cultural Spectacle of *Seinfeld*'s Last Episode." *Journal of Popular Film and Television* 28:3 (fall 2000). 108–15. Reprinted in Morreale, *Critiquing the Sitcom*, 274–85.

Newitz, Annalee. "No Exit for Seinfeld: A Consideration of the Final Episode." *Bad Subjects: Political Education for Everyday Life*. July 30, 1998. http://eserver.org/bs/reviews/1998-07-30-2.46PM.html.

Nietzsche, Friedrich. *The Portable Nietzsche*. Translated by Walter Kaufman. New York: Viking Press, 1954.

Novak, William, and Moshe Waldoks. *The Big Book of Jewish Humor*. New York: Harper and Row, 1981.

O'Brien, Geoffrey. "Sein of the Times." *The New York Review of Books*, August 12, 1997: 12–14. Republished as "The Republic of *Seinfeld*" in *Castaways of the Image Planet: Movies, Show Business, Public Spectacle*. Washington, D.C.: Counterpoint, 2002: 162–72.

Oppenheimer, Jerry. *Seinfeld: The Making of an American Icon*. New York: Harper Collins, 2002.

"Patterns of Behavior." Seinfeld *Forever*. 49.

Payne, David E., and Christy A. Peake. "Cultural Diffusion: The Role of U.S. TV in Iceland." *Journalism Quarterly* 54 (1977). 523–531.

"Peter Melhman." *So Long*, Seinfeld. 34.

Pierson, David. P. "A Show About Nothing: *Seinfeld* and the Modern Comedy of Manners." *Journal of Popular Culture* 34:1 (Summer 2000): 49–64.

Pingree et al. "Television Structures and Adolescent Viewing Patterns: A Swedish-American Comparison." *European Journal of Communication* 6 (1991). 417–440.

Pinkser, Sanford. *The Schlemiel as Metaphor: Studies in Yiddish and American Jewish Fiction*. Carbondale, Illinois: Southern Illinois University Press, 1971.

Pleck, Joseph H. *The Myth of Masculinity*. Cambridge, Massachusetts: MIT Press, 1981.

Rachlin, Jill. "What's the Deal with Jerry Seinfeld?" *Ladies' Home Journal*, September 1992. 66–69.

Radavich, David. "Man Among Men: David Mamet's Homosocial Order." Edited by Peter F. Murphey. *Fictions of Masculinity: Crossing Cultures, Crossing Sexualities*. New York: New York University Press, 1994.

"Remembrance of Nothings Past." *So Long*, Seinfeld. 88–89.

Rensin, David. "Julia's Delightful Talk About . . . Nothing." *TV Guide*, December 18, 1993. 18–22.

"Rent Control." Seinfeld *Forever*. 40–41.

Robb, David. "On a Role: SAG Residuals Post Another High in '96." *Hollywood Reporter*, February 20, 1997. 1+.

Rosten, Leo. *The Joys of Yiddish*. New York: McGraw-Hill, 1968.

Samuelson, Robert J. *The Good Life and its Discontents: The American Dream in the Age of Entitlement, 1945–1995.* New York: Times Books, 1995.

Sartre, Jean Paul. *L'Idiot de la famille: Gustave Flaubert de 1821 à 1857, tome 1.* Paris: Gallimard, 1971.

———. *No Exit* and *The Flies.* New York: Knopf, 1954.

Savran, David. *Taking It Like a Man: White Masculinity, Masochism, and Contemporary American Culture.* Princeton: Princeton University Press, 1998.

"Say It Ain't So! A Stunned Nation Prepares for Life without *Seinfeld.*" *People Weekly* (January 12, 1998).

Schick, Theodore. "The Final Episode: Is Doing Nothing Something?" Irwin, 183–92.

Schilling, Mary Kaye and Mike Flaherty. "The *Seinfeld* Chronicles." *So Long,* Seinfeld. 18–90.

Schneider, Alfred R, with Kaye Pullen. *The Gatekeeper: My 30 Years as a TV Censor.* Syracuse: Syracuse University Press, 2001.

Schumacher, Owen. "*De geschiedenis van de* stand-up comedy," *Comedytrain Homepage,* 2002, http://www.toomler.nl/achtergronden/geschiedenis/geschie.htm, January 2, 2003.

Schwarzbaum, Lisa. "Elaine Style." *So Long,* Seinfeld. 35.

———. "The Jewish Question." *So Long,* Seinfeld. 80–81.

———. "Much Ado about Nothing." *Entertainment Weekly,* April 9, 1993. 15–19.

"Season 1: The Year Nothing Began." Seinfeld *Forever.* 10, 12, 14–15.

"Season 2: The Year of the Busboy." Seinfeld *Forever.* 18, 20–22.

"Season 3: The Year of Pez." Seinfeld *Forever.* 26, 28–29, 32–35.

"Season 4: The Masterful Year." Seinfeld *Forever.* 38, 40–45.

"Season 5: The Year of the Bris." Seinfeld *Forever.* 46, 48–55.

"Season 6: The Year of the Soup." Seinfeld *Forever.* 58, 60–64.

"Season 7: The Sponge-Worthy Year." Seinfeld *Forever.* 68, 70–75.

"Season 8: The Bizarro Year." Seinfeld *Forever.* 78, 80–85.

"Season 9: The Last Year." Seinfeld *Forever.* 86, 88–91.

Sedgwick, Eve Kosofsky. *Between Men: English Literature and Male Homosocial Desire.* New York: Columbia University Press, 1985.

"Sein of the Times." Seinfeld *Forever.* 63.

"The Seinfeld Guide to Sex." Seinfeld *Forever.* 21.

"Seinfeld Hitched at Last, No Joke." *Herald Sun* December 27, 1999.

Seinfeld, Jerry. Interview. *Playboy,* October 1993.

———. *Jerry Seinfeld on Comedy.* Interview by Larry Wilde. Compact Disc. Laugh.com, 2001.

———. *SeinLanguage.* New York: Bantam Books, 1993.

———. Julia Louis-Dreyfus, Michael Richards, Jason Alexander, and David Hume Kennerly. *Sein Off: The Final Days of Seinfeld.* New York: HarperCollins, 1998.

"*Seinfeld* Biographies." Sony Pictures Entertainment. 4 pp. Online. Netscape. September 15, 1995. Available at http:spe.sony.com/Pictures/tv;seinfeld/seinfeld.html.

The Seinfeld Scripts: The First and Second Seasons. New York: HarperPerennial, 1998.

Silvers, Phil, with Robert Saffron. *The Laugh Is on Me,* Englewood Cliffs, New Jersey: Prentice Hall, 1973.

Silverstone, Roger. *Television and Everyday Life.* London and New York: Routledge, 1994.

Simeauer, Jacqueline and David Carroll. *Singles: The New American.* New York: Simon & Schuster, 1982.

Simon, Richard Keller. *"Friends, Seinfeld, and Days of Our Lives." Trash Culture: Popular Culture and the Great Tradition.* Berkeley: University California Press, 1999. 44–57.

Singer, Isaac Bashevis. *The Collected Stories.* New York: FSG, 1982.

"Smart Women, Foolish Choices." *So Long,* Seinfeld, 69.

Smith, Steven Cole. "*Seinfeld* Suits Syndication: Next Year up in the Air." *Tampa Tribune,* December 17, 1995, metro edition, Florida television. 45.

So Long, Seinfeld. The Definitive Viewer's Guide. Special Collector's Issue of *Entertainment Weekly,* May 4, 1998.

"Spit on Seinfeld's Grave." *Alligator Online:* http://www.alligator.org/edit/issues/98-sumr/ 980514/co2eddy.htm

Stark, Steven D. "A Tale of Two Sitcoms." *Glued to the Set: The 60 Television Shows and Events That Made Us Who We Are Today.* New York: Free Press, 1997. 282–87.

"The Stars Sein Up." Seinfeld *Forever.* 66–67.

Sterne, Hilary. "Please, Mr. Postman." *Gentlemen's Quarterly,* November 1991. 78.

Stichting Kijkonderzoek. www.kijkonderzoek.nl, March 14, 2003.

Stratton, Jon. "Not Really White—Again: Performing Jewish Difference in Hollywood Films Since the 1980s." *Screen* 42.2 (2001). 142–166.

———. "*Seinfeld* is a Jewish Sitcom, Isn't It? Ethnicity and Assimilation on 1990s American Television." *Coming Out Jewish: Constructing Ambivalent Identities.* New York: Routledge, 2000.

——— and Ien Ang. "Multicultural Imagined Communities: Cultural Differences and National Identity in Australia and the USA." *Continuum* 8.4 (1994). 124–138. Reprinted in David Bennett, ed., *Multicultural States: Rethinking Difference and Identity.* London: Routledge. 1998.

Strauss, Gary. "J. Peterman's Travails." *USA Today,* January 27, 1999. 1B–2B.

———. "'One Mistake After Another' Finishes J. Peterman." *USA Today,* February 24, 1999. 2B.

———. "'Seinfeld' Gives Mixed Signs.'" *USA Today,* February 24, 1999. 1B.

Sweetzer, Norton. "No Writers, No Script, No Rehearsal: Is This Any Way to Direct a Sitcom?" (Interview with Robert Weide). http://www.duckprods.com/projects/cye/ cye-sweetzerinterview.html.

Telushkin, Rabbi Joseph. *Jewish Humor.* New York: William Morrow, 1992.

"Thin, Neat—and Married." *Who Weekly,* January 10, 2000.

Thomas, Calvin, ed. *Straight with a Twist: Queer Theory and the Subject of Heterosexuality.* Urbana and Chicago: University of Illinois Press, 2000.

Thompson, Stephen. "Larry David Interview." *The Onion AV Club* 33 (April 23, 1998). 15.

Thorburn, David. "Television Melodrama." *Television: The Critical View.* Edited by Horace Newcomb. 6th edition. New York: Oxford University Press, 2000.

"To be or not to be . . . Jewish," *Jewish News of Greater Phoenix,* at http://www.jewishaz .com/jewishnews/970905/tv.sctml.

"Tom Azzari." *So Long,* Seinfeld. 54.

"Total Recall." *So Long,* Seinfeld. 85.

Tracy, Kathleen. *Jerry Seinfeld: The Entire Domain.* Secaucus, New Jersey: Birch Lane Press, 1998.

Travis, John. "The Brain's Funny Bone: *Seinfeld, The Simpsons* Spark Same Nerve Circuits." *Science News Online: The Weekly Newsmagazine of Science.* http://www.sciencenews.org/20021116/fob4.asp

Tucker, Ken. "The Fantastic 4." *So Long,* Seinfeld. 12–15.

"Up Close and Personal with Elaine." Seinfeld *Forever.* 36.

"Up Close and Personal with George." Seinfeld *Forever.* 56.

"Up Close and Personal with Jerry." Seinfeld *Forever.* 16.

"Up Close and Personal with Kramer." Seinfeld *Forever.* 76.

"The Usual Suspects." Seinfeld *Forever.* 24–25.

Visser, Margaret. *The Rituals of Dinner.* New York: Grove, 1991.

Walley, Wayne. "Barter Craze Entrenched in Syndication." *Advertising Age,* June 13, 1994. S18.

Weide, Robert B. interview, part 1. http://www.hbo.com/larrydavid/interviews/weide1.html.

———. interview, part 2. http://www.hbo.com/larrydavid/interviews/weide2.html.

Weimann, Gabriel. "Images of Life in America: The Impact of American TV in Israel." *International Journal of Intercultural Relations* 8 (1984). 185–197.

Wernblad, Annette. *Brooklyn is Not Expanding: Woody Allen's Comic Universe.* Rutherford, New Jersey: Fairleigh Dickinson University Press, 1994.

Wexman, Virginia Wright. "Return from the Moon: Jackie Gleason and the Carnivalesque." In *Morreale.* 56–68.

"Whine and Dine." Seinfeld *Forever.* 92–94.

White, Mimi. "Crossing Wavelengths: The Diegetic and Referential Imaginary of American Commercial Television." *Cinema Journal* 25 L2 (Winter 1986), pp. 51–64.

Wild, David. *Seinfeld: The Totally Unauthorized Tribute (Not That There's Anything Wrong With That).* New York: Three Rivers Press, 1988.

Wilhoit, Cleveland, and Harold de Bock. *Archie Bunder Goes to Holland: Selective Exposure and Perception in the Dutch Television Audience.* Hilversum, Netherlands: Netherlands Broadcasting Foundation (NOS), Audience Research Service, 1975.

Williams, Raymond. *Television: Technology and Cultural Form.* London: Wesleyan University Press, 1992.

Winship, Frederick M. "Series Syndication Cuts Network Viewing." *United Press International,* December 12, 1995, BC cycle, domestic news. *Lexis-Nexis,* June 2005.

Wisse, Ruth R. *The Schlemiel as Modern Hero.* Chicago: University of Chicago Press, 1971.

Wolcott, James. "Blows and Kisses." *The New Yorker,* November 15, 1993. 107–109.

"The World According to *Seinfeld:* A Handy Master Guide to the Domain of Four Neurotic New Yorkers." Seinfeld *Forever.* 14–15.

Worth, Sarah E. "Elaine Benes: Feminist Icon." In Irwin, 27–37.

Wyman, Bill. "Seinfeld." Salon.com. http://www.salon.com/ent/masterpiece/2002/01/07/seinfeld/index.html

Zehme, Bill. "May the Thsouris Be With You." Seinfeld *Forever* 4–7, 8.

Zurawik, David. *The Jews of Prime Time.* Hanover, New Hampshire: Brandeis University Press/University Press of New England, 2003.

———. "The World According to *Seinfeld.*" *Baltimore Sun,* May 3, 1998: 10E–F.

Index